To Henry, Christmas 2003.

All G... ...ing.

Dad

THE OFFICIAL
LIVERPOOL FC
ILLUSTRATED ENCYCLOPEDIA

Jeff Anderson with Stephen Done

First published in Great Britain in 2003 by
Carlton Books an imprint of Carlton Publishing Group
20 Mortimer Street
London W1T 3 JW

10 9 8 7 6 5 4 3 2 1

ISBN 1 84222 950 8

Project Editor: Nigel Matheson
Art Director: Jim Lockwood
Design: David Ashford
Picture Research: Marc Glanville
Production: Lisa French

Printed in Great Britain

THE OFFICIAL
LIVERPOOL FC
ILLUSTRATED ENCYCLOPEDIA

Jeff Anderson with Stephen Done

CARLTON
BOOKS

CONTENTS

Foreword by Ronnie Moran   6

Author's Introduction   8

A   A'Court – Autographs   10

B   Babb – Byrne   19

C   Cadden – Crossley   35

D   Dabbs – Dunlop   50

E   Eastham – Everton   61

F   FA Cup – Furnell   70

G   Gayle – Gunson   82

H   Hairstyles – Hyypia   90

I   Ince – Irwin   109

J   Jackson – Jones   111

K   Kay – Kvarme   116

L   Lacey – Lucas   121

M   Macs – Museum   131

N   Neal – Northern Ireland   148

O   Ogrizovic – Owen   151

P   Pagnam – Pursell   154

Q   Quotes   164

R   Race – Rush   166

S   Sandon Hotel – Supporters' Clubs   177

T   Tallest Players – Twentyman   197

U   UEFA Cup – Uren   204

V   Venison – Vignal   206

W   Waddle – Wright   207

X   Xavier   218

Y   Yeats – Youngest Players   218

Z   Ziege   221

Bibliography   222

Useful Contacts   223

Acknowledgements   224

May 1990: manager Kenny Dalglish and assistants Ronnie Moran (left) and Roy Evans with the Division One trophy after beating Derby County 1-0

FOREWORD

With 49 years' service under his belt, Ronnie Moran is arguably the greatest servant the club has ever had – both out on the pitch and behind the scenes. When it comes to Liverpool FC, few people are better equipped to give insight into the Reds.

THE WORLD WAS A DIFFERENT place when I joined the club straight from school in 1949 – there was nothing like the Academy back then.

In those days, we trained at Anfield because there was no training ground. I turned pro in January 1952 on part-time terms: which meant £5 a week in the winter and £3 in the summer. All you could hope for then was a 12-month contract. You'd have to wait until April every year, when an envelope was pushed through your door telling you whether you were going to be kept on or not. Try telling that to players today.

The person responsible for the biggest changes at Anfield was Bill Shankly. Without his influence, I don't think the club would be where it is today. We were in the Second Division when he arrived in 1959, and by 1962 he had got us out of it. Then we really started moving forward. Bill had real presence; if he walked into a room, it would fall quiet – but he wasn't aloof or big-headed or anything like that. He enjoyed being outspoken and letting the fans know what was going on. Nowadays, if he was still going, you would never get him off the TV.

When I was coming to the end of my playing days, I didn't know what I was going to do and Bill came up to me and asked, "Would you like a job on the backroom staff?" I coached the kids for three years, the reserves for another three and then I was with the first team for 24.

Bill wanted the club run his way, a philosophy which lasts to this day. Players had to give 110 per cent at all times – even in training – and pass the ball to the nearest red shirt. That was his recipe for success. Simple really.

Without him, who knows how many European nights there would have been at Anfield? These have always been so special to the club and to English football too. I played in the first-ever European game against Reykjavik in 1964 and was lucky enough to be there when Liverpool lifted the European Cup for the first time in 1977. It was an amazing, emotional night and the supporters were out of this world. The cup itself was massive: I know that because I had it overnight at my house for safekeeping when we got back.

You can read all about Liverpool's amazing exploits in Europe – including the European Cup and UEFA Cup triumphs – on pages 64-67 of this encyclopedia. It was during Bill's time that another great Anfield tradition, the Boot Room, started. Players never went in there without knocking – an unwritten rule. It was only a small room but the coaching staff had a few lively discussions there I can tell you, and after games you would invite the opposition in to have a friendly drink. You can discover the history of the Boot Room for yourself on page 30.

Over the years, Liverpool FC has had more than its share of characters and great players. When we buy new players, though, the bottom line is, will we win anything with them? Do they hate losing? With players like Kevin Keegan, we won a few things, with Kenny Dalglish, we won a few trophies too. If you have good players with the right attitude, you can't go wrong. There have been so many here: Ron Yeats, Roger Hunt, Ian St John, Tommy Smith, Ian Callaghan, Steve Heighway, Emlyn Hughes, Graeme Souness, John Barnes, Alan Hansen, Mark Lawrenson... the list goes on and on and they're all in this book. Thumbing through the pages with its great illustrations, the memories come flooding back. And you remember what makes the place tick. It's sink or swim together at Liverpool – one for all and all for one.

Continuity is the key. The kids nowadays are coached by people fostered within the club: such as Phil Thompson, Sammy Lee and Steve Heighway. That is why success continues. I still go to Melwood three times a week just to have a walk around. I was there when Steven Gerrard was breaking through and when Michael Owen played his first game in the first team. They are out of the same mould as Keegan and Dalglish.

That's the beauty of Liverpool FC. All the kids who make it through the system to become regulars want to win with real desire. That's the vital element. It's no good playing well all season and winning nothing. You have got to win trophies, which is the true legacy of Bill Shankly, Bob Paisley, Joe Fagan and all the others who have helped make Liverpool the most successful English football club side ever.

Ronnie Moran,
Liverpool, 2003

INTRODUCTION

At the age of six, Jeff Anderson saw his first Liverpool match and came face to face with his hero of heroes. Since then, he's seen many golden years of Liverpool history in the making, which made choosing the contents of this book a daunting assignment.

THE 1968–69 SEASON HOLDS few special memories for Liverpool fans. The team that had won two League titles, lifted the FA Cup and stormed to a first European final had fallen into decline. For a third successive year, there were no major trophies bound for Anfield and even the great Bill Shankly was attracting unfamiliar criticism.

But, for me, that season will always be magical. That was when I first caught sight of the Anfield turf, having convinced my dad that – at the age of six – I was big enough to borrow his season ticket.

After taking me through the turnstile he led me to his regular place (Row 1, Block L, Seat 189). It was just before 3pm. The Kop was finishing a deafening rendition of 'You'll Never Walk Alone'. The players were warming up on the pitch. And the man whose face was plastered across every inch of my bedroom wall just happened to be standing three feet away from my seat. "H" was for "hero"; "H" was for "Hunt".

Typically, 'Sir' Roger was on target that day, scoring one of the 245 goals that still keep him top of the list of Liverpool's leading League marksmen. Not long afterwards he was gone, bound for a new career with Bolton Wanderers. But, more than three decades after his departure, nobody can argue with his status as an all-time Anfield great. Which is why – like Liddell, Shankly, Paisley, Dalglish and Owen, among others – he merits an extended entry in this official encyclopedia of the club.

But including the legends was the easy part. When Stephen Done and I began planning this book, we knew there wouldn't be room for every player who has pulled on a Liverpool shirt, particularly as we wanted to feature many other colourful aspects of LFC's history and culture. We looked at a number of criteria for inclusion but, in the end, opted for the simple yardstick of appearances.

Under this formula, those who played up until Shankly's arrival had to have appeared in at least 30 games, while those who played between 1960 and 1983 needed to have featured in 20 matches. As for those who've been on the books since Bob Paisley's departure, all qualify for a mention – provided they have at least one senior game to their credit. But there are some exceptions. During our research we found quite a few players who were at the centre of fascinating stories, despite their limited number of matches. Hence the entries for Olympic gold medal-winner Joe Dines, who lost his life in the First World War after making just one appearance for the Reds. The "B" section includes an entry for 1950s player Keith Burkinshaw, another one-game-wonder who was to find much fame and success as manager of Tottenham Hotspur two decades later.

And in "G", there's a reference to Howard Gayle. He may only have appeared in a handful of games, but one of those was against Bayern Munich in 1981, when his dazzling substitute's performance on the wing helped Liverpool on their way to a third European Cup final.

Players aside, we hope you enjoy the other interesting, entertaining – and occasionally slightly bizarre – entries in this book.

Sections like 'Anfield', 'Houlding', 'Pre-Season Tours' and 'Testimonials' give a real insight into the club's origins and development. Others, like 'Singing', 'Fightbacks' and 'Homecomings' provide inspirational stories of players and fans alike.

Those who like to smile should look up entries such as 'Hairstyles', 'Pop Songs' and 'Dr Fun'. And anyone wanting to settle a football argument can check out all the comprehensive statistics, along with headings like 'Ever Presents', 'Goalscorers' and 'Honours'.

The statistics themselves were compiled at the end of the 2002–03 season, largely thanks to the efforts and fearsome dedication-to-detail of lifelong Reds fan Eric Doig. Thanks are also due to Adrian Killen, George Sephton and Freddy O'Connor for their assistance with various facts and figures, as well as the staff of the Liverpool FC Museum for allowing access to their vast collection of club treasures.

Finally, a special thank you to my dad for giving me that ticket back in 1968... and to Rory, Ciaran, Rosie and Mairead Anderson for their patience and support today.

Jeff Anderson
Liverpool, 2003

Number eight with a bullet: Roger Hunt was indisputably one of the all-time Anfield greats

That's your lot... the referee abandons the 1973 UEFA Cup final first leg after just 17 minutes

A'Court, Alan

1952/3-1964/5 (Striker) **B** 30.9.1934, Rainhill **S** 1952 from Prescot Cables, no fee **D** 7.2.53 v Middlesbrough, lg **L** 1964 to Tranmere R, £4,500 **Apps** 381, 63 gls **Hons** Div2 CH 1961–62; 5 caps for England **OC** Prescot Celtic, Prescot Cables, Tranmere R, Norwich C (player-coach), Chester C (assistant manager), Crewe Alexandra (assistant manager, twice), Ndola Utd (coach), Stoke C (trainer)

HIS RUGBY-MAD FAMILY were reportedly upset when he chose a football career, but Liverpool fans were thankful for his decision. The Rainhill-born winger signed on his 18th birthday and became a crowd favourite, playing through the eras of Don Welsh, Phil Taylor and Bill Shankly. Although A'Court spent most of his career in Division Two, he was talented enough to win five England caps while in the lower reaches. Career high points included an international debut goal, replacing the injured Tom Finney during the 1958 World Cup finals, and playing every game in Liverpool's promotion-winning 1961–62 season. He found the going tougher in the top flight, and soon lost his regular place to Peter Thompson. He joined Tranmere for £4,500 in 1964, then coached various clubs in England, Zambia and New Zealand.

Abandoned Matches

IN MORE THAN a century of Anfield games, only two have been abandoned. In 1973, torrential rain stopped the UEFA Cup final first leg against Borussia Moenchengladbach after 17 minutes. Liverpool won the replayed tie 3-0, going on to win the final 3-2 on aggregate. A 1903 League match against Wolves was also stopped due to rain. And, away from Anfield, three FA Cup ties have been abandoned. In 1899, crowd incursions caused a semi-final against Sheffield United to be stopped at Manchester's Fallowfield ground. In 1989 the referee halted the semi-final against Nottingham Forest, due to the unfolding tragedy on the Hillsborough terraces. And in 1994, a tie at Bristol City was called off due to second-half floodlight failure.

Ablett, Gary I

1986/7-1991/2 (Full-back) **B** 19.11.1965, Liverpool **S** LFC apprentice, professional 1983–84 **D** 20.12.1986 v Charlton Athletic, lg **L** January 1992 to Everton, £750,000 **Apps** 146, 1 gl **Hons** Div1 CH 1987–88, 1989–1990; FAC 1988–89; CS 1988, 1990; Littlewoods Cup finalist 1988–89 **OC** Derby County (loan), Hull C (loan), Everton, Sheffield Utd (loan), Birmingham C, Blackpool

TALL, VERSATILE DEFENDER who won two Championships and an FA Cup winners' medal during a 146-game Anfield career. Ablett made his debut in a 0-0 draw at Charlton in December 1986, and marked his second appearance with a spectacular goal in a 3-0 win over Nottingham Forest. He played 17 games in the title-winning season of 1987–88, then missed just three matches of the following campaign. Despite his fine track record, the occasional lapse in concentration made Ablett a target for crowd criticism. Kenny Dalglish kept faith, but new boss Graeme Souness was happy to accept a surprise £750,000 bid from Everton in 1991. He won a second FA Cup winners' medal while at Goodison, and later joined Steve McMahon's Blackpool.

Academy, The

MCMANAMAN, FOWLER, Owen, Gerrard... the names on Liverpool's youth production line could hardly be more impressive. To maintain a steady flow of home-grown talent, the club has spent £12 million on its purpose-built Academy, based in Kirkby, some seven miles from Anfield. Under the directorship of seventies star Steve Heighway, a 50-strong team of scouts identify and recruit the best young talent in the north. Once installed at the Academy, youngsters are given intensive coaching sessions, technical excellence courses, plus all the facilities and staff for their educational needs. The Kirkby centre, opened in 1999, boasts ten grass pitches and a specialist goalkeeping area. There's also an indoor synthetic pitch, plus an advanced outdoor floodlit arena with its own spectator accommodation. The club may have laid out millions on importing players from around the world, but this investment may well prove to be the most important and valuable of all.

Top Graduates: (back) McManaman, Carragher, Matteo, Gerrard; (front) Owen, Thompson, Fowler

Adelphi Hotel

LIVERPOOL CITY CENTRE landmark since 1826, the Adelphi was the well-appointed venue for some of the club's earliest civic receptions.

KEY Apps Appearances | **B** Born | **CH** Championship | **CWC** Cup Winners' Cup | **CS** Charity Shield | **D** Debut | **d** Died | **EC** European Cup | **FAC** FA Cup | **gls** Goals | **Hons** Honours | **lg** League

The hotel, lavishly refurbished in 1912, became one of the most luxurious in Europe, catering for passengers of the transatlantic liners that once docked at the Pier Head. The Sefton Suite – a replica of the First Class Smoking Lounge on the *Titanic* – hosted Liverpool's Championship Celebration dinners in 1922 and 1923, attended by players, officials and club dignitaries, the Lord Mayor and city MPs.

Aldridge, John W

1986/7-1989/90 (Striker) **B** 18.9.1958, Liverpool **S** January 1987 from Oxford Utd, £750,000 **D** 21.2.1987 v Aston Villa, lg **L** September 1989, Real Sociedad, £1.1 million **Apps** 104, 63 gls **Hons** Div1 CH 1987–88; FAC 1988–89; FAC finalist 1987–88; CS 1988; 69 caps for Rep Ireland **OC** South Liverpool, Newport County, Oxford Utd, Real Sociedad, Tranmere R (player-manager).

FEW FANS THOUGHT Ian Rush could be replaced – until his scouse-lookalike capped a magical Anfield debut with a flying header past Southampton's England 'keeper Peter Shilton. Aldridge's goals had already propelled little Oxford United into the top flight. But once at Anfield, in the company of Barnes, Beardsley and Houghton, he achieved his full outstanding potential. He was on target in all nine opening games of the brilliant 1987–88 Championship season, finishing with 26 goals in 36 League matches. His FA Cup Final penalty miss ensured the trophy went to Wimbledon that year. But he made amends in 1989, scoring in the 3-2 Wembley victory over Everton. By then, though, Rush was back from Juventus, and Liverpool were keen to cash in on their phenomenal, but ageing, talent. The club collected £1.1 million from Spain's Real

Sociedad the following season, but only after "Aldo" marked his farewell by coming off the bench to score a penalty in Liverpool's 9-0 destruction of Crystal Palace... then threw his shirt and boots into the Kop. "It was an emotional thing," he explained later. "I was going to walk off the pitch when I realised I had to say thanks to the fans who had been so great to me. I wanted to give something back. I would love to have given 10,000 shirts out instead of one."

A short but successful period in Spain ended with a return to Merseyside, and an Indian Summer with Tranmere Rovers. He equalled the club scoring record, hitting 40 goals in his first season, then played in Jack Charlton's Republic of Ireland side at the 1994 USA World Cup Finals.

A year later he became player-manager at Prenton Park, and in 1998 – just short of his 40th birthday – he finally hung up his boots. As manager he brought new excitement to Tranmere, guiding the team all the way to the 2000 Worthington Cup Final. But promotion to the Premiership never seemed a realistic prospect, and after his team slumped to the foot of the First Division in 2001, Aldridge resigned. He now works as a media pundit.

A

Carried away by the occasion: 'Aldo' is lifted shoulder-high by delirious fans after his contributions to victory over Nottingham Forest at Hillsborough in 1988

Allan, George H

1895/6-1896/7, 1898-1899 (Centre-forward) **B** Linlithgow Bridge,
Scotland, 23.8.1875 **S** September 1895 from Leith Athletic
D 14.9.1895 v Newcastle Utd, lg **L** May 1897 to Celtic **Apps** 96,
58 gls **Hons** Div2 CH 1895–96 **OC** Broxburn Shamrock, Bo'ness,
Leith Athletic, Celtic **d** 17.10.1899 of TB

PROLIFIC SCOTTISH STRIKER from the
Victorian era – and the first Liverpool player to
net four goals in a game. Allan spent three years
at Anfield, with one season at Celtic in-between.
He was top scorer in the 1895–96 promotion-
winning season, and leading marksman the following year. He went on to collect a Scottish
League Championship medal with the Glasgow
club, then returned to help Liverpool to a runners-up spot in 1899. Tragically, Allan died
the same year – a victim of tuberculosis at the
tender age of 24.

Anderson, Eric

1952/3-1956/7 (Inside forward) **B** 12.3.1931, Manchester
S Liverpool amateur, professional December 1951 **D** 28.3.1953 v
Charlton Athletic, lg **L** July 1957 to Barnsley, £4,000 **Apps** 76, 22 gls
Hons none **OC** Army football, Barnsley, Bournemouth & Boscombe
Athletic, Macclesfield **d** 1990

Anelka, Nicolas

2001-2002 (Striker) **B** 14.3.1979, Versailles, France **S** December
2001, Paris St Germain, loan **D** 26.12.2001 v Aston Villa, lg
L Summer 2001, Manchester C **Apps** 22, 5 gls **Hons** none
OC Arsenal, Real Madrid, Paris St Germain, Manchester C

AS THE SURPRISE recruit of the 2001–02
season, Anelka was keen to banish his image
as a moody loner. And by the time the campaign ended the Kop had taken 'Nico' to
their hearts – only to see him deemed
surplus to requirements by Gerard
Houllier. Three years earlier, the
Frenchman had been the star of
Arsenal's Double-winning side,
earning himself the PFA
Young Player Of The
Year award. A contro-
versial transfer to
Real Madrid fol-
lowed, along with a
dip in form and a
further switch to
Paris St Germain.
Houllier, who had
previously worked
with him at
France's Youth
Academy, brought
him back from the
wilderness in December 2001, offering him a loan deal to replace
Robbie Fowler.

Anelka seized the chance,
scoring a crucial
equaliser against
Everton in the
Anfield derby,
and putting on
a stunning
display in the
3-0 win over
Newcastle. With
more impressive
performances under
his belt, most fans
thought the deal would
become permanent. But
Houllier obviously thought he'd
seen the best of the mercurial forward and, when Manchester City
came in with a close-season cash
offer, the Liverpool manager decided
not to bid.

Anfield

⮕ See pages 14-15

Anfield Road End

THE LEGENDARY twin-tiered terrace opposite the Kop goal. Like all other Anfield enclo-
sures, it's undergone major changes throughout
the years, with the latest refurbishment boosting the capacity to 9,400. It's been the regular
gathering place for opposing fans since the
1960s, although thousands of Liverpudlians
also count the "Annie Road" as their home.

"Anfield South"

⮕ See Wembley

Anthems

⮕ See Fields Of Anfield Road
See Scouser Tommy
See You'll Never Walk Alone

KEY **Apps** Appearances | **B** Born | **CH** Championship | **CWC** Cup Winners' Cup | **CS** Charity Shield | **D** Debut | **d** Died | **EC** European Cup | **FAC** FA Cup | **gls** Goals | **Hons** Honours | **lg** League

Arnell, Alan J

1953/4-1960/1 (Centre-forward) **B** 25.11.1933, Chichester **S** 1953 from Worthing **D** 5.12.1953 v Blackpool, lg **L** 1961 to Tranmere R **Apps** 75, 35 gls **Hons** none **OC** Worthing, Tranmere R, Runcorn, Halifax T

EX-AMATEUR WHO joined from non-league Worthing in 1953, scored on his debut and averaged a goal every two games. Good enough for Division Two, but new manager Bill Shankly wanted a stronger, more effective striker to lead his promotion charge. Arnell was transferred to Tranmere Rovers in 1961, and subsequently finished his career at Runcorn and Halifax.

Arphexad, Pegguy

2000/1-2002/3 (Goalkeeper) **B** 18.5.1973, Abymes, Guadeloupe **S** Summer 2000 from Leicester C **D** 1.11.2000 v Chelsea, LC rd 3 **Apps** 6 **Hons** none **OC** Lens, Leicester City, Portsmouth (loan)

A

CAUGHT THE EYE of Gerard Houllier while keeping goal for Worthington Cup-winning Leicester City, and became an able deputy to former Number 1, Sander Westerveld.

Arphexad made a handful of appearances following his arrival in 2000, but the double signings of Jerzy Dudek and Chris Kirkland severely restricted the Guadaloupe-born 'keeper's first-team chances and he was released by the club in May 2003.

Above: the view from the Kop; below: "Anfield South" – the 1977 Cup Final against Man Utd

A drawing by Tom Preston depicting the ground in 1894–95; the photograph (right) was taken in 1996

Anfield

THE HOME OF Liverpool Football Club since its formation. Back in the 19th Century the land belonged to two brothers, John and James Orrell. They leased it to fellow brewer John Houlding, whose house stood opposite, and whose team, Everton, had recently been evicted from their pitch on nearby Priory Road. For an annual rent of £100, Houlding enclosed the ground, then staged its first-ever match – Everton's 5-0 win against Earlestown on September 28th, 1884. Eight years later, Houlding bought Anfield outright and told his fellow Everton members he was increasing their rent to £250 a year. They refused to pay and left for Goodison Park, taking their team with them. Houlding started from scratch, forming a new club – Liverpool FC – which played its first home game on September 1st, 1892.

Anfield has undergone a series of fundamental changes in the 111 years since then. A Main Stand, seating 3,000, was built in 1895. A barrel-roof was added later, and the mock-Tudor gable bearing the club's name would become one of English football's best-known landmarks for the next 75 years. In 1903 a timber and corrugated iron terrace was constructed on Anfield Road, then – in 1906 – the club unveiled the Spion Kop, a vast bank of cinders and rubble behind the goal of the Walton Breck Road End.

The Kop was covered in 1928, and, at the Kemlyn Road corner, a white flagpole was installed, originally the top mast of Brunel's mighty iron-ship *The Great Eastern*, which had been broken up in Liverpool docks in 1888. When the Kop was completed, the pole was floated across the Mersey. A fleet of horses carried it to Anfield, where it remains to this day.

The first floodlights were installed in 1957. Six years later the old standing Kemlyn Road terrace was rebuilt to seat 6,700 spectators.

In 1965 the club used profits from its first FA Cup final victory to build a new covered Anfield Road enclosure. Then, in 1970, the original Main Stand was torn down and gradually replaced.

Apart from minor alterations – new roof-mounted floodlights, perimeter fencing and the seating of the Paddock – Anfield remained largely unchanged for the next two decades. Replacing the Kemlyn Road with the two-tiered Centenary Stand in 1992 was an undoubted landmark, but the demolition of the Kop terrace two years later provided the most fundamental change. The move to an all-seater stadium, and the tearing down of perimeter fences, was an inevitable outcome of the Taylor report into the Hillsborough disaster. Today's Kop holds less than half the 30,000 fans who once stood, sung and swayed on the old concrete steps. But it's an impressive structure that remains at the heart of one of the most famous and atmospheric arenas in the entire world of sport.

With a capacity of 45,522, plus executive boxes and state-of-the-art broadcasting facilities, Anfield is once again capable of staging international fixtures. However, as a club venue, it may have outlived its usefulness. Unable to expand it further, the club plan to build a 60,000-plus-seater stadium at Stanley Park, 300 yards from the current site. Moving from the ground will be an emotional wrench for many. However, the club has pledged that traditional features, such as a single-tiered Kop, will be included in the development. Most importantly, the ground will still bear the name "Anfield".

Right: Anfield employees card from the Shankly era

Arrowsmith, Alf

1961/2-1968/9 (Centre-forward) **B** 11.12.1942, Manchester **S** Aug
1960 from Ashton Utd, £1,500 **D** 7.10.1061 v Middlesbrough, lg
L 1968 to Bury, £25,000 **Apps** 56, 24 gls **Hons** Div1 CH 1963–64
OC Ashton Utd, Bury, Rochdale, Macclesfield

LETHAL MARKSMAN
whose Liverpool career was
cut short by injury. The
teenage Arrowsmith was
spotted playing for Ashton
United alongside future
England captain Alan Ball,
and brought to Anfield for a
£1,500 fee. Shankly
declared that the youngster
was "born to score goals",
and gave him his debut in
the promotion-winning
1961–62 season. But he
really began to fulfil his
promise during the
1963–64 Championship
campaign, scoring 15
goals in 20 League games – and hitting four in
an FA Cup tie against Derby County. The future
looked bright until he suffered serious knee
damage in the 1964 Charity Shield clash with
West Ham. He returned to the first team midway through the season but never recaptured
his goalscoring form. Four years later he joined
Bury for £25,000, and later finished his career
with Rochdale and Macclesfield.

Ashcroft, Charlie

1943-1954/55 (Goalkeeper) **B** 3.7.1926 **S** December 1943
from Eccleston Juniors.**D** 7.9.1946 v Chelsea, lg **L** June 1955
to Ipswich Town **Apps** 89 **Hons** Sundry caps for England
OC Eccleston Juniors, Ipswich Town, Coventry City, Chorley
d 25.12.1984

Ashworth, David

1920/1-1922/3 (Manager) **B** 1868, Waterford
S Summer 1920 from Oldham Ahtletic
D 28.8.1920 v Manchester C, lg **L** February
1923 to Oldham Athletic **Hons** (as manager)
Div1 CH 1921–22, 1922–23; CS finalists
1922 **OC** (as manager) Oldham A, Stockport
C, Manchester C, Walsall; Blackpool (scout)

FORMER LEAGUE REFER-
EE who became LFC manager
after World War One, then
landed the 1921–22 title. Ashworth was
on the verge of clinching a second successive
Championship when he sensationally quit to
rejoin his old club, Oldham, who had made him

a lucrative offer to help them stave off relegation. But his acceptance proved to be a personal
disaster. As Liverpool went on to win the
League, Ashworth couldn't prevent his new club
from going down. He lasted only a year at
Boundary Park before a series of unhappy spells
at Manchester City, Stockport and Walsall.
Finally he dropped out of management altogether, and finished his days as a talent scout
with Blackpool.

Attendances

LIVERPOOL'S BIGGEST HOME GATE was on
February 2nd, 1952 when 61,905 supporters
packed into Anfield to see a 2-1 FA Cup Fourth
Round victory over Wolverhampton Wanderers.
The highest seasonal attendance came in
1972–73 when an average crowd of 48,103
watched each home League game. The lowest
post-war average was in 1960–61 when
Liverpool were in the Second Division. But, surprisingly, the lowest post-war gates while in the
top flight came in 1983–84 – when the Reds won
a League, European Cup and Milk Cup Treble.
Their average home attendance that season was
just 32,021.

**The highs and lows for post-war Anfield
matches in all competitions are as follows:**

League
Highest: v Chelsea, 27 Dec, 1949: **58,757**
Lowest: v Scunthorpe, 22 Apr, 1959: **11,976**

FA Cup
Highest: v Wolves, 2 Feb, 1952: **61,905**
Lowest: v Chester, 9 Jan, 1946: **11,207**

League Cup
Highest: v Nottm Forest, 12 Feb, 1980: **50,880**
Lowest: v Brentford, 25 Oct, 1983: **9,902**

UEFA Cup
Highest: v Barcelona, 14 April, 1976: **55,104**
Lowest v Swarovski, Tirol, 1991: **16,007**

European Cup Winners' Cup
Highest: v Honved, 8 March, 1966: **54,631**
Lowest: v Apollon Limassol 1992: **12,769**

European Cup
Highest: v St. Etienne, 16 Mar, 1977: **55,043**
Lowest: v Dundalk, 28 Sept, 1982: **12,021**

The old-fashioned way of avoiding queues at the turnstiles – a big game at Anfield during season 1946–47

KEY **Apps** Appearances | **B** Born | **CH** Championship | **CWC** Cup Winners' Cup | **CS** Charity Shield | **D** Debut | **d** Died | **EC** European Cup | **FAC** FA Cup | **gls** Goals | **Hons** Honours | **lg** League

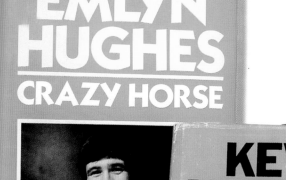

Autobiographies

GIVEN THEIR CAREER SUCCESS, it's unsurprising that many Reds stars have been asked to put their life stories down on paper. In 1960, Billy Liddell wrote *My Soccer Story*, charting his rise from teenage prodigy to Liverpool and Scotland legend. Since then, a succession of players have given their own account of life inside Anfield. They include:

John Aldridge – *My Story*
John Barnes – *The Autobiography*
Bruce Grobbelaar – *Bring On The Clown*
Alan Hansen – *A Matter Of Opinion*
Emlyn Hughes – *Crazy Horse*
Roger Hunt – *Hunt For Goals*
Craig Johnston – *Walk Alone*
Ray Kennedy – *Ray Of Hope*
Phil Neal – *Life At The Kop*
Michael Owen – *In Person*
Ian Rush – *Rush*
Ian St John – *Boom At The Kop*
Tommy Smith – *I Did It The Hard Way*
Graeme Souness – *No Half Measures*

A

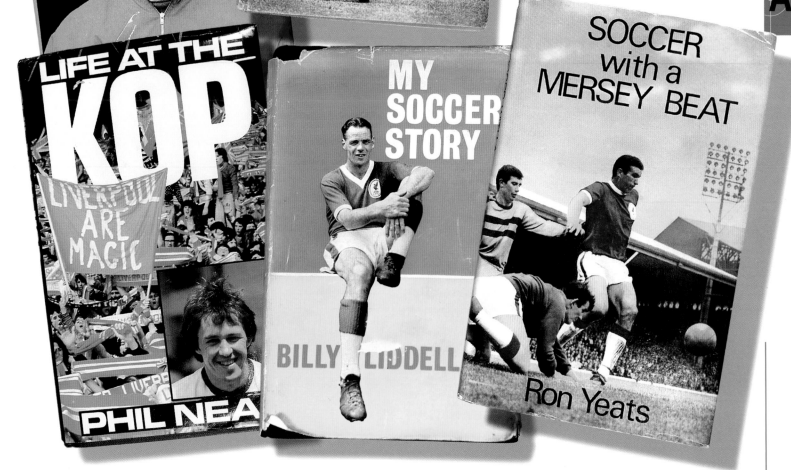

Autographs

FROM THE STYLISH to the unreadable, fans have been collecting footballers' signatures for decades. There's a thriving market for mint-condition autographs of the famous – and some of the best examples are to be found in fans' scrapbooks donated to the Liverpool FC Museum. Can you match the squiggle to the star?

Babb, Phil

1994/5-2000/1 (Central defender) **B** 30.11.1970, Lambeth **S** From
Coventry C for £3.6 million **D** 17.9.1994 v Manchester Utd, lg
L Summer 2000 to Sporting Lisbon **Apps** 170, 1 gl **Hons** LC
1994–95; 34 caps for Rep I **OC** Bradford C, Coventry C, Tranmere R
(loan), Sporting Lisbon, Sunderland

ROY EVANS PAID a record £3.6 million for the
Irish international following his impressive displays at the 1994 World Cup Finals.
Unfortunately the ex-Coventry City centre-back
didn't always reproduce that sort of form at
Anfield. He remained a regular for most of the
Evans era, but injuries and some erratic performances meant he was relegated to the
fringes of the first team by the end of the
1998–99 season. At the end of Gerard Houllier's
first season in charge, Babb was loaned to
Tranmere Rovers. He then took advantage of
the Bosman ruling and joined Sporting Lisbon.
At the end of his first year – when he was voted
'Best Defender' by Portuguese sportswriters –
he rejoined the Premiership with a move to
Sunderland.

Power behind the throne: Sammy Lee, Patrice Bergues, Phil Thompson, Gerard Houllier and Joe Corrigan

Babbel, Markus

2000/1-2002/3 (Right-back) **B** 8.9.1972, Munich **S** 2000 from Bayern
Munich, free **D** 19.8.2000 v Bradford C, lg **Apps** 73, 6 gls
Hons LC 2000–01; FAC 2000–01; UEFA 2000–01; Super Cup 2001;
CS 2001; 51 caps for Germany **OC** Bayern Munich

POLISHED GERMAN FULL-BACK, captured
on a free transfer from Bayern Munich in the
summer of 2000. On arriving, Babbel, who had
won 51 international caps while with Munich,
announced his
retirement from
the international
scene, choosing
instead to concen-
trate on the
rigours of English
football. He need-
ed to. He played
in all but three
matches during
the marathon
63-game Treble campaign,
chipping in with six goals, including the opener
in the UEFA Cup Final.

As one of the most consistent performers
during that historic season, Babbel was an automatic choice for the team to face Manchester
United in the 2001 Charity Shield clash.

But that proved to be his last game for a full
year. Struck down with a rare virus, the potentially fatal Guillan-Barre syndrome, the super-
fit 29-year-old suffered nerve damage and paral-
ysis – at one point he could not even walk.
Confined to a wheelchair for several months,
it looked like his career might well be over. But
following intensive treatment in his native
Germany, he returned to the Liverpool squad
and made an appearance in a pre-season friendly against Le Havre.

Backroom Staff

ABILITY ON THE PITCH is all very well, but
any successful manager also needs a talented
behind-the-scenes team. Apart from the ultra-
passionate Phil Thompson, Gerard Houllier's
staff currently includes:

Sammy Lee – boyhood Reds fan who enjoyed
a trophy-laden career with the club in the late
1970s and early 1980s. Lee was in charge of the
reserves during Roy Evans' reign and promoted
to first-team coach under Houllier. In 2001 the
FA asked him to work alongside Sven-Goran
Eriksson with the full England squad, which
was quite an honour for the club.

Christian Damiano – former Fulham assistant boss, who replaced Jacques Crevoisier as
first-team coach at Anfield after he left in May
2003. Damiano was Houllier's assistant when
the pair took the France Under-18 side to
European Youth Championship victory in 1996.

Hugh McAuley – reserve team manager with
a wealth of experience working with up-and-
coming youngsters. He led the Under-19s to the
title in 2001–02 and helped develop the talents
of Owen, Gerrard and Carragher.

Joe Corrigan – goalkeeping coach who works
with the squad's three 'keepers. As a player,
Corrigan enjoyed a distinguished career with
Manchester City.

Ian Rush – legendary goalscorer with
responsibility for Liverpool's first-team strikers.
Rush joined the staff after winning his coaching
badge at the start of 2003. Could the Anfield forward line ever be in better hands?

In addition to the coaching and admin staff,
Liverpool also employ a number of specialists on
the medical side. They include physios Dave
Galley and Mark Browes, club doctor Mark
Waller and masseurs John Wright, Stuart
Welsh and Paul Small.

A shattered Peter Beardsley can't believe his bad luck after the 1988 Cup Final against Wimbledon

Bad Decisions

LUCK MAY EVEN itself out over time but some refereeing decisions continue to rankle years afterwards. One of the most notorious came at Arsenal on the last day of the 1971–72 season, with the Reds needing a win to claim the Championship. With two minutes left, John Toshack put them ahead, sending Liverpudlians in the Highbury crowd into temporary ecstasy. As the TV evidence later showed, Toshack was clearly onside when he struck. But, after consulting with his linesman, Roger Kirkpatrick disallowed the goal, denying Liverpool two points and effectively handing the title to Brian Clough's Derby County.

In 1978, Clough benefited from another refereeing gaffe, as his Nottingham Forest side were awarded a vital penalty in the League Cup Final replay at Old Trafford. Forest's John O'Hare was at least a yard outside Liverpool's 18-yard area when Phil Thompson brought him down. But the official pointed to the spot, and the Reds duly lost.

One referee who admitted his error was Brian Hill, the man in charge of the 1988 FA Cup Final against Wimbledon. Just a minute before the Dons' winning goal, Peter Beardsley had put the ball in their net with an audacious chip past Dave Beasant. However, the ref refused to let it stand, having blown for a foul on the Liverpool winger seconds earlier. "I suppose there was every opportunity to play the advantage and, perhaps, in hindsight, I should have done," he said later.

But however unfair those decisions, no referee has achieved greater notoriety than Ortiz de Mendibil, the Spaniard who took charge of the 1965 European Cup semi-final at Inter Milan. His handling of the game, in which the Italians grabbed two highly dubious first-half goals, led to widespread claims of bribery, and – even 15 years later – Bill Shankly complained of being haunted by Mendibil's face. Perhaps he should have followed Tommy Smith's example. Walking off the San Siro pitch in disgust, the Anfield Iron gave full vent to his anger… by kicking the ref in the knee.

Badges

→ See opposite, also Club Crest

Ballon D'Or

THE EUROPEAN FOOTBALLER of The Year accolade is decided by 52 sports journalists brought together annually by *France Football* magazine. Until recently they had never honoured a serving Liverpool player, so who knows what games they were watching when Dalglish and Rush were terrorising continental defences in the early 1980s. In 2002, they put matters right, recognising Michael Owen's role in the Treble triumph, and his superb hat-trick for England in the 5-1 defeat of Germany. Receiving the *Ballon D'Or* put him in the company of some of the game's all-time greats, including Sir Stanley Mathews, Johan Cruyff, Beckenbauer, Eusebio and Zidane. It also ranked him alongside Kevin Keegan, who was twice voted European Footballer Of The Year after leaving the Reds for Hamburg.

Golden Boy: Michael Owen with *Le Ballon d'Or*

Badges

BADGES GIVE FANS the chance to wear their hearts on their sleeves, their lapels or even on their bobble hats. They also act as campaign medals for games and seasons past. Here are a few from the vast collection that has been produced over the years…

B

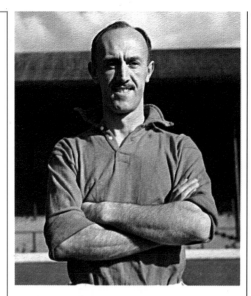

Balmer, Jack

1935/6-1951/2 (Inside-forward) **B** 6.2.1916, Liverpool **S** May 1935 from Everton as amateur **D** 21.9.1935 v Leeds Utd, lg **L** December 1951 – retired **Apps** 313, 111 gls **Hons** Div1 CH 1946–47; FAC 1950 finalist; unofficial England honours **OC** Collegiate School, guested for Brighton, Newcastle Utd during WW2 **d** 25.12.1984

LOCAL-BORN STRIKER who became the first Liverpool player to score three consecutive hat-tricks. Balmer, whose two uncles had both played for Everton, started out as a Goodison amateur. But in 1935 he crossed Stanley Park, forcing himself into the first team while still a teenager. By the 1938–39 season he was an ever-present, tipped for England honours. But the outbreak of war restricted his appearances to 'unofficial' internationals in the early 1940s.

When League football resumed in 1946, Balmer slotted back into Liverpool's first team, captaining the side and forming a deadly strike partnership with Albert Stubbins. That November he made history, hitting three against Portsmouth, four at Derby, then another three past Arsenal. As if that wasn't enough, he went on to score another five in his next four games, a grand total of 15 goals in seven matches. With him and Stubbins finishing the season as joint top-scorers, the team lifted the League Championship. But, in a Liverpool career lasting 17 years, that would be his only medal.

Bamber, John

1915/6-1923/4 (Right-half) **B** 11.4.1895, Peasley Cross, St Helens **S** December 1915 from Heywood **D** 4.12.1915 v Bolton W, Lancashire section Principal Tournament, wartime league; 13.9.1919 v Aston Villa, full lg debut **L** February 1924 to Leicester C **Apps** 62, 2 gls (plus 116 apps, 8 gls in wartime) **Hons** Injury denied him two Div1 CHs (1921–22, 1922–23); 1 England cap **OC** St Helens Recreation, Heywood, Leicester C, Tranmere R, Prescot Cables **d** August 1971

Barclay, William E

1892/3-1895/6 (Secretary/manager) **B** n/k **S** On original Everton board **D** Debut as manager 3.9.1892 v Higher Walton, Lancashire league **L** 1896 to become a headmaster **Hons** Div2 Ch 1893–94, 1895–96; Lancashire League CH 1892–93 **d** n/k

FORMER EVERTON VICE-PRESIDENT who stayed loyal to chairman John Houlding following his split with the club in 1892. When Houlding decided to set up a new club, it was Barclay who came up with the name "Liverpool". Within three months he and John McKenna were installed as LFC's first joint bosses, with Barclay taking the title "secretary-manager". He stayed in that position for another four years, looking after the administration of the club and helping to recruit the famous "Team of all the Macs" – the ten Scots who formed the bulk of the squad in the mid-1890s. Like Houlding, Barclay was involved in several charities to help the city's destitute. He raised money for the Industrial Schools' (Victorian skill centres designed for children from "unwholesome" backgrounds destined for a life of crime). After leaving the club he became headmaster of the movement's school in Everton.

Barmby, Nick

2000/1-2001/2 (Wing/midfield) **B** 11.2.1974, Hull **S** From Everton, £6 Million **D** 19.8.2000 v Bradford C, lg **L** 8.8.2002 to Leeds Utd, £2.5 million **Apps** 58, 8 gls **Hons** LC 2000–01; FAC 2000–01; UEFA 2000–01; CS 2001; 23 England caps **OC** Tottenham, Middlesbrough, Everton, Leeds Utd

FEW TRANSFERS HAVE caused more anger on Merseyside than Barmby's switch from Everton to Liverpool in the summer of 2000. It was the first time a Blues player had moved directly across the park for 40 years… and their fans were in unforgiving mood when he stepped out for the Anfield derby. The £6 million signing answered their "Judas" taunts with a goal in a 3-1 victory that helped secure a Champions' League place. And as the 2000–01 season progressed, Barmby produced stunning UEFA Cup displays, scoring four times in the opening three rounds. Later, fighting to regain fitness, he had to settle for a place on the bench against Alaves. The following season was a big disappointment for Barmby, who made just nine appearances before ankle surgery ruled him out for the rest of the campaign. He moved to Leeds United just before the start of the 2002–03 season.

Barmby celebrates his goal in the UEFA Cup 3rd round game against Olympiakos, December 2000

KEY Apps Appearances | **B** Born | **CH** Championship | **CWC** Cup Winners' Cup | **CS** Charity Shield | **D** Debut | **d** Died | **EC** European Cup | **FAC** FA Cup | **gls** Goals | **Hons** Honours | **lg** League

Barnes, John C B (MBE)

1987/8-1996/7 (Striker/midfield) **B** 7.11.1963, Kingston, Jamaica
S June 1987 from Watford, £900,000 **D** 15.8.1987 v Arsenal, lg
L Summer 1997 to Newcastle Utd **Apps** 403, 106 gls **Hons** Div1 CH
1987–88, 1989–90; FAC 1988–89; FAC finalist 1987–88, 1995–96;
LC 1994–95; CS 1988, 1989, 1990; MBE; Footballer of the Year
1988, 1990; PFA Player of the Year 1988; 79 England caps.
OC Watford, Newcastle Utd, Charlton A, Celtic (manager)

BRILLIANT LEFT-SIDED forward who lit up Anfield and packed out stadiums around the country in a glittering nine-season spell. Three years before joining, he announced his arrival on the international scene with a dazzling goal for England in Brazil's Maracana Stadium. Some doubted such an individualist would fit in at Liverpool, but the £900,000 signing soon silenced them. In a team bulging with talent he was the undoubted star of the 1987–88 campaign, scoring 15 goals, winning a Championship medal, plus the Footballer Of The Year and PFA Player Of The Year awards.

"John was a key figure in that side because he could take on three or four defenders or, at least, hold the ball long enough to disrupt the opposition's attacking momentum and rhythm," said skipper Alan Hansen. "The last Liverpool player who could beat defenders as easily as Barnes had been Steve Heighway in the 1970s. But John was possibly even better. His strength meant that, even if he was dispossessed, or did not have full control of the ball, he could be relied upon to win a throw-in or a corner."

Unsurprisingly, he became a target for the game's hard men. Yet he remained remarkably free from injury during his peak years: "If a really hard tackle came in I took evasive action," he wrote later. "I knew when bad tackles were imminent. It's animal instinct. In the jungle, animals sense when a lion prowls nearby. Humans have similar intuition on the football field. I never suffered a bad injury from a tackle: solely pulled muscles. I anticipated and reacted quicker than most players."

Barnes attributed his speed, suppleness and agility to his Caribbean childhood. The Jamaican Army officer's son came to Britain when his father received a London posting. Achieving fame with Watford, he rose above the racism evident at many grounds in the 1980s to become Britain's first black soccer superstar. And, by making himself a hero to youngsters from all backgrounds, he helped break down racial barriers, paving the way for a whole new generation of ethnic footballers.

But it's his play for which he'll always be remembered at Anfield. After that initial title, he helped the Reds to another Championship and FA Cup success. He was also a key figure in

John Barnes kisses the old First Division trophy after the Reds wrapped up the title at Anfield in 1987–88

the 1995 Coca-Cola Cup Final, linking up brilliantly with the two-goal match-winner Steve McManaman. By then, he had moved into a deeper role, supplying inch-perfect passes for the likes of McManaman and Robbie Fowler. But, after defeat by Manchester United in the following season's FA Cup Final, Roy Evans decided on a change in tactics, bringing in the

midfield ball-winner Paul Ince. It was the signal for Barnes to leave. In 1997, with more than 400 Liverpool games and 106 goals to his credit, he joined Kenny Dalglish's Newcastle United side. He was awarded an MBE, and later played for Charlton Athletic. After an unhappy spell coaching at Glasgow Celtic, he established a new career in the media.

Baron, Kevin M P

1944/5-1953/4 (Inside-forward) **B** 19 7.1926, Preston **S** August
1945 from Preston NE (amateur) **D** 5.1.1946 v Chester City, FAC
L May 1954 to Southend Utd **Apps** 153, 32 gls **Hons** FAC finalist
1950 **OC** Preston North End (amateur), Southend Utd, Northampton T,
Gravesend & Northfleet, Wisbech T, Aldershot, Cambridge C, Bedford
T, Maldon T **d** 5.6.1971

A DECADE WITH Liverpool may have produced nothing more than an FA Cup losers'
medal, but the Preston-born forward was a firm
favourite among post-war fans. He joined the
club in 1944 and spent three years in the
reserves before finally getting his first-team
break. Standing at just 5ft 6in, he was a tricky
and elusive dribbler who kept Jack Balmer out
of the 1950 FA Cup Final side, then remained a
regular for another four years. When his Anfield
career began to fade he moved on to Southend,
then Northampton and Aldershot.

Anfield favourite: Kevin Baron

Baros, Milan

2001/2-present (Striker) **B** 28.10.1981, Ostrava, Czech Republic
S From Banik Ostrava, £3.4 million **D** 13.3.2002 v Barcelona, CH
League **Apps** 48, 11 gls **Hons** LC 2002–2003, 12 caps for Czech
Republic **OC** Banik Ostrava

CZECH INTERNATIONAL STRIKER
SIGNED in 2001, despite strong competition
from Juventus and Inter Milan. Strong, fast and
skilful, the 20-year-old's form with Banik
Ostrava had even led to comparisons with
Maradona. He made his Liverpool debut in
March 2002, replacing Emile Heskey as a substitute in the Champions League tie at
Barcelona. He pressed his claim for a regular
first-team place during the 2002–03 season, hitting 11 goals, and forming an increasingly pro-
ductive partnership with Michael Owen.

Milan Baros, the 'Ostravan Maradona'

Barton, Harold

1929/30-1933/4 (Outside-right) **B** 30.9.1911, Leigh **S** November
1928 from Whitegate Juniors **D** 9.10.1929 v Blackburn Rovers, lg
L June 1934 to Sheffield Utd **Apps** 109, 29 gls **Hons** none
OC Whitegate Juniors (Blackpool), Sheffield Utd, wartime guest for
Bradford C, Chesterfield, Lincoln C, Rotherham Utd, Sheffield Wed
d n/k

SPEEDY AND SKILFUL right-winger who
made more than 100 appearances between the
wars. Barton once scored four goals in an FA
Cup tie against Chesterfield, but his most memorable game came in February 1933 when
Liverpool beat Everton 7-4 in the League derby
at Anfield. Scoring legend Dixie Dean turned
out for the Blues – but it was Barton who
bagged a hat-trick.

Bartrop, Wilfred

1914-1915 (Winger) **B** 1889, Worksop **S** May 1914 from Barnsley
D 19.12.1914 v Oldham Athletic, lg **Apps** 3, 0 gls **Hons** none
OC Worksop T, Barnsley **d** 7.11.1918, four days before war ended

One of three Liverpool players killed in action
during World War One. Born in Worksop,
Bartrop played for his hometown team before
signing for Barnsley in 1909. He became a regular on the wing and was part of the Yorkshire
club's 1912 FA Cup-winning side. Bartrop
moved to Liverpool at the start of the 1914–15
season but made only three appearances before
enlisting as a gunner with the Royal Field
Artillery. He was killed in action in Belgium on
November 7th, 1918 – just four days before the
war ended.

Beardsley, Peter A

1987/8-1990/1 (Forward) **B** 18.1.1961, Newcastle **S** July 1987 from
Newcastle Utd, £1.9 million **D** 15.8.1987 v Arsenal, lg **L** Summer
1991 to Everton FC **Apps** 173, 59 gls **Hons** Div1 CH 1987–88,
1989–90; FAC 1988–89; CS 1988, 1989, 1990; 59 caps for
England **OC** Wallsend Boys Club, Carlisle Utd, Vancouver Whitecaps
(twice) Manchester Utd, Newcastle Utd (twice), Everton, Bolton W,
Manchester C, Fulham, Hartlepool, Doncaster R, Melbourne Knights

A CRUCIAL COG in the most entertaining side
in Liverpool's history. Beardsley arrived from
Newcastle for £1.9 million – a record deal
between British clubs. Along with the recently
recruited John Barnes and John Aldridge, he
took his place in an explosive forward line that
no defence could hold. Inheriting Kenny
Dalglish's No. 7 shirt, the little Geordie's skills
and finishing instincts helped Liverpool go 29
games unbeaten. And, by the end of the campaign, he'd picked up a Championship medal.
"Peter had as good a debut season for Liverpool
as any player I have seen," said skipper Alan
Hansen. "His most spectacular show came in
the 5-0 win over Nottingham Forest, one of our
closest Championship rivals, when he deceived
the Forest defence with an array of feints and
dummies that probably sent most of the crowd
the wrong way, too."

Beardo on the rampage against Manchester United's Gary Pallister and Clayton Blackmore

feat of scoring for both sides in Merseyside derbies – Beardsley returned to a prodigal's welcome at Newcastle. There were further moves to Bolton and Manchester City followed by a number of lower-league clubs before he finally decided to hang up his boots in 1999.

Beatles, The

THEY MAY HAVE been raised in a soccer-mad city, but John, George and Ringo had little interest in the game. As for Paul, his first loyalties were with Everton.

Still, they did more than most to spread Liverpool FC's fame worldwide. In 1967, they stuck Albert Stubbins on the cover of their *Sgt Pepper* album, putting him in the company of 20th Century icons such as Albert Einstein and Marilyn Monroe. A year later, they posed for photos wearing Liverpool rosettes (perhaps Macca had a change of heart after all).

But it was their rise to fame in the early 1960s that first put Liverpool under a global spotlight. The Beatles-inspired 'Mersey Sound' helped spark singing at Anfield, and made the city the capital of pop and youth culture. The Kop, packed with 25,000 suited mop-tops was its epicentre. The BBC's *Panorama* film, showing their version of *'She Loves You'*, defined the era of Merseybeat. And it led to copycat behaviour on every terrace in Britain.

Just weeks later, The Beatles conquered the USA, drawing record TV audiences for an appearance on *The Ed Sullivan Show*. With the Americans suddenly captivated by all things Liverpudlian, Bill Shankly took his the team on a promotional tour across the Atlantic. They were treated as major celebrities – and Sullivan promptly booked them as his next guests.

Back in Britain, the new singing craze transformed the atmosphere at soccer grounds throughout the 1964–65 season, and – having started it all – the Anfield fans continued to lead the pack.

In the studio, no one could match the Beatles' creativity; on the terraces, the Kopites were equally ahead in terms of wit and invention. Adapting pop songs into homages to LFC became their art form. Even Lennon himself was said to be impressed when he heard the words "Yellow Submarine" transformed into "Red And White Kop".

→ Also See "Singing"

Beardsley, who won 39 of his 59 England caps while with the Reds, went on to collect a second Championship in 1990, along with an FA Cup winners' medal a year earlier. Fans were puzzled when they saw him being relegated to the bench in Dalglish's last season. But they were in for a nastier surprise when Graeme Souness arrived as boss – and accepted a £1 million bid from Everton. After two seasons at Goodison – where he repeated David Johnson's

The Spice Beatles: Steve McManaman, Rob Jones, Stan Collymore and Jason McAteer pay homage to the original Beatles (inset)

Becton, Francis

1894/5-1897/8 (Inside-left) **B** 1873, Preston **S** 25.3.1895 from Preston NE, £100 **D** 25.3.1895 v Sunderland, lg **L** 7.10.1898 to Sheffield Utd **Apps** 86, 42 gls **Hons** Div 2 CH 1895–96 **OC** Preston Junior Football, Fishwick Ramblers, Preston N E (twice), Sheffield Utd, Bedminster, Swindon T (twice), Nelson, Ashton T, New Brighton Tower **d** 6.11.1909 of TB

LANCASTRIAN INSIDE-LEFT who signed from Preston for £100, then helped Liverpool clinch the Second Division Championship in 1896. Hitting the target 37 times in 74 appearances, he maintained a strike rate of a goal every two games. Already an international when he arrived, Becton made one more England appearance while at Anfield, becoming the first-ever LFC player to be capped. He left for Sheffield United in 1898, but wound up his career back on Merseyside with New Brighton Tower.

Beglin, James 'Jim' M

1983/4-1988/89 (Left-back) **B** 29.7.1963, Waterford, Rep I **S** May 1983 from Shamrock Rovers, £20,000 **D** 10.11.1984 v Southampton, lg **L** 1989 to Leeds Utd **Apps** 90, 3 gls **Hons** Div 1 CH 1985–86; FAC 1985–86; 15 caps for Rep I **OC** Bolton W, Bohemians, Shamrock Rovers, Leeds Utd, Plymouth Argyle (loan), Blackburn R (loan)

FORMER SHAMROCK ROVERS full-back, signed in Bob Paisley's last transfer deal. Paisley's successor Joe Fagan gave him his debut, but it was Kenny Dalglish who finally

Czech that out: Patrik Berger slams home a picture-perfect penalty in October 2000 as Evertonians watch on

made Beglin a regular. After displacing Alan Kennedy at No.3, he made 53 appearances in the 1985–86 Double-winning season. A combination of tough tackling and intelligent passing brought him over a dozen Republic of Ireland caps, but his Anfield career effectively ended on a cold night at Goodison Park when he broke a leg in a clash with Everton's Gary Stevens. Although he battled his way back to fitness, Beglin never regained a regular first-team place. He joined Leeds in 1989, helping them win promotion from the old Second Division. But in 1991, at the age of just 27, he was forced to retire, concentrating his energies on a new career as a football pundit for TV and radio.

Bennett, Reuben

FEARSOME SCOT WHO joined Liverpool's coaching staff in 1959 and became one of the original members of the Boot Room. The former Motherwell manager was widely tipped to take over from Phil Taylor as boss, but when the board opted for Shankly he asked him to remain as part of the backroom team. Bennett acted as club 'spy', travelling the country to compile dossiers on opposing teams. He also took charge of the Melwood training sessions, and acted as a blatantly biased referee in the legendary five-a-sides between players and staff. In the mid-1970s, Bennett handed over his coaching duties to Joe Fagan. He died in December 1989, at the age of 75.

Berger, Patrik

1996/7-2002/3 (Midfield/forward) **B** 10.11.1973, Prague, Czech Republic **S** 1996 from Borussia Dortmund, £3.2 million **D** 7.9.1996 v Southampton, lg **L** July 2003 on free transfer **Apps** 196, 35 gls **Hons** LC 2000–01; FAC 2000–01; UEFA 2000–01; Super Cup 2001; CS 2001; 44 Czech caps **OC** Slavia Prague, Borussia Dortmund

THE ATTACKING CZECH MIDFIELDER made an explosive start to his Liverpool career

of his career. Injuries kept him out of for much of the 2000–01 campaign, but he did feature as an FA Cup Final substitute, supplying the killer pass for Michael Owen's winner. Less than a week later he again came off the bench to help the Reds to UEFA Cup victory over Alaves.

Sadly, the injuries returned, making it impossible for him to reclaim a regular first-team place. He left in the summer of 2003.

Berry, Arthur

1907/8-1908/9 and 1912/3-1913/4 (Winger) **B** 3.1.1888, Liverpool **S** 1907 from Oxford University **D** 11.4.1908 v Newcastle United, lg **L** September 1909 for Fulham **Apps** 4, 0 gls **Hons** Great Britain Olympic Gold: 1908, 1912 **OC** Oxford University, Fulham, Everton (twice), Oxford C, Northern Nomads **d** 15.3.1953

ONE OF TWO FORMER Liverpool players to have won Olympic gold. The local born right-winger won his medals representing Great Britain's soccer team at the 1908 and 1912 Games before the World Cup was a twinkle in anybody's eye. Berry, whose father also served as Liverpool chairman between 1904 and 1909, enjoyed two spells at the club, with moves to Fulham and Everton in between. An Oxford law graduate, he gave up football at the end of the 1912–13 season to practise as a barrister.

Bimpson, J Louis

1952/3-1959/60 (Centre-forward) **B** 14.5.1929, Rainford, Lancashire **S** January 1953 from Burscough **D** 7.3.1953 v Aston Villa, lg **L** November 1959 to Blackburn R, £6,500 **Apps** 102, 39 gls **Hons** none **OC** Burscough, Blackburn R, Bournemouth & Boscombe Athletic, Rochdale, Wigan Athletic

LOUIS BIMPSON
Liverpool

with four goals in three games. He later established himself as one of the most exciting Anfield players of the nineties.

Berger first made his name alongside Vladimir Smicer at Slavia Prague, where he caught the attention of Borussia Dortmund. After helping them to the Bundesliga title, he enjoyed a starring role in Euro 96, scoring a penalty in his country's 2-1 Final defeat by Germany. Roy Evans pounced as the tournament ended, bringing him to Merseyside in a £3.2 million deal.

Berger's pace, work rate, passing ability and thunderous shot earned him praise from Kopites, while his Hollywood looks brought him an army of female fans. But despite his popularity on the terraces, he fell out of favour with Evans and, with the 1997–98 season coming to a close, he looked to be on his way to Roma.

However, new boss Gerard Houllier decided to nurture his undoubted talent and the player responded with some of the best performances

HEFTY CENTRE-FORWARD who inherited Albert Stubbins' No.9 jersey to become the leading marksman in the 1953–54 relegation season. He kept his place for most of the Second Division era, but was transferred to Blackburn when Roger Hunt broke into the side.

Biscan, Igor

2000/1-present (Midfield) **B** 4.5.1978, Zagreb, Croatia **S** December 2000 from Dinamo Zagreb, £5.5 million **D** 10.12.2000 v Ipswich Town, lg **Apps** 44, 1 gl **Hons** LC 2000–01, 2002–2003; FAC 2000–01; UEFA 2000–01; Super Cup 2001; CS 2001; 14 Czech caps **OC** Dinamo Zagreb

THE 6FT 3 CROATIAN caught the attention of Europe's top clubs at the European Under-21 Championships in the summer of 2000, but it was Liverpool who finally won the race for his signature.

Arriving from Zagreb for £5.5 million that December, Biscan slotted into a defensive midfield role and made 21 appearances in the Treble-winning season. First-team opportunities were limited during the following campaign but he fought his way back in the 2002–03 season, proving his versatility by playing in defence, midfield and attack.

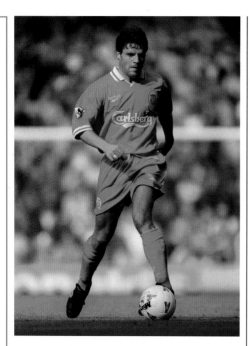

Bjornebye, Stig Inge

1992/3-1999/00 (Full-back/midfield) **B** 11.12.1969, Trondheim, Norway **S** From Rosenborg, 1992 **D** 19.12.1992 v Coventry C, lg **L** Summer 2000 to Blackburn R **Apps** 184, 4 gls **Hons** LC 1994–95; 75 Norway caps **OC** Strommen, Kongsvinger, Rosenborg (twice), Blackburn Rovers

AFTER AN ANFIELD DEBUT ending in a 5-1 defeat by Coventry City, Bjornebye's Liverpool career seemed to be cursed by bad luck. An unconvincing start at left-back led to a period on loan back at his former club, Rosenborg. Then, after displacing Julian Dicks during the 1994–95 season, he was among the team that lifted the Coca-Cola Cup… only to break a leg in a match with Southampton just a few days later. A series of other injuries sidelined him, while the likes of Steve Staunton and Rob Jones established themselves as regulars. He fought his way back into contention but, after finding his opportunities more limited under Gerard Houllier, he moved to Blackburn.

Blenkinsop, Ernest

1934/5-1937/8 (Left-back) **B** 20.4.1902, Cudworth, nr Barnsley **S** March 1934 from Sheffield Wed, 'four-figure fee' **D** 17.3.1934 v Birmingham C, lg **L** 1937 **Apps** 71, 0 gls **Hons** 26 England caps **OC** Cudworth United Methodists, Hull C, Sheffield Wed, Cardiff C, Buxton, wartime guest for Halifax T, Bradford C, Hurst **d** 24.4.1969

ONE OF THE FINEST left-backs England has ever produced, with an international reputation for hard but fair tackling. Blenkinsop had won 26 caps by the time he joined Liverpool from Sheffield Wednesday in 1934, going on to partner his fellow international full-back Tom Cooper for the next three seasons.

Boersma, Phil

1969/70-1975/6 and 1990/1-1993/4 (Forward) **B** 24.9.1949, Liverpool **S** Liverpool amateur, professional September 1968 **D** 24.9.1969 v Manchester C, LC **L** December 1975 to Middlesbrough, £72,000 **Apps** 121, 30 gls **Hons** Div1 CH 1972–73; UEFA 1972–73 **OC** Liverpool Amateur, Wrexham (on loan), Middlesbrough, Luton T, Swansea C; on coaching staff: Liverpool, Southampton, Benfica, Blackburn R; physio: Rangers

LOCAL-BORN STRIKER who had the bad luck to emerge at the same time as Steve Heighway, John Toshack and Kevin Keegan. Despite that handicap, Boersma always made the most of his limited first-team opportunities. An injury to Toshack led to 19 games and seven goals in the 1972–73 title-winning campaign. An appearance as substitute for Heighway against Borussia Moenchengladbach brought him a UEFA Cup Winners' Medal in the same season. Perhaps his best spell came at the start of the 1974–75 campaign when he scored six goals in the first eight League games, including a first-half hat-trick against Spurs. But after again failing to gain a regular first-team place he decided to move on, transferring to Middlesbrough in December 1975. A close friend of Graeme Souness, Boersma teamed up with the Scot on his return to Anfield in 1990, serving as physio and first-team coach. He's since worked with Souness at Southampton, Benfica, and Blackburn Rovers.

Bogey Teams

SEVERAL CLUBS APPEAR to have had a jinx on Liverpool throughout the years, even if only temporarily. In the early 1960s, newly promoted Leicester won five out of six League games against Bill Shankly's men, along with an FA Cup semi-final. Nottingham Forest made Bob Paisley's life a misery in the late 1970s – taking over as Champions, beating his team in the hotly disputed 1978 League Cup Final replay, then knocking them out of the European Cup a year later. For Kenny Dalglish and his successors, it was Wimbledon who proved the stuff of nightmares. Not content with supplying one of the biggest Wembley shocks of all time by beating Liverpool in an FA Cup Final, the Dons won at Anfield three times between 1987 and 1992, before dumping them out of the League Cup in a 1993 penalty shoot-out.

Boot Room

➔ See pages 30, 31

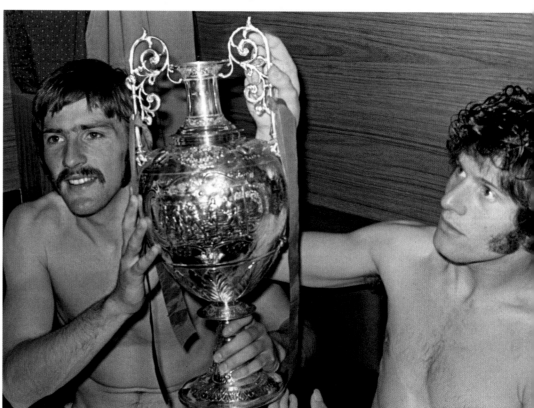

Phil Boersma and Steve Heighway with the 1973 Championship (the sideburns give away the year)

Bogey Team: John Robertson is mobbed by his Nottingham Forest team-mates after scoring the winner in the 1978 League Cup Final replay at Old Trafford

Boxing

LIVERPOOL FC'S LINKS with the fight game go right back to the 1920s when Anfield was sometimes used as a venue for British championship bouts. The biggest of them all came in 1934 when world featherweight champion Freddie Miller retained his crown by beating Nelson Tarleton in front of a packed house.

A decade later the club had an even more distinguished boxing visitor. Legendary American world heavyweight champ Joe Louis called in at Anfield after taking part in a three-round exhibition match at Liverpool Stadium. In a memorable publicity stunt, manager George Kay invited the so-called 'Brown Bomber' to sign professional terms for the club. Louis agreed and was unveiled to the press as Liverpool's newest star player. But, as the forms weren't submitted to the Football League, the signing was never made official. One man who would have been glad to have Louis was Bob Paisley. As a keen fight fan, he advocated boxing training for players, and encouraged goalkeepers to strengthen their hands on the Anfield punch-ball. He also offered his services to local fighters, helping coach Alan Rudkin and Kirkby's world-champion, light-heavyweight John Conteh.

Boys' Pen

TERRIFYING, FENCED-IN enclosure, originally part of the Kemlyn Road terrace, but moved to a rear corner of the Kop in the 1950s. Offering cut-price admission to Under-16s, the Pen also attracted many suspiciously old-looking 'schoolboys'. Big games would also see hundreds of Kopites climbing over the fence to escape the crush on the main terrace – and forcing the youngsters to make way. "The Pen was ridiculous – Britain's own Dodge City," wrote Liverpudlian author Alan Edge. "To term it a jungle would be an affront to all self-respecting lions, sabre-toothed tigers and orang-utans." Thousands of frightened youngsters got their first glimpse of Anfield from inside the wild and lawless Pen. Some even came out alive.

A 1950s Anfield boxing photo call: future Beatles manager, Brian Epstein, with LFC'S Cyril Done (r)

Boot Room

SMALL CUBBY-HOLE underneath Anfield's Main Stand that took on an almost mythical status during the Shankly and Paisley eras. It was here that the manager's backroom staff would meet to discuss form and tactics, while dissecting the strengths and weaknesses of upcoming opposition. It was also the home of the 'black books' – exhaustive dossiers on every LFC player, detailing their injuries, treatments, absenteeism records, even notes on their attitudes during training. The list of Boot Room personnel may have changed over the years, but some names are synonymous: Bob Paisley, Joe Fagan, Ronnie Moran, Reuben Bennett, Roy Evans, former chief scout Geoff Twentyman, and ex-Youth Development Officer Tom Saunders.

The 'Boot Room Boys' achieved fame throughout the football world but, as Graeme Souness later recalled, they also guarded their privacy. "The room is not very big and the carpet could do with replacing but it has an atmosphere all of its own and it is a big honour to be invited inside. Sometimes the players may wander in to beg a glass of pop, which they pay for, but if the door is closed you stay out. This is the place where all the playing decisions are made and where the big pow-wow takes place after every home game when it is strictly out of bounds to us mere players. When that door is locked and bolted, you can imagine what goes on inside only, for – though you may pause – you never hear a word. It is not a shouting room. It is a place for whispers, secrets and, especially, those black books."

Ironically it was Souness who was later blamed for getting rid of the Boot Room. But in fact its demolition – to make way for a press facilities room during Anfield's hosting of Euro 96 matches – had already been decided by the Board. It was a symbolic loss but, by that stage, the Boot Room's influence had waned. The departure of Roy Evans, followed by the retirement of Ronnie Moran, finally brought an end to another Shankly-inspired tradition.

John Aldridge looks a little apprehensive in the inner sanctum of the Liverpool FC backroom boys

"The job's yours" – Kenny Dalglish is warmly welcomed into the boot room by longtime residents Ronnie Moran, Bob Paisley and Roy Evans

Bradley, James 'Jim' E

1905/6-1910/1 (Left-half) **B** 1881 Goldenhill, Staffs, 1881 **S** September 1905 from Stoke **D** 23.9.1905 v Birmingham, lg **L** 1911 for Reading **Apps** 185, 8 gls **Hons** Div 1 CH 1905–06, Dewar Shield 1906 **OC** Stoke (twice), Reading **d** 12.3.1954

Bradshaw, T Henry 'Harry'

1893/4-1897/8 (Forward) **B** 24.8.1873, Liverpool **S** October 1893 from Northwich Victoria **D** 28.10.1893 v Arsenal, lg **L** May 1898 for Tottenham **Apps** 138, 53 gls **Hons** Div 2 CH 1893–94, 1895–96; 1 England cap **OC** Northwich Victoria, Tottenham, Thames Ironworks **d** 25.12.1899 of TB

ONE OF THE FIRST Liverpool internationals, Bradshaw turned out for England in 1897 – a year after helping his club win promotion from Division Two for the second time. He left for Tottenham in 1898 but died before the century was out, aged just 26.

Bradshaw, Thomas 'Tiny'

1929/30-1937/8 (Centre-half) **B** 7.2.1904, Bishopton, Renfrewshire **S** January 1930 from Bury, £8,000 **D** 25.1.1930 v Manchester Utd, lg **L** September 1938 for Third Lanark **Apps** 291, 4 gls **Hons** Lancashire Senior Cup 1930–31; 1 Scottish cap (he was one of the 1928 'Wembley Wizards') **OC** Woodside Juniors, Hamilton Academical, Bury, Third Lanark, South Liverpool; Chief scout: Norwich City **d** 22.2.1986

NICKNAMED 'TINY' BECAUSE of his huge 6ft 2 in frame, Bradshaw stood out as a massive, commanding figure at the heart of Liverpool's Depression-era defence.

Everton scoring legend Dixie Dean rated the Scottish international his most difficult opponent, and Bradshaw's outstanding form almost certainly helped the club stave off relegation in the lean 1930s. He left for Third Lanark in 1938 but later returned to Merseyside with non-league South Liverpool.

Brierley, Ken

1947/8-1953/4 (Winger/Inside-left) **B** 3.4.1926, Ashton-U-Lyne **S** April 1945 from Oldham Athletic, £7,000 **D** 6.3.1948 v Huddersfield T, lg **L** 1953 to Oldham Athletic, £2,750 **Apps** 61, 8 gls **Hons** none **OC** Range Boilers FC (Oldham), Oldham Athletic (twice), Stalybridge Celtic, Mossley

Bromilow, Tom

1919/20-1929/30 (Left-half) **B** 7.10.1894, Liverpool **S** Summer 1919, from wartime service **D** 25.10.1919 v Burnley, lg **L** Left summer 1930 for managment in Holland **Apps** 374, 11 gls **Hons** Div1 CH 1921–22, 1922–23; CS finalist 1922; 5 caps for England **OC** Fonthill Road School, West Dingle, Army Football; manager: in Amsterdam, Burnley Crystal Palace (twice), Leicester C, Newport; scout: Leicester C **d** 4.3.1959 at Nuneaton whilst returning by train from watching Wrexham play Merthyr Tydfil in a cup tie

FIRST WORLD WAR veteran who turned up one day at Anfield wearing full army uniform and asking for a trial. Assistant manager George Patterson quickly agreed to the soldier's request – and never regretted it either, as he watched Bromilow's game blossom. Progress happened fast as the left-half developed into an England international within three years.

Bromilow was a vital member of the post-WW1 side, building a reputation as a hard tackler and fine distributor of the ball. He missed just two games in each of the title-winning seasons in the early 1920s, and won the first of his five England caps in 1921. After retirement he coached abroad, before returning to manage Burnley, Crystal Palace, Newport and Leicester.

'Tiny' Bradshaw – the big Scottish centre-half

KEY **Apps** Appearances | **B** Born | **CH** Championship | **CWC** Cup Winners' Cup | **CS** Charity Shield | **D** Debut | **d** Died | **EC** European Cup | **FAC** FA Cup | **gls** Goals | **Hons** Honours | **lg** League

Burkinshaw, Keith H

1953/4-1957/8 (Centre-half) **B** 23.6.1935, Higham, Barnsley
S November 1953 from Denaby Utd (amateur) **D** 11.4.1955 v Port
Vale, lg **L** December 1957 for Workington, £2,500 **Apps** 1, 0 gls
Hons None **OC** Denaby Utd (Wolves amateur), Workington,
Scunthorpe Utd; Assistant coach: Newcastle Utd; chief coach/manag-
er: Tottenham, Bahrain national team, West Bromwich Albion,
Gillingham; director: Aberdeen

THE ONLY FORMER Liverpool player to lead out a team against the Reds at Wembley. Burkinshaw made just one appearance for the club during the 1950s, before continuing his playing career at Workington and Scunthorpe. He emerged from obscurity in 1976 when Tottenham Hotspur appointed him as manager – a position he held for eight years. During that time, he signed the Argentinian World Cup winners Osvaldo Ardilles and Ricky Villa, won the FA Cup twice in succession and guided his team to UEFA Cup glory. But facing Liverpool in the 1982 League Cup, Spurs lost 3-1 as Ronnie Whelan struck twice and Ian Rush added the third. Burkinshaw left White Hart Lane in 1984 and later coached the Bahrain national squad. He went on to manage West Bromwich Albion, Gillingham and Aberdeen, where he served as a director until 2001.

Burrows, David

1988/9-1993 (Full-back) **B** 25.10.1968, Dudley **S** October 1988 from
West Bromwich Albion, £500,000 **D** 22.10.1988 v Coventry C, lg
L October 1993 to West Ham **Apps** 190, 6 gls **Hons** Div 1 CH
1989–90; FAC 1991–92; England U21 caps **OC** West Bromwich
Albion, West Ham, Everton, Coventry C, Brimingham, Sheffield Wed

HALF-MILLION POUND signing from West Bromwich Albion in October 1988. Although a skilful full-back, Burrows was also noted for over-enthusiastic challenges that often got him into trouble with referees. His commitment also led to a succession of injuries sustained in rugged challenges.

Burrows missed out on a place against Everton in the 1989 FA Cup Final as Kenny Dalglish opted for the more thoughtful style of Steve Staunton. But despite that disappointment, 'Bugsy' bounced back to play a useful role in the 1989–90 Championship-winning campaign.

Under new manager Graeme Souness, the player's first-team appearances became less regular and he soon found himself being offered in the exchange deal that brought West Ham's Julian Dicks to Anfield. After just a year at Upton Park he joined Everton, then Coventry and Birmingham, before switching to Sheffield Wednesday in 2002.

B

Liverpool FC's greatest contribution to Manchester United… Matt Busby was once an Anfield favourite

Bush, Tom

1933/4-1947 (Left-back/centre-half) **B** 22.2.1914, Hodnet, Shropshire **S** March 1933 from Shrewsbury Amateurs **D** 30.12.1933 v Wolverhampton Wanderers, lg **L** Retired summer 1947, joined LFC office staff **Apps** 72, 1 gl **Hons** None **OC** Shrewsbury Amateurs; wartime guest: Brighton & Hove Albion, Leeds Utd, Fulham **d** 20.12.1969

Byrne, Gerry

1957/8-1968/9 (Left-back and coach) **B** 29.8.1938 Liverpool **S** From Liverpool Schools **D** 28.9.1957 v Charlton Athletic, lg **L** Retired December 1969 to become LFC coach **Apps** 330, 3 gls **Hons** Div2 CH 1961–62; Div1 CH 1963–64, 1965–66; FAC 1964–65; CWC Finalist 1965–66; CS 1966; 2 caps for England **OC** Liverpool Schools

"THE BRAVEST THING I've ever seen," was how Tommy Smith described Byrne's performance at the 1965 FA Cup final. A clash with Leeds captain Bobby Collins had left him with a broken collarbone after just nine minutes. But, with no substitutes allowed, he chose to play on, defying the agony until the end of extra-time, and supplying the cross for Roger Hunt's opening goal along the way.

"I couldn't lift my hand; I was running with it across my chest," the heroic full-back said afterwards. "I made the mistake of trying to take a throw-in and it nearly killed me. At that point I knew something was broken. But no one tried to get me to come off. And I didn't want to come off anyway."

Unsurprisingly, Bill Shankly rated him as the hardest player he'd ever come across. Yet, when the new boss arrived at Anfield, the local-born defender was up for sale. After seeing him train, Shankly took him off the transfer list and promptly gave him a regular first-team place. Byrne then became an ever-present in the 1962 promotion-winning season.

Although finally forced to retire because of injury, Byrne never let pain affect his performances. Less than a year after his Wembley heroics, he dislocated an elbow in a European game at Celtic Park. Defying the club doctor's advice, he stayed on the field until ten minutes before the end. Two days later – his arm black from shoulder to wrist – he played the full 90 minutes of a League match at Stoke.

Busby, Matt

1935/6-1944/5 (Right-half) **B** 26.5.1909, Orbiston, Lanarks **S** 11.3.1936, from Manchester C, £8,000 **D** 14.3.1936 v Huddersfeld T, lg **L** Retired October 1945, to manage Manchester Utd **Apps** 125, 3 gls (26 apps WWII) **Hons** none **OC** Alpine Villa, Denny Hibernian, Manchester C; wartime guest Chelsea, Middlesbrough, Reading, Brentford, Bournemouth & Boscombe Athletic, Hibernian; manager: Manchester Utd **d** 21.1.1994

ALTHOUGH FOREVER remembered for his managerial success at Old Trafford, Busby was once a firm playing favourite at Anfield. The ex-Man City half-back joined for £8,000 in 1936, just in time to help new boss George Kay put up a successful fight against relegation, and to cement his reputation as one of the game's most elegant players. "Matt was captain of Liverpool when I came down from the North-East to join them," Bob Paisley wrote later. "We certainly had a lot of respect for him… as a player he was cultured, methodical, precise and very deliberate in his distribution." He was also a born leader. After serving with Merseyside's 9th King's Regiment in World War Two, several clubs tried to tempt him into management. The Liverpool board countered with an offer to make him first-team coach, but that wasn't enough to prevent him taking on the top job at Manchester United.

At Old Trafford he went on to lift the 1948 FA Cup and 1952 Championship, while laying the foundations for the "Busby Babes" – a team of youngsters who looked set to dominate the domestic game from the late 1950s onwards. The death of eight of them in the 1958 Munich air disaster robbed the game of some its best and brightest talents. Yet Busby, who was himself seriously injured in the crash, bounced back to construct another team that won the European Cup in 1968. "When you think about it, it was only right that United, under Matt, should be the first English club to win the trophy," added Paisley. "There was the style with which his United teams played – and the character of the man, shown at its greatest when he and the club fought back after the tragedy of Munich." In all, Busby guided United to a European Cup, two FA Cup and five League Championship triumphs. Knighted for his services to football, he went on to serve the club as a director, then President, until his death in 1994.

Cadden, Joe Y

1950/1-1951/2 (Centre-half) **B** 13.4.1920, Glasgow **S** June 1948 from Brooklyn Wanderers **D** 23.9.1950 v Fulham, lg **L** June 1952 to Grimsby T **Apps** 5, 0 gls **Hons** none **OC** Brooklyn Wanderers, Grimsby T, Accrington Stanley, New Brighton **d** 5.6.1981

LIVERPOOL RETURNED FROM their second American pre-season tour with healthy tans – and a brand-new centre-back. Cadden was a Scot who moved to the USA after being demobbed from the Army at the end of World War Two. He turned out against the Reds for Brooklyn Wanderers in 1948, playing so well that manager George Kay promptly signed him on. Back in England, though, his form was nowhere near as impressive. Cadden made just four appearances before moving to Grimsby in 1952. He later played for Accrington Stanley and New Brighton.

Callaghan, Ian (MBE)

1959/60-1977/8 (Winger/midfield) **B** 10.4.1942 Liverpool **S** From youth team **D** 16.4.1960 v Bristol R. lg **L** Summer 1978 to Swansea **Apps** 857, 69 gls **Hons** EC 1976–77; UEFA 1972–73, 1975–76; Super Cup 1977; CWC Finalist 1965–66; Div1 CH 1963–64, 1965–66, 1972–73, 1975–76, 1976–77; Div2 CH 1961–62; FAC 1964–65, 1973–74, finalist 1970–71; CS 1966, 1974, 1976; 4 caps for England **OC** Swansea, Cork Hibernian, Soudifjord, Crewe Alexandra

WITH A RECORD 857 senior outings, no player comes near to Callaghan's longevity at the game's highest level. The Liverpool-born teenager took the place of his idol Billy Liddell, then stayed in the team as it rose from Division Two obscurity to the pinnacle of Europe. A mark of his consistency is that he was chosen for England in 1966 – before getting a recall 11 years later, aged 35.

Fast, direct and possessing incredible stami- na, Callaghan was a raiding right winger until suffering knee damage in the 1970–71 season. When he regained his place it was in the centre of midfield, later playing alongside Peter Cormack, then Ray Kennedy and Terry McDermott. In 1974 his performances earned him the Footballer Of The Year award and an MBE, but his best moment came three years later as part of the team that lifted the European Cup for the first time.

In a Liverpool career spanning nearly two full decades, Callaghan was never sent off, and was booked only once. Added to the honour picked up in Rome, he also collected five League Championships, a European Super Cup, two FA Cup and two UEFA Cup medals. His outstanding service came to an end in 1978 when he moved to Swansea City. He later joined Crewe Alexandra, setting an all-time record of 88 FA Cup appearances.

February 19, 1977: Mr Consistency, Ian Callaghan, is applauded on to the pitch by both Liverpool and Derby County players for his 800th appearance

Camara, Aboubacar 'Titi'

1999/2000-2000/01 (Striker) **B** 17.11.1972, Donka, Guinea
S From Olympique Marseille, 1 June 1999, £2.8 million **D** 7.8.1999
v Sheffield Wed, lg **L** 21.12.2000 to West Ham, £1.3 million
Apps 37, 10 gls **Hons** None **OC** St Etienne, Lens, Olympique
Marseille, West Ham, Al-Ittihad (loan)

THE FIRST FOOTBALLER from Guinea to play in England, Camara finished his debut season second only to Michael Owen in the Anfield scoring charts. The former Olympic Marseille striker was a huge Kop favourite who showed his commitment by playing and scoring in a 1-0 win against West Ham, just hours after the death of his father. But his demand for a more regular first-team place set him on a collision course with Gerard Houllier, who agreed to a £1.3 million bid from the Hammers shortly before Christmas 2000.

Campbell, Donald

1950/1-1957/8 (Left-half) **B** 19.10.1932, Bootle **S** November 1950
from Liverpool Schools **D** 14.11.1953 v Sunderland, lg **L** July 1958
to Crewe Alexandra, £4,000 **Apps** 47, 2 gls **Hons** England Youth
caps **OC** Liverpool Schools, Crewe Alexandra, Gillingham (trial),
Folkestone T

Campbell, Kenny

1911/12-1919/20 (Goalkeeper) **B** 6.9.1892,
Glasgow **S** May 1911 from Cambuslang Rovers
D 10.2.1912 v Blackburn R, lg **L** April 1920 to
Partick Thistle, £1,750 **Apps** 142 (plus 37
WWI games) **Hons** FAC finalist 1913–14;
8 caps for Scotland **OC** Rutherglen Glencairn,
Cambuslang Rovers, Partick Thistle, New
Brighton (twice), Stoke C, Leicester C
d 28.4.1977

SUPERB SCOTTISH
INTERNATIONAL who kept
goal between the eras of two
other outstanding 'keepers – Sam Hardy and the legendary Elisha Scott. Campbell joined from Cambuslang Rovers in 1911, became the first-choice No.1 and appeared in the 1914 FA Cup Final. Despite the emergence of Scott, Campbell kept hold of the 'keeper's jersey until the outbreak of World War One. He resumed his place when the fighting was over, but within a season the Irishman had taken over. He went on to play for New Brighton and later opened a sports shop in the town.

Caps

→ See International Caps

Captains

EVER SINCE Andrew Hannah led out the team for their first Lancashire League fixture in 1892, Liverpool have produced a line of outstanding skippers. They include the Scottish international Alex Raisbeck, who lifted the first Championship trophies in 1901 and 1906, and Don MacKinlay, who led the team to two successive League triumphs in the early 1920s. Striker Jack Balmer captained the post-World War Two title winners, with future boss Phil Taylor taking charge in time for the 1950 FA Cup Final.

It was Taylor's managerial successor, Bill Shankly, who launched the club on the road to unprecedented success, building a team around his "Captain Colossus" Ron Yeats – the first Liverpool player to get his hands on the FA Cup. Later captains have included Emlyn Hughes, the first to lift the UEFA and European Cups, as well as the most decorated skipper in the history of the English game; Phil Thompson and Graeme Souness, who also led their sides to European Championship glory; and Alan Hansen, who was captain when the Reds clinched their first League and FA Cup Double.

During the relatively barren 1990s, only Mark Wright (FA Cup) and Ian Rush (Coca-Cola Cup) managed to hold trophies aloft. And during the Treble-winning season, the armband passed from the injured Jamie Redknapp to Robbie Fowler and finally to the current skipper, Sami Hyypia.

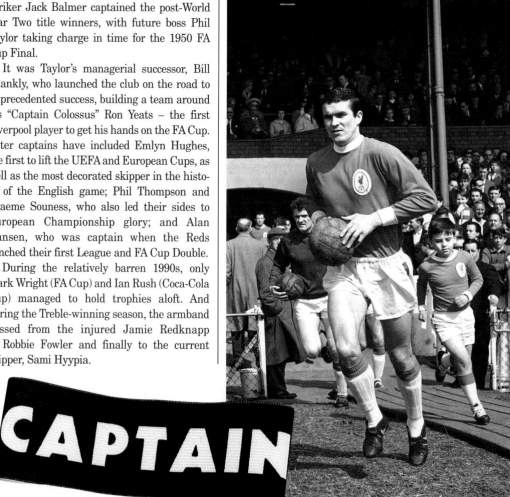

CAPTAIN

KEY Apps Appearances | **B** Born | **CH** Championship | **CWC** Cup Winners' Cup | **CS** Charity Shield | **D** Debut | **d** Died | **EC** European Cup | **FAC** FA Cup | **gls** Goals | **Hons** Honours | **lg** League

Captains clockwise from top left: Souness with the First Division trophy, 1982; Emlyn Hughes at Anfield, 20.2.1973; Phil Thompson in Paris with the European Cup after victory over Real in 1981; Phil Taylor greeting a bowler-hatted George VI before the 1950 Cup Final; Hansen after the 3-1 FA Cup win over Everton in 1986; Ron Yeats at Chelsea, 16.4.1965

Carlin, John

1902/3-1906/7 (Inside-forward) **B** Liverpool **S** 1902 from Merseyside
Junior Football **D** 17.1.1903 v Stoke C, lg **L** 1907 to Preston NE
Apps 35, 8 gls **Hons** Div2 CH 1904–05; Div1 CH 1905–06; Dewar
Shield 1906; Liverpool Cup 1905–06 **OC** Preston NE **d** n/k

Carragher, Jamie

1996/7-present (Defender/midfield) **B** 28.1.1978, Liverpool **S** From
LFC Academy, summer 1996 **D** 8.1.1997 v Middlesbrough, LC
Apps 274, 2 gls **Hons** LC 2000–01, 2002–03; FAC 2000–01; UEFA
2000–01; Super Cup 2001; CS 2001; CS finalist 2002; FA Youth Cup
19955/6; 8 caps for England **OC** none

A wispy Carragher with coach Hugh McAuley

STRONG, COMMITTED DEFENDER who's
filled every position in the back four. Bootle-
born Carragher played in Liverpool's 1996 FA
Youth Cup-winning side, graduating to captain
England's Under-21s. He marked his senior
debut with a goal against Aston Villa in 1997
before establishing himself as a regular two seasons later.

Markus Babbel's arrival forced him to move
from right- to left-back, but he still became an
essential member of the Treble-winning side.
His consistent form brought him an England
cap in 2000, and he only missed out on the 2002
World Cup squad because of knee surgery. After
spending the summer recuperating, he went
into the 2002–03 season as the player with most
Liverpool appearances under his belt.

Carter, Jimmy

1990/1-1991/2 (Winger) **B** 9.11.1965, Hammersmith **S** Jan 1991
from Millwall, £800,000 **D** 12.1.1991 v Aston Villa, lg **L** Oct 1991 to
Arsenal **Apps** 4, 0gls **OC** Millwall, Arsenal, Oxford Utd, Portsmouth

Case, Jimmy R

1973/4-1980/1 (Forward) **B** 18.5.1954, Liverpool **S** May 1973 from
South Liverpool, £500 **D** 26.4.1975 v QPR, lg **L** August 1981 to
Brighton, £350,000 **Apps** 267, 46 gls **Hons** EC 1976–77, 1977–78,
1980–81; UEFA 1975–76; Super Cup 1978 finalist; Div1 CH
1975–76, 1976–77, 1978–79, 1979–80; FAC finalist 1976–77;
LC 1980–81; LC finalist 1977–78; CS 1976, 1977, 1979, 1980
OC South Liverpool, Brighton, Southampton, Bournemouth, Halifax

FIERCE-TACKLING MIDFIELDER with possibly the most powerful shot in the club's entire
history. He joined as an amateur from South
Liverpool FC in 1972, making his debut on the
last day of the 1974–75 season. Within a year
he'd taken his place in one of the best Liverpool
midfield line-ups ever: Case, Kennedy,
Callaghan and McDermott.

His phenomenal shooting power brought
many spectacular goals, often from free-kicks.
He hit a hat-trick in a UEFA Cup tie against
Poland's Slask Wroclaw in 1975, and another
three in a 1978 League match against Bolton.

In between came his unstoppable volley past
Manchester United in the 1977 FA Cup Final –
a game the Reds eventually went on to lose 2-1.
But Case picked up plenty of other honours
along the way, helping lift the 1976 UEFA Cup,
four League Championships and three
European Cups. He joined Brighton in 1981,
returning to Anfield to score a stunning FA Cup
winner that put his new team on the road to
Wembley. He played for Southampton, and a
host of lower-league clubs before returning to
Brighton as manager.

Celebrity Fans

LIVERPOOL SUPPORTERS PREFER watch-
ing their heroes on the pitch to star-spotting in
the stands. Still, anyone looking to fill the half-
time void could look out for: Ricky Tomlinson
and Sue Johnston, the *Royle Family* actors
who've been fans since Shankly's day; singer
Elvis Costello, who's been an Anfield regular
since his boyhood on the Kop; and radio DJ
John Peel, who used to wear a neck-locket containing a patch of Anfield turf.

There are many more supporters from the
worlds of film and TV, including *Austin Powers*
star Mike Myers (whose father came from
Liverpool), Scottish actor Robert Carlyle, the
television and theatre playwright Alan
Bleasdale, BBC newsreader Peter Sissons and
Sky One presenter Kirsty Gallacher.

Meanwhile, from the world of music, the list
is virtually endless: from Gerry & The
Pacemakers and Eminem's American producer
Dr Dre – who was captivated by John Barnes in
the 1980s – to local bands such as Cast, Echo &
The Bunnymen, sundry members of Atomic
Kitten and The Lightning Seeds, to the Irish
ballad king Chris de Burgh.

Although politics and sport are best kept
apart, Bill Shankly was always happy to welcome former PM Harold Wilson to Anfield, even
though the Huyton MP's first allegiance was to
his native Huddersfield. And what supporter
wasn't proud when Nelson Mandela met John
Barnes in South Africa – to reveal that he'd
been a Liverpool fan since the 1960s?

Royle reds: Heskey, Hyypia, Gerrard, Murphy and Riise with *The Royle Family's* Ricky Tomlinson

KEY Apps Appearances | **B** Born | **CH** Championship | **CWC** Cup Winners' Cup | **CS** Charity Shield | **D** Debut | **d** Died | **EC** European Cup | **FAC** FA Cup | **gls** Goals | **Hons** Honours | **lg** League

Casing the joint: Jimmy Case salutes the Anfield crowd after scoring the third goal against West Bromwich Albion in the 3-0 win in August, 1977

Centenary Stand

BUILT IN 1992, a hundred years after Liverpool FC was formed. The impressive two-tiered block, including executive boxes and banqueting facilities, was officially opened by UEFA President Lennart Johanssen. It replaced the old Kemlyn Road stand and can seat 11,400 spectators.

Chadwick, Edgar W

1902/3-1903/4 (Inside-forward) **B** 14.6.1869, Blackburn **S** 1902 from Southampton **D** 6.9.1902 v Blackburn R, lg **L** May 1904 to Blackpool **Apps** 45, 7 gls **Hons** 7 England caps **OC** Little Dots FC, Blackburn Olympic, Blackburn R, Everton, Burnley, Southampton, Blackpool, Glossop, Darwen; coached Germany/Holland **d** 14.2.1942

Chambers, Harry 'Smiler'

1915/6-1927/8 (Inside-forward) **B** 17.11.1896, Willington Quay, Northumberland **S** April 1915 from North Shields Athletic **D** 30.8.1919 v Bradford C, lg **L** March 1928 to West Bromwich Albion **Apps** 339, 151 gls **Hons** Div1 CH 1921–22, 1922–23; CS 1922 finalist; 8 England caps **OC** Willington Utd Methodists, North Shields Athletic, Belfast Distillery (wartime guest), Glentoran (wartime guest), West Bromwich Albion, Oakengates T (player-manager), Hereford Utd **d** 29.6.1949

BOW-LEGGED GEORDIE whose goals powered Liverpool to successive League titles in 1922 and 1923. He was on target 41 times in those two seasons and finished as the club's top marksman for three years in a row. The left-footed Chambers arrived just after the First World War, staying for nine years and averaging a goal almost every other game. He won eight England caps throughout his career, getting on the mark five times at international level. He left Anfield in 1928 bound for West Brom and, later, the Shropshire non-league side Oakengates, where he played until he was 52.

The Class of '88: Kenny Dalglish and his men bring the Championship trophy back to Anfield again

Championship – Winners

WITH 18 TITLE SUCCESSES, Liverpool have won the League Championship more times than any other English club. The years they have lifted the trophy are as follows:

1900–01, 1905–06, 1921–22, 1922–23, 1946–47, 1963–64, 1965–66, 1972–73, 1975–76, 1976–77, 1978–79, 1979–80, 1981–82, 1982–83, 1983–84, 1985–86, 1987–88, 1989–90

Championship – Runners–Up

OVER THE YEARS, the team has finished second in the title race on 11 separate occasions. The years they have come in as runners–up are as follows:

1898–99, 1909–10, 1968–69, 1973–74, 1974–75, 1977–78, 1984–85, 1986–87, 1988–89, 1990–91, 2001–02

From the top: 1900–01 Title medal; home-made card and pennant from 1963–64

Peter Cormack holds the Charity Shield aloft after Liverpool's victory over Leeds in 1974

Charity Shield

LIVERPOOL FIRST TOOK part in the traditional annual League curtain-raiser in 1922 when they were beaten by Huddersfield at Old Trafford. They have since made another 19 appearances, winning the trophy outright nine times, and sharing it on five occasions.

The 1966 victory over Everton at Goodison Park proved historic – the one and only time the League Championship, FA Cup and World Cup were displayed together at a British stadium.

In 1974 Liverpool became the first club to win the Shield on penalties, beating Leeds 6-5 in a match that stuck in the mind for a long time.

That fixture was notable for two features: Bill Shankly led out Liverpool for the last time, and both Kevin Keegan and Billy Bremner received red cards for fighting. In 2001 the Reds beat Manchester United in Cardiff, the first time the fixture had been held outside England.

Cheyrou, Bruno

2002/3-present (Left-midfield) **B** 10.5.1978, Suresnes, France **S** July 2002 from Lille, £3.7 million **D** 11.8.2002 v Arsenal, CS **Apps** 28, 1 gl **Hons** none **OC** RC Lens, Racing Club Paris, Lille

CREATIVE LEFT-SIDED MIDFIELDER signed from the French club Lille in the summer of 2002. Cheyrou comes from a footballing family, with a grandfather who was President of Racing Club Paris, and a brother still at Lille. Fine performances in the Champions League caused a rush for his signature, but in the end he opted for Anfield. He made his debut in the 2002–03 season but didn't play enough games to get used to the frenetic pace of the Premiership but did show some signs of class for the future.

Chisnall, J.Phillip

1964/5-1966/7 (Centre-forward) **B** 27.10.1942, Manchester **S** April 1964 from Manchester Utd, £25,000 **D** 22.8.1964 v Arsenal, lg **L** August 1967 to Southend Utd, £12,000 **Apps** 9, 2 gls **Hons** 8 England schoolboy caps; England U23 caps **OC** Stretford Schools, Manchester Utd, Southend Utd, Stockport County

IF MOVES ACROSS Stanley Park are rare, transfers between Liverpool and Manchester United are almost unheard of. It's nearly 40

years since Chisnall left Old Trafford for Anfield, and no one has followed that direct path since. Bill Shankly may have had high hopes when he paid £25,000 for the ex-England schoolboy international in 1964. But Chisnall – who scored in the club's first-ever European game in Reykjavik – never became a regular face in the legendary mid-1960s line-up. He finally left for Southend in 1967.

Clarke, John R

1928/9-1930/1 (Forward) **B** 6.2.1903, Newburn, Newcastle upon Tyne **S** January 1928 from Newcastle Utd **D** 4.2.1928 v West Ham **L** July 1931 to Nottingham Forest **Apps** 42, 11 gls **Hons** none **OC** Spencer's Welfare, Hawthorn Leslie, Newburn Grange, Newburn FC, Pruhoe Castle, Newcastle Utd, Nottingham Forest, North Shields (player-coach) **d** 1977

Clean Sheets

LIVERPOOL'S BEST SEASON for clean sheets came in 1978–79 when the opposition were shut out 28 times. Among the club's 'keepers, only two – John McConnell and Harold McNaughton – never conceded a goal (although both managed just one appearance each between the sticks).

Of the others, the best records belong to Elisha Scott, who boasted 137 clean sheets in 468 appearances, and Bruce Grobbelaar, who kept the opposition out 267 times during his 628 games with Liverpool. But, with no goals against in 323 of his 665 matches, the undisputed "clean sheet king" is Ray Clemence. Talking of whom… see next entry.

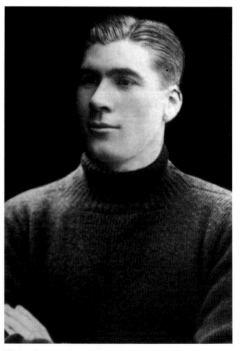

Elisha Scott, whose sheets were often clean…

The ultimate safe pair of hands: defenders could always depend on Clemence's technique and reflexes

Clemence, Ray N (MBE)

1967/8-1980/1 (Goalkeeper) **B** 5.8.1948, Skegness **S** June 1967 from Scunthorpe, £18,000 **D** 31.1.1970 v Nottingham Forest **L** August 1981 to Tottenham, £300,000 **Apps** 656 **Hons** EC 1976–77, 1977–78, 1980–81; UEFA 1972–73, 1975–76; Div1 CH 1972–73, 1975–76, 1976–77, 1978–79, 1979–80; FAC 1973–74; FAC finalist 1970–71; LC 1980–81, 1977–78 finalist; Super Cup 1977, 1978 finalist; CS 1974, 1976, 1977, 1979, 1980; 61 caps for England **OC** Scunthorpe Utd, Tottenham; England goalkeeping coach

BOB PAISLEY RANKED HIM as Liverpool's best-ever goalkeeper, while many others would rate him the bargain of the century. Signed from Scunthorpe for just £18,000, Clemence succeeded Tommy Lawrence in the 1969–70 season, and immediately displayed the amazing agility, reflexes and exceptional handling for which he would become famous.

The one-time Skegness deckchair attendant was an ever-present in six seasons throughout the 1970s and – during the 1978–79 Championship year – conceded just 16 goals. Clemence made 61 appearances for England and would have won more caps had he not being competing for a place with another great 'keeper, Peter Shilton. In 1981, after collecting 12 major honours with Liverpool, he moved to Tottenham for £300,000 where he won another FA Cup medal and picked up an MBE. He played on until he was almost 40, and was always guaranteed a deafening reception when returning to Anfield with Spurs.

Clough, Nigel

1993/4-1995/6 (Forward/midfield) **B** 19.3.1966, Sunderland **S** June 1993 from Nottingham Forest, £2.75 million **D** 14.8.1993 v Sheffield Wed, lg **L** 1996 to Manchester C, £1 million **Apps** 44, 9 gls **Hons** 14 caps for England **OC** Nottingham Forest (twice), Manchester C, Sheffield Wed (loan), Manchester C; manager: Burton Albion

GRAEME SOUNESS VIEWED HIM as the ideal partner for Ian Rush, and it seemed the striker would live up to the billing after four goals in his opening four matches. But following a sudden loss of form and confidence, he also lost his place – that was when a young striker named Robbie Fowler exploded on to the first-team scene.

Clough, who had earlier played under his father Brian at Nottingham Forest, forced his way back into the side, settling into a midfield role that suited his vision and passing. His finest Anfield moment came in January 1994 when he scored twice to help Liverpool cancel out a 3-0 deficit against Manchester United. But when Roy Evans took over, Clough found himself out of favour and relegated to the subs' bench. Frustrated by his lack of opportunities, he opted for a move to Manchester City.

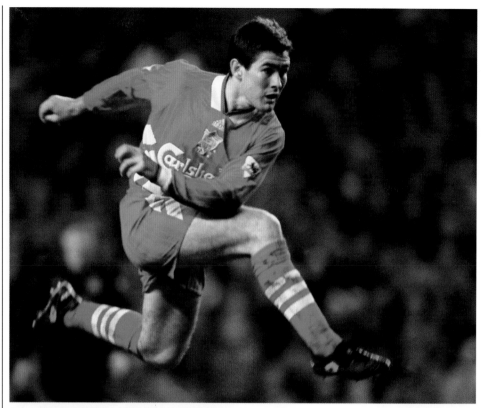

Is it a bird, is it a plane? When Nigel Clough first arrived at Anfield, supporters thought he was Superman

Club Crest

THE CENTREPIECE OF Liverpool's badge is the Liver Bird, a mythical creature that is the symbol of the city itself. Historians believe the bird probably derives from a case of mistaken identity. When the city was granted its first charter in 1207, an artist was asked to make Liverpool's official seal, based on King John's heraldic eagle. Unfortunately, he did such a bad job that by the 17th Century most people thought the bird on the seal was a cormorant, common to the Mersey estuary. The sprig of broom in the mouth of the King's eagle was also widely mistaken for seaweed. Confusion reigned, but the locals gradually grew to like the idea of a bird exclusive to their own city. Other artists started to embellish its shape and image further and, by 1911, the widely accepted version had taken its place on top of the newly built Liver Buildings at the Pier Head.

It first appeared on Liverpool's shirts for the 1950 FA Cup final, and became a permanent feature five years later. That simple crest – initially a red bird on a white, oval-shaped background – remained until 1992.

Today's more intricate design still has the Liver Bird at its centre, but there are important other elements. The wrought-ironwork of the Shankly Gates, featuring the words 'You'll Never Walk Alone', is at the top, while the date 1892 – the year of the club's formation – is at the bottom.

At either side of the crest are two burning flames: in remembrance of the 96 fans who died in the Hillsborough disaster.

Coca-Cola Cup

➡ See League Cup

Cohen, Abraham 'Avi'

1979/80-1981/2 (Left-back) **B** 14.11.1956, Cairo **S** May 1979 from Maccabi Tel Aviv, £200,000 **D** 15.9.1979 v Leeds Utd **L** November 1981 to Maccabi, £100,000 **Apps** 24, 1 gl **Hons** caps for Israel **OC** Maccabi Tel Aviv (twice), Rangers

ISRAELI INTERNATIONAL full-back signed from Maccabi Tel Aviv for £200,000 in May 1979. He was in the team that clinched the Championship against Aston Villa at the end of the 1979–80 season, scoring in front of the Kop to cancel out an earlier own goal. But, unfortunately, he didn't get a medal as he had only made four appearances during the campaign. Never able to dislodge Alan Kennedy from the left-back berth, Cohen returned to Israel in 1981 and later joined Graeme Souness at Glasgow Rangers.

Collymore, Stan

1995/6-1996/7 (Striker) **B** 22.1.1971, Stone, Staffs **S** August 1995 from Nottingham Forest, £8.5 million **D** 19.8.1995 v Sheffield Wed, lg **L** Summer 1997 to Aston Villa, £7 million **Apps** 81, 35 gls **Hons** 3 caps for England **OC** Walsall, Wolves, Stafford R, Crystal Palace, Southend Utd, Nottingham Forest, Aston Villa, Leicester C, Bradford C, Real Oviedo

THE RECORD £8.5 MILLION capture from Nottingham Forest made a terrific start with a stunning goal on his debut in 1995. But spectacular strikes – including the winner in a legendary 4-3 Premiership win over Newcastle – weren't the only hallmarks of his Anfield career. Reluctant to leave his home in the Midlands, Collymore fell out with with boss Roy Evans over absenteeism and attitude. He hardly helped his case by criticising his manager in print and refusing to play for the reserves.

Despite his off-the-field problems, he was a crowd favourite who hit 26 goals in 61 Premiership games and who created many more for Robbie Fowler and others. However, with the emergence of Michael Owen, the club decided they could live without such a wayward character. Collymore transferred to Aston Villa for £7 million, and later moved on to Leicester and Bradford, although personal problems continued to dog him at all three clubs. He attempted a fresh start with Spain's Real Oviedo but, after being told he was overweight and unfit, he decided to quit the game at the age of 30. Footballing potential unfulfilled, he now works as a pundit for television.

Stan the Man started life at Anfield like a whirlwind. But his career soon hit choppy waters as Michael Owen arrived on the scene

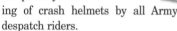

Cooper became a sergeant in the military police. He played for Liverpool in an Anfield friendly against Stoke in April 1940. But, while on military duty two months later, he was killed when his motorcycle collided with a bus. An inquiry into his death led to the compulsory wearing of crash helmets by all Army despatch riders.

"Yes, boss" – Phil Neal was always first on the LFC teamsheet and didn't miss an appearance in 417 games

Community Shield

THE SUCCESSOR TO the FA Charity Shield. Liverpool faced Arsenal to contest the prize in 2002, but were beaten 1-0.

➲ See Charity Shield

Consecutive Appearances

PHIL NEAL HOLDS Liverpool's record for most matches on the run. He was an ever-present for eight consecutive League seasons and, in all competitions, played 417 times without a break. Three others have made more than 300 consecutive appearances: Ray Clemence (336), Chris Lawler (316) and Bruce Grobbelaar (310).

Cooper, Tom

1934/5-1939/40 (Right-back) **B** 9.4.1904, Fenton, Stoke-on-Trent **S** December 1934 from Derby County, £7,500 **D** 8.12.1934 v Chelsea, lg **L** Killed on war service **Apps** 169, 0 gls **Hons** England caps **OC** Trentham, Port Vale, Derby County, Wrexham (wartime guest) **d** 25.6.1940

FORMER REDS CAPTAIN who lost his life in World War Two. The Stoke-born defender had won 15 England caps when Liverpool paid £7,500 to sign him in December 1934. He formed a famous full-back pairing with England colleague Ernie Blenkinsop and went on to make 160 appearances – without ever getting on to the scoresheet. With the outbreak of war,

Cormack, Peter B

1972/3-1976/7 (Midfield) **B** 17.7.1946, Granton, Edinburgh **S** July 1972 from Nottingham Forest, £110,000 **D** 2.9.1972 v Derby Co, lg **L** November 1976 to Bristol C, £50,000 **Apps** 178, 26 gls **Hons** UEFA 1972–73; Div 1 CH 1972–73, 1975–76; FAC 1973–74; 9 caps for Scotland **OC** Tynecastle Boys Club, Heart of Midlothian, Hibernian (twice), Nottingham Forest, Bristol C; Partick Thistle (manager), Anartosi FC, Cyprus (manager), Botswana (national coach)

ELEGANT MIDFIELDER recommended to the club by Bill Shankly's brother, Bob. Liverpool paid Hibernian £110,000 for the Scottish international who became the last piece of Shankly's jigsaw in the triumphant 1972–73 season. Scoring eight times in 30 outings, Cormack helped the club to their first League Championship and UEFA Cup double. He was among the team that destroyed Newcastle in the FA Cup final the following year, and went on to collect another Championship and UEFA Cup medal in 1976. But with Ray Kennedy increasingly edging him out of the first-team picture, Cormack decided to move on to Bristol City. He later managed Partick Thistle, then coached in Cyprus and Botswana, before returning to his native Edinburgh.

Cox, Jack

1897/8-1908/9 (Outside-right/left) **B** 21.11.1876, Blackpool **S** February 1898 from Blackpool **D** 12.3.1898 v Notts County, lg **L** 1909 to Blackpool as player-manager **Apps** 361, 81 gls **Hons** Div1 CH 1900–01, 1905–06; Div2 CH 1904–05; Liv Cup 1905–06; 3 England Caps **OC** South Shore Standard, Blackpool South Shore FC, Blackpool (twice) **d** n/k

ONE OF THE CLUB'S earliest stars who won three England caps as an outside-left. Cox was a superb sprinter and, in his prime, was reputed to be the fastest footballer in the land. He joined from Blackpool in 1898 and spent 12 seasons at Anfield, scoring 81 goals. As well as collecting two Championship medals, he helped the club to the 1904–05 Second Division title .

Crawford, Robert S

1908/9-1914/5 (Right/left-back) **B** 4.7.1886, Blythswood, Renfrewshire **S** January 1909 from Arthurlie **D** 13.2.1909 v Leicester Fosse, lg **L** December 1915 **Apps** 114, 1 gl **Hons** none **OC** Arthurlie, **d** n/k

Midfielder with an eye for goal, Peter Cormack played a vital role at Anfield for a couple of seasons

C

Springbok Gordon Hodgson in Lancashire guise

Batsman John Barnes in a Middlesex sweater

Cricketers

RED IN WINTER, whites in summer... the football-cricket mix is well-established at Anfield. Perhaps the most successful player was the interwar striker Gordon Hodgson, who combined scoring goals for Liverpool with taking wickets for Lancashire. The South African hat-trick king made more than fifty first-class appearances as a fast bowler, and formed part of the County Championship teams of 1930 and 1931.

Other cricketing LFC players include the Victorian-era 'keeper Harry Storer, who turned out for Derbyshire in 1895, wartime striker Cyril Done – a regular with Bootle – and ex-boss Phil Taylor who once played for Gloucestershire. Former understudy 'keeper Steve Ogrizovic also has a cricketing claim to fame. He may have had little success breaking into Liverpool's first team, but he was a Shropshire hero when he dismissed the legendary West Indian batsman Viv Richards in a NatWest Trophy match.

A combined Liverpool and Everton cricket team played against Bootle Cricket Club in 1936: Gordon Hodgson and Dixie Dean sit together, front row, far left

'Crossing The Park'

THE PHRASE TO DESCRIBE a direct transfer between Liverpool and Everton. Although quite common in the early days, the practice of switching from one side of Stanley Park to the other became more unusual as the rivalry between the two clubs – and in particular their fans – intensified.

Of the Liverpool players who have made the short journey, very few have managed to improve their careers as a result. Johnny Morrissey, with two League Championship medals, and 1980s midfielder Kevin Sheedy – who collected a European Cup Winners' Cup, as well as two Title-winning honours – are the most successful.

The 1920s forward Dick Forshaw won a Championship medal with Everton, after two earlier triumphs at Anfield. And in the 1990s, Everton's Gary Ablett collected a second FA Cup winners' medal to add to the honours he had won with Liverpool.

Transfer deals between the clubs have often been controversial. There were loud Evertonian protests when their gifted Irish international winger Bill Lacey went to Liverpool in a 1912 exchange deal. And in 1934 the Anfield directors were ready to accept Everton's audacious £250 bid for veteran goalkeeper Elisha Scott – only to shelve the idea when Reds fans bombarded the *Liverpool Echo* with letters of denunciation.

Two deals that did go ahead caused much disgust and anger over at Goodison Park. In November 1959, Dave Hickson arrived at Anfield for £12,000. Forty years later, Nick Barmby incensed Evertonians by pulling on a red shirt, then announcing that he'd been a Liverpool fan since childhood. The level of abuse directed at Barmby prompted fears that he may

It may not be far, but the journey across Stanley Park isn't one many players undertake

Goalkeeper to the rescue: Russell Crossley clears the danger from Chelsea during a 1953 match

have to go into hiding. It also gave new manager Gerard Houllier an early lesson in football's place on Merseyside. "Are we talking about a change of religion here or just a change of football club?" asked the bemused Frenchman.

Several players have found it easy to change childhood loyalties. Among the famous schoolboy Evertonians who went on to wear a red shirt are Steve McManaman and Robbie Fowler. And – as Michael Owen's dad played for the Blues – he could so easily have ended up in the wrong place.

Crossley, Russell

1947/8-1953/4 (Goalkeeper) **B** 25.6.1927, Hebden Bridge, Yorkshire **S** June 1947 from Army Football **D** 21.10.1950 v Middlesbrough, lg (clean sheet) **L** July 1954 to Shrewsbury T **Apps** 73 **Hons** none **OC** Army football, Shrewsbury T, Kettering T

Alan Hansen goes up to lift the League trophy after the Reds suffered only two defeats in 1987–88

Dabbs, Ben E

1932/3-1937/8 (Right/left-back) **B** 17.4.1909, Oakengates, Shropshire **S** June 1932, from Oakengates T **D** 26.8.1933 v Wolvehampton W, lg **L** June 1938 to Watford **Apps** 56, 0 gls **Hons** none **OC** Oakengates T, Watford **d** n/k

Dalglish, Kenny M (MBE)

➡ See pages 52–53

Davidson, David L

1928/9-1929/30 (Centre-half) **B** 4.6.1905, Aberdeen **S** July 1928 from Forfar Athletic **D** 25.8.1928 v Bury, lg **L** January 1930 to Newcastle Utd, £4,000 **Apps** 62, 2 gls **Hons** none **OC** Garthdee FC, Aberdeen Argyle, Forfar Athletic, Newcastle Utd, Hartlepool Utd, Gateshead, Whitley Bay (manager), Ashington (manager) **d** June 1969

Defeats

LIVERPOOL'S HIGHEST NUMBER of reverses came during the 1953–54 campaign. They lost 23 times and won only nine games as they slid towards relegation. The following season brought their heaviest individual defeat as Birmingham City mauled them 9-1 at St Andrews.

Moving swiftly on… the Reds went through the entire 1893–94 promotion season without losing a single match. They were unbeaten at Anfield throughout the 1978–79 Championship campaign. And in 1987–88, Kenny Dalglish's title-winners suffered just two losses, equalling Leeds United's First Division record.

Derby Matches

"THERE ARE SOME events along life's waysides that never pale. And an Everton-Liverpool meeting is one of them. Today all roads lead to Goodison: the stage is set for yet another mighty, pulsating struggle for supremacy."
– Everton v Liverpool match programme, October 1932

The Merseyside derby is one of the oldest fixtures in the football calendar, and few games continue to create more passion and excitement. The inaugural clash came in the final of the Liverpool Senior Cup on April 22nd, 1893 – a game Liverpool won 1-0 in front of 10,000 spectators at Bootle Cricket Club. But the first-ever League match came on October 13th, 1894, when a then-record English crowd of 44,000 saw the Blues win 3-0 at Goodison Park. By the end of the 2002–03 season, there had been 168 League meetings between the two clubs, with

Liverpool winning 61, losing 54 and drawing 53. With more success in knock-out tournaments, too, the red half of Merseyside has definitely had more reasons to celebrate over the last 109 years.

The history of the derby is packed with incident. In 1933, Liverpool put their highest number of goals past Everton to win the Anfield match 7-4. Two years later they won 6-0, recording their biggest-ever margin against their neighbours. In 1982, Ian Rush hit four goals at Goodison as a rampant Reds went on to win 5-0. Nine years later, Liverpool took the lead four times in an FA Cup fifth round replay – only for the home side to continually strike back and level the game 4-4.

The derby's unpredictabilty is also legendary, with results always too difficult to call. In 1955, when Liverpool were languishing in the bottom half of Division Two, they beat high-flying Everton 4-0 in an FA Cup tie.

A time to
Remember..........
Date 25th September 1965
Place ANFIELD
Time Five past West

5-0!

AT THIS TIME OF CHRISTMAS CHEER,
IT IS WRONG OF ME TO JEER,
BECAUSE I THINK YOU'RE CRYING STILL,
FROM WHEN WE BEAT YOU 5-TO NIL!
SO CHRISTMAS EVE WHEN YOU'RE IN BED,
REMEMBER SANTA TOO WEARS RED,
AND HIDE YOUR BLUE & WHITE ROSETTE
OR NIL AGAIN IS WHAT YOU'LL GET
!!!

EE-AYE-ADDIO
we also won the cup!
All the best -(from the Best)

Price—ONE PENNY
LIVERPOOL F.C.
Official Programme
The only Official Programme Issued by the authority of
THE LIVERPOOL FOOTBALL CLUB CO., LTD.
LORD MAYOR OF LIVERPOOL'S WAR FUND.
Liverpool v. Everton
AT ANFIELD. SATURDAY, 21st AUGUST, 1943.
KICK-OFF 3 p.m.

LIVERPOOL (Red Jerseys)

NEXT WEEK'S GREAT ATTRACTION.
FOOTBALL LEAGUE MATCH.
Liverpool v. Manchester City
AT ANFIELD. SATURDAY, 28th AUGUST, 1943.
KICK-OF 3 p.m.

D

Derby derring-do:
(above left) Steven Gerrard
celebrates at Goodison,
September 2001;
(above right) Sagar tips
over from Liddell to save
Everton's bacon

In 1978, Everton ended a run of 14 winless games by taking the points off unbeaten Liverpool.

And in 1988, Liverpool were on the verge of beating Leeds United's magnificent record of 29 games unbeaten from the start of a season… before going down to a single Everton goal at Anfield.

Dramas like those that make every derby match an automatic sell-out, wherever it's played. The record crowd for a League match between the two came in September 1948 when more than 78,000 packed into Goodison Park. In 1984, a capacity 100,000 crowd were at Wembley for the Milk Cup Final. And in 1967, when Everton hosted a fifth round FA Cup tie between the two clubs, the match was beamed back to giant screens at Anfield via closed-circuit TV. A crowd of 64,851 were at Goodison to see the action live, while another 40,109 packed into the terraces across Stanley Park.

Dalglish, Kenny M (MBE)

1977/8-1990/1 (Forward) **B** 4.3.1951, Glasgow **S** August 1977 from Celtic, £440,000 **D** 20.8.1977 v Middlesbrough, lg **L** Retired February 1991, later went to Blackburn R as manager **Apps** 496, 168 gls **Hons** EC 1977–78, 1980–81, 1983–84; Super Cup 1977, 1978 finalist; WCCH 1981 and 1984 finalist; Div1 CH 1978–79, 1979–80, 1981–82, 1982–83, 1983–84, 1985–86; FAC 1985–86; FAC finalist 1987–88; LC 1980–81, 1981–82, 1982–83, 1983–84; CS 1977, 1979, 1980, 1982, 1988, 1989, 1983 and 1984 finalist; 102 caps for Scotland **OC** Celtic (twice, as player and manager), Blackburn R (manager), Newcastle Utd (manager)

SUPREMELY GIFTED AS an individual, but the ultimate team player – many consider Dalglish the best they've ever seen in a red shirt. Bought by Bob Paisley in 1977, he instantly banished the pain of Kevin Keegan's departure and brought a whole new dimension to Liverpool's style of play.

Four hundred and forty thousand pounds was a laughable price for a man who unlocked defences throughout Britain, and led his teammates to continuing domination of Europe. Even when his playing days were over he remained an architect of Liverpool's unprecedented success, putting together its most entertaining team ever and inspiring a loyalty in the fans second only to Shankly.

Yet he could have been an Anfield player much earlier. As a teenager he twice travelled down for trials, making a big enough impression to be asked back a third time. But by then, Celtic had moved in. Dalglish chose to stay in his native Glasgow, then spent a decade collecting medals and carving his name into Scottish football legend.

By the age of 26 he was ready for his move south. A ten-minute meeting with Paisley convinced him Liverpool was the right club, and he duly took his place in the manager's line-up for the start of the 1977–78 season. His impact was staggering. He was on target in his first four games, scored an unforgettable winner in the 1978 European Cup Final, and found the net 50 times in just 101 appearances. He displayed a touch and vision like no other. A magnificent shielder of the ball, he could turn defenders or hold play up before sending a killer pass to striking partners like David Johnson and Ian Rush. Even when a colleague delivered him a sloppy ball, he could usually be relied upon to get to it first. "Kenny's not the fastest – but the first five yards are in his head," said Paisley.

According to captain Graeme Souness, Dalglish's courage was also beyond compare. "He is one of the greatest competitors I have ever come across. He is exceptionally brave and physically a lot tougher than the critics give him credit for. For me, his bravery is often over- looked. He is kicked all game long but I have never once seen him accept it and admit that he was beaten."

Dalglish won 55 of his record-breaking 102 Scotland caps while with Liverpool. His 172 first-team goals, and countless superb perform- ances, would be enough to make him an all- time Anfield hero. But the fact that he went on to manage the club, and guarantee it further suc- cess, makes him a man apart. When Joe Fagan stepped down in 1985 he was invited to become the club's first play- er-manager. He repaid the board's faith by landing a League and FA Cup Double, two further Championships and three Manager Of The Year awards – all in the space of five seasons. He also showed brilliant judgement in the trans- fer market, signing the likes of John Barnes, Peter Beardsley and Ray Houghton, and bring- ing in John Aldridge to replace Ian Rush.

Amid all the success, though, came tragedy. Dalglish and his family responded magnificent- ly to the Hillsborough disaster, attending many funerals and offering personal comfort to the bereaved and traumatised. But, in the long term, it took a huge toll on his own health and outlook. Amid continuing emotional distress, he resigned suddenly in February 1991, leaving a void that was impossible to fill.

After a period of recuperation, he did return to football management, taking charge at Blackburn and leading them to Championship success in 1995. He later moved to Newcastle United, then had a short spell as Director of Football at Celtic before retiring from the game and working as an occasional media pundit.

Whatever his associ- ation with other clubs, Liverpool fans will always count Dalglish as one of their own. But where exactly does he rank among the Anfield greats, and – more specifically – how does he compare to his Number 7 predecessor Kevin Keegan? Writing in his autobiography, former boss Paisley finally gave his verdict: "If I had to choose one of them, it would have to be Kenny. As individuals he and Kevin are on a par. But Kenny can make a team spark collec- tively with his gifted ability to read situations, and offers players so many options with his wide-ranging distribution and vision. Of all the players I have played alongside, managed and coached in more than forty years at Anfield, he is the most talented. When Kenny shines, the whole team is illuminated."

King Kenny – when the man from Glasgow shone, the whole team basked in the warm glow of success

D

Devlin, William A

May-December 1927 (Centre-forward) **B** 30.7.1899, Bellshill, Lanarkshire **S** May 1927 from Huddersfield **T** 7.5.1927 v West Ham, lg **L** December 1927 to Heart of Midlothian **Apps** 19, 15 gls **Hons** none **OC** Clyde Junior football, Cowdenbeath (twice), Huddersfield T, Heart of Midlothian, Macclesfield, Mansfield T, Burton T, Shelbourne, Bangor, Boston Utd, Ashton National, Olympique Marseille **d** July 1972

Diao, Salif

2002-present (Defensive-midfielder) **B** 10.2.1977, Kedougou, Senegal **S** August 2002 from Sedan, £4.3 million **D** 28.8.2002 v Blackburn R, lg **Apps** 40, 2 gls **Hons** 24 caps for Senegal **OC** Epinal, Monaco, Sedan

DEFENSIVE MIDFIELDER who emerged as one of the stars of Senegal's 2002 World Cup campaign.

His role in the win against Denmark – which included a brilliant goal as well as a red card – sent many of Europe's top clubs in search of his signature. But by then he was already Liverpool-bound, having agreed a £4.3 million move from the French club Sedan before the tournament had even started.

Diao, who had been a French Championship winner with Monaco, made his Liverpool debut against Blackburn Rovers in the 2002/3 season, and was soon given an extended first-team run.

Diarra, Alou

2002- present (Defensive midfielder) **B** 15.7.1981, Villepinte, France **S** 9 July 2002 from Bayern Munich **D** not yet **Apps** 0, 0 gls **Hons** none **OC** Freiburg, Bayern Munich, Le Havre (loan)

BECAME GERARD HOULLIER'S first summer 2002 recruit by joining from Bayern Munich. Seen as a player for the future, Diarra has already appeared in the French Under-20 side. He went on a year's loan to Le Havre at the beginning of the 2002–03 season to gain experience.

Dicks, Julian

1993-1994 (Full-back) **B** 8.8.1968, Bristol **S** September 1993 from West Ham, £2.5 million **D** 18.9.1993 v Everton **L** October 1994 to West Ham, £1 million **Apps** 28, 3 gls **Hons** none **OC** Birmingham C, West Ham (twice), Canvey Island

AN AWESOME COLLECTION of red and yellow cards didn't deter Graeme Souness from targeting West Ham's 'bad boy' full-back in 1993. In fact he was so determined to get him, he offered David Burrows and Mike Marsh in return. The controversial exchange deal angered many fans, and Dicks did little to win them over. He suffered knee problems, struggled with his weight and never managed to adapt to the Reds' passing game. He did score a memorable penalty against Ipswich – Liverpool's last

goal in front of the standing Kop – but by then Souness had gone and the player's Anfield future looked bleak.

When new boss Roy Evans criticised his attitude and left him out of the 1994–95 pre-season squad, he decided to leave, returning to Upton Park before an injury-enforced retirement two seasons later.

The Terminator: Julian Dicks in mid-snarl

Diet

"YOU CAN'T PUT DIESEL in a Rolls Royce," said Gerard Houllier when asked about Premiership footballers' eating habits. Houllier had just arrived in England and appeared shocked at the lack of importance given to players' diets. As French football's technical director he'd had a huge influence on nutrition, overseeing the schools of excellence where youngsters were given detailed advice about liquids, proteins and carbohydrates.

Not that his Anfield predecessors didn't understand the link between food and performance. As long ago as 1896, Tom Watson issued his players with instructions on what foods to eat and avoid. A typical recommended dinner was:

"Plain roast or boiled joints of mutton or beef, with an occasional fowl, fresh vegetables, rice or tapioca pudding, plus a glass of beer or claret." Breakfast should be *"preceded by a half hour stroll"*, while *"butter, sugar milk, potatoes and tobacco should be sparingly used".*

KEY Apps Appearances | **B** Born | **CH** Championship | **CWC** Cup Winners' Cup | **CS** Charity Shield | **D** Debut | **d** Died | **EC** European Cup | **FAC** FA Cup | **gls** Goals | **Hons** Honours | **lg** League

During wartime, players would be lucky to find those sort of foods, and, even when hostilities ended, Britain was still subject to rationing. It was because of the food shortage that Liverpool's chairman Bill McConnell led his team on a six-week tour of America and Canada in 1946. Fed a diet of unrationed T-bone steaks, fish and fruit, the players returned weighing an average of seven pounds heavier… then went on to win the Championship.

More than a decade on, Bill Shankly arrived at Anfield. A man with definite views on everything, he was having no arguments about what his players should eat: "Shanks was a big boxing fan, and he loved the big boxers and the way they trained," recalled Ian St John, "Because he'd heard that Joe Louis used to eat steaks, we ate steaks for 10 years, every meal."

Tommy Smith remembered how Shankly even checked through the players' hotel breakfast orders to make sure his instructions were followed. When he found that Smith and Chris Lawler had ordered black puddings, he promptly cancelled them.

The dietary regime was a little more relaxed during the Paisley era, as Graeme Souness once explained: "Dinner before a game would consist of tomato or mushroom soup, followed by either fish, steak or eggs, usually with chips and milk, orange or tea to drink with it… one thing they would watch very carefully, however, was bread. That was stodge and it took too long to digest."

It was Souness's own experience of playing in Italy that led to Liverpool adopting a "pasta and chicken" diet in the 1990s. Houllier's arrival meant more continental menus, regular nutritional lectures from club doctor Mark Waller, plus a team of Melwood chefs who now tailor specific diets to each individual's needs. But whatever the advantages of such a scientific approach, some players have always preferred to go their own way at meal times. Terry McDermott apparently existed on sandwiches alone. And as for Steve Nicol: "He's a walking advert for the benefits of junk food," said team-mate Mark Lawrenson. "He'll eat five packets of crisps and wash it down with Coke and Mars bars."

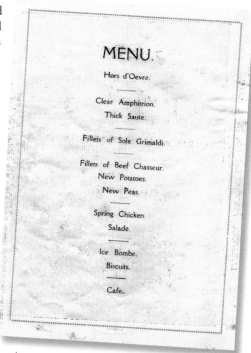

Posh nosh: celebratory menu from 1922

Dressing for dinner: Matt Busby (front, right) is among the players enjoying a formal pre-match meal back in the Thirties

Dines, Joe

1912/3-1913/4 (Left-half) **B** 12.4.1886, King's Lynn **S** May 1912 as amateur **D** 9.9.1912 v Chelsea, lg **L** enlisted 1914 **Apps** 1, 0 gls **Hons** England amateur, Olympic Gold winner 1912 **OC** King's Lynn FC, Ilford, England amateur **d** killed in action, 27.8.1918

OLYMPIC GOLD MEDAL winner who signed after representing Great Britain's amateur football team at the 1912 Games, along with another Reds' player, Arthur Berry.

Dines gave up his teaching job to turn professional, but only managed one senior game before the outbreak of World War One, when he joined the Ordnance Corps.

He later served with the King's Liverpool Regiment on the Western Front. There, in September 1918, the player once described as "the smiling footballer, thoughtful young man and master of the art of dribbling" became one of the many thousands to lose their life in the fighting.

Diomede, Bernard

2000/1-present (Wing/midfield) **B** 23.1.1974, Saint-Doulchard, France **S** Summer 2000 from Auxerre, £3 million **D** 14.9.2000 v Rapid Bucharest, UEFA **L** June 2003 **Apps** 5, 0 gls **Hons** World Cup Winner 1998 **OC** Auxerre, Ajaccio

LIVELY, DREADLOCKED winger who won a French League and Cup double with Auxerre before collecting a 1998 World Cup winners' medal with his country. His former national coach Gerard Houllier paid £3 million to bring him to Anfield in the summer of 2000.

Despite his undoubted natural dribbling ability, Diomede never made a particularly convincing claim for a first-team place. An appearance against FC Haka in the Champions League qualifier was all he had to show for the 2001–02 season. He was confined to the reserves for the the following campaign, then joined French side Ajaccio on long-term loan before being released by the Reds in June 2003.

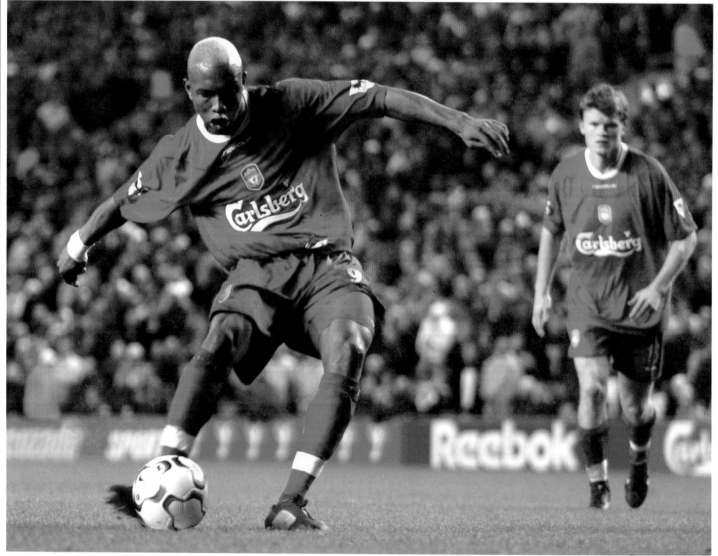

El Hadji Diouf has a tattoo of a lion showing his commitment to Senegal's cause – after improved displays at Anfield, he should soon have a Liver Bird to match

His master's voice: Doctor Fun is a well-known face at Anfield but who exactly is controlling who?

Diouf, El Hadji

2002-present (Forward) **B** 15.1.1981, Dakar, Senegal **S** Summer 2002 from Lens **D** 11 8.2002 v Arsenal, CS **Apps** 46, 6 gls **Hons** LC 2002–03; CS finalist 2002; 27 caps for Senegal; African Footballer of the Year 2001 and 2002 **OC** ASC Kaani Gui, Socheaux, Rennes, Lens

HAILED AS THE JEWEL in Senegal's crown during the 2002 World Cup qualifiers, hitting nine goals and collecting the African Footballer Of The Year award along the way. His performances during the actual finals added further gloss, particularly his outstanding display in the victory over France. But, pursued by the likes of Valencia and AC Milan, Diouf elected instead for the five-year contract on offer from Gerard Houllier.

"He's a talented player, he's strong and covers a lot of ground," said the boss, before warning, "It may take time to settle in the Premiership, as it's different to any other league." Houllier was right. After a patchy start, Diouf adapted his game to the English style, and ended the 2002–03 season as one of the Premiership's most improved players.

Doctor Fun

LEGENDARY KOPITE who brightens up home matches by wearing top hat and tails, red shoes and a glove puppet named "Liverpool Charlie" on his right hand.

Doctor Fun is really Lenny Campbell, from Huyton. The eccentric lifelong Liverpudlian is a former seaman, lifeguard and nightclub compere, among other professions.

He's even had a spell working as an entertainer at Butlin's holiday camp… where he obviously developed his love for red coats.

L Left Liverpool | **LC** League Cup | **n/k** not known | **OC** Other Clubs | **P** Premiership | **S** Signed | **Sb** Substitute | **SSSC** Screen Sport Super Cup | **UEFA** UEFA Cup | **WCCH** World Club Championship

57

Doig, J Edward 'Ned'

1904/5-1908/9 (Goalkeeper) **B** 29.10.1866, Letham, Forfarshire
S August 1904 from Sunderland **D** 1.9.1904 v Burton Utd, lg (clean
sheet) **L** 1908 to St Helena Recreation **Apps** 53 **Hons** Div2 CH
1904–05; 6 caps for Scotland **OC** St Helena FC (Arbroath), Arbroath,
Blackburn R, Sunderland, St Helens Recreation **d** 7.11.1919

THE SCOTTISH INTERNATIONAL kicked off
Liverpool's tradition of great goalkeepers – and
still ranks as the club's oldest-ever player. As
part of Sunderland's 'Team Of All Talents', Doig
had already won four Championship medals –
three of them under future Reds manager Tom
Watson. When Watson's Liverpool were relegated in 1904 he persuaded Doig to join for a fee of
£150. It was an inspired move. With the 38-
year-old 'keeper an ever-present in the 1904–05
season, Liverpool conceded just 25 goals and
regained their place in Division One. He also
helped them lift the Championship the following year, and played on until 1908. He later
played for St Helens Recreation.

Done, Cyril C

1938/9-1951/2 (Centre-forward/inside-left) **B** 21.10.1920, Bootle
S January 1938 from Bootle Boys Brigade **D** 2.9.1939 v Chelsea, lg
(scored) **L** May 1952 to Tranmere R **Apps** 111, 38 gls **Hons** Div1 CH
1946–47; FAC finalist 1950 **OC** Bootle Boys Brigade, Tranmere R,
Port Vale, Winsford Utd; manager: Skelmersdale **d** 24.2.1993

FORMER BOOTLE BOYS BRIGADE player
who scored on his debut – then had to wait
seven years for his next League match. The
burly striker's first appearance was on
September 2nd, 1939, when he scored in a 1-0
win against Chelsea. But just a day later
Britain declared war on Germany and the
League programme was abandoned. Done
proved to be a prolific striker in the wartime
friendlies, scoring 14 times against Everton

alone. But his follow-up First Division game
didn't come until October 1946, when he was on
target in the 1-1 home draw with Charlton.

Powerful in the air and possessing a fierce
left-foot drive, Done hit ten League goals in that
Championship season, even though the partnership of Stubbins and Balmer restricted him
to 17 appearances. He went on to score a total of
37 for the club before joining Tranmere in 1952.
Two years later, while with Port Vale, he faced
Liverpool in the FA Cup – and hit all his team's
goals in a shock 4-3 win. When his professional
career came to an end he appeared for Winsford
United, managed Skelmersdale and continued
to play cricket for Bootle.

Done, Robert

1926/7-1934/5 (Right/left-back) **B** 27.4.1904, Runcorn **S** April 1926
from Runcorn **D** 1.1.1927 v Bolton W, lg **L** May 1935 to Reading
Apps 155, 13 gls **Hons** none **OC** Runcorn FC, Reading, Chester C,
Accrington Stanley, Bangor **d** Sept 1982

Double, The

LIVERPOOL'S ONLY League and FA Cup
Double came in the 1985–86 season – Kenny
Dalglish's first as manager. Critics had written
off his team's chances after an indifferent opening. Then, after losing at home to Everton, it
looked like the title was heading to Goodison for
the second year running. But the team put
together a superb late run, collecting 31 points
from 11 games. They clinched the
Championship on the last day of the League
programme with Dalglish himself volleying a
superb winner against Chelsea at Stamford
Bridge. Exactly a week later, he led the team
out at Wembley for the first all-Merseyside FA
Cup Final. Everton took the lead, but a goal
from Craig Johnston and a memorable double
strike by Ian Rush put the trophy safely in the
Anfield cabinet.

Other years when the club has won two or
more trophies include:

1973 and 1976
League Championship and UEFA Cup
1977
League Championship and European Cup
1981
European Cup and League Cup
1982 and 1983
League Championship and League Cup
1984
League Championship, European Cup
and League Cup
2001
FA Cup, League Cup, UEFA Cup

Skipper Alan Hansen loses his cool for once as he and his team-mates celebrate another title after beating Chelsea 1-0 at Stamford Bridge in 1986

L Left Liverpool | **LC** League Cup | **n/k** not known | **OC** Other Clubs | **P** Premiership | **S** Signed | **Sb** Substitute | **SSSC** Screen Sport Super Cup | **UEFA** UEFA Cup | **WCCH** World Club Championship

Jerzy Dudek has shown he can command the box and stop shots with the best of them since his transfer from Feyenoord

KEY Apps Appearances | **B** Born | **CH** Championship | **CWC** Cup Winners' Cup | **CS** Charity Shield | **D** Debut | **d** Died | **EC** European Cup | **FAC** FA Cup | **gls** Goals | **Hons** Honours | **lg** League

Dudek, Jerzy

2001/2-present (Goalkeeper) **B** 23.3.1973, Rybnik, Poland **S** August
2001 from Feyenoord **D** 8 9.2001 v Aston Villa, lg **Apps** 94 **Hons**
LC 2002–2003; 24 caps for Poland; Dutch Goalkeeper of the Year
1998–99; Polish Player of the Year 2000–2001 **OC** Sokol Tychy,
Feyenoord

SIGNED FOR LIVERPOOL in August 2001,
instantly replacing 'keeper Sander Westerveld.
The miner's son had made his Poland debut in
1998, catching the eye of Feyenoord scouts. He
moved to the Rotterdam club, quickly establishing himself as a fans' cult hero and carrying off
the Dutch Goalkeeper Of The Year award. His
move to Anfield was quickly hailed as a success.
He helped instil confidence and discipline into
the defence and rounded off a terrific first year
by representing his country in the World Cup
finals. Some uncharacteristic errors led to him
briefly losing his place the following season. But
he returned to the side showing the form of old
– and putting in a Man Of The Match performance in the Worthington Cup final victory over
Manchester United.

Dundee, Sean

1998-1999 (Striker) **B**:7.12.1972, Durban, SA **S** August 1998 from
Karlsruhe, £2 million **D** 27.10.1998 v Fulham, LC 3rd rd (sub for
Michael Owen) **L** Summer 1999 to VFB Stuttgart, £1 million **Apps** 5, 0
gls **Hons** none **OC** Karlsruhe, VFB Stuttgart

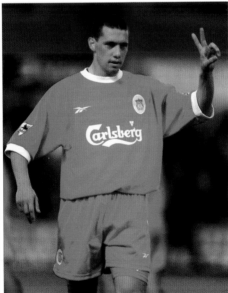

TELLING NEWSPAPERS he was as fast as
Michael Owen, the tall South African certainly
knew how to build up expectations. Sadly his
form on the pitch never came close to matching
the hype. Signed from German side Karlsruhe
for £2 million, Dundee arrived at Anfield just
before Gerard Houllier became joint manager.

He made his debut as a substitute for Owen in
a Worthington Cup win over Fulham in October
1998. But, after coming off the bench another
four times, he failed to impress, and spent the
remainder of his short Anfield career in the
reserves. In 1999, the club cut their losses, sell-
ing him to VFB Stuttgart for £1 million.

Dunlop, Billy

1894/5-1908/9 (Left-back) **B** 14.7.1871, Kilmarnock **S** 19.10.1894
from Abercorn, £35.00 **D** 25.3.1895 v Sunderland, lg **L** 1909
Apps 363, 2 gls **Hons** Div1 CH 1900–01, 1905–06; Div2 CH
1895–96, 1904–05; Dewar Shield 1906 **OC** Sandyford, Hurlford,
Annbank, Kilmarnock, Abercorn, Sunderland (assistant manager/train-
er) **d** n/k

SCOTTISH INTERNATIONAL DEFENDER
who joined the club in 1894 and stayed for the
next 15 years.

Dunlop twice helped the team win promotion from Division Two and was part of Tom
Watson's Championship-winning sides of 1901
and 1906. When his playing days were over, he
joined Watson's former club Sunderland as
assistant trainer.

Eastham, Harry

1935/6-1947/48 (Forward) **B** 30.6.1917, Blackpool **S** February 1936
from Blackpool, amateur **D** 31.10.1936 v Arsenal, lg **L** May 1948 to
Tranmere R **Apps** 68, 4 gls **Hons** Div1 CH 1946–47 **OC** Junior foot-
ball, Blackpool (amateur); wartime guest for: New Brighton, Southport,
Brighton & Hove Albion, Bolton W, Leeds Utd, Newcastle Utd &
Blackpool, Tranmere R, Accrington Stanley **d** September 1998

Edmed, Richard 'Dick' A

1926-1931/32 (Outside-right) **B** 14.2.1904, Gillingham **S** January
1926 from Gillingham, £1,800 **D** 28.8.1926 v Manchester Utd, lg
L May 1932 to Bolton W **Apps** 170, 46 gls **Hons** none **OC** Chatham
Centrals, Rochester FC,
Gillingham, Bolton W (retired
through injury); Gillingham (trainer)
d 14.3.1983

SPEEDY RIGHT-
WINGER who supplied
the crosses for many of
Gordon Hodgson's goals
between the wars. The
£1,800 buy from
Gillingham, was also a
decent marksman him-
self, hitting 46 goals during his five years with the
club. But, after a series of
injuries reduced his effectiveness, Edmed was transferred to Bolton.

DICK EDMED

1966 was a very good year for England and LFC

England

A TOTAL OF 53 PLAYERS have won England caps during careers with Liverpool. The first to represent his country was Francis Becton who played against Ireland in March 1895, scoring twice in a 9-0 victory. Eph Longworth was the first to captain England, leading the side out for a 1921 fixture against Belgium. Subsequent skippers supplied by the club include Tom Lucas, Emlyn Hughes, Ray Clemence, Phil Thompson and Michael Owen.

Hughes, with 59 appearances, is the Liverpool player with most England caps. On the scoring front, Roger Hunt led the way with 18 goals in 34 matches for his country. However, Owen – on the mark 20 times in 47 games – overtook him in 2002.

England have played many matches with more than one Liverpool player in the side. In 1977, six of them – Callaghan, Clemence, Hughes, Ray Kennedy, McDermott and Neal – were called up to face Switzerland at Wembley. Kevin Keegan was also in the team, just a month after leaving Liverpool for Hamburg.

English, Sam

1933/4-1934/5 (Centre-forward) **B** 1910, Coleraine, Co Derry, NI
S August 1933 from Yoker Athletic Rangers, £8,000 **D** 26.8.1933 v
Wolverhampton W, lg **L** July 1935 to Queen of the South, £1,700
Apps 50, 26 gls **Hons** caps for N Ireland **OC** Rangers, Queen of the
South, Hartlepool Utd **d** April 1967

RECORD-BREAKING goalscorer in Scotland who was on target 44 times for Rangers in 1930–31. But, after a freak goalmouth collision that led to the death of Celtic's keeper, English reckoned Liverpool offered a better chance of personal safety. Anfield boss George Patterson paid £8,000 for the Northern Ireland international, who began with 19 goals in 29 starts in 1933–34. But his scoring knack then deserted him and, after just six goals in 19 games, he was transferred to Queen Of The South.

It's "That Goal" from France 1998 as Owen slots the ball beyond Carlos Roa and England lead Argentina 2-1 in St Etienne

Above right: Kevin Keegan and his patriotic friend with their own version of the football double

KR Reykjavik

Oulo Palloseura

Brann

FC Kuusysi Lahti
FC Haka
MYPA 47
HJK Helsinki

Stromsgodset IF

BK Odense

Aberdeen
Borussia
Moenchengladbach

Brondby IF
Spartak Moscow

Celtic
Hibernian
Malmo FF

Vitesse
Arnheim
Hamburger SV

Crusaders
AZ67 Alkmaar
Dynamo Berlin

Dundalk
Leeds United
KKS Lech Poznan

Nottingham Forest
Bayer 04 Leverkusen
RTS Widzew Lodz

BV Borussia Dortmund
WS Slask Wroclaw

Ajax
Dynamo
Dresden
FC Slovan WSK Liberec
FC Dynamo Kyiv

Tottenham Hotspur
1FC Köln

RSC Anderlecht
Eintracht Frankfurt

Standard Liege
TSV Munich 1860
FC Bayern Munich
1FC Kosice

Club Brugge KV
FC Basel
Ferencvarosi TC

AS Jeunesse D'Esch
Strasbourg
Honved
Spartak Vladikavkaz

Paris St-Germain
FC Zurich
FK Austria Vienna

FC Swarovski Tirol

AJ Auxerre
Servette
Geneva
Sion

AS St Etienne
Internazionale
Petrolul Ploiesti

Juventus
Crvena Zvezda
Dinamo Bucuresti
CS Rapid Bucuresti

Athletic Bilbao
Genoa

Real Sociedad
CSKA Sofia

Celta Vigo
AS Roma

FC Porto
Boavista
FC Barcelona
Galatasaray SK

Valencia CF
Trabzonspor

SL Benfica
Vitoria Setubal
AEK Athens
Panathinaikos
Olympiakos Piraeus
Dynamo Tbilisi

Apollon Limassol

KEY Apps Appearances | B Born | CH Championship | CWC Cup Winners' Cup | CS Charity Shield | D Debut | d Died | EC European Cup | FAC FA Cup | gls Goals | Hons Honours | lg League

RED EUROPE

Like typical English tourists of the time, Liverpool initially found they couldn't always stand the heat on the continent, but slowly they learned to adapt and soon they were painting the whole place red.

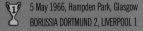

EUROPEAN FINALS

EUROPEAN CUP WINNERS' CUP

🏆(1) 5 May 1966, Hampden Park, Glasgow
BORUSSIA DORTMUND 2, LIVERPOOL 1

UEFA CUP

🏆(1) 9 May 1973, Anfield, 1st Leg
LIVERPOOL 0, BORUSSIA MOENCHENGLADBACH 0 (abandoned)
10 May 1973, Anfield, 1st Leg (replay)
LIVERPOOL 3, BORUSSIA MOENCHENGLADBACH 0
23 May 1973, Bokelberg, Moenchengladbach, 2nd Leg
BORUSSIA MOENCHENGLADBACH 2, LIVERPOOL 0

🏆(2) 28 April 1976, Anfield, 1st Leg
LIVERPOOL 3, CLUB BRUGGE KV 2
19 May 1976, Olympiastadion, Bruges, 2nd Leg
CLUB BRUGGE KV 1, LIVERPOOL 1

🏆(3) 16 May 2001, Westfalenstadion, Dortmund
LIVERPOOL 5, ALAVES 4 (aet)

EUROPEAN CUP

🏆(1) 25 May 1977, Stadio Olimpico, Rome
LIVERPOOL 3, BORUSSIA MOENCHENGLADBACH 1

🏆(2) 10 May 1978, Wembley, London
LIVERPOOL 1, CLUB BRUGGE KV 0

🏆(3) 27 May 1981, Parc des Princes, Paris
LIVERPOOL 1, REAL MADRID 0

🏆(4) 30 May 1984, Stadio Olimpico, Rome
LIVERPOOL 1, AS ROMA 1 (aet, Liverpool won 4-2 on pens)

🏆(5) 29 May 1985, Heysel, Brussels
JUVENTUS 1, LIVERPOOL 0

EUROPEAN SUPER CUP

(1) 22 November 1977, Volksparkstadion, Hamburg, 1st Leg
SV HAMBURG 1, LIVERPOOL 1
6 December 1977, Anfield, 2nd Leg
LIVERPOOL 6, SV HAMBURG 0

(2) 4 December 1978, Heysel, Brussels, 1st Leg
RSC ANDERLECHT 3, LIVERPOOL 1
19 December 1978, Anfield, 2nd Leg
LIVERPOOL 2, RSC ANDERLECHT 1

(3) 16 January 1985, Stadio Delle Alpi, Turin
JUVENTUS 2, LIVERPOOL 0

(4) 8 August 2001, Stade Louis II, Monaco
LIVERPOOL 3, BAYERN MUNICH 2

Europe

LIVERPOOL'S LENGTHY domination of English football can be traced to the team's years of unbroken experience in Europe, a journey that began on a freezing night in Iceland and ended amid the ruins of Heysel. In the intervening 21 years, the club faced every continental giant, pitting themselves against the world's best players and learning new formations and playing styles. Ian Callaghan, who made a record 88 European appearances for the club, has no doubt about their value: "They were much more than a chance to win trophies abroad. We learned so much in terms of technique and tactics, and that was to help us immensely on the domestic scene."

Although the sheer self-belief and momentum of Bill Shankly's mid-1960s team nearly brought early European success, their limitations were soon visible. A 5-1 drubbing by Ajax in 1966 exposed the team's tactical naivety. Another six barren continental campaigns convinced even Shankly that the traditional 'attack, attack, attack' approach had to change.

And it did. By the decade's end, speed and fury had been replaced by patient build-ups and endless passing. Away from home, precious goals were grabbed by lightning counter attacks – then fiercely protected by defensive play. Preparations for European games had changed too. Before one early tie against Anderlecht, Shankly famously threw a dossier on the Belgian side into the dustbin, without even bothering to read it. By the early 1970s, he was dispatching Reuben Bennett and Tom Saunders all over Europe to check on upcoming opposition. Their notes – highlighting weaknesses and recommending styles of play that could be adapted by Shankly's own team – became gospel.

The more professional approach began to pay off. On the road to the 1973 UEFA Cup Final, the Reds conceded only one goal on foreign soil. In the first leg of the final, Shankly employed John Toshack at the front, ruthlessly – and successfully – exploiting an aerial weakness in the Borussia Moenchengladbach defence. In the second leg, Liverpool came under severe pressure, but their improved defensive discipline restricted the Germans to two goals. Liverpool won 3-2 on aggregate – and the first European trophy was on its way to Anfield.

Under Paisley, the team grew stronger and yet more tactically aware. A 1976 UEFA Cup tie at Barcelona marked their true coming of age as one of Europe's premier sides. Obeying the boss's orders to "keep the home crowd quiet", they stifled the Spanish opposition, then went ahead through a Toshack goal. The Nou Camp fans turned on their own team – while Liverpool marched on to a famous victory and, ultimately, a second piece of silverware.

But the greatest prize was still to come. In 1977 – roared on by around 25,000 travelling Liverpudlians – the Reds lifted the European Cup in Rome's Olympic Stadium, after what Paisley described as "the best performance in the history of the club". A year later, a sublime Kenny Dalglish goal was enough to retain the trophy. And in 1981, Alan Kennedy's shot sealed victory in the Parc des Princes Stadium in Paris – and a hat-trick of European Cups. By the time they won the fourth, again in Rome, Liverpool were the most-feared team on the continent. But 1985 brought the Heysel Stadium disaster and the club's six-year ban from European tournaments. Kenny Dalglish's great sides of the late 1980s were prevented from competing; and Liverpool were thus denied the chance of overtaking Real Madrid as Europe's most successful side ever.

When the ban was finally lifted, Dalglish had gone, along with most of those with any continental experience. Some supporters may have looked forward to the club resuming their place at the top of the pile, but inside Anfield, wiser heads knew it wouldn't be that simple. Coach Ronnie Moran had watched them gradually fall behind the Italians, Germans and Spaniards and he predicted it would take years for them to make up the necessary ground and win trophies once more.

Ten years to be exact. A decade after their readmission, a new-look team – complete with six foreign players and a French manager – strode out in Dortmund to win the most thrilling UEFA Cup Final ever. And just a few months afterwards the team went into the draw for the Champions League for the first time. It had been a long wait, but Liverpool were finally back among Europe's elite.

European Cup

THE CLUB'S FIRST foray into Europe's premier competition came in August 1964 when they travelled to Iceland for a first-round tie with Reykjavik. Almost 17 years later – on May 25th, 1977 – they lifted the trophy for the first time, thanks to a 3-1 victory over Borussia Moenchengladbach. That victory in Rome lives on in the memories of the thousands who were there, along with the millions who watched it on live television.

The club went on to win the trophy for a second successive year, overcoming FC Bruges 1-0 at Wembley. They made it a hat-trick of successes in 1981 by beating Real Madrid in Paris. And in 1984 they returned to the Olympic Stadium for a fourth Cup success, this time thanks to a dramatic penalty shoot-out against AS Roma.

Liverpool's last appearance in the old tournament was at Heysel Stadium, Brussels, in May 1985, when rioting by some fans led to the club being expelled from Europe. By then they had competed in the Champions Cup in 11 different seasons. Their record of four trophies is equalled by Ajax and Bayern Munich and bettered only by Real Madrid and AC Milan.

European Champions League

THE LEAGUE-BASED competition replaced the straight knock-out version of the European Cup in 1992. However, with entry at first restricted to the top two in the Premiership, Liverpool didn't qualify for a place until 2001.

Their first match was against the Finnish side FC Haka in a preliminary round in August that year. The Reds won the away leg 5-0 – with half the Finns in the crowd apparently being part of the LFC Scandinavian Supporters' Club.

Liverpool progressed to the knockout stages of the competition but exited from the quarter-finals after losing to Germany's Bayer Leverkusen. The following year, two defeats at the hands of Valencia led to the team's elimination during the league stage.

European Cup Winners' Cup

THE ONLY MAJOR piece of silverware never to have appeared in the Anfield trophy cabinet. The Reds came closest to capturing the trophy at the first time of asking, going all the way to the 1966 final, only to lose 2-1 to Borussia Dortmund at a rain-soaked Hampden Park.

They last took part in the 1996–97 season, progressing to the semi-finals before defeat by Paris St Germain. The extension of the Champions League led to the competition finally being scrapped in 1999 – with Chelsea's name being the last to go on the trophy.

European Super Cup

TRADITIONAL PLAY-OFF between the European Champions and the holders of the Cup Winners' Cup, more or less a European version of the Charity Shield. Liverpool first took part in 1977, thrashing Kevin Keegan's new team SV Hamburg 7-1 on aggregate.

The following year they won 2-1 at home against Anderlecht, but lost the away leg 3-1. The 1985 final was a one-off game against Juventus, which the Reds lost 2-0 in Turin. And in 2001 they faced Bayern Munich in Monaco, beating the European Cup holders 3-2.

All goals lead to Rome: Jimmy Case and Ray Kennedy

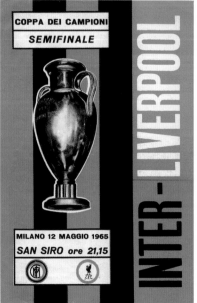

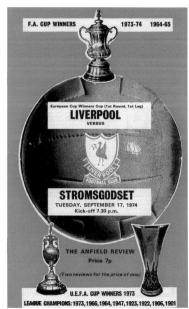

KEY Apps Appearances | **B** Born | **CH** Championship | **CWC** Cup Winners' Cup | **CS** Charity Shield | **D** Debut | **d** Died | **EC** European Cup | **FAC** FA Cup | **gls** Goals | **Hons** Honours | **lg** League

bask in the glory of Liverpool's first European Cup final win over Borussia Moenchengladbach

Evans, Alun W

1968/9-1971/2 (Centre-forward, inside-right) **B** 30.4.1949, Bewdley, Worcs **S** September 1968 from Wolverhampton W, £100,000 **D** 21.9.1968 v Wolverhampton W, lg (scored twice) **L** June 1972 to Aston Villa, £70,000 **Apps** 111, 33 gls **Hons** FAC finalist 1970–71; England U-23 caps **OC** Mid-Worcester Schools, Birmingham Schools, Wolverhampton W, Aston Villa, Walsall, Hellas FC (Melbourne)

BECAME BRITAIN'S first £100,000 teenager after Shankly saw him run Ron Yeats ragged in a 1968 match against Wolves. The 18-year-old Evans joined shortly afterwards, scoring on his debut and hitting two against his former club just a week later. But the England Under-23 international never fulfilled his huge potential. Knee injuries and a loss of confidence – the result of a nightclub attack that left him facially scarred – led to long lay-offs. He did make a spectacular return with a hat-trick against Bayern Munich in a 1971 Fairs Cup tie. But a year later, the man the German press called 'Der Bomber', was on his way out of Anfield to Aston Villa. He later played for Walsall before retiring from the game and starting a new life in Australia.

Evans, John W

1953/4-57/8 (Inside-left) **B** 28.8.1929, Tilbury, Essex **S** December 1953 from Charlton Athletic, £12,500 **D** 26.12.1953 v West Bromwich Albion, lg **L** 25.11.1957 to Colchester Utd, £4,000 **Apps** 107, 53 gls **Hons** none **OC** Bata Sports, Tilbury FC, Charlton Athletic, Colchester Utd, Romford, Ford United

SCORED ALL LIVER-POOL'S goals in a 5-3 win over Bristol Rovers in 1954 – the first Reds player to hit five in a game for more than half a century. The ex-Charlton forward kept up an impressive strike rate of more than a goal every two games during the 1950s, but it wasn't enough to lift the team out of Division Two. He was chosen to represent the Football League against Scotland in 1955, and left for Colchester two years later.

Evans, Roy Q

1965/6-1998/9 (Left-back, reserve coach, manager) **B** 4.10. 1948, Bootle **S** October 1965 from Bootle Schools **D** 16.3.1970 v Sheffield Wed, lg **L** August 1974 – retired to become LFC reserve team coach **Apps** 11, 0 gls **Hons** LC 1994–95 (manager); FAC finalist 1995–96 (manager); 11 Central League championships (coach); England Schoolboys **OC** Bootle Schools

ONE OF THE FINEST servants in Liverpool's history – a former fan, player, coach and manager. The ex-England Schoolboys full-back became an Anfield apprentice in 1965, making his full debut four years later. He hung around the fringes of the first team until Bob Paisley took over as manager and persuaded him to join the Boot Room. He was only 25, but club Chairman John Smith was confident enough to declare, "We have not made an appointment for the present but for the future. One day Roy Evans will be our manager." He was right. As Reserve Team coach, Evans showed his potential by winning the Central League Championship in his first season – then lifting it seven times in nine years. Paisley's retirement led to a subsequent appointment as senior coach, a position he also held under Joe Fagan and Kenny Dalglish. As newly promoted assistant to Graeme Souness he was seen as a calming influence who represented a link with the club's glorious past. And, when Souness left, the board looked to him to plan a brighter future.

For a while it seemed he would deliver. Under Evans, the team returned to the passing game which had brought so much success in earlier years. Liverpool won the Coca-Cola Cup in 1995 and, with Redknapp, Fowler and McManaman in the team, looked set to challenge for the biggest honours again. But it never worked out. After a poor display and defeat at the 1996 FA Cup Final, the League position worsened. There was criticism of his players' attitude and underachievement, while high-profile signings like Paul Ince and Stan Collymore never fulfilled their promise.

By the summer of 1998 the team had fallen further behind Manchester United – whose growing dominance of English football was hard for many Liverpudlians to stomach. Evans agreed to share his managerial responsibilities with the former French national coach Gerard Houllier. But, as widely predicted, the arrangement proved difficult and, after just four months, the former Boot Room Boy decided to dissolve the partnership and leave Anfield after 33 years.

Evans' reign may have only yielded one trophy, but the superb football he brought to Anfield in the mid-1990s should not go without mention. For a while, Liverpool were the best passing team in Britain, and certainly the most

Faithful servant to the club: Roy Evans brought many exciting youngsters into the first team

In Memoriam
Treasured Memories of
Everton F.C.
who "Fell Asleep" 29th January, 1955
at Goodison Park.

'Peacefully sleeping, free from all pain
We wouldn't wake them to suffer again'

Sadly missed by all at Anfield Road.

"Dear Departed Friends"

Everton

THE ORIGINAL TENANTS of Anfield – and Liverpool FC's oldest rivals. Everton were formed in 1878 as the St Domingo Football Club. They moved to Anfield in 1884 and became one of the founding members of the Football League four years later. They won their first Championship in 1891, but suffered a boardroom split soon afterwards when their chairman John Houlding bought the ground outright and proposed a major increase in rent. When the majority of directors voted to leave for pastures new, Houlding tried to keep the name Everton for his new club. But the Football League vetoed that plan, leaving him to christen his new team Liverpool FC, and allowing Everton to make a fresh start at Goodison Park.

➲ See also: Anfield, Houlding, John

Enthusiasm gives you legs: Ian Callaghan was an ever-present in five different League campaigns

attractive to watch. Some of his big signings failed to shine, but he helped develop youngsters like Robbie Fowler, Jamie Redknapp and Steve McManaman into world-beaters. And let no one forget he was the manager who gave an unknown 17-year-old his big first-team break. The youngster's name was Michael Owen.

Ever-Presents

TODAY'S ROTATION SYSTEMS lessen the chances of a player appearing in every League game throughout a season. Since the launch of the Premiership, only eight Liverpool players – Rush, Fowler, James, McManaman, Bjornebye, Hyypia, Babbel and Westerveld – have managed to do it. It's a far cry from the 1965–66 season when the Reds used just 14 players throughout the entire campaign, with five – Lawrence, Byrne, Yeats, Callaghan and Smith – not missing a single match.

Phil Neal holds the club record for 100 per cent appearance records. He was an ever-present for eight successive seasons between 1975 and 1983. He missed just one game in the 1983-84 campaign, but appeared in all 42 League matches the season afterwards. Aside from Neal, three players – Chris Lawler, Ray Clemence and Bruce Grobbelaar – played in every match in six different League campaigns. Ian Callaghan and Kenny Dalglish were ever-presents in five.

The Toffee Lady hands out sweets before a derby

FA Cup – Winners

IT TOOK THE REDS 73 years to land English football's most glittering trophy, But since Bill Shankly guided his men to victory against Leeds in 1965, the Cup has been displayed in the Anfield cabinet another five times.

In 1974 the Scot led out his second great team at Wembley. In what was to be his penultimate match in charge, they overwhelmed Newcastle and ran out 3-0 winners. Twelve years later, Kenny Dalglish completed his League and Cup double with a magnificent 3-1 triumph over Everton. And in 1989 his side tasted a second victory against the Blues – dedicating their 3-2 win to the fans who lost their lives at the semi-final in Sheffield.

The team's last FA Cup win at Wembley came in 1992, when they beat Sunderland 2-0. And in 2001 they became the first club to lift the trophy outside of England, thanks to a 2-1 victory over Arsenal at Cardiff's Millennium Stadium.

FA Cup – Runners-Up

THE TEAM HAVE been defeated finalists six times. In 1914 they lost to Burnley at Crystal Palace. Arsenal (1950 and 1971) and Manchester United (1977 and 1996) have since beaten them twice at Wembley, along with Wimbledon in 1988.

FA Youth Cup

LIVERPOOL'S YOUNGSTERS have enjoyed only one triumph in this 40-year-old competition. In 1996, with a team including Michael Owen and Jamie Carragher among others, they lifted the trophy after a brilliant 4-1 final win against West Ham. The Liverpool youth team had previously been runners-up in 1963 and 1972.

First time for everything: the FA Youth Cup win in '96 | The 39 Steps: Ron Yeats leads his team away from the royal box after victory over Leeds in 1965

Joe Fagan – a Treble-winner in his first season as manager

KEY **Apps** Appearances | **B** Born | **CH** Championship | **CWC** Cup Winners' Cup | **CS** Charity Shield | **D** Debut | **d** Died | **EC** European Cup | **FAC** FA Cup | **gls** Goals | **Hons** Honours | **lg** League

Boss from the Boot Room: Joe Fagan flanked by Roy Evans and Ronnie Moran, Rome 1984

Although his reshaped team dropped out of the title race relatively early, he did manage to lead them to a second successive European Cup final in 1985. But it was there – amid the shame and ruins of Heysel – that he announced his decision to retire, walking away from the club, and the game, that he loved. After a period of quiet exile, Fagan began to show his face around Anfield and Melwood again. He turned up to offer help and advice when his old Boot Room colleague Roy Evans inherited the boss's chair. But it wasn't until 1994 that he strode out on to the Anfield turf again, saying his goodbyes before the last game in front of the standing Kop.

Joe Fagan died at the age of 80 in July 2001, still held in huge affection by players and fans alike.

Fagan, Willie

1937/8-1951/2 (Centre-forward) **B** 20.2.1917, Musselburgh, Midlothian **S** October 1937, from Preston NE, £8,000 **D** 23 October 1937 v Leicester C, lg **L** January 1952 to Belfast Distillery **Apps** 185, 57 gls **Hons** Div1 CH 1946–47; FAC finalists 1950; Scotland wartime honours **OC** Celtic, Preston NE, wartime guest for Aldershot, Leicester C, Northampton T, Newcastle Utd, Chelsea, Millwall, Reading & Crystal Palace, Belfast Distillery, Weymouth (player-manager) **d** 29.2.1992

OCCASIONAL CAPTAIN and one of only three players to score in three different decades. Fagan signed in 1937, a few months after playing alongside Bill Shankly in Preston's FA Cup Final defeat by Sunderland. He chipped in nine goals in his first campaign, and in 1938–39 – the last season before war broke out – he finished as joint leading scorer. As a soldier, he guested for various clubs, including Newcastle, Chelsea and Millwall, and was called up for a number of Scottish wartime friendlies. He was a valuable member of the 1946–47 Championship squad, finding the net seven times in 18 appearances, and scored his final goal in May 1950

WILLIAM FAGAN LIVERPOOL

– 13 years after his first. Fagan left Anfield in 1952 to play for Belfast club Distillery, then manage non-league Weymouth. After retiring from football he worked as a Borstal officer, and died in 1992, aged 75.

Fagan, Joe

1958-1984/5 (coach, manager) **B** 12.3.1921, Liverpool **S** 1958 from Rochdale (trainer) **D** First game as manager v Wolves Aug 27th 1983, drew 1-1 **L** Retired 1985 **Hons** (as manager) EC 1983–84; EC finalist 1984–85; Div1 CH 1983–83; LC 1983–84 **OC** Nelson, Altrincham, Bradford Park Avenue, Manchester C, Rochdale (trainer) **d** 30 7.2001

STALWART OF THE BOOT ROOM who emerged from the background to make English football history: the first-ever manager to win a treble of major honours. Down-to-earth and as scouse as they come, it was hard to believe that Fagan hadn't spent his whole professional life at Anfield. In fact, he arrived just 18 months before Shankly, following a playing career at Manchester City, Bradford Park Avenue and management with Rochdale.

As Shankly's coach he was often in charge of Melwood training sessions and, along with Ronnie Moran, he formed one of the noisiest dug-out duos in Anfield history. After working as Number Two to Bob Paisley, it was inevitable he would be asked to take the top job when his boss retired. He accepted the role, but refused to let the power and status change him. A few months into his reign, the board had to almost force him to trade in his modest Ford car for a Jaguar.

His own attentions were focused solely on the pitch. To bolster his inherited squad, he signed Gary Gillespie and Michael Robinson within his first few weeks. He then guided his team to an unprecedented year of success: a Milk Cup Final win over Everton, victory in the Championship race, followed by the triumph in Rome that landed a fourth European Cup. It was a phenomenal achievement for a man in only his first season at the helm. And Fagan rounded off a glorious 12 months by collecting the Manager Of The Year award.

After seeing his inspirational captain Graeme Souness move to Italy, the next campaign was always going to be more difficult. However, Fagan showed a real talent in the transfer market, recruiting Ipswich's free-scoring midfielder John Wark, the Danish passmaster Jan Molby and the exciting Luton Town striker Paul Walsh. He also demonstrated his willingness to take tough decisions – even opting to drop Kenny Dalglish at one point in the season.

Fairclough, David

1974/5-1982/3 (Forward) **B** 5.1.1957, Liverpool **S** January 1974
from LFC apprentice **D** 1.11.1975 v Middlesbrough, lg **L** July 1983
to Lucerne **Apps** 155, 55 gls **Hons** EC 1977–78; UEFA 1975–76;
Super Cup 1977, 1978 finalist; Div1 CH 1975–76, 1976–77,
1979–80; LC 1980–81, 1982–83, 1977–78 (finalist); CS 1977 **OC**
Toronto Blizzard, Lucerne, Norwich C, Oldham Athletic, Beveren SK,
Tranmere R, Wigan Athletic

FOREVER KNOWN AS 'supersub' for his astonishing ability to score after coming off the bench, Fairclough is also remembered as the star of Anfield's greatest European night. The flame-haired forward first made headlines in 1976 when he came on late in a Merseyside derby, hitting the winner following a dazzling run past six Everton defenders. It was one of his seven goals in the team's last eight games – four of them as substitute – and they were to prove crucial in bringing Bob Paisley his first title. Paisley continued to use him as a sub through-out the following campaign, often to lethal effect. The most famous occasion came in March 1977 when he sent him on to replace John Toshack in the European Cup quarter final tie against St Etienne. With just six minutes left the gangly striker collected a Ray Kennedy pass and went on a trademark blistering run into the opposition penalty box. His shot past the French 'keeper put Liverpool into the semi-finals, sending 55,000 Anfield spectators into a frenzy.

Although he started more than 90 matches, Fairclough often proved more menacing in the Number 12 jersey. The sight of him warming up on the touchline brought a buzz of anticipation around Anfield and often unnerved defences. Not surprising: in 61 appearances as a substitute, he found the net 18 times. But for all his pace and shooting ability, the boyhood Reds fan could never count himself as an automatic first-team choice. He continued to collect medals (including two Championships, plus a European and UEFA Cup), but by 1983 he was yearning for a regular start-ing place. Unable to get it at Anfield, he moved on to the Swiss club Lucerne, later returning to England with Norwich and Oldham.

➔ **Also see: Fightbacks**

The Original Supersub: David Fairclough puts Liverpool into the semi-final of the European Cup against St Etienne

Fairfoul, Tom

1913/4-1914/5 (Right-half) **B** 16.1.1881, West Calder, Midlothian
S 1913 from Third Lanark **D** 1.9.1913 v Derby County, lg **L** 1915
banned from professional football **Apps** 71, 0 gls **Hons** FAC finalist
1913-14 **OC** Junior football, Kilmarnock, Third Lanark **d** 1952

SCOTTISH WING-HALF who joined in 1913 and became embroiled in a match-rigging scandal two years later. On Good Friday 1915, Liverpool lost 2-0 to Manchester United at Old Trafford. After falling behind, newspapers reported how several Liverpool players

seemed to simply give up. Further suspicions arose when bookmakers found that a large number of bets had been placed on a 2-0 United win. A subsequent Football League inquiry found that four Liverpool players – Fairfoul, Jackie Sheldon, Tom Miller and Bob Pursell – had got together with another four of the United team to fix the result beforehand. Like the others, Fairfoul was suspended for life but had the ban lifted after the war. By then, though, he was too old to resume playing and became a Liverpool taxi owner instead.

Fanzines

SIXTIES SUPPORTERS had *Kop* magazine, complete with homages to Bill Shankly and a weekly list of songs to learn and sing.

Later fans had *The End*, an all-in-one football, music and style bible. Then came *Another Wasted Corner*, *Our Days Are Numbered*… and a host of others.

Today's match-goers have three well-established fanzines to choose from, all fiercely independent from the club and each with its own character and humour. The longest-established is *Through The Wind And Rain*, produced in Bootle and published four times a year. Next comes the Loughborough-based *Red All Over The Land*, which – as the name suggests – celebrates Liverpool FC's appeal to fans on Merseyside and much further beyond. Finally there's *The Liverpool Way*, first published in August 1999.

For those who prefer computer screens to paper, each fanzine has its own website. Other non-official fan sites online include: www.redandwhitekop.net www.lfconline.com www.koptalk.co.uk and www.shankly.com

Fastest Goal

SEVERAL EARLY LIVERPOOL players are reported to have scored "in the first minute", but none is likely to have found the target as quickly as Jack Balmer. On February 16th, 1938, he hit the opener at Goodison after just 10 seconds. The Reds went on to win the derby game 3-1. Twenty years later Billy Liddell got Liverpool off to a flyer at Bristol City – getting on the scoresheet 16 seconds after kick off.

Ferguson, Robert

1912/3-1914/5 (Centre-half) **B** 1886, Cleland, Lanarkshire **S** May 1912 from Third Lanark **D** 4.9.1912 v Oldham Athletic, lg **L** 1915, emigrated to the USA **Apps** 103, 2 gls **Hons** FAC finalist 1913–14 **OC** Junior football, Third Lanark **d** n/k

Ferns, Phil

1961/2-1964/5 (Full-back/left-half) **B** 14.11.1937, Liverpool **S** August 1961 from Junior football **D** 29.8.1962 v Manchester C, lg **L** August 1965 to Bournemouth **Apps** 28, 1 gl **Hons** Div1 CH 1963–64 **OC** Bournemouth, Mansfield T, Rhyl

LEFT-SIDED LOCAL who survived Bill Shankly's early clear-out to make his debut during the Reds' first season back in Division One. Managed 18 appearances in 1963–64.

Bill Liddell leads 'Liddellpool' out of the tunnel; on one occasion he scored 16 seconds into the game!

'Fields Of Anfield Road'

THE KOPITES' NEWEST anthem is based on the Irish folk ballad 'Fields of Athenry' – a song long associated with Celtic fans. Liverpool's travelling supporters adopted the tune in the late 1990s, perhaps in response to Celtic's growing fondness for 'You'll Never Walk Alone'. But it wasn't until the 2002–03 season that this scouse version began to echo loudly around Anfield.

Lyrics:

Outside the Shankly Gates
I heard a Kopite calling
Shankly, they have taken you away
But you left a great eleven
Before you went to Heaven
Now it's glory round the fields of Anfield Road

All round the fields of Anfield Road
Where once we watched the King Kenny play
(and he could play!)
We had Heighway on the wing
We had dreams and songs to sing
Of the glory round the fields of Anfield Road

Outside the Paisley Gates
I heard a Kopite calling
Paisley, they have taken you away
You led the great eleven
Back in Roma 77
And the Redmen, they're still playing the same way

All round the fields of Anfield Road
Where we watched the King Kenny play
(and he could play!)
We had Heighway on the wing
We had dreams and songs to sing
Of the glory round the fields of Anfield Road

Fightbacks

THEY MAY HAVE made managers prematurely grey, but they've provided fans with some of the most rousing tales in the club's history. Nothing causes as much excitement around Anfield as the prospect of an epic fightback. When the Kop struck up the "no surrender" chant in the 1960s, it often stirred the players into action. No wonder Shankly regarded the Liverpool crowd as his twelfth man.

Never was their power more in evidence than in November 1970 when his transitional team of youngsters faced League champions at Everton at home. Two-nil down with just 15 minutes left, the Kopites watched Steve Heighway finish an awesome run down the left with a shot past Andy Rankin. Minutes later John Toshack levelled the scores with a bullet header. Spurred on by the loudest Anfield roars

for years, the Reds ran Everton ragged in the closing stages. And just a minute from time, Chris Lawler brought the house down with a fiercely struck winner.

The ground has witnessed many brilliant comebacks since then. Who can forget the 1991 UEFA Cup tie with Auxerre when Liverpool cancelled out a 2-0 first leg defeat, then grabbed a brilliant 83rd minute winner through Mark Walters? Or the 1994 Premiership clash with Manchester United, when Nigel Clough's shots and Neil Ruddock's unstoppable header stopped Ferguson's team from taking the points after leading 3-0?

But the most memorable Anfield fightback was on March 16th, 1977 – the night French champions St Etienne came to town. Leading 1-0 from the first leg, the away side replied to Kevin Keegan's opener on 51 minutes, leaving Liverpool in need of two more goals for victory. Ray Kennedy came up with one of them on the hour. Then, with only six minutes left, he played the ball into the path of 'supersub' David Fairclough, who outran his markers to slide the ball home into the Kop net.

Twenty-four years later Michael Owen sparked the same scenes when he single-handedly overturned Arsenal's 1-0 lead at Cardiff's Millennium Stadium in the last eight minutes. The FA Cup was heading back to Anfield and another chapter in Liverpool's stirring book of fightbacks had been written.

➤ Also see: Fairclough, David
Owen, Michael

Flag Days & Nights

ALTHOUGH HUGE BANNERS are a feature of the Kop at most home matches, Anfield has also become noted for specially designated 'flag days', when they're unfurled on all sides of the ground. Fans organised the inaugural event in 1994 to mark the last day of the standing Kop. Since then, leaflets have been handed out around the stadium advertising upcoming matches when banners should be displayed in force. One of the most memorable was the UEFA Cup clash with Roma in 2001. Designated a special 'Paisley Night', Anfield was a riot of colour and noise as a capacity crowd waved their specially made banners honouring the most successful manager in British football history.

Fleming, George

1901/2-1905/6 (Left-half) **B** 20.5.1869, Bannockburn, Stirlingshire
S May 1901 from Wolverhampton W **D** 21.9.1901 v Sunderland, lg
L 1906 became LFC asst trainer **Apps** 83, 5 gls **Hons** Div2 CH
1904–05; Dewar Shield 1906 **OC** East Stirling, Wolves **d** Aug 1922

In 1973, Anfield lost its floodlight pylons and new spotlights were recessed into the roofs of the stands, in line with furnishing trends of the time

Floodlights

THE FIRST ANFIELD MATCH under floodlights was on October 1957 when 46,724 saw the Reds beat Everton in a friendly to mark the 75th anniversary of the Liverpool County FA. Three weeks earlier, Everton hosted the same fixture as the Goodison lights were switched on for the first time. The home side ran out 3-2 winners in front of a 58,771 crowd.

The Anfield floodlights – mounted on four pylons at each corner of the ground – were removed in 1973 and replaced by two new sets, stripped across the roof of the Kemlyn Road and Main Stands. The Kemlyn Road lights were changed in 1992 due to the building of the Centenary Stand.

Floodlit Challenge Cup

DUE TO THE SUCCESS of the first floodlit-friendlies, Liverpool and Everton decided to make the two-legged tie an annual event.

It was, in part, a way of keeping the Merseyside derby fixture alive during Liverpool's Division Two days, and the games continued to attract huge crowds at both grounds.

Despite their lower position, Liverpool won the Cup four times between 1957 and 1962, the year the tournament was discontinued. The Reds got to keep the trophy, which now rests in the LFC Museum.

Kevin Keegan receives his Footballer of the Year award in 1976 from Everton legend Dixie Dean

Footballer Of The Year

Ian Callaghan was the first Liverpool player to be honoured by the Football Writers' Association. Since he picked up the award in 1974, another seven Anfield men have followed suit:

Kevin Keegan (1976)
Emlyn Hughes (1977)
Kenny Dalglish (1979 & 1983)
Terry McDermott (1980)
Ian Rush (1984)
John Barnes (1988 & 1990)
Steve Nicol (1989)

➲ Also see PFA Player Of The Year

Foreign Players

FORMER LIVERPOOL manager George Patterson pioneered the use of overseas players by importing a number of South Africans between the two world wars.

Goalkeeper Arthur Riley, signed by Patterson in 1925, was the first player from outside the UK and Ireland to pull on a Liverpool jersey. He was followed later that same year by fellow Springbok, Gordon Hodgson.

The South African connection died out in the early 1950s (although it was later revived with the arrival of Bruce Grobbelaar and Craig Johnston) and it wasn't until the signing of the Israeli international Avi Cohen in 1979 that the club ventured back into the foreign market.

Jan Molby signalled the start of the Scandinavian influx in the mid-1980s. And by the end of the 1990s – due to the introduction of the Premiership, and more relaxed rules on the number of foreigners that could be fielded – there had been a pretty dramatic rise in overseas playing staff.

By the start of 2003, a total of 52 players, from 21 non-UK and Ireland countries, had made senior appearances for the club:

Cameroon: Rigobert Song
Czech Republic: Patrik Berger, Vladimir Smicer, Milan Baros
Croatia: Igor Biscan
Denmark: Jan Molby, Torben Piechnik
Finland: Sami Hyypia, Jari Litmanen
France: Djimi Traore, Bernard Diomede, Gregory Vignal, Nicolas Anelka, Bruno Cheyrou
Germany: Karl-Heinz Riedle, Dietmar Hamann, Markus Babbel, Christian Ziege
Guadaloupe: Pegguy Arphexad
Guinnea: Titi Camara
Holland: Erik Meijer, Sander Westerveld
Hungary: Istvan Kozma
Israel: Avi Cohen, Ronny Rosenthal
Jamaica: John Barnes
Mozambique: Abel Xavier
Norway: Stig Inge Bjornebye, Bjorn Tore Kvarme, Oyvind Leonhardsen, Vegard Heggem, Frode Kippe, John Arne Riise
Poland: Jerzy Dudek
Senegal: El-Hadji Diouf, Salif Diao
South Africa: Arthur Riley, Gordon Hodgson, Charles Thompson, Lance Carr, Berry Nieuwenhuys, Dirk Kemp, Harman Van Den Berg, Bob Priday, Hugh Gerhardi, Doug Rudham, Craig Johnston, Sean Dundee
Sweden: Glenn Hysen
Switzerland: Stephane Henchoz
USA: Brad Friedel
Zimbabwe: Bruce Grobbelaar (b South Africa)

Happy days for the foreign legion: (clockwise from top left) Meijer, Westerveld, Smicer, Camara, Henchoz, Houllier, Thompson and Hyypia

Forshaw, Dick

1919/20-1926/7 (Inside-right/centre-forward) **B** 20.8.1895, Preston, Lancashire **S** 1919 from army football **D** 8.9.1919 v Arsenal, lg **L** March 1927 to Everton **Apps** 288, 124 gls **Hons** Div1 CH 1921–22, 1922–23; CS 1922 finalist **OC** Gateshead Schools football, St George's Church Lads' Brigade, Gateshead St Vincent's; wartime guest: Nottingham Forest and Middlesbrough, Army football, Everton, Waterford, Wolverhampton W, Hednesford T, Rhyl Athletic **d** n/k

THE ONLY MAN to win Championship medals with both Liverpool and Everton. Preston-born Forshaw was an ever-present in the sides that won the 1922 and 1923 titles, hitting 36 goals in both campaigns. He was top scorer in the 1925–26 season but was, surprisingly, sold to Everton a year later. He appeared in the same forward line as Dixie Dean and collected his third Championship medal after just one season. He joined Wolves in 1929 and later played for Hednesford Town and Rhyl Athletic.

Fowler, Robbie

1993/4-2000/01 (Striker) **B** 9.4.1975, Toxteth, Liverpool **S** 1993 from youth team **D** 22.9.1993 v Fulham, LC **L** November 30 2001 to Leeds United, £11 million **Apps** 330, 171 gls **Hons** UEFA 2000–01; FAC 2000–01; FAC finalist 1995–96; LC 1994–95, 2000–01; CS 2001; Super Cup 2001; Young Player of the Year, 1995, 1996; 22 caps for England **OC** Leeds Utd, Manchester C

WIDELY REGARDED AS one of the game's most natural finishers, the Toxteth teenager gave notice of his awesome scoring talents just a fortnight after breaking into the first team. Fresh from shooting England's Under-18s to glory in the 1993 European Championships, Fowler lined-up for a League Cup clash with Fulham – and hit every goal in Liverpool's 5-0 win. He was on the mark 18 times in his debut campaign, broke the 30-goal barrier for the following two seasons and picked up the PFA's Young Player Of The Year award twice running.

One of us: Robbie Fowler enjoyed an incredible rapport with the Anfield faithful

Fowler enjoyed a rapport with the Anfield crowd like no other during the 1990s. The prime example of a local lad made good, he seemed to live out the dreams of thousands of Kopites every time he pulled on a red shirt. When press controversy about his on and off-the-field behaviour erupted – as it frequently did – the fans only rallied round him even more. To them, he was the man who had topped the Anfield scoring charts for three years, and whose devastating shooting power earned him the ultimate nickname – 'God'.

But even the most glittering careers have their troughs. Fowler's *annus horribilis* came in the 1997–98 season when two serious injuries restricted him to just a handful of club appearances and ruled him out of the World Cup. At the same time, Michael Owen was emerging as an equally brilliant Anfield talent and achieving national hero status with his performance for England against Argentina.

Fowler's return coincided with the arrival of Gerard Houllier, and a rotation system that meant his automatic place in Liverpool's starting-line-up was a thing of the past. The subsequent signings of Emile Heskey and Jari Litmanen also intensified competition, and led to him frequently starting matches on the subs' bench.

Still, Houllier made him captain when Jamie Redknapp was injured and, in February 2001, he became the first Liverpool skipper to lift a

Friedel, Brad

1997/8-2000/01 (Goalkeeper) **B** 18.5.1971, Lakewood, Ohio, USA
S December 1997 from Columbus Crew **D** 28.2.1998 v Aston Villa, lg
L November 2000 to Blackburn R **Apps** 31 **Hons** 45 caps for USA
OC Brondby, Galatasaray, Columbus Crew, Blackburn R

LIVERPOOL LANDED the American goalkeeper's signature after a three-year wait for a work permit.

He joined from Columbus Crew at the end of 1997 but kept his No.1 jersey for less than a year, due to the arrival of David James. Although the club were interested in keeping him on, a law restricting the number of non–EC nationals meant his future at Anfield was doomed. He went home to the US in 1999, but later returned to Premiership action with Blackburn.

Furnell, Jim

1962-1963 (Goalkeeper) **B** 23.11.1937, Clitheroe, Lancashire
S February 1962 from Burnley, £18,000 **D** 3.3.1962 v Walsall, lg
L November 1963 to Arsenal, £15,000 **Apps** 28 **Hons** Div2 CH
1961–62 **OC** Burnley, Arsenal, Rotherham Utd, Plymouth Argyle, Blackburn R (assistant manager)

TOOK OVER AS GOALKEEPER mid-way through the 1961–62 season and helped Shankly's team win promotion. But the £18,000 signing from Burnley managed just 13 apearances in Division One before breaking a finger and losing his place to Tommy Lawrence. He played two final games in the 1963–64 Championship campaign before moving to Arsenal. Later in his career he played for Rotherham and Plymouth, and worked as part of Blackburn's coaching staff.

trophy for six years. His brilliant volley at the Millennium Stadium had helped Liverpool to Worthington Cup victory. His performances would soon help bring further triumphs in the FA and UEFA Cups. And his two goals against Charlton on the last day of the season helped land a first Champions League spot.

But he didn't stay long enough to enjoy that European campaign. In November 2001 – a month after hitting his final hat-trick against Leicester – he confirmed months of press speculation by opting for an £11 million transfer to Leeds United.

However, his career at Elland Road never managed to take off, and, in 2003, he moved to Manchester City.

"U-S-A, U-S-A": Brad Friedel was Anfield's all-American hero until football red tape forced his departure

Howard Gayle with an avuncular Bob Paisley

Gayle, Howard

1977/8-1982/3 (Forward) **B** 18.5.1958, Toxteth, Liverpool
S November 1977 from Merseyside Sunday football **D** 4.10.1980 v
Manchester C, lg **L** January 1983 to Birmingham C, £75,000 **Apps** 5,
1 gl **Hons** England U21 caps **OC** Merseyside Sunday football, Fulham
(loan), Newcastle Utd (loan), Birmingham C, Sunderland, Dallas
Sidekicks (American Indoor League), Stoke C, Blackburn R

THE FIRST BLACK PLAYER to wear a Liverpool first-team jersey – and the man who helped the Reds turn in one of their greatest European Cup performances. Munich's Olympic Stadium was the scene of his triumph, as Liverpool faced Bayern in the 1981 semi-final second leg after a goalless draw at Anfield. They were under sustained attack from the Germans – until Gayle replaced a limping Kenny Dalglish and began terrorising the Bayern defence with his blistering pace. They subjected the Toxteth teenager to a barrage of fouls, and manager Bob Paisley eventually replaced him with Jimmy Case. But by then the Germans were in disarray, allowing Ray Kennedy to put Liverpool through to the final with a cool strike seven minutes from time.

It was Gayle's second appearance for the senior team, but despite his heroics he played only three more games. In a squad featuring Dalglish, Johnson, Fairclough – and a young Ian Rush – competition for forward places was just too fierce. He left for Birmingham in 1983 and gained England Under-21 honours, before spells with Sunderland and Blackburn.

Geary, Fred

1895/6-98/9 (Forward) **B** 23.1.1868, Hyson Green, Nottingham
S May 1895 from Everton, £60.00 **D** 7.9.1895 v Notts C, lg
L Retired 1899 **Apps** 45, 14 gls **Hons** Div2 CH 1895–96
OC Nottingham schoolboy football, Balmoral FC, Notts Rangers,
Grimsby T, Notts C, Everton **d** 8.1.1955

AN EARLY RECRUIT from Everton, the Scottish striker arrived in 1895, four years after helping the former Anfield club to their first Championship. He retired in 1899, became a Liverpool pub landlord and represented Lancashire at bowls.

Gerrard, Steven

1998/9-present (Midfield) **B** 30.5.1980, Liverpool **S** LFC Academy
D 29.11.1998 v Blackburn R, lg **Apps** 192, 22 gls **Hons** UEFA 2000-
–01; FAC 2000–01; LC 2000–01, 2002–03; Super Cup 2002; CS
2002, 2003 finalist; 14 caps for England

PUNDITS ALMOST RAN OUT of superlatives to describe the Academy graduate's early games, but ex-skipper Alan Hansen still had one in reserve: "Gerrard is Souness with pace – and that's one hell of a player."

No-one could disagree. From his teenage debut in 1998, Gerrard showed the tenacity and skill that have made him one of Liverpool – and England's – most prized assets. A ferocious tackle, awesome stamina and pinpoint passing all combined to make the complete midfielder. By 1999 he was a first team regular; by 2000, an international; by 2001, he had become Young Player of The Year.

That award was due to his brilliant form in the Treble-winning season – a campaign when he featured in 50 games and scored 10 goals. And it came just a few months before his crucial role in England's 5-1 win over Germany – capped with a magnificent 25-yard strike.

Unfortunately, Gerrard's next season was blighted by a series of niggling injuries. After suffering back problems he damaged a groin, then had to pull out of England's 2002 World Cup squad. But by the following campaign he was back to fitness and fulfilling all the promise he had shown as a teenager.

The undoubted highlight of that rollercoaster 2002–03 season was the Worthington Cup final against Manchester United. Gerrard's opening goal, and his powerhouse performance in midfield, put United's Roy Keane in the shade – and helped the Reds to victory over their great north-west rivals.

Gerry and the Pacemakers

→ See You'll Never Walk Alone

Gillespie, Gary T

1983/4-90/1 (Centre-back) **B** 5.7.1960, Bonnybridge, Stirling
S July 1983 from Coventry C, £325,000 **D** 7.2.1984 v Walsall, LC
L 1991 to Celtic, £925,000 **Apps** 212, 16 gls **Hons** Div1 CH
1985–86, 1987–88, 1989–90; Super Cup 1985 finalist, WCCH 1984
finalist, SSSC 1984–85, CS 1988; 13 caps for Scotland
OC Falkirk, Coventry C (twice), Celtic

AT 17, THE SCOTTISH centre-back captained
Falkirk to become the youngest skipper in world
professional football. But an illustrious past
counts for nothing at Anfield and, when
Gillespie joined Liverpool, he found the towering figures of Alan Hansen and Mark
Lawrenson blocking his route to the first team.
A £325,000 capture from Coventry, he was Joe
Fagan's first buy, but had to wait for two years
– and the appointment of Dalglish as manager
– before becoming a regular. From then on, he
was a vital link in the teams that lifted the
Championships in 1986, 1988 and 1990. Tall
and cultured, he was a perfect partner for
Hansen at the heart of the Reds defence and his
cool consistency brought him the first of his
Scotland caps in 1987. But, like several other
experienced players, Gillespie found himself out
of favour following the appointment of Graeme
Souness as boss. After moving to his boyhood
favourites Celtic for £925,000, he resumed his
English League career with Coventry.

Gilligan, Samuel A

1910/1-1913 (Inside-forward) **B** 18.1.1882, Dundee **S** 1910 from
Bristol C **D** 24.9.1910 v Manchester C, lg **L** 1913 to Gillingham as
player-manager **Apps** 40, 16 gls **Hons** none **OC** Belmont Athletic
(Dundee), Dundee, Celtic, Bristol C, Gillingham (player-manager) **d** n/k

Glover, John W

1900/1-1902/3 (Right-back) **B** 22.10.1876, West Bromwich **S** 1900
from New Brompton, £350 **D** 20.10.1900 v Notts C, lg **L** June 1903
to Small Heath **Apps** 59, 0 gl **Hons** Div1 CH 1900–01 **OC** West
Bromwich A, Blackburn R, New Brompton, Small Heath **d** 20.4.1955

Goalkeepers

CHRIS KIRKLAND is the 51st player to keep
goal for Liverpool since the club's formation.
Several No.1s – like Kirkland and Jerzy Dudek
– have been genuinely world-class. Many others
have been outstanding.

Veteran Scot Ned Doig kicked off the Anfield
tradition of great 'keepers. When he arrived in
1904 he'd already amassed four Championship
medals with Sunderland and seven international caps. His goal was breached just 25 times in
his first season and it was thanks to his superb
form that Liverpool climbed out of Division Two

But the Candyman can – Gary Gillespie was a classy and more-than-competent defender

KEY Apps Appearances | **B** Born | **CH** Championship | **CWC** Cup Winners' Cup | **CS** Charity Shield | **D** Debut | **d** Died | **EC** European Cup | **FAC** FA Cup | **gls** Goals | **Hons** Honours | **lg** League

Goalscoring Celebrations

BRUCE GROBBELAAR USED to turn cartwheels when one of his team-mates found the net, but he wasn't the first with the celebratory gymnastics. In fact, Reds winger Billy Lacey was delighting the crowds with his post-scoring rituals as far back as 1914. "Lacey scored a glorious goal – a real old-fashioned effort," reported the *Liverpool Echo*. "Billy was so pleased he performed a somersault, to the amazement and amusement of the spectators."

Nothing so spectacular is on show at Anfield these days. But either a Steven Gerrard full-length dive, a Michael Owen hand-rub, an Emile Heskey DJ routine or a John Arne Riise shirt-strip is more than enough to keep a Kopite happy.

G

at the first attempt.

After Doig came Sam Hardy, who won 14 England caps during his seven years at Anfield. He was followed by Scottish international Kenny Campbell, then the legendary Elisha Scott, who stayed at the club for an incredible 21 years. In 1920, Scott and Campbell faced each other in a Scotland v Northern Ireland match – the first time two 'keepers from a single club had appeared in the same international fixture.

Other internationals down the years have included Tommy Younger and Tommy Lawrence (Scotland), Cyril Sidlow (Wales), Bruce Grobbelaar (Zimbabwe), David James (England), Brad Friedel (USA), Sander Westerveld (Holland) and Jerzy Dudek (Poland). Ray Clemence, probably the club's greatest No.1 of all time, made 56 appearances for his country. In a 1981 game against Brazil he became the first goalkeeper to captain England since Frank Swift, back in the 1940s.

Goalscorers

IAN RUSH TOPS Liverpool's all-time scoring record with 229 League goals and 117 more in other competitions. The striker with the highest League total is Roger Hunt, with a total of 245 in Division One and Two matches.

Michael Owen, with 139 goals in all competitions, is the club's current top scorer. The all-time table of leading marksmen – as at the end of the 2002–03 season – is as follows:

		League	Other	TOTAL
1	Ian Rush	229	117	346
2	Roger Hunt	245	40	286
3	Gordon Hodgson	233	8	241
4	Billy Liddell	216	13	229
5	Robbie Fowler	120	53	173
6	Kenny Dalglish	118	54	172
7	Harry Chambers	135	16	151
8	Michael Owen	102	37	139
9	Jack Parkinson	125	5	130
10	Sam Raybould	119	8	127

Clockwise from top left: Ray Clemence's jersey from the European Cup Final, 1981; Gerrard celebrates his winner against Manchester United at Anfield; John Arne Riise bares all after scoring at Villa Park; Ray Celemence's gloves from 1977

Goddard, Arthur M

1902/3-1914 (Right-wing) **B** Heaton Norris, Stockport, date n/k
S 24.2.1902 from Glossop North End, £460 **D** 8.3.1902 v
Wolverhampton W, lg **L** September 1914 to Cardiff C **Apps** 464, 77
gls, (plus 49 apps, 7 gls as wartime guest) **Hons** Div1 CH 1905–06,
Div2 CH 1904–05; Dewar Shield 1906; Liverpool Senior Cup
1904–05, 1908–09, 1912–13, 1911–12 (shared); Lancashire Cup
finalist **OC** Heaton Albion (amateur), Stockport C, Glossop North End,
Cardiff C, Barnsley **d** n/k

KNOWN AS 'GRACEFUL ARTHUR' because
of his speed and fluency, Goddard was a super-

GALLAHER'S CIGARETTES.

ARTHUR GODDARD, LIVERPOOL, 1909-10.

consistent performer
during his 12 years
at Anfield. He made
more than 300
League appear-
ances, won a 1906
Championship
medal and later
served as captain.
A 1914 testimoni-
al raised the then
substantial sum
of £250, helping
to set him up in
business on
Merseyside.

Golden Boot

AWARDED BY *FRANCE FOOTBALL* magazine to Europe's leading scorer, with points
given for the number of goals, and the relative
difficulty of each country's league. Only one
Liverpool player has won the award since its
inception in 1966: that was Ian Rush, for his 32
First Division goals in the 1983–84 season.

'Golden Goal'

'*GOLDEN GOAL: During the period of extra
time played at the end of normal playing time,
the team which scores the first goal is declared
the winner.*'
– FIFA Rule Book.

Since it was introduced as an alternative to
penalty shoot-outs, the controversial Golden
Goal has settled a number of high-profile cup
clashes. In 2001 it provided the climax to the
most exciting European game ever: Liverpool's
5–4 victory over Alaves in the UEFA Cup Final.

With the scores level at the end of normal
time, the Reds went into the added-on period
knowing that conceding just one more goal
would spell the end of the Treble dream. But,
with the clock showing 116 minutes, Garry
McAllister's free kick was headed into the

Golden Own Goal: Delfi Geli of Alaves looks back in disbelief as his misdirected header gives Liverpool the UEFA Cup

KEY Apps Appearances | **B** Born | **CH** Championship | **CWC** Cup Winners' Cup | **CS** Charity Shield | **D** Debut | **d** Died | **EC** European Cup | **FAC** FA Cup | **gls** Goals | **Hons** Honours | **lg** League

Alaves net by the Spanish defender Delfi Geli… and the trophy was bound for Anfield.

"I've always said I'm not in favour of the golden goal," said Gerard Houllier afterwards. "The rule is still unfair, because it doesn't give the chance to the opposition to get back into the match. I'm against the rule, but I'm still pleased we won by it."

"Pleased" doesn't begin to describe the feelings of more than 20,000 Liverpudlians in Dortmund that night!

Goldie, Archibald

1895/6-1899/00 (Right-back) **B** 5.1.1874, Hurlford, Ayrshire **S** June 1895 from Clyde **D** 28.9.1895 v Burslem Port Vale, lg **L** May 1900 to New Brighton Tower **Apps** 149, 1 gl **Hons** Div2 CH 1895–96 **OC** Clyde, New Brighton Tower, Crewe A, Small Heath **d** 2.4.1953

Ayrshire-born defender from the club's early days. Goldie played alongside his younger brother Bill (see below) at Anfield, before joining Small Heath – later renamed Birmingham FC.

Goldie, William Glover

1897/8-1903/4 (Left-half) **B** 22.1.1878, Hurlford, Ayrshire **S** 25.11.1897 from Clyde **D** 2.4.1898 v Nottingham County, lg **L** January 1904 to Fulham **Apps** 174, 6 gls **Hons** Div1 CH 1900–01 **OC** Clyde, Fulham, Leicester Fosse **d** n/k

Gordon, Patrick

1893/4-94 (Right-wing) **B** Scotland **S** 1893 from Everton **D** 2.9.1893 v Middlesbrough, lg **L** Oct 1894 to Blackburn R **Apps** 30, 8 gls **Hons** Div2 CH 1893–94 **OC** Renton, Everton, Blackburn R **d** n/k

SPEEDY SCOTTISH WINGER, believed to be the first player to 'cross the park' from Goodison to Anfield. He joined at the start of the 1893–94 season – Liverpool's first in the Football League – just a few months after lining up for Everton in the FA Cup Final. He helped his new club to the Second Division Championship, but left for Blackburn after little more than a year.

Gracie, Tom

1912/3-1913/4 (Centre/inside-forward) **B** 12.6.1889, Gasgow **S** February 1912 from Everton **D** 24.2.1912 v Bury, lg **L** 1914 to Hearts **Apps** 34, 5 gls **Hons** none **OC** Morton, Everton, Hearts **d** 23.10.1915

EX-EVERTON INSIDE-LEFT who joined Liverpool in a 1912 exchange deal. He struggled to find the net at either club and was transferred to the Edinburgh club Hearts in 1914. Gracie joined the Royal Scots Guards at the outbreak of World War One, and died in his native Glasgow in 1915.

Graham, Bobby

1960/1-1971/2 (Forward) **B** 22.11.1944, Motherwell **S** From schools football, 1960 apprentice with LFC **D** 14.9.1964 v Reykjavik, EC (scored) **L** March 1972 to Coventry C, £70,000 **Apps** 137, 42 gls **Hons** none **OC** Coventry C, Tranmere R (loan), Motherwell, Hamilton Academical, Queen of the South

AFTER MARKING HIS DEBUT with a European Cup goal against Reykjavik, the young Scot had an even more memorable first League outing – hitting a hat-trick against Aston Villa. But, despite his obvious ability in front of goal, the one-time Anfield apprentice never managed more than a handful of appearances in Shankly's great mid-1960s team.

Graham had played junior football alongside Ian St John in Motherwell, and it was his old friend's form that kept him out of the first team picture at Liverpool. He finally got his chance in 1969–70, going through the season as an ever-present, and finishing as top scorer with 21 goals in all competitions.

But, after waiting so long for that breakthrough, Graham suffered the cruel blow of a broken ankle in an Anfield clash with Chelsea. He was on the treatment table for five months, and it was shortly after he made his comeback that John Toshack and Kevin Keegan established a deadly new partnership.

With his first-team prospects again looking bleak, he opted for a £70,000 move to Coventry in 1972. He then had a short spell at Tranmere before moving to Motherwell. At the start of the 1977–78 season, Hamilton Academical paid a club record £18,000 for his signature.

G

Greatest Goal

STEVEN GERRARD'S 30-YARD screamer against Manchester United in 2001? Robbie Fowler's breathtaking volley in the Worthington Cup Final? Or was it Gary McAllister's unbelievable free-kick winner at Goodison... from all of 44 yards out?

Young fans will have their own opinion on Liverpool's greatest goal. But the true test is, will it be remembered and talked about for years afterwards?

Like Albert Stubbins' low-flying header in a fifth-round FA Cup tie against Birmingham in 1947? The *Liverpool Echo* described it as the "best ever seen at Anfield", and Stubbins was still giving interviews about his so-called "goal in the snow" more than 40 years later. The generation of supporters who saw it also witnessed many spectacular goals from Billy Liddell. But one that lived on long in the memory was a 1948 bullet header against Portsmouth – from outside the penalty area.

Fans who came of age in the 1970s have plenty of TV and video evidence to back up their own candidates for greatest-ever goal. Some may point to Kenny Dalglish's strike against Bruges in the 1978 European Cup Final. Collecting a pass at the edge of the penalty box, Dalglish delayed his shot until the 'keeper had committed himself, making – in Bob Paisley's words – "time stand still".

Others may cite a dazzling 1987 John Barnes goal against Queens Park Rangers, which started in the centre circle, included a dazzling dribble past five defenders and ended with a low, angled shot past David Seaman. "Liverpool's official handbook described it as one of the most memorable goals Anfield had seen in years," Barnes wrote later. "I scored a good goal at Arsenal where I dribbled past four players, but that second against QPR was the most unforgettable."

But organise a supporters' vote on this question and the goal likely to be chosen as the greatest of all time is the one that completed a 7-0 rout of Tottenham back in 1978.

Twelve seconds was all it took for the ball to pass from Ray Clemence to Kenny Dalglish, to David Johnson and Steve Heighway. His pinpoint left-wing cross was then met by Terry McDermott, who headed into the Anfield Road net – after sprinting all the way from the Kop goalmouth.

"I've still got a video of that goal and I watch it whenever I'm feeling low," says McDermott, 25 years on. "It's not because I scored it, but because of the way it came about. The brilliant build-up, the passing, the movement – it's what dreams are made of."

Grobbelaar, Bruce

1981/2-1993/4 (Goalkeeper) **B** 6.10.1957, Durban, South Africa
S March 1981, from Crewe Alexandra, £250,000 **D** 29.8.1981 v
Wolverhampton W, lg (clean sheet) **L** Summer 1994 to Southampton
Apps 619 **Hons** EC 1983–84, 1984–85 finalist; Div1 CH 1981–82,
1982–83, 1983–84, 1985–86, 1987–88, 1989–90; FAC 1985–86,
1988–89, 1991–92; LC 1981–82, 1982–83, 1983–84; Super Cup
1985 finalist; WCCH 1984 finalist; CS 1982, 1988, 1989, 1990;
1982 finalist, 1984 finalist; SSSC 1985–86; 42 caps for Zimbabwe
OC Vancouver Whitecaps, Crewe Alexandra (loan), Stoke C (loan),
Southampton, Plymouth Argyle, Oldham A

COLOURFUL – AND SOMETIMES eccentric –
goalkeeper who took over from Ray Clemence to
become one of the most decorated players in
Liverpool's history.

Although born in South Africa, Grobbelaar
had served as a soldier in the Zimbabwean
army during that country's brutal civil war in
the late 1970s. He later played for the national
team, joined the Canadian club Vancouver
Whitecaps and moved to Anfield in a £250,000
deal in March 1981.

With Clemence as consistent as ever, few
expected Grobbelaar to break into the first team
for many years. But when the first-choice 'keeper asked for a move that summer, Bob Paisley
was forced to throw him in at the deep end.
Erratic performances in his debut season
caused much dismay on the Kop, and
Grobbelaar had to contend with "clown" taunts
from opposing fans. But Paisley kept his faith
and was rewarded as his new No.1 began to
show the athleticism and lightning reflexes that
would later make him famous.

A born entertainer, Grobbelaar
could never resist stopping
shots with spectacular dives:
"Hollywood saves", as his
team-mates called them. He
celebrated Liverpool goals
by performing cartwheels
and marked the 1983
League Cup final win
against Manchester
United by walking
around Wembley on his
hands.

But such showmanship
could be used to serious
effect. His fake nervousness
during the 1984 European Cup
Final penalty shoot-out – complete
with wobbling knees on the goal-
line – undoubtedly distracted
Roma's spot-kickers.

When their penalty king
Graziani fired high and wide,
Grobbelaar became as big a hero

as Alan Kennedy, who went on to hit the eventual winner. While most supporters would still
choose Clemence ahead of his successor, it's
worth noting that Grobbelaar won four more
medals while at Anfield. He equalled
Clemence's feat of being ever-present in six seasons. And – with 34 clean sheets in all competitions for the 1983–84 campaign – he matched
his predecessor's record set in 1970–71.

After 13 years with Liverpool, Grobbelaar
left for Southampton. Soon afterwards he was
embroiled in allegations of match-fixing and,
along with Wimbledon's John Fashanu and
Hans Segers, forced to defend himself in the
courts. He was eventually found not guilty but
then got embroiled in a series of lengthy and
expensive libel cases. He is now involved in
coaching in South Africa.

Guest Players

THE OUTBREAK OF World War Two meant
hundreds of professional footballers being called
up for the armed forces. In an effort to keep the
game going, the Football league allowed clubs to
field players from other teams, if their barracks
were nearby.

Dozens of non-LFC players guested at
Anfield between 1939 and 1945, including
Manchester City's international 'keeper Frank
Swift and Wolves' England star Stan Cullis. But
Liverpool's most illustrious guest of all
appeared in May 1942. As the Reds
beat Everton 4-1 in a wartime
derby, the man wearing the No.4
shirt was Preston's Bill Shankly.

Gunson, Gordon J

1929/30-1933/4 (Outside-left) **B** 1.7.1904, Chester **S** March 1930
from Sunderland **D** 15.3.1930 v Bolton W, lg **L** June 1934 to Swindon
T **Apps** 87, 26 gls **Hons** none **OC** Brickfields FC, Nelson (amateur),
Wrexham (twice), Sunderland, Bangor C (manager), Swindon T, Crewe
Alexandra (trainer), Flint Town (manager), Welshpool (trainer), Dolgellau
FC (manager) **d** 13.9.1991

AN EVER-PRESENT in the 1931–32 season,
but a victim of cartilage damage that blighted
the rest of his career. Gunson was a former
Chester schoolboy who made his name as a lively, goalscoring winger with Wrexham
and Sunderland.

Once at Anfield he was equally
happy to play on either flank, supplying crosses for the great Gordon Hodgson
and regularly finding the net himself.

With injuries restricting his appearances,
the club sold him to Swindon in 1934. He later
managed a string of Welsh League clubs, including Bangor City and Flint Town.

G

Hall, Brian

1968/9-1975/6 (Midfield) **B** 22.11.1946, Glasgow **S** July 1968 from Manchester University **D** 7.4.1969 v Stoke C, lg **L** July 1976, to Plymouth Argyle, £35,000 **Apps** 224, 21 gls **Hons** UEFA 1972–73; Div1 CH 1972–73; FAC 1973–74, 1970–71 finalist **OC** Lancashire Schoolboy football, Manchester University, Plymouth Argyle, Burnley, non-league

TERRIER-LIKE MIDFIELDER with endless invention and energy. Teaming up with fellow graduate Steve Heighway, Hall broke into the side in 1970 and was soon causing headaches for opposition defences with his raiding runs down the flanks. The following season he got on to the scoresheet for the first time, hitting the winner in a 2-1 FA Cup semi-final victory over Everton. From then on, he was a valuable squad player, always ready to replace injured colleagues or to give the team different attacking options.

Hall played 224 games in eight seasons but, ironically, may be best remembered for his non-appearance at the start of 1973's UEFA Cup Final first leg at Anfield. Although part of the original line-up against Borussia Moenchegladbach, the match was soon abandoned because of torrential rain. It was during the 17 minutes of play that Bill Shankly spotted an aerial weakness at the heart of the Borussia defence. And when the match was replayed 24 hours later, Hall found himself replaced by 6ft 1in John Toshack, whose heading power helped Liverpool take a commanding 3-0 lead to Germany. Despite that disappointment, he was sent on as a late substitute, allowing him to claim a medal. The following season he was also an FA Cup winner, playing the full 90 minutes as Liverpool demolished Newcastle at Wembley. Hall left Liverpool for Plymouth in 1976, then began a new career as a teacher. However, he later returned to Anfield, where he now works as the club's public relations manager.

Hamann, Dietmar 'Didi'

1999/00-present (Midfield) **B** 27.8.1973, Waldasson, Germany **S** July 1999 from Newcastle Utd, £8 million **D** 7.8.1999 v Sheffield W, lg **Apps** 172, gls 7 **Hons** UEFA 2000–01; FAC 2000–01; LC 2000–01, 2002–03; Super Cup 2001; CS 2001, 2002 finalist; 48 caps for Germany **OC** FC Waker Munich, Bayern Munich, Newcastle Utd

TWO BUNDESLIGA TITLES, a UEFA Cup medal and a string of international caps were all evidence of Hamann's talent. But it was his commanding midfield displays in Liverpool's Treble season that confirmed the 6ft 2in German as a natural-born winner on the field.

Hamann got his first taste of English football at Newcastle following the 1998 World Cup. The

Hairstyles

"I was the first one to get my perm done. The lads all laughed, but one by one they started having it done themselves. I kept mine for five years."
– TERRY MCDERMOTT

DID HE REALLY once go around with a perm like that? Afraid so. As did Phil Neal. And Phil Thompson.

In fact, Liverpool's players have always been slaves to fashion in the salon. In the late 1950s, Roger Hunt and Dave Hickson vied with each other for the biggest Elvis-style quiff. A decade later, Alun Evans' mop-top made him look like the fifth Beatle. And, in the 1990s, John Barnes pioneered the 'Number One' close-shave. But those cuts are still considered cool by some. Unlike Barry Venison's 'mullet', or Nicky Tanner's 'wedge'. Other fashion-crimes include Robbie Fowler's bleach-blond circa 1997, David James's peroxide crop and any one of the styles favoured by Abel Xavier.

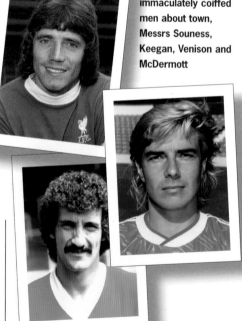

Regulars under the hairdryer – immaculately coiffed men about town, Messrs Souness, Keegan, Venison and McDermott

KEY Apps Appearances | **B** Born | **CH** Championship | **CWC** Cup Winners' Cup | **CS** Charity Shield | **D** Debut | **d** Died | **EC** European Cup | **FAC** FA Cup | **gls** Goals | **Hons** Honours | **lg** League

former Bayern Munich man had only a brief stay on Tyneside, but his ability to guard the defence and break up opposition attacks marked him out as one of the most effective players in the Premiership. Barcelona, Borussia Dortmund and Arsenal all declared an interest in his signature, but in July 1999 he opted for Anfield. Gerard Houllier agreed a then record £8million fee but was quick to announce that he'd found "a player who has everything".

Injuries blighted his first season with Liverpool, but by the 2000–01 campaign he was an automatic choice, excelling on the biggest of occasions, notably in Europe. He also showed how well he was suited to the big stage at international level, scoring the last-ever goal at Wembley in Germany's 1-0 win over England, then, in 2002, becoming the first Reds player since Roger Hunt to appear in a World Cup Final. Hamann's huge influence on the team was shown during the 2002–2003 season when his absence through injury coincided with Liverpool's worst run of results for half a century. He made a belated return but ended the season by returning to Germany for shin surgery.

Hannah, Andrew

1892/3-1894/5 (Right-back) **B** 17.9.1864, Renton, Dumbartonshire
S 1892 from Renton **D** 3 .9.1892 v Higher Walton, Lancs, lg
L October 1895 to Rob Roy **Apps** 69, 1 gl **Hons** Div2 CH 1893–94;
Lancashire League 1892–93 **OC** Renton FC, Everton, Rob Roy
d 1.6 1940

ONE OF LIVERPOOL'S original 1892 recruits, and the team's first-ever captain. Hannah joined from the Scottish club Renton, but had previously been part of Everton's 1891 League Championship-winning side. A powerfully built defender with a famously strong tackle, he was also an all-round sportsman who had won prizes at the Highland Games. As Liverpool skipper, he led the team to promotion from the Lancashire league, then to the Second Division title. He returned to his native Scotland a year later.

Hannah, Davy

1894-1896/7 (Inside-left) **B** 28.4.1867, Raffrey, Co, Down
S November 1894 from Sunderland AFC **D** 10.11.1894 v Stoke C, lg
L 1897 to Dundee **Apps** 33, 12 gls **Hons** Div 2 CH 1895–96
OC Renton FC, Sunderland, Dundee, Woolwich Arsenal **d** Jan 1936

Didi Hamann exhibits his technical prowess with a typically skilful dragback at Anfield

Hansen, Alan

1977/8-1989/90 (Centre-half) **B** 13.6.1955, Sauchie **S** May 1977 from Partick Thistle, £100,000 **D** 24.9.1977 v Derby C, lg **L** retired 1991 **Apps** 616, 14 **Hons** EC 1977–78, 1980–81, 1983–84, 1984–85 finalist; Div1 CH 1978–79, 1979–80, 1981–82, 1982–83, 1983–84, 1985–86, 1987–88, 1989–90; FAC 1985–86, 1988–89, 1987–88 finalist; LC 1980–81, 1982–83, 1983–84; Super Cup 1978 finalist; SC 1985 finalist; WCCH 1981 and 1984 finalist; CS 1979, 1980, 1982, 1988, 1989; 1983 and 1984 finalist; SSSC 1985–86; 26 caps for Scotland **OC** Sauchie Juniors, Partick Thistle

AS SMOOTH ON THE PITCH as he is in the TV studio, Hansen was among the most skilful defenders British football has ever produced. He arrived as a ridiculously cheap £100,000 buy from Partick Thistle and left with the second biggest medal haul in English football history.

A brilliant all-round sportsman who also excelled at basketball, squash and golf, Hansen established himself at centre-back at the start of the 1977–78 season. His superb tackling was evident from the beginning, and within a few games he had gained a reputation for starting counter-attacks with lightning-fast bursts through the middle. "Alan gave me kittens when he came into the side because he had so much composure on the ball," said goalkeeper Ray Clemence. "He would dribble out of defence, which I had not heard of before. You would shout, 'Away!' and he would bring it down, beat the attacking player and dribble it out."

But his team-mates soon got accustomed to his style of play, and Hansen himself was able to form a unique understanding with others. His partnership with Phil Thompson was the defensive rock on which two European Cup victories were built. His later pairing with Mark Lawrenson was probably the greatest in the team's history. After a medal-laden career under Paisley and Fagan, Hansen was offered the captaincy by new boss, and close friend, Kenny Dalglish. With his on-the-field leadership, Liverpool won their first League and FA Cup Double. And when Dalglish finally decided to call it a day, many fans – and the majority of players – wanted the authoritative Scot to take his place. By his own admission, though, Hansen never felt cut out for the stress and

Cool as a cucumber – Hansen in action (above) and in the BBC studio (left)

commitment required of football management. "So many things can go wrong – so many things that are out of your control – which would never appeal to me. Basically I wanted to keep my hair relatively black. Also, I had a lot of friends in that Liverpool dressing room and I'm not sure that I'd have been able to separate myself from them as their boss."

Suffering with increasingly serious knee problems, Hansen chose to bow out of the game altogether in 1991. He took up the offer of media work and soon became the most celebrated and articulate of all television football pundits.

Hanson, Adolf J 'Alf'

1931/2-1937/8 (Outside-left) **B** 27.2.1912, Bootle, Liverpool **S** November 1931 from Bootle JOC **D** 21.1.1933 v Aston Villa, lg **L** July 1938 to Chelsea, £7,500 **Apps** 177, 52 gls **Hons** England wartime international honours **OC** Bootle JOC, Chelsea; wartime guest: Liverpool, New Brighton, Chester, Wrexham, Mancester C, Bolton W, Crewe Alexandra, Rochdale, Tranmere R, Southport, South Liverpool (player-manager), Shelbourne Utd (player-manager), Ellesmere Port Town (player-manager) **d** 6.10.1993

SPOTTED WHILE PLAYING in a Bootle amateur league, the ship's plumber joined Liverpool in 1931 and broke into the first team little more than a year later. A useful goalscorer himself, Hanson was famed for his pinpoint crosses, moving one columnist to write, "A slip of a lad, he was not entirely a one-footed player but it was that left boot which put fear into the hearts of goalkeepers when they saw Alf prancing down the wing."

During wartime, Hanson – an ex-England baseball international – was called up for his country's soccer friendly against Scotland. After leaving Anfield, he played on for Chelsea, but later returned to Merseyside to manage South Liverpool and Ellesmere Port Town.

'Hard Men'

WHILE NEVER REGARDED as a 'dirty' team, the Reds have a long tradition of players able to mix it with the opposition. One of the most noted was 1960s full-back Gerry Byrne, whose bone-crunching tackles often had wingers begging to switch flanks by half-time.

"He was one of the hardest fellas in football, but he never used to speak during a game," said team-mate Geoff Strong. "He'd kick people up in the air and they'd start mouthing off, 'You little…', but Gerry would just walk away like nothing had happened. And then kick them up in the air again."

A decade later it was Joey Jones who wore Byrne's No.3 jersey. His way of dealing with any foul play by the opposition was summed up by

Alf Hanson: "a slip of a lad… it was [his] left boot which put fear into the hearts of goalkeepers"

the Kop's regular chant: "Joey's Going To Get Yer."

The midfield has also thrown up its crop of hard men. From Jimmy Case – with perhaps the thickest thighs the game has ever seen – to Graeme Souness, Steve McMahon, Steven Gerrard and Dietmar Hamann. Souness, like Gerrard, combined sublime skill with raw aggression, and was never a player to be messed with. In one European Cup tie with Dynamo Bucharest, his Russian midfield counterpart paid for a night of cynical fouls – by exiting Anfield with a broken jaw.

But pride of place in the ranks of Liverpool hard men must go to Tommy Smith. He may not have been able to "start a riot in a graveyard", as Bill Shankly once claimed, but he could easily spread panic on the pitch. Everton's Duncan McKenzie, known as one of the great entertainers of the 1970s, recalled Smith's words in his ear as they were warming up for an Anfield derby clash. "Try anything fancy today, lad, and I'll snap your back." Not surprisingly, McKenzie changed wings before kick-off.

Even in an era when Chelsea's Ron 'Chopper' Harris and Leeds United's Norman Hunter terrorised attackers, the so-called 'Anfield Iron' stood out. By his own admission, he relished coming up against other known hard men. One of them – Manchester United's Joe Jordan – found himself felled by a crunching tackle, then picked up off the floor, held upside down and dusted off by a beaming Smithy.

"This hard man image of mine came about through a conscious decision I made as a youngster," he later wrote in his autobiography. "I figured out the only way to win was never to let the other fellow see you were beaten in any way. So

I didn't shirk tackles and it seemed to work. I found people admired me more for getting stuck in, not necessarily kicking the other fellow, but tackling hard."

With a face even his mother would hesitate to call handsome, Smith also learned how to use his features to terrifying effect: "I soon realised the way to win was to frighten the opposition. So I used to growl at them and show my teeth – what's left of them – and it seemed to work. It was a tough guy reputation that took me about twelve months to forge, and twelve years to live down."

Hardy, Sam

1905-12 (Goalkeeper) **B** 26.8.1883, Newbold, Chesterfield **S** May 1905 from Chesterfield T, £500 **D** 21.10.1905 v Nottingham Forest, lg **L** May 1912 to Aston Villa **Apps** 240 **Hons** Div1 CH 1905–06; Dewar Shield 1906; Liv Cup 1905–06; 21 England caps **OC** Newbold White Star, Chesterfield T, Aston Villa, Nottingham Forest **d** 24.10.1966

ONE IN A LONG line of great Liverpool 'keepers, Hardy's career spanned 22 years. 'Safe And Steady Sam' spent seven of those at Anfield, where he collected not only a 1906 Championship medal but also 14 of his 21 England caps. After joining Aston Villa in 1912, he picked up two FA Cup winners' medals, then, while with Forest, he helped his team to the Second Division Championship.

It takes two to tango: Steve Harkness and Noel Whelan, then of Coventry City, tussle for the ball

around Anfield in 1958. Unfortunately, Harrower's ball skills weren't matched by speed and consistency and the crowd's support for the ex-Hibernian man soon wore thin. But his talents remained in demand elsewhere. When Bill Shankly sold him to Newcastle in 1961, the club made a profit of £4,000 on the player.

Hateley, Tony

1967-1968 (Centre-forward) **B** 13.6.1941, Derby **S** June 1967 from Chelsea, £96,000 **D** 19.8.1967 v Manchester C, lg **L** Sept 1968 to Coventry C, £80,000 **Apps** 56, 28 gls **Hons** none **OC** Normanton Sports, Notts C (twice), Aston Villa, Chelsea, Coventry C, Birmingham C, Oldham, Bromsgrove Rovers, Prescot, Barrow, Keyworth Utd

A TRUE SOCCER NOMAD who appeared for seven clubs in a League career spanning 14 years. The giant centre-forward arrived from Chelsea in a record-breaking deal during the summer of 1967. He began repaying his £96,000 fee almost immediately, hitting 27 goals – including two hat-tricks – in his first season. Fast, direct and brilliant in the air, Hateley was a menacing figure at the forefront of Liverpool's attack. His aerial ability also provided many opportunities for Roger Hunt to feed on, and between them the two strikers shared 61 goals during the campaign.

But opposition defences soon got wise to Hateley's threat and he was the subject of some vicious tackling that led to injury lay-offs. His weakness in build-up play also forced the team into a long-ball game that Shankly personally disliked. The new boss went on the look-out for a replacement, identifying the teenage Alun Evans as a better prospect for the future. After just four appearances in the 1968–69 season, Hateley was sold to Coventry for £80,000.

Harkness, Steve

1989/90-1998/9 (Midfield/defender) **B** 27.8.1971, Carlisle **S** July 1989 from Carlisle Utd, £75,000 **D** 27.8.1991 v Queens Park Rangers, lg **L** March 1999 to Benfica **Apps** 139, 4 gls **Hons** England Youth international **OC** Carlise Utd, Huddersfield T (loan), Southend Utd (loan), Benfica, Blackburn R

VERSATILE ENGLAND YOUTH international, signed as a 17-year-old from his hometown club, Carlisle United, in 1989. Harkness made his debut as a defender but was later switched to a midfield role under Graeme Souness.

He made a good impression in the senior team but, after an absence with a broken leg, found it difficult to displace the returning Steve Staunton. In 1998, Souness persuaded him to move to his new club Benfica. He returned to the Premiership after a transfer to Blackburn Rovers and later moved on to pastures new with Sheffield Wednesday.

Harley, Jim

1934/5-1948/9 (Right/left-back) **B** 21.2.1917, Methil, Fife **S** April 1934 from Hearts o' Beath **D** 28.9.1935 v West Bromwich A, lg **L** retired through injury 1948/9 **Apps** 134 **Hons** Div1 CH 1946–7; Scotland wartime international honours **OC** Hearts o' Beath **d** 1989

LIGHTNING-FAST DEFENDER who arrived at Anfield fresh from winning Scotland's famous Powderhall Sprint race. After playing through the Depression era, Harley joined the Royal Navy, managed to put in a few wartime Anfield appearances and gained Scotland recognition. He returned to the club full-time when the fighting was over, and collected a Championship medal in the 1946–47 season.

Harrop, Jim

1907/8-1911/2 (Centre-half) **B** Sept 1884, Sheffield **S** Jan 1908 from Rotherham, £250 **T** 18.1.1908 v Bolton W, lg **L** 1912 to Aston Villa **Apps** 139, 4 gls **Hons** Football league honours **OC** The Wednesday, Denaby United, Rotherham T, Aston Villa, Sheffield Utd **d** 1958

Harrower, Jimmy

1957/8-1960/1 (Inside-forward) **B** 18.8.1935, Alva, Clackmannanshire **S** January 1958 from Hibs, £11,000 **D** 11.1.1958 v Fulham, lg **L** March 1961 to Newcastle Utd, £15,000 **Apps** 105, 22 gls **Hons** Scotland Under-21s **OC** Sauchie Juveniles, Kilsyth Rangers, Bo'ness Utd, Hibs, Newcastle Utd, Falkirk, St Johnstone, Albion Rovers

TALENTED INSIDE FORWARD whose £11,000 signing caused much anticipation

Dazzling dribbler, fifties forward Jimmy Harrower never quite brought his skills to bear at Anfield

Hat-Tricks

LIVERPOOL'S ALL-TIME hat-trick hero is Gordon Hodgson, who hit 17 of them between 1926 and 1935. Jack Balmer is the only player to score three consecutive hat-tricks (in 1946–47) and Roger Hunt, with five hat-tricks in 1961–62, holds the record for scoring the most in one season.

Although Ian St John hit three on his first outing for the Reds, it was in a Liverpool Senior Cup game. Bobby Graham, on the other hand, managed a hat-trick on his League debut against Aston Villa in 1964.

Only four Liverpool players – Phil Boersma, Ian Rush, Robbie Fowler and Michael Owen – have ever managed to score three before the half-time whistle. Fowler's 1994 first-half hat-trick against Arsenal came in the space of just 4 minutes and 33 seconds, making it the fastest in the club's history.

Heggem, Vegard

1998/9-2002/03 (Right-back) **B** 13.7.1975, Trondheim, Norway **S** July 1998 from Rosenborg, £3.5 million **D** 16.8.1998 v Southampton, lg **L** May 15 2003 to Norway **Apps** 65, 3 gls **Hons** 20 caps for Norway **OC** Rennebu, Orkdal, Rosenborg

AS THE FIRST SIGNING of joint managers Roy Evans and Gerard Houllier, the Norwegian international went straight into first-team action as an effective overlapping full-back. Unfortunately his impressive performances at the start of the 1998–99 season were soon interrupted by a long series of hamstring injuries. By the time he was fit, his place had been taken by Markus Babbel and he left Anfield in May 2003.

Tony Hateley was a great partner for Roger Hunt – on the terraces they were known as the "H Bombers"

Brian Hall and Steve Heighway scrutinize the back pages before their game against AEK Athens in 1972

for John Toshack and Kevin Keegan and, displaying a keen scent for goal himself, he found the net 76 times. The rewards were 34 Republic of Ireland caps, four Championship medals, plus victories in two UEFA Cup and two European Cup Finals. At Wembley in 1974 he was also on target as Liverpool beat Newcastle 3-0 to win the FA Cup for the second time.

Heighway's contribution to Liverpool FC is impressive enough as a player. But, after returning to Anfield as Youth Development Officer, he has helped to nurture a new generation of legends. Fowler, McManaman, Owen, Gerrard – and a host of others – all came under his care and tuition as youngsters. Now, as director of the club's world-leading Academy, he's charged with finding even more stars of the future. "I love the job and I feel a great sense of responsibility towards the club," he said, as the Academy opened in 1999. "The board have shown considerable foresight by investing so heavily in the Academy and we each have a role to play now to repay that faith. Our record over the years of bringing our own players through is magnificent and we hope there are many more to come in the next few years."

Henchoz, Stephane

1999/00-present (Defender) **B** 7.9.1974, Billens, Switzerland
S Summer 1999 from Blackburn R, £3.5 million **D** 21.9.1999 v Hull
City, LC **Apps** 174, 0 gls **Hons** UEFA 2000–01; FAC 2000–01; LC
2000–01, 2002–03; Super Cup 2001; CS 2001, 2002 finalist; 55
caps for Switzerland **OC** Stade Payerne, Bulls, Xamax Neuchatel,
SV Hamburg, Blackburn R

ONE OF SEVEN SIGNINGS in the summer of 1999 and one of the defensive rocks on which Gerard Houllier built his Treble-winning side.

Heighway, Steve D

1970/1-1980/1 (Forward) **B** 25.11.1947, Dublin, Rep I **S** 1970 from
Skelmersdale (as amateur) **D** 29.8.1970 v WBA, lg **L** 1981 to
Minnesota Kicks, USA **Apps** 475, 76 gls **Hons** EC 1976–77,
1977–78; UEFA 1972–73, 1975–76; Super Cup 1977; Div 1 CH
1972–73, 1975–76, 1976–77, 1978–79; FAC 1973–74, 1970-71,
1976–77 finalist; 34 caps for Rep I **OC** Manchester C (amateur),
Warwick University, Skelmersdale Utd (amateur), Minnesota Kicks

OUTSTANDING WINGER whose dazzling runs down the left flank electrified Anfield for a decade. In 1970, Bob Paisley's son spotted the young graduate playing amateur football for Skelmersdale. Paisley Snr persuaded him to sign professional forms, then saw him become a key part of Bill Shankly's second great team.

One of his finest early games was the famous 1970 Anfield League derby. With Champions Everton 2-0 up, and just 15 minutes left on the clock, he inspired an incredible Liverpool fightback that resulted in the Reds winning the game 3-2. Six months later he opened the scoring in the FA Cup Final, capping a brilliant run past the Arsenal defence with an angled shot past Bob Wilson. Sadly, the Gunners managed a spectacular late equaliser from Charlie George.

Throughout the 1970s, Heighway's speed and trickery opened up countless defences. His crosses created hatfuls of scoring opportunities

KEY Apps Appearances | **B** Born | **CH** Championship | **CWC** Cup Winners' Cup | **CS** Charity Shield | **D** Debut | **d** Died | **EC** European Cup | **FAC** FA Cup | **gls** Goals | **Hons** Honours | **lg** League

The big Swiss international was a bargain £3.5million capture from newly relegated Blackburn Rovers, where fans had just named him as the club's Player of The Season.

Once at Anfield, the Liverpool supporters could easily understand why. Seeing him team up with Sami Hyypia, they were able to revel in the most effective defensive partnership for more than a decade. Henchoz proved himself to be strong in the air and his sense of timing in a tackle was reminiscent of Mark Lawrenson at his best. His willingness to stay back throughout the game also allowed Hyypia to move up for set-pieces, causing chaos in opposition defences. Although he played a major part in the 2003 Worthington Cup win, he had surgery afterwards, and his absence seriously damaged Liverpool's push for the Champions League.

Henderson, David

1893/4-1894/5 (Centre-forward) **B** 1868, Stirling
S September 1893 from King's Park **D** 23.9.1893 v Small
Heath, lg **L** November 1894 Partick Thistle **Apps** 23,
12 gls **Hons** Div2 CH 1893–94 **OC** King's Park (Stirling),
Partick Thistle **d** n/k

Heskey, Emile I

2000/01-present (Striker) **B** 11.1.1978, Leicester
S March 2000 from Leicester C, £11 million **D**
11.3.2000 v Sunderland **Apps** 175, 48 gls
Hons UEFA 2000–01; FAC 2000–01; LC 2000–01,
LC 2002–03; Super Cup 2001; CS 2001, 2002 finalist; 30 caps for
England, as well as U-21 caps **OC** Leicester C

THE FAST AND POWERFUL Leicester striker became Liverpool's costliest player when he arrived in March 2000. But thanks to his all-action performances in the Treble-winning season, the £11 million man won an army of admirers on the Kop. He weighed in with 22 goals in that campaign, including a sensational opening day goal against Bradford and a crucial header against Wycombe in the FA Cup semi-final.

A few months later he hit a brilliant goal in the Super Cup victory over Bayern Munich, and his performances throughout the season made him the natural choice to partner Michael Owen at the 2002 World Cup Finals. The exertions of the tournament took a personal toll on the player the following season, as his ability to find the net diminished. However, his pace and power to unsettle defences was still there and it was easy to see why both Houllier and England boss Sven-Goran Eriksson preferred him in their starting line-ups. Houllier was rewarded when Heskey scored the winner at Southampton, bringing a run of 11 goalless games to an end, and then equalised against Arsenal weeks later.

Goalward-bound, Liverpool's £11 million record signing Emile Heskey in full flight

Hewitt, Joe

1903/4-1909/10 (Centre-forward) **B** 3.5.1881, Chester **S** 11.2.1904 from Sunderland **D** 13.2.1904 v Stoke City, lg **L** August 1910 to Bolton W **Apps** 164, 71 gls **Hons** DIV 1 CH 1905–06; Dewar Shield 1906; Liv Cup 1905–06 **OC** Chester works team, Sunderland, Bolton W, LFC (coaching staff) **d** 1971

CHESTER-BORN FORWARD and leading scorer in the 1905–06 title-winning season. He left for Bolton in 1910 but later became a long-serving member of the Anfield coaching staff.

Heydon, John 'Jack'

1948/9-1952/3 (Right/centre-half) **B** 19.10.1928, Birkenhead **S** December 1948 from Everton (amateur) **D** 7.10.1950 v Stoke C, lg **L** May 1953 to Millwall, £3,000 **Apps** 67, 0 gls **Hons** none **OC** junior football, Everton (amateur), Millwall, Tranmere R

Heysel Disaster

ON MAY 29TH, 1985, Liverpool faced Juventus in their fifth European Cup Final. The venue was Heysel Stadium, Brussels – a dilapidated ground that was patently unsuitable for such a fixture. Club officials had lodged objections with UEFA about its choice of venue. But fears about the state of repair, policing arrangements and the lack of proper crowd segregation were waved aside.

In the hour leading up to the game there were skirmishes between Liverpool and Juventus fans, who had both been sold tickets for the same end of the stadium. Security was shambolic, there were no stewards to enforce an alcohol ban and all that separated the two sets of supporters was a flimsy length of chicken wire. Around 30 minutes before kick-off, that wire was torn down by a group of Liverpool fans who then began a violent charge into the Juventus section. As the Italians fled in fear, a huge crush led to the collapse of a wall at the front of the terrace. Hundreds were injured; 39 people died.

The disaster caused a wave of revulsion towards English football followers. Liverpool FC and Merseyside Police vowed to help the Belgian authorities track down many of the so-called fans who had caused the fatal crush. But UEFA slapped an indefinite ban on all English clubs and ruled that Liverpool must stay out of Continental competition for another three years once it was lifted.

It wasn't until September 1991 that the club were eventually allowed to play in a European tournament again. By that time the overwhelming shame and grief of Heysel had dimmed, but the memories – particularly for those who witnessed the tragedy first hand – remained as stark.

Today, a plaque in memory of the 39 victims hangs in the Liverpool FC Museum.

Hickson, Dave

1959/60-1960/1 (Centre-forward) **B** 30.10.1929, Salford, Cheshire **S** November 1959 from Everton, £40,500 **D** 7.11.1959 v Aston Villa, lg (scored twice) **L** July 1961 to Cambridge C, £500 **Apps** 67, 38 gls **Hons** none **OC** Ellesmere Port Town FC (three times including manager), Everton (three times, amateur and professional and PR/tour guide), Aston Villa, Huddersfield T, Cambridge C, Bury, Tranmere Rovers, Ballymena Utd, Northwich Victoria, Winsford Utd, Fleetwood, Bangor City

AN IMPRESSIVE TEDDY-BOY quiff and a fiery temper were two of 'Dashing' Dave's trademarks. But he'll be best remembered for his £40,500 transfer across Stanley Park, which left Evertonians in despair and led to some Kopites threatening to tear up their season tickets. The Ellesmere Port-born centre-forward had been the undisputed darling of Goodison's Gladwys Street and the man the Anfield crowd loved to hate. But fears that he would be barracked at his new home soon evaporated, as Hickson put 15,000 on the gate for his first game, then scored twice in a 2–1 win over Aston Villa. He went on to notch 21 goals in 27 League outings in the 1959–60 season, and another 16 the following year. However, new boss Bill Shankly was keen to offload the 31-year-old and clear the way for a new generation of strikers. Hickson moved to Cambridge City in 1961, then spent several years in non-League football, before quitting the game to become a bookmaker.

Hillsborough Disaster

ANFIELD'S HILLSBOROUGH Memorial honours the 96 people who died as a result of the darkest day in the club's history. Saturday April 15th, 1989, should have been an afternoon of joy: a day when thousands of fans celebrated another passage to Wembley. Instead, what they – and millions of TV viewers – witnessed was an avoidable tragedy of epic proportions.

Thirty minutes before the FA Cup semi-final against Nottingham Forest, senior police officers were told of a heavy build-up of Liverpool fans outside the entrance to the Leppings Lane end. By 2.45pm, with the waiting crowd esti-

mated at 5,000, a decision was taken to open a single steel door into the stadium. The resulting surge into two already full sections of the terrace created a crush. When the match got under way, the pressure in the enclosure was intense and suffocating: hundreds of fans were pressed against the perimeter fences designed to stop pitch invasions.

At 3.06pm, with desperate fans running on to the field to plead for help, the referee stopped the game. Neither the police nor emergency services appeared to know how to respond. It was left to spectators to pull their fellow fans from the crush, to tear down advertising boards for use as makeshift stretchers and to administer the kiss of life to those who had lost consciousness. Mass confusion reigned. By the end of the day, 94 supporters had been pronounced dead. Another two would later lose their battle for life.

Within hours of the tragedy, the focus of mourning switched from Sheffield Wednesday's ground to Anfield. The club threw open its doors for friends and relatives of the victims, for fans and the shocked general public of Merseyside. An estimated 250,000 people passed through the stadium over the next few days, as the green turf disappeared under a blanket of flowers and

Merseyside United: Liverpool and Everton players bow their heads in remembrance of Hillsborough

scarves. The following Saturday the ground was packed to capacity for a special minute's silence at 3.06pm. Every player was there; Steve Nicol stood on the Kop.

Lord Justice Taylor's official report into the tragedy later cleared the fans of any blame, despite the shameful press coverage in the immediate aftermath. However, he did accuse senior police officers of "a failure of control", and his recommendations on improved ground safety led to the removal of perimeter fences and the compulsory introduction of all-seater stadia.

Hobson, Alfred

1935/6-1938/9 1944/5-1945/6 (Goalkeeper) **B** 9.9.1913, Co Durham **S** April 1936 from Shildon Colliery **D** 29.8.1936 v Stoke C, lg **L** October 1938 to Chester C **Apps** 28 + 171 WW2 **Hons** none **OC** Shildon Colliery, Chester C, Southport & Burnley, **S** Liverpool **d** n/k

Hodgson, David J

1982/3-83/4 (Forward) **B** 6.8.1960, Gateshead **S** August 1982 from Middlesbrough, £450,000 **D** 21.8.1982 v Tottenham CS **L** August 1984 to Sunderland, £125,000 **Apps** 47, 10 gls **Hons** Div1 CH 1982–83; CS 1982; England U-21 caps **OC** Redleugh Boys Club (Gateshead), Middlesbrough, Sunderland AFC, Norwich C, Jerez (Spain), Sheffield Wed

FORMER MIDDLESBROUGH striker who followed Graeme Souness and Craig Johnston from Ayresome Park to Anfield. But despite the hefty £450,000 price tag, Hodgson never reached the heights of his predecessors. He did win a Championship medal in 1983, making more than 20 appearances alongside Kenny Dalglish and Ian Rush. But the following season his first-team opportunities were strictly limited and, after the arrival of Michael Robinson in attack, he decided to move to Sunderland. He became a nomadic player afterwards, with spells at Norwich, Sheffield Wednesday, Swansea and even Jerez in Spain.

Hodgson, Gordon

1925/6-35/6 (Inside-right) **B** 16.4.1904, Johannesburg, S.Africa **S** December 1925 from the South Africa national team (Springboks) **D** 27.2.1926 v Manchester C, lg **L** January 1936 to Aston Villa, £3,000 **Apps** 377, 241 gls **Hons** 3 caps for England; caps for South Africa **OC** Transvaal FC, South Africa, Aston Villa, Leeds Utd (twice, player then coaching staff), Hartlepool Utd (wartime guest), Port Vale (manager), Everton Baseball Club, Lancashire County Cricket Club, Forfarshire Cricket Club **d** 14.6.1951

PROLIFIC MARKSMAN WHOSE achievements in front of goal set club records that would last for nearly half a century. One of them – an incredible total of 17 hat-tricks – still stands to this day. One of three touring South African internationals signed by the club in 1925, Hodgson topped the Anfield scoring charts for seven years, hitting an amazing 36 goals in 40 appearances during the 1930–31 season. Despite his goals, Liverpool spent much of this period in the Division One doldrums, or even fighting to avoid relegation. The team's overall performances – plus the presence of Dixie Dean over at Goodison Park – can be the only reasons why he won a mere three England caps. In 1936, with 241 Liverpool goals to his credit, he left for Aston Villa and later joined Leeds.

Away from the football field, Hodgson was a brilliant all-round sportsman who excelled in baseball and cricket. As a fast bowler, he once took 10 wickets for 13 runs in an amateur match against Liverpool Police. Seeing his obvious potential, Lancashire CCC soon recruited him to their County Championship-winning sides of the early 1930s, and he later turned out for the Scottish club Forfarshire. During World War Two, he retired from playing both cricket and football, taking up the offer of a coaching position at Leeds. In 1947 he was appointed manager of Port Vale, where he stayed until his premature death four years later.

Holmes, John

1895/6-1897/8 (Left-half) **B** date n/k, Preston, Lancs **S** June 1895 from Preston NE **D** 14.9.1895 v Newcastle Utd, lg **L** 1898 to Burton Swifts **Apps** 44, 0 gls **Hons** Div2 CH 1895–96 **OC** Junior football, Preston NE, Burton Swifts, New Brighton Tower **d** n/k

Homecomings

"CHAIRMAN MAO HAS never seen such a show of red strength in all his life," said Bill Shankly, surveying the 300,000 people who turned out to welcome his victorious team back from the 1974 FA Cup final. And that homecoming wasn't even the biggest.

In fact, official police estimates have put the figures for three homecomings – the 1965 FA Cup final, the 1977 European Cup and the 2001 Treble parade – at around the half-million mark. The parades have traditionally featured an open-topped bus tour around the city, followed by a civic reception at one of Liverpool's grandest buildings.

The earliest recorded homecoming was in 1901, when Liverpool returned from their first Championship-clinching victory at West Brom. According to local newspapers, thousands gathered at Central Station as the team's train arrived in the early hours. A drum and fife band played on the platform and the players were then hoisted shoulder-high on to horse-drawn carriages that took them on a tour up and down Bold Street.

The club's first two FA Cup Finals were also marked by significant homecoming events, even though the games themselves ended in disappointment. There was a parade and Adelphi Hotel reception for the 1914 team. Then, in 1950, the players came back from their defeat

To cross or to dribble: Hodgson's choices led to a nomadic football life, wandering from club to club

KEY Apps Appearances | **B** Born | **CH** Championship | **CWC** Cup Winners' Cup | **CS** Charity Shield | **D** Debut | **d** Died | **EC** European Cup | **FAC** FA Cup | **gls** Goals | **Hons** Honours | **lg** League

by Arsenal to find tens of thousands of fans lining the route from Lime Street to Anfield. "That was a night I shall never forget," wrote Billy Liddell. "Even the most hardened members of our party were really touched by this amazing expression of loyalty to the club bearing the city's name."

It was the ecstatic 1965 reception that set the standards for all those that have followed. With Liverpool landing the FA Cup for the first time in their history, the players were expecting something special. But as the chief constable pronounced it the largest gathering the city had ever experienced – bigger than Everton's 1933 Wembley victory, bigger than VE Day, bigger than the Beatles a year earlier – even Shankly had to admit he was "frightened to death" by the size of the crowd.

But for those too young to witness that – or any of the many fantastic receptions in the 1970s and 1980s – there was the unforgettable 2001 homecoming. Surveying the 500,000 well-wishers from the team's 'Triple Decker Tour Bus', Sammy Lee summed up the mood when he said: "This is for them. These people are what it's all about."

Honours

THE FULL LIST OF major domestic and European honours won by Liverpool Football Club up until, and including, April 2003, is as follows below:

Welcome back... the 1950 FA Cup homecoming. They lost the final but fans cheered them as heroes

Division One Champions – 18 (20)
1900-01, 1905–06, 1921–22, 1922–23, 1946–47, 1963–64, 1965–66, 1972–73, 1975–76, 1976–77, 1978–79, 1979–80, 1981–82, 1982–83, 1983–84, 1985–86, 1987–88, 1989–90. (Wartime: 1916–17, 1943–44).

Division Two Champions – 4
1893–94, 1895–96, 1904–05, 1961–62

Lancashire League Champions – 1
1892–93

FA Challenge Cup Winners – 6
1964–65, 1973–74, 1985–86, 1988–89, 1991–92, 2000–01

FA Challenge Cup Runners-up – 6
1913–14, 1949–50, 1970–71, 1976–77, 1987–88, 1995–96

League Cup Winners – 7
1980–81, 1981–82, 1982–83, 1983–84, 1994–95, 2000–01, 2002–03

League Cup Runners-up – 2
1977–78, 1986–87,

FA Charity Shield Winners – 15
1964 (shared), 1965 (shared), 1966, 1974, 1976, 1977 (shared), 1979, 1980, 1982, 1985, 1986 (shared), 1988, 1989, 1990 (shared), 2001

FA Charity Shield Runners-up – 6
1922, 1971, 1983, 1984, 1992, 2002

European Champions Cup Winners – 4
1976–77, 1977–78, 1980–81, 1983–84

European Champions Cup Runners-up – 1
1984–85

UEFA Cup Winners – 3
1972–73, 1975–76, 2000–01

European Cup Winners Cup Runners-up – 1
1965–66

European Super Cup Winners – 2
1977, 2001

European Super Cup Runners-up – 2
1978, 1985

World Club Championship Runners-up – 2
1981, 1984

Screen Sport Super Cup Champions – 1
1985–87 (played over two seasons)

Central League (Reserves) Champions – 16
1956–57, 1968–69, 1969–70, 1970–71, 1972–73, 1973–74, 1974–75, 1975–76, 1976–77, 1978–79, 1979–80, 1980–81, 1981–82, 1983–84, 1984–85, 1989–90

FA Premier Reserve League North Champions – 1
1999–2000

FA Youth Cup Winners – 1
1996

Dubai Super Cup Winners – 1
(English v Scottish league Champions) 1986
Runners-up 1989

Hooper, Mike D

1985/6-1992/3 (Goalkeeper) **B** 10.2.1964, Bristol **S** October 1985 from Wrexham, £4,000 **D** 16.8.1986 v Everton, CS **L** September 1993 to Newcastle Utd, £550,000 **Apps** 70 **Hons** CS 1986 **OC** Bristol C, Wrexham, Newcastle Utd

UNDERSTUDY GOALKEEPER who enjoyed his senior debut outing at Wembley. Hooper came on as a second-half substitute in the 1986 Charity Shield against Everton, but it wasn't until the 1988–89 season that the English Literature graduate got an extended run in the first team. With Bruce Grobbelaar out through meningitis, 'Hooperman' put on a series of impressive displays. He lost his place when Grobbelaar regained his health, but he continued to provide able cover for both him and David James. As the 'keeper on duty in Liverpool's shock 2-0 FA Cup defeat by Bolton in 1993, Hooper probably shouldered more than his fair share of the blame. He never played for the first team again and was sold to Newcastle later that year.

Hopkin, Fred 'Polly'

1921/2-1930/1 (Outside-left) **B** 23.9.1895, Dewsbury, Yorkshire **S** 1921 from Manchester Utd, £2,800 **D** 27.8.1921 v Sunderland, lg **L** August 1931 to Darlington **Apps** 360, 12 gls **Hons** Div1 CH 1921–22, 1922–23; England triallist **OC** Darlington, Manchester Utd, Darlington **d** 1970

SKILFUL WINGER known as the man whose goal set the Anfield Road stand on fire. Although a key figure in the Championship sides of the early 1920s, Hopkin was noted for his

lack of goals. When he finally did hit the target in a 1923 game against Bolton, there were riotous celebrations on the terraces. Seconds later, flames and smoke rose from the stand and the entire crowd had to be evacuated. Hopkin, who died in 1970, was the last surviving member of Liverpool's 1922 and 1923 title-winning teams

Houghton, Ray

1987/8-1991/2 (Midfield) **B** 9.1.1962, Glasgow **S** October 1987 from Oxford Utd, £825,000 **D** 24.10.1987 v Luton T, lg **L** July 1992 to Aston Villa, £825,000 **Apps** 200, 37 gls **Hons** Div1 CH 1987–88, 1989–90; FAC 1988–89, 1991–92, 1987–88 finalist; CS 1988, 1989; 73 caps for Rep I **OC** West Ham, Fulham, Oxford Utd, Aston Villa, Crystal Palace, Reading

ALTHOUGH A SURPRISE buy in 1987, the Republic of Ireland international immediately slotted into one of the club's greatest-ever sides, winning a Championship medal in his first Anfield season. The workaholic midfielder was a brilliant crosser of the ball and became noted for the service he gave to John Barnes, as well as his old Oxford United team-mate John Aldridge.

But Houghton could also find the net himself, often spectacularly. His first goal for the Reds involved a jinking run past three Wimbledon defenders and a perfectly placed shot past their giant 'keeper Dave Beasant. He was also on the mark in that season's famous 5-0 victory over Nottingham Forest, a performance described by the legendary Tom Finney as the best he'd ever seen. Most memorably of all, he converted a superb header that settled an FA Cup fifth round tie against Everton.

Following that triumphant first campaign, Houghton collected a 1989 FA Cup winners' medal, along with a second Championship a year later. He was also in the side that beat Sunderland in the 1992 Cup final but, sadly, that Wembley appearance proved to be his last in a red shirt. Disagreements with Graeme Souness and a dispute over pay led to the new boss putting him up for sale and, by the start of

Ray Houghton was born in Scotland and represented the Republic of Ireland while playing in England

the following season, Houghton had moved on to Aston Villa for £825,000. Many fans still point to his departure as one of Souness's biggest mistakes. The fact that he went on to represent his country in the 1994 World Cup Finals in the USA – and score the winner in a famous 1-0 win over Italy – is evidence that he was still in his prime when sold.

Houlding, John

BUSINESSMAN, FREEMASON, politician... and the founder of Liverpool Football Club. Few Victorians have had such a lasting impact on Liverpool life as John Houlding. Born into a humble farming family in the city's Scotland Road area, he used his brilliant mathematical brain to go into business and make his fortune. By the time he was 40 – with a brewery and string of pubs to his name – he was wealthy enough to retire. Instead, he threw his energies into a political career that made him Lord Mayor – and into a sporting hobby that made him chairman of the most powerful football club in the land.

That club was Everton, the original tenants of Anfield. Houlding had secured the ground for his fellow directors, thanks to a leasehold deal struck with the owners in 1884. But eight years later, having bought the land outright, Houlding himself became the club's landlord, incurring the anger of the Everton board by asking for a 150 per cent increase in the annual rent. He defended this demand by pointing out how much he had personally invested in the club over the previous years. Thanks to his generosity, Everton had been able to buy the best players in the country, land their first Championship in 1890–91 and start to turn a handsome profit.

His directors didn't see it that way. They revolted against his rent demands and actually offered a reduced payment for the next 12 months. A split between the two was inevitable, and on March 12th, 1892, the board announced that they – and their playing staff – were moving to a new ground at Goodison Park.

Houlding would always continue to claim that their decision had as much to do with alcohol as it had to do with rent. Many of the Everton members were strict teetotal Methodists who had a profound distaste for their chairman's line of business. His decision to sell his beer at the ground and to run the club's affairs from his own Sandon Hotel on Oakfield Road, only added to their objections. Tellingly, when they moved to Goodison, they announced that the stadium would be alcohol-free.

But whatever the real reasons for the split, it was Houlding's reaction that mattered most.

The man who started it all – Victorian entrepreneur and Liverpool FC founder, John Houlding

Without a football club to his name, many thought he would simply sell Anfield and concentrate on his burgeoning business and political career.

Instead, the man known as 'King John' decided to form an entirely new club, Liverpool FC, and once again use his personal fortune to get it off the ground. The rest is history. After just one season, his expensively recruited team were elected to the Football League. A year later they won promotion to Division One. Within a decade they were English Champions.

By then Houlding was an elderly man who had effectively handed over control of the club to his family and fellow directors.

A year later, following a long period of serious illness, he died while convalescing in the south of France. 'King John of Anfield' was gone. But the club he left behind would one day go on to conquer Europe.

Houllier, Gerard (OBE)

THE APPOINTMENT of the former French national coach marked a break with Anfield tradition, but, back in 1998, the board had no choice other than radical action.

The situation was critical: the club had won just two trophies in eight years, and an under-achieving squad was heading for the club's worst League finish for three decades. The memories of success were fading. It was clear that Liverpool needed to look forward rather than back.

In Houllier they correctly identified the man to lead them to new glories. Since the short joint-managerial experiment with Roy Evans ended, he has led an Anfield revolution, introducing stronger discipline, improved fitness and a fierce desire to win.

He has also used his vast knowledge of continental football to land outstanding buys such as Hyypia, Henchoz and Riise. And, as befits a man who once oversaw the French FA's national academy, he has encouraged the burgeoning talent of exceptional home-grown youngsters like Owen and Gerrard.

Most importantly, he has delivered the silverware that Reds fans crave so badly. A unique treble of Cups in 2001 was quickly followed by Charity Shield and European Super Cup success. Even in the relatively disappointing 2002–03 season – when his team missed out on a third consecutive Champions League qualifying place – he was able to show off the Worthington Cup after a sweet and emphatic victory over Manchester United in Cardiff.

A youthful Houllier and team-mates at Le Touquet

Houllier's time in charge has not lacked drama. From his ruthless, early clear-out of players no longer needed at the club, to the Treble triumph, to the life-saving heart surgery that sidelined him during the 2001/2 campaign, to his emotional return before the spine-tingling Anfield clash with Roma – life under 'le boss' is never dull.

His passion for Liverpool is as strong as when he first stood on the Kop as a young visiting schoolteacher back in 1970, and his dreams of winning the Premiership and Champions League remain as vivid as any fan's. In the summer of 2003, he promised new faces in his squad to help turn those dreams into reality.

Howe, Fred

1934/5-1937/8 (Centre/inside-forward) **B** 24.9.1912, Bredbury, Cheshire **S** March 1935 from Hyde Utd, £400 **D** 6.4.1935 v Derby C, lg **L** June 1938 to Manchester C, £1,000 **Apps** 94, 36 gls **Hons** none **OC** Wilmslow, Stockport C, Hyde Utd, Manchester C, Grimsby T, Oldham Athletic **d** n/k

CENTRE-FORWARD LARGELY responsible for Liverpool's biggest victory in a derby. The Reds beat Everton 6-0 in September 1935 – with Howe scoring four times. After taking over the main striker's role from Gordon Hodgson, the former Hyde United player topped the club's scoring charts for two seasons running.

Howell, Raby 'Rab'

1898-1900/1 (Right-half) **B** 12.10.1869, Wincobank, Sheffield **S** 14.4.1898 from Sheffield Utd, £200 **D** 16.4.1898 v Aston Villa, lg **L** June 1901 to Preston NE **Apps** 67, 0 gls **Hons** 2 caps for England **OC** Ecclesfield, Rotherham Swifts, Sheffield Utd, Preston North End **d** 1937

DIMINUTIVE MIDFIELDER, famed for being the first full-blooded Romany to play for England. Standing at just 5ft 5in, Howell joined Liverpool for £200, shortly after winning an 1898 Championship-winners' medal with Sheffield United.

He stayed for three seasons but found his appearances restricted by a series of injuries. In 1903, while playing for Preston, a broken leg brought an end to his career.

'Huddle', The

LIVERPOOL FANS GOT THEIR first sight of the rugby scrum-like huddle in the 1999–2000 season. The tradition had started at Celtic, but it quickly became an established pre-match ritual at Anfield.

Although originally designed as a bonding exercise for Houllier's multi-national squad, captain Sami Hyypia says he now uses the huddle to "pump up" his team-mates in the minute before kick-off.

One for all and all for one: the Reds huddle before the Champions League game v Borussia Dortmund, 2001

Hats off to Emlyn, Liverpool's skipper celebrates the Rome '77 triumph in time-honoured fashion

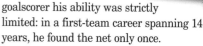

Hughes, Emlyn W (OBE)

1966/7-1978/9 (Midfield) **B** 28.8.1947, Barrow-in-Furness **S** February 1967 from Blackpool, £65,000 **D** 4.3.1967 v Stoke C, lg **L** August 1979 to Wolverhampton W, £90,000 **Apps** 665, 49 gls **Hons** EC 1976–77, 1977–78; UEFA 1972–73, 1975–76; Div1 CH 1972–73, 1975–76, 1976–77, 1978–79; FAC 1973–74, 1970–71 finalist, 1976–77 finalist; LC 1977–78 finalist; Super Cup 1977, 1978 finalist; CS 1974, 1976, 1977, 1971 finalist; 62 caps for England **OC** Roose FC, Blackpool, Wolverhampton W, Rotherham Utd (twice, once as manager), Hull C, Mansfield T, Swansea C

ONE OF THE GREAT Liverpool captains, the club's record holder of England caps and the first Reds player to hold the European Cup aloft. The son of a Rugby League international, Hughes arrived from Blackpool in a record £65,000 deal in 1967.

He'd made only 31 League and Cup appearances for the Lancashire club, but his strength, skill and bravery quickly moved manager Bill Shankly to declare, "This boy is the future captain of England."

The boss was right. With the new season under way, Hughes brought a new dimension to Liverpool's play, breaking up opposition attacks, then finishing off surging runs with powerhouse shots. His ability to barge through the midfield earned him the nickname 'Crazy Horse', and his endless enthusiasm made him an inspirational figure to all around him. In 1970, he was called up for England's Mexico World Cup squad. Five years later, Hughes – by then Liverpool skipper – was wearing the armband for his country.

Under his captaincy, Liverpool developed into English football's dominant force. He lifted the FA and UEFA Cups once, the European Cup twice and the League Championship trophy three times. He also matured from a ball-of-energy midfielder into an accomplished centre-half and an effective full-back. But in 1979, with his pace and ability beginning to wane, Wolves paid £90,000 for his signature. He later turned out for a number of lower-league clubs, and had a spell as Rotherham's player-manager, before retiring from the game and setting up an event-management business in Yorkshire.

Hughes, John 'Geezer'

1903/4-1905/6 (Left-half) **B** 1877, Flint **S** May 1903 from Aberdare **D** 19.9.1903 v Sunderland, lg **L** 1906 to Plymouth Argyle **Apps** 32, 2 gls **Hons** Dewar Shield 1906; Liv Cup 1905–06; caps for Wales **OC** New Brighton T, Aberdare, Plymouth, Harrowby FC (trainer) **d** 5.7.1950

Hughes, Laurie

1943/4-1959/60 (Centre-half) **B** 2.3.1924, Everton, Liverpool **S** February 1943 from Tranmere R (amateur) **D** 5.1.1946 v Chester C, FAC **L** retired 1960 **Apps** 326, 1 gl + 113 WW2 apps **Hons** Div1 CH 1946–47; FAC 1949–50 finalist; 3 caps for England **OC** Tranmere R

AS PART OF ENGLAND'S 1950 squad, Hughes became the first Liverpool player to take part in the World Cup Finals. He made three appearances for his country at the Brazil tournament, including an embarrassing defeat by the USA. The ex-Tranmere Rovers amateur signed professional forms with his hometown club in 1943 and was a regular member of the Liverpool team that won the first post-war title four years later. He also appeared in the 1950 FA Cup Final and stayed with the team during their slow and painful decline over the next decade. Big and powerful, Hughes could play at the heart of defence or as a wing-half. However, as a goalscorer his ability was strictly limited: in a first-team career spanning 14 years, he found the net only once.

Hunt, Roger (OBE)

1959/60-1969/70 (Centre-forward) **B** 20.7.1938, Glazebury, Lancashire **S** July 1959 from Stockton Heath **D** 9.9.1959 v Scunthorpe, lg (scored) **L** December 1969 to Bolton Wanderers, £31,000 **Apps** 492, 285 gls **Hons** CWC 1965–66 finalist; Div1 CH 1963–64, 1965–66; Div2 CH 1961–62; FAC 1964–65; CS 1966; 34 caps for England; World Cup winner 1966 **OC** Lancashire Schools Football, Bury, Stockton Heath, Bolton Wanderers, Warrington Town

ALL-TIME SCORING LEGEND and idol to the generation who saw Liverpool sweep all before them in the 1960s. As the spearhead of Bill Shankly's first great team, Hunt smashed virtually every scoring record, reaching 100 goals in just 144 games, then eclipsing Billy Liddell as the club's leading marksman. He went on to amass 245 League goals – still a record – and his 41 goals in 1961–62 remain unsurpassed.

Born near Warrington, Hunt was discovered while playing for the Cheshire League side Stockton Heath. He broke into the Anfield first team as a 21-year-old and his triumphant debut had one local newspaper purring, "Liverpool followers have a new star in the making. It was not only Roger Hunt's goal, cracked home with the punch of a champion from over 20 yards range, that created the happiest of impressions, but how he used the ball, how he fought for possession – and so often won – that stamped him as a youngster extraordinary."

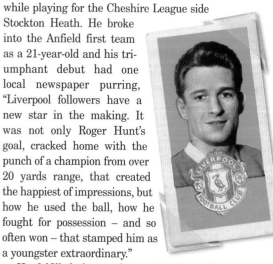

He fulfilled that early promise in spades. After marking his first League appearance with a goal, Hunt also scored on his FA Cup, European Cup and England debuts. He finished his opening campaign with 21 goals, then spent another eight years as the club's top scorer. On the way, he netted 12 hat-tricks, including five in a single season. He was also prolific at inter-

As the Kopites will always remember him, 'Sir Roger' on target yet again, this time against Newcastle United at Anfield in August 1967

national level, finding the net 18 times in 34 appearances.

Yet, despite that ratio of a goal every other game, he was often attacked by a London-based press who preferred to see Tottenham's Jimmy Greaves in the national side. In 1966, when Greaves was left out of the World Cup Final, the campaign against Hunt reached new heights. The criticism hurt. But, writing in 1969, he was able to reflect on what really mattered. "I don't think I have done too badly. With no false modesty, I can point to a pretty good record. While with Liverpool I have won one Second Division Championship medal, two First Division Championship medals and an FA Cup medal, as well as helping the club to the semi-final of the European Cup and the final of the Cup Winners'

Cup. I have played nearly 500 games for the Reds and scored more goals for them than anyone in history. I have made more international appearances than any other Liverpool player, and during my 34 matches for England, I only finished on the losing side twice. And, of course, I helped my country win the World Cup, even if I didn't top any popularity polls in doing so."

On Merseyside, though, it would be hard to think of a player more popular. Respected for his honesty and integrity, as much as for his skill and bravery, Hunt was one of the game's gentlemen. In 1969, to the huge sadness of all supporters, the man the Kop called 'Sir Roger' moved on to Bolton. Three years later, 56,000 adoring fans flocked to Anfield for his testimonial match.

Hunter, John 'Sailor'

1899/1900-1901/2 (Centre/inside-forward) **B** 6.4.1878, Johnstone, Renfrewshire **S** Sept 1899 from Abercorn **D** 2.9.1899 v Stoke C, lg (scored) **L** May 1902 to Hearts, c.£300 **Apps** 45, 13 gls **Hons** caps for Scotland **OC** Westmarch XI , Abercorn, Hearts, Woolwich Arsenal,Portsmouth, Dundee, Motherwell (manager) **d** 12.1.1966

TURN-OF-THE-CENTURY striker, signed after impressive performances in the Scottish amateur leagues. After three seasons at Anfield, Hunter was transferred to Heart of Midlothian for a then substantial fee of £300.

On retiring as a player, he embarked upon a long career as manager of Motherwell in the west of Scotland, where he landed the Scottish Championship in 1932.

Hutchison, Don

1990/1-1993/4 (Midfield) **B** 9.5.1971, Gateshead **S** November 1990 from Hartepool Utd, £300,000 **D** 31.3.1991 v Nottingham C, lg **L** August 1994 to West Ham, £1.5 million **Apps** 60, 10 gls **Hons** 23 caps for Scotland **OC** Hartlepool U, West Ham (twice) , Sheffield Utd, Everton, Sunderland

TALL, COMPETITIVE GEORDIE, who was given the opportunity to impress in the 1992–93 season. Partnering another up-and-coming star, Jamie Redknapp, the youngster took his chance, scoring 10 goals from midfield. He looked set for a golden future at Anfield, but a loss of form and off-the-field disciplinary problems brought his Liverpool career to an abrupt end in 1994. He's since played for West Ham, Sheffield United, Everton and Sunderland.

Hysen, Glenn

1989/90-1991/92 (Centre-half) **B** 30.10.1959, Gothenburg, Sweden **S** July 1989 from Fiorentina, £650,000 **D** 12.8.1989 v Arsenal, CS **L** January 1992 to GAIS Gothenburg, Sweden **Apps** 93, 3 gls **Hons** Div1 CH 1989–90; caps for Sweden **OC** Warta, IFK Gothenburg (twice), PSV Eindhoven, Fiorentina, GAIS Gothenburg

COOL CENTRE-BACK, snatched from under the noses of Manchester United in 1989. The silver-haired Swede, whose cultured performances with Fiorentina had attracted attention all over Europe, looked all set to go to Old Trafford – until Kenny Dalglish stepped in with a £650,000 bid. He partnered Alan Hansen during the 1989–90 Championship season, making 35 appearances and getting on the scoresheet in the famous 9-0 rout of Crystal Palace. Hysen

Attack from the back – Glen Hysen in his pomp

was strong in the tackle and powerful in the air, but the following year his outstanding form slipped. Captaining the side in the injured Hansen's absence, he seemed to struggle under the responsibility and his decreasing pace was exploited mercilessly by opposition strikers. As Liverpool threw away lead after lead, new boss Graeme Souness identified a younger and faster centre-half as his top priority. Mark Wright was bought in from Derby County – and the Swedish international returned home.

Hyypia, Sami

1999/00-present (Centre-back) **B** 7.10.1973, Porvoo, Finland **S** July 1999 from Willem II, £2.6 million **D** 7.8.1999 v Sheffield Wed, lg **Apps** 212, 16 gls **Hons** UEFA 2000–01; FAC 2000–01; LC 2000–01, 2002–03; Super Cup 2001; CS 2001, 2002 finalist; 51 caps for Finland **OC** Pallo-Peikot, KuMu, MyPa Anjalankoski (all Finland), Willem II (Holland)

AT A COST OF JUST £2.6million, the giant Finn probably ranks as Gerard Houllier's best signing. Hyypia was captured from Willem II, the Dutch side he had captained to a Champions League place in 1999. He was about to play his part in Europe's premier cup competition when Houllier came knocking, and immediately decided on a move to Anfield instead.

It was an inspired choice for both player and club. After forming a superb early understanding with Stephane Henchoz, he helped Liverpool to the best defensive record in the Premiership during the 1999–2000 season.

At 6ft 3in, few strikers could match Hyypia's power in the air. His strong tackling, calmness under pressure and an ability to score from set-pieces made him an automatic choice. And, with the absences of the injured Jamie Redknapp and vice-captain Robbie Fowler, he was the natural man to gradually take on the responsibilities of skipper during the Treble-winning campaign.

Hyypia, who was nominated as Player of the Year at the end of his first season, made it into the PFA's Premiership Select XI at the end of 2001–02. Two months later, he delighted Reds fans by signing a new contract which will keep him at the club until 2006.

His success on Merseyside has made him a national hero in Finland and,

unsurprisingly, an international regular. One of his best performances for his country came in April 2003 when he scored the only goal in a 1-0 win against Northern Ireland in Belfast.

Yet despite his ultra-consistent form at both domestic and international level, Hyypia remains a perfectionist who always strives for improvement. "I'm my own worst critic," he says, "I hate making any kind of mistake and I get angry with myself when that happens. If I feel I haven't played to the best of my ability, then it does get me down."

The man who would be king: 'The Guvnor' Paul Ince wears the captain's armband in a UEFA cup match against Celtic

Ince, Paul

1997/8-1998/9 (Midfield) **B** 21.10.1967, Ilford, Essex **S** July 1997 from Inter Milan, £4 million **D** 9.8.1997 v Wimbledon, lg **L** August 1999 to Middlesbrough **Apps** 81, 17 gls **Hons** 53 caps for England **OC** West Ham, Manchester Utd, Inter Milan, Middlesbrough, Wolverhampton W

TOUGH BALL-WINNER whose recruitment from Inter Milan in 1997 marked a profound change in tactics for Roy Evans' side. After another trophyless season the former boss dispensed with the passing game that had made his team so attractive to watch. Instead, with Ince driving the midfield, Liverpool became more physical and harder to penetrate. For a while, the £4million signing looked to be a shrewd one, with Ince taking over the role of captain and playing well enough to win a further 12 England caps.

But, as the team's fortunes faded, his did too. Ince's famously short temper caused disciplinary problems and fans grew impatient waiting for him to recapture the form that made him such a star at Old Trafford before his move to Italy. When Evans left, the new management team also showed their dissatisfaction. Houllier questioned his attitude and Phil Thompson told him to justify his chosen nickname of 'Guvnor' by adding to his medals haul.

With such tensions in the dressing room, it came as no surprise when Ince was sold to Middlesbrough in 1999. The ex-England skipper spent three years at the Riverside before moving on to Wolves.

Inter Cities Fairs Cup

IT WASN'T UNTIL after this tournament changed its name to the UEFA Cup in 1972 that Liverpool enjoyed any success.

Before that the Reds had competed four times, going out to Ferencvaros, Athletic Bilbao and Vittoria Setubal in the early rounds. They reached the semi-final in 1971 but were then beaten by the eventual cupwinners Leeds United.

International Caps

LIVERPOOL'S MOST-CAPPED player of all time is Ian Rush, who played 67 games for Wales during his Anfield career. Emlyn Hughes won 59 England caps while with the club and Ray Clemence 56.

Of Kenny Dalglish's record 102 Scotland appearances, 55 where made when he was a Liverpool player. Elisha Scott – with 27 caps – has played the most games for Northern Ireland

and Ronnie Whelan's 51 international matches make him the club's record holder of caps for the Republic. The first Liverpool player to win England honours was Francis Becton in 1895. Since then, eight of Anfield's English internationals – Ephraim Longworth, Tom Lucas, Emlyn Hughes, Kevin Keegan, Ray Clemence, Phil Thompson, Paul Ince and Michael Owen – have served as captain.

Michael Owen, who made his international debut aged 18 years and 59 days, was England's youngest player of the twentieth century but has since been superseded by 17-year-old Wayne Rooney this millennium.

Keegan, England boss between February 1999 and October 2000, is the only former Reds player to manage the national team.

Above: Francis Becton's 1895 England cap; Bill Shankly's Scotland cap; Toshack's Wales cap

For club and country: Michael Owen has now scored more England goals than any Liverpool player in history

International Matches

ANFIELD STAGED ITS first international fixture in 1889 when England beat Ireland 6-1. There were four more England games between 1905 and 1931, but it wasn't until 1977 that another senior international match was played at the ground. That was the electric World Cup qualifying clash between Scotland and Wales, when nearly 51,000 spectators saw Kenny Dalglish seal a 2-0 tartan victory.

Nearly two decades later, major ground improvements led to Anfield being chosen as one of the venues for Euro 96. It hosted two of Wales' Euro 2000 qualifiers and was also the scene of England's victory over Finland in 2001, when Michael Owen got the first of his country's two goals.

The full list of Anfield international matches is as follows:

1889:	England 6 Ireland 1
1905:	England 3 Wales 1
1922:	England 1 Wales 0
1926:	England 3 Ireland 3
1931:	England 3 Wales 1
1977:	Wales 0 Scotland 2
1995:	Holland 2 Republic of Ireland 0
1996:	Italy 2 Russia 1
1996:	Italy 1 Czech Republic 2
1996:	Russia 3 Czech Republic 3
1996:	France 5 Holland 4 (on penalties)
1998:	Wales 0 Italy 2
1999:	Wales 0 Denmark 2
2001:	England 2 Finland 1
2002:	England 4 Paraguay 0

Irwin, Colin T

1974/5-1980/1 (Defender) **B** 9.2.1957, Liverpool **S** December 1974 from Merseyside Junior football **D** 25.8.1979 v West Bromwich A, lg **L** August 1981 to Swansea C, £350,000 **Apps** 44, 3 gls **Hons** none **OC** Merseyside Junior football, Swansea C – retired 1984

THE LIVERPOOL-BORN centre-back made the first of his few outings in 1979 and played in the League Cup Final against West Ham in 1981. That year saw the highlight of his Anfield career, in the 1-1 European Cup semi-final at Bayern Munich. Describing his performance as "outstanding", the injured Phil Thompson made him man of the match. However, it was the skipper's return that convinced Irwin his future lay elsewhere. He moved to Swansea City, before injuries caused his early retirement.

Jackson, Brian

1951/2-1957/8 (Outside-right) **B** 1.4.1933, Walton-on-Thames, Surrey **S** November 1951 from Leyton O, £6,500 plus Donald Woan **D** 10.11.1951 v Bolton W, lg (scored) **L** 25.7.1958 to Port Vale, £3,000 **Apps** 133, 11 gls **Hons** England schoolboy caps **OC** Weybridge Schools, Chase of Chertsey, Leyton O, Port Vale, Peterborough Utd, Lincoln C, Burton Albion, Boston Utd

NEWS CHRONICLE AND DISPATCH POCKET PORTRAIT

BRIAN JACKSON
Liverpool A.F.C.

THE EX-LEYTON ORIENT winger was just 18 when he made his Anfield debut, but predictions that he'd become one of the outstanding talents of the 1950s proved to be nothing more than newspaper talk. In Jackson's defence, he did play for one of the least successful Liverpool sides in history, so it was always going to be difficult for him to prosper. After spending several years in Division Two, he left for Port Vale.

Jackson, Rev James 'Parson'

1924/5-1932/3 (Right-back/centre-half) **B** 4.12.1903, Newcastle **S** May 1925 from Aberdeen **D** 14.11.1925 v West Brom, lg **L** Retired 1933 **Apps** 224, 2 gls **Hons** represented Scottish League, Football League **OC** Queen's Park, Motherwell, Aberdeen **d** 1977

MAVERICK EX-CAPTAIN who spent much of his Anfield career reading philosophy and Greek… and studying to be a Presbyterian minister. A former star with Motherwell and Aberdeen, Jackson appeared in every outfield position, although he excelled in defence. As befitted a potential man of the cloth, 'The Parson' took great exception to swearing and his on-the-field arguments with Liverpool's famously foul-mouthed 'keeper Elisha Scott were legendary. In reality, though, the two were great friends who were equally competitive and who lined up as team-mates for eight years.

After taking over from the great Don MacKinlay as skipper in 1928, Jackson began a regular column for the *Liverpool Weekly Post* – one of the first footballers to supplement his income by writing. When he finished playing in 1933, he continued his religious studies at Oxford and later became a practising church minister in Liverpool and Bournemouth.

James, David

1992/3-1998/9 (Goalkeeper) **B** 1.8.1970, Welwyn Garden City **S** July 1992 from Watford, £1.3 million **D** 16.8.1992 v Nottm Forest, lg **L** June 1999 to Aston Villa, £1.8 m **Apps** 277 **Hons** LC 1994–95; 9 caps for England **OC** Watford, Aston Villa, West Ham

STANDING AT 6FT 5IN, James was one of the biggest players in the club's history. And, when the ex-Watford 'keeper arrived in the summer of 1992, his reputation was equally towering. Some of his early displays between the posts were truly outstanding and his debut performance against Nottingham Forest – Sky TV's first live Premiership game – brought him the Man of the Match award, and nationwide plaudits.

But as the season wore on, James's spectacular saves became overshadowed by some embarrassing mistakes. He had increasing difficulty in dealing with crosses and had a bizarre explanation for his lapses in concentration: "I realise now that computer games have affected my performance badly," he said after one match. "I had a nightmare at Middlesbrough… and I had played Nintendo for eight hours beforehand."

After conceding four goals in an incredible League Cup tie draw with Chesterfield, James was dropped and Bruce Grobbelaar reinstated as first team 'keeper.

Manager Graeme Souness immediately then tried to exhange him for Southampton's Tim Flowers – a deal that only fell through when Flowers chose to go to Blackburn Rovers. It was new manager Roy Evans who revived James' Anfield career, bringing him back from the Reserves in 1994. A year later, he enjoyed his finest moments as a Reds player, as he made a series of crucial saves in the Coca-Cola Cup Final victory over Bolton.

Despite that display, his confidence always seemed to be fragile, and when basic errors crept back into his game he found himself dubbed 'Calamity James' by the media.

Even Evans, who had so publicly backed him, began to lose faith, bringing in Brad Friedel as his new first choice. In 1999, with Sander Westerveld arriving to inherit the jersey, James left Anfield for Aston Villa. He later moved to West Ham, where his rejuvenated form soon put him in regular contention for the England team.

A giant between the sticks, David James displays the form that brought him England caps

J

Jerseys – The History Of The Red Shirt

FANS OF REPLICA SHIRTS are used to design changes, but they'll be surprised to find that the original LFC top wasn't even red. When the club was formed in 1892, the jersey was blue and white quarters, similar to the colours worn by Blackburn today.

The switch to red came c1895 and, while there have been many alterations since, the basic colour has remained the same. Here's a guide to the red jersey from the late 19th Century to the present day.

1895 – 1901: Red top with single-button collar

1901 – 1914: Ribbed jersey with lace-up neck

1918 – 1933: Plain cotton with lace-up neck

1934 – 1946: Rugby-style jersey with red collar

1946 – 1953: A brief experiment with white roundneck collar and cuffs in the 1946–47 season. The team reverted to an all-red shirt with button-up collar midway through the campaign. A special one-off 1950 FA Cup Final jersey featured the Liver Bird badge.

1955 – 1958: White open-neck collar with white oval badge containing the Liver Bird crest

1958 – 1960: White V-neck collar

1961 – 1962: White V-neck collar and short sleeves.

1963 – 1964: Long sleeves with white round-neck collar and cuffs

1965 – 1968: Red collars and cuffs

1968 – 1976: Oval badge changed to a simple embroidered Liver Bird

1976 – 1978: White V-neck with gold badge

1978 – 1982: 'Hitachi' sponsor-name, white badge

1982 – 1985: 'Crown Paints' sponsor-name, white pin-stripes, double V-neck

1986 – 1987: Pin-stripes removed, white round neck, 'adidas' manufacturer's name visible

1988 – 1991: Candy-sponsored shirt, red with white flecks

1991 – 1992: All red with three diagonal stripes across right shoulder.

1993 – 1996: Carlsberg-sponsored shirt featuring new Centenary crest. First use of squad numbering and players' surnames

1996 – 1998: Reebok-manufactured shirt, red and white collar

2000 – 2001: V-neck with white piping, club crest moved to the centre of the jersey

1892-c1894–95
Liverpool successfully re-used Everton's blue-and-white quarters

Early 20th century
Enter the red men! Plain jersey with no logo or badge

1950
First-ever use of the club badge for the 1950 FA Cup Final

1955-1963
The oval badge became a fixture on all jerseys

1960s
Echoing the 1946–47 design, the classic round neck arrives

1976-78
Another design classic – think Keegan, Hughes, Heighway

1978-82
History is made as a sponsor's name appears for the first time

1982-1985
The skinny-fit red pinstripe remains an all-time favourite

1989–1990
Eighteen times League Champions!

1991–1992
Adidas stripes, Carlsberg and the FA Cup – a winning combination

1998–1999
Back to first principles: homage to the 1960s

2000-2002
Five trophies later, this one will live in the memory

Johnson, David E

1976/77-1981/82 (Centre-forward) **B** 23.10.1951, Liverpool **S** August 1976 from Ipswich T, £200,00 **D** 21.8.1976 v Norwich C, lg **L** 1982 to Everton, £100,000 **Apps** 213, 78 gls **Hons** EC 1980–81; Div1 CH 1976–77, 1978–79, 1981–82; FAC finalist 1976–77; 8 caps for England **OC** Liverpool Schools, Everton (twice), Ipswich T, Barnsley (loan), Manchester C, Tulsa Roughnecks, Preston NE, Barrow

AS A TEENAGE STAR with Everton, he was a sensation – scoring on his League, FA Cup and European Cup debuts, as well as in his first Merseyside derby. But it was Liverpool who eventually saw the best of the home-grown striker. After his early spell at Goodison, Johnson moved to Ipswich, helping Bobby Robson establish the East Anglian club as a major First Division force. Bob Paisley paid a record £200,000 for his signature in the summer of 1976 and the player went on to win a Championship medal in his first season.

Johnson was an impressive forward: strong, energetic, with superb balance and an unerring eye for the net. He established a deadly partnership with Kenny Dalglish and averaged almost a goal every other game at Anfield. According to Paisley, though, he played a much wider role in the team's success: "His strong

From blue to red, ex-Everton star David Johnson became a massive Anfield favourite

running and mobility not only produce goals but also allow him to act as a decoy to move players around and create chances for others," said his manager. "His goals, in fact, have been a bonus – I always saw his main task as disturbing defences."

Despite collecting three Championship medals, the England striker suffered desperate disappointment when he missed out on Liverpool's first two European Cup Finals. However, in the last of 40 appearances in the 1980–81 season, he was in the team that beat Real Madrid in Paris.

During his six years at Anfield, Johnson became the first player to score for both sides in Merseyside derbies. He moved back to Everton in 1982 and enjoyed later spells with Manchester City, Preston, American side Tulsa Roughnecks and Barrow, before retiring.

Johnson, Richard 'Dick', K

1920/1-1924/5 (Centre-forward) **B** 1895, Gateshead **S** January 1920 from Felling Colliery **D** 5.4.1920 v Derby County, lg **L** February 1925 to Stoke C, £1,200 **Apps** 82, 30 gls **Hons** Div1 CH 1922–23 **OC** Felling Colliery, wartime guest: Sunderland, Stoke C, New Brighton Tower, Connah's Quay **d** January 1933

GEORDIE STRIKER WHO joined Liverpool from the amateur side Felling Colliery in 1919. Knee injuries kept him sidelined during the entire 1921–22 Championship campaign, but he helped the team retain the title the following season with a grand total of 14 goals in 37 games. The ex-miner decided to move to Stoke in 1925 and later played for New Brighton Tower as well as Connah's Quay.

DICK JOHNSON

Johnson, Thomas 'Tosh' C.F.

1933/4-1935/6 (Centre-forward/inside-left) **B** 19.8.1901, Dalton-in-Furness **S** March 1934 from Everton, £450 **D** 3.3.1934 v Middlesbrough, lg **L** August 1936 to Darwen **Apps** 38, 8 gls **Hons** 5 caps for England **OC** Dalton Athletic, Dalton Casuals, Manchester C, Everton, Darwen **d** 29.1.1973

THE EX-SHIPYARD worker crossed the park from Goodison fresh from winning a 1932 Championship medal and the 1933 FA Cup. Previously he'd led the line for Manchester City, where his eight League goals during the 1928–29 season set a club record that stands to this day. The England international was less effective at Anfield, finding the target just eight times in 38 appearances. With his best days clearly behind him, he moved to non-League Darwen in 1936.

J

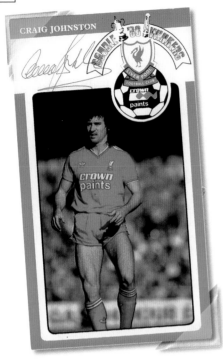

Johnston, Craig P

1980/1-1987/88 (Midfield) **B** 8.12.1960, Johannesburg, SA **S** April 1981 from Middlesbrough, £575,000 **D** 29.8.1981 v Wolverhampton W, lg **L** May 1988 retired from football **Apps** 271, 40 gls

Hons EC 1983–84; Div1 CH 1981–82, 1982–83, 1983–84, 1985–86, 1987–88; FAC 1985–86, FAC finalist 1987–88; LC 1982–83, 1983–84; CS 1982, 1988; England U21 caps

OC Lake McQuarrie FC, Sydney City, Middlesbrough

SURFER, PHOTOGRAPHER, inventor, businessman… and one of the most popular Anfield characters of the 1980s. Although born in South Africa, Johnston was raised in Australia where he played for Sydney City and Lake McQuarrie FC. In 1977 he wrote to Middlesbrough asking for a trial and within a year made his debut with the English First Division club.

In April 1981, Bob Paisley paid £575 ,000 for the livewire midfielder. He struggled for a regular place, but developed a knack of scoring crucial, and sometimes spectacular, goals as Liverpool swept all before them over the next three years. Despite his contributions, Johnston felt frustrated at not playing a bigger part in Joe Fagan's plans and, at the end of the 1984–85 season, looked set to leave. However, with Kenny Dalglish installed as boss, the player was given a new lease of life. He played in almost every game of the 1985–86 Double-winning campaign and capped his most memorable year with a Wembley goal in the FA Cup victory over Everton.

Although Ray Houghton began to edge him out of the senior team, Johnston remained a valuable squad player. It therefore came as a shock to Liverpool fans when, in 1988, he announced his retirement from the game at the age of 27. At the time, he said he was quitting to look after his sick sister back in Australia. But, as he later explained in his autobiography, there were other reasons too. "I didn't need much incentive to return home. For almost 13 years, and in spite of the great friendships and hospitality we'd encountered in Britain, I'd never really mastered the chronic homesickness that had dogged me since my arrival."

His teammates were probably less surprised at his decision. Throughout his Anfield career he was a maverick figure with a range of interests outside the game. He took his cameras on the club's tours throughout Europe, cataloguing what went on behind the scenes. In 1988 he also showed off his talent as a songwriter, penning *The Anfield Rap*. A few years later, following spells as a TV executive, he resurfaced as the designer of the revolutionary Predator football boot.

But the Anfield crowd will always remember him for his ability, his enthusiasm – and his decision to fly 12,000 miles to help comfort the bereaved in the immediate aftermath of Hillsborough. That gesture, as much as his brilliant playing career, led to the huge ovation he received on the last day of the standing Kop.

Jones, William H 'Bill'

1938/39-1953/54 (Utility player) **B** 13.5.1921, Whaley Bridge **S** September 1938 from Hayfield St Matthews **D** 31.8.1946 v Sheffield Utd, lg **L** May 1954 to Ellesmere Port Town **Apps** 277, 17 gls **Hons** Div1 CH 1946–47; FAC finalist 1949–50; 2 caps England **OC** Hayfield St Matthews (Derbyshire), wartime guest: York C, Leeds Utd & Reading, Ellesmere Port Town (player-manager); LFC (scout)

ONE OF LIVERPOOL'S finest post-war utility players, and the man later responsible for bringing Roger Hunt to Anfield. Jones joined the

Reds from Derbyshire side Hayfield St Mathews in 1938 and won a Military Medal during the Allied crossing of the Rhine in World War Two. Although he could play in any position, he was at his best on the half-back line. At the end of the 1946–47 Championship campaign, the *Sports Spectator* magazine reported, "Jones is over six feet high and could be the best back in the world – a big thing to say. Heading, tackling or clearing with rare-length deliveries, he has been the outstanding player of the season."

Jones, whose grandson Rob would also later play for Liverpool, won two England caps during his time at Anfield. He was in the 1950 FA Cup Final team – chosen ahead of Bob Paisley – but left the club four years later to join Ellesmere Port Town as player-manager. It was while there that he spotted the young Hunt playing in the Mid-Cheshire League, then recommended him to the Liverpool management. His obvious eye for talent later led to the club offering him a full-time scouting role.

Jones, Joey

1975/76-1977/78 (Left-back) **B** 4.3.1955, Llandudno, Wales **S** July 1975 from Wrexham, £110,000 **D** 16.8.1975 v Queen's Park Rangers, lg **L** 19.10.1978 to Wrexham, £20,000 **Apps** 97, 3 gls **Hons** EC 1976–77; Div1 CH 1975–76, 1976–77; 72 caps for Wales **OC** Junior football, Wrexham (twice), Chelsea, Huddersfield T

ULTRA-COMPETITVE full-back, forever remembered for the banner he inspired at the 1977 European Cup final, after Liverpool had beaten St Etienne and FC Zurich in the earlier rounds: "Joey Ate The Frogs Legs, Made The Swiss Roll, Now He's Munching Gladbach."

A £110,000 signing from Wrexham in 1975, Jones inherited the No.3 jersey from Alec Lindsay. His style was a world away from his cultured predecessor, but his up-and-at-'em attitude made him an instant favourite with the fans he once stood amongst. Although he played just enough games to qualify for a 1976 Championship medal, it was during the following season that he established himself as an automatic choice in Bob Paisley's team. He missed only three League fixtures, played through the entire FA and European Cup runs and ended the campaign with the two most prized honours of all.

A regular Welsh international with 72 caps, Jones returned to his former club Wrexham in 1978, before enjoying further spells with Chelsea and Huddersfield. But whatever he did afterwards, the highlight of his career will always be that night in Rome. As for the immortal banner, "The fans presented it to me afterwards," says Joey. "I think as much of that as I do my medal."

Jones, Lee

1992/2- 1994/5 (Forward) **B** 29.5.1973, Wrexham **S** 1March 1992 from Wrexham **D** 19.8.1996 v Arsenal, lg **L** 1995 to Wrexham on loan **Apps** 4 (sub) apps, 0 gls **Hons** none **OC** Wrexham (three times), Tranmere R, Barnsley

WREXHAM-BORN STRIKER who made four substitute appearances alongside his namesake, Rob, in 1994. He joined Wrexham in January 2002 and scored all five goals in their win over Cambridge three months later.

Jones, Rob

1991/2-1998/9 (Full/wing-back) **B** 5.11.1971, Wrexham, Wales **S** 4.12.1991 from Crewe Alexandra, £300,000 **D** 6.10.1991 v Manchester Utd, lg **L** 1999 to West Ham **Apps** 243, 0 gls **Hons** FAC 1991–92; LC 1994–95; 8 England caps **OC** Crewe A, West Ham

THE EX-CREWE DEFENDER was so impressive on his 1991 Old Trafford debut that Ryan Giggs later rated him as his most difficult opponent. Within six months, Jones won his first England cap and, by the end of the season, he'd collected an FA Cup winners' medal. Soon he became the best right-back in the country, linking brilliantly with Steve McManaman and moving effortlessly into the new wing-back position established by Roy Evans. He was in the side that lifted the 1995 Coca-Cola Cup and, in a team packed with passing experts, his accuracy and precision were outstanding.

Sadly, back problems restricted him to three appearances in the 1996–97 season and a series of other complaints continued to sideline him. Finally, in 1999, he was released to try his luck with West Ham, but injuries persisted and he was forced to retire from the game prematurely.

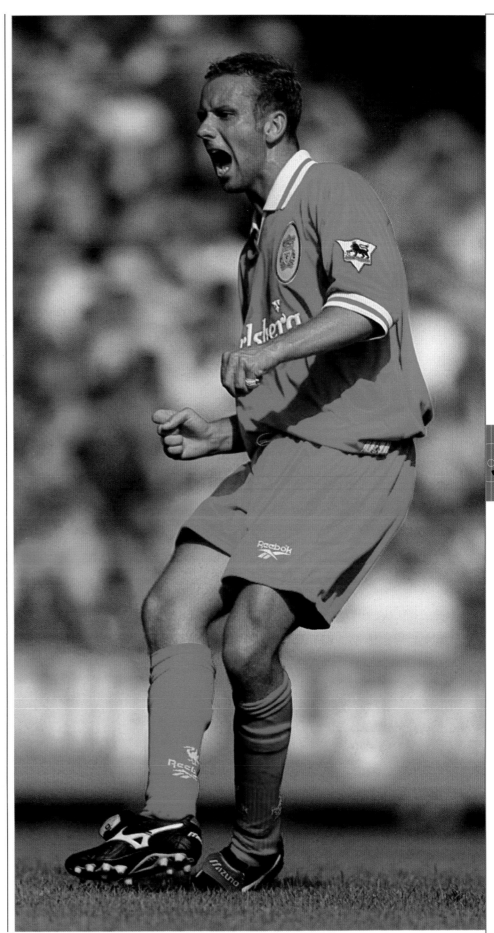

Kay, George

1936/7-1950/1 (Manager) **B** 21.9.1891 **S** Summer 1936 from Southampton **D** 29.8.1936 v Stoke C, lg **L** Retired 1951 **Hons** Div1 CH 1943–44, 1946–47; FAC finalists 1949–50 **OC** Bolton, Belfast Celtic, West Ham, Stockport, Luton Town (trainer-manager), Southampton (manager), **d** 18.4.1965

ONE OF LIVERPOOL'S longest-serving managers, and the architect of the club's first postwar title triumph. The ex-Southampton boss had enjoyed a distinguished playing career, captaining West Ham and Belfast Celtic. He came to Anfield in 1936, just after Matt Busby arrived from Manchester City to help shore up the midfield. "Liverpool were really struggling then and in danger of being relegated to the Second Division," the legendary Old Trafford boss later recalled. "It was a time when men who had been great players were coming towards the close of their illustrious careers… George Kay worked like a Trojan to put things right."

And he succeeded. By the end of the decade Liverpool were re-emerging as a top-flight force. But for the outbreak of war, many believed they would have been among the major honours of the early 1940s. As it was, Anfield fans had to settle for one wartime title in 1944. But, as soon as peace descended, they were able to celebrate their first League Championship victory for 24 years – and Kay was the man to thank.

"He understood the game from A-Z, and he was the type of man who understood the characteristics of each player," said former defender Laurie Hughes. "He knew what every player was capable of achieving, and he got together a wonderful side." Players recruited by Kay included Bob Paisley, Albert Stubbins and Billy Liddell, all of whom helped power the team to Wembley for the 1950 FA Cup Final. But by then, the stresses of management had taken a

Father and son relationship – Keegan and Shankly shared huge respect and affection for one another

huge personal toll on the workaholic Kay. He collapsed on the morning of the game and was unable to lead his players out against Arsenal. Six months later he was ordered to retire on medical grounds. In 1954 he died in hospital after a long illness.

Liddell, a long-time personal friend, was deeply upset by Kay's death and blamed his health problems on his "obsessive dedication" to his job. But he later admitted that, without the manager's driving force, Liverpool faced a long period of decline. "When he was laid to rest, I felt that something vital had gone from Anfield."

Keegan, Kevin

1971/2-1976/7 (Striker) **B** 14.2.1951, Doncaster **S** May 1971 from Scunthorpe Utd, £33,000 **D** 14.8.1971 v Nottingham Forest, lg (scored) **L** Summer 1977 to SV Hamburg, £500,000 **Apps** 323, 100 gls **Hons** EC 1976–77; UEFA 1972–73, 1975–76; Div1 CH 1972–73, 1975–76, 1976–77; FAC 1973–74, 1970–71 finalist; CS 1974, 1976; Footballer of the Year 1976; 63 England caps **OC** Lonsdale Hotel FC, Scunthorpe Ut, SV Hamburg, Southampton, Newcastle Utd (twice: player and mgr), Fulham; England (manager), Man C (manager)

WHEN BILL SHANKLY paid Scunthorpe £33,000 for their dynamic little midfielder, he knew he was getting a bargain. But within a matter of months, the manager described the deal as "daylight robbery". And captain Tommy Smith compared the little Yorkshireman to a precious work of art. "Kevin is like the Mona Lisa – beyond price."

After his mesmerising debut on the opening day of the 1971–72 season, Shankly declared him to be "a born winner – all action and energy". For the next six years, Keegan stamped that personality all over the club, inspiring his teammates to victory throughout England and Europe. Although not the most naturally gifted footballer, no other player could match him for effort, determination and workrate. On the pitch he seemed to be everywhere, winning the ball in midfield, getting back early to defend and leading the line when it was time to attack. He could carry the ball, dribble and shoot with both feet. He could also beat most defenders for speed and, despite his 5ft 8in frame, in aerial duels.

"I was never a fancy player and could never have competed with the likes of George Best or Rodney Marsh for ball-juggling," he wrote later. "I did have a lot of personal little tricks in my cupboard, but I preferred to pour all my energy into working for the team. I wanted to be totally involved at all times and not just flit in and out of games as it suited me. There was no room in the Liverpool system for showing off with flashy ball-conjuring tricks. Shanks put it in a nutshell: 'If I'd wanted a juggler I'd have gone to the bloody circus.'"

Keegan was the undoubted star of the 1972–73 Championship-winning campaign, finishing joint top scorer with 13 League goals and hitting two in the UEFA Cup Final win against Borussia Moenchengladbach. But it was his 1974 FA Cup Final performance against Newcastle that marked him out as a special talent. In front of a 100,000 Wembley crowd – and millions more watching on television – Keegan ran riot, covering every blade of grass and scoring two of his team's three goals. From then on, every top club in Europe wanted his signature.

But there was still more to do with Liverpool. When Shankly quit, Bob Paisley looked to Keegan and his strike partner John Toshack to spearhead his own charge for honours. The pair then delivered in spades, forming a near-telepathic understanding in attack, sharing 39 goals in the 1975–76 season and helping land a second League/UEFA Cup double. By then, the England captain and newly crowned Footballer Of the Year had finally given in to the temptation to move abroad. He was keen to take up a £500,000 offer from Germany's SV Hamburg but, after discussions with Paisley, agreed to stay at Anfield for one more season in a bid to land the European Cup. A year later, on the greatest night in the club's history, Keegan put on the performance of his life as Liverpool beat Borussia Moenchengladbach 3–1 in Rome's Olympic Stadium.

As Paisley plotted a new Liverpool system based around his replacement Kenny Dalglish, Keegan himself carved out an equally successful future. At Hamburg he helped his team to the Bundesliga Championship and was twice named European Footballer Of The Year. He returned to England to spark a Southampton revival, then inspired Newcastle United to promotion in 1984. On retirement Keegan dropped out of the game to live in Spain and concentrate on his business interests. After being lured back to manage Newcastle, he again led them out of the Division Two wilderness and turned them into a major Premiership force. He quit after five years at St James' Park and helped lead Fulham to the top-flight. Then, after a short and disappointing spell as England boss, he took over as manager at Manchester City.

Keegan was one of the first of the game's superstars

Shoot-out king: Alan Kennedy slots home the winning penalty against Roma in 1984 after extra-time finished 1-1. The Reds won 4-2 on penalties

Kemlyn Road Stand

ANFIELD'S IMPRESSIVE Centenary Stand was originally nothing more than a narrow bank of cinders squeezed between the pitch and a row of terraced houses. A number of seats were fitted in 1906, but it also retained a standing area that later housed the original Boys' Pen. When Bill Shankly guided Liverpool back to Division One he persuaded his directors to begin reconstruction work on Kemlyn Road. The result – a 6,700-seater cantilevered grandstand – was in place for the start of the 1963–64 Championship season.

Apart from new floodlights being mounted on the roof in the early 1970s, the stand remained unchanged for almost 30 years. However, in 1991 the club gained permission to buy and demolish the remaining back-to-back former council homes on Kemlyn Road and construct a new top tier of seats, complete with executive boxes and suites. Twelve months later the 11,400-seater new stand was completed – with its name changed to mark Liverpool's Centenary year.

Kemp, Dirk J

1936/7-1944 (Goalkeeper) **B** date n/k, Cape Town, SA **S** December 1936 from SA national team (Springboks) **D** 27.3.1937 v Manchester Utd, lg (clean sheet) **L** retired 1944 **Apps** 33 + 10 WW2 apps **Hons** South African caps **OC** S A National Team (Springboks), wartime guest: York C, Brighton, Scunthorpe Utd, Southport, Jo'burg Rangers

SOUTH AFRICA-BORN 'keeper who inherited the No.1 jersey from fellow Springbok Arthur Riley. He made his debut in a 2-0 win over Manchester United and went on to make 30 appearances for the club. During wartime he guested for York, Brighton and Scunthorpe.

Kennedy, Alan P

1978/9-1985/6 (Left-back) **B** 31.8.1954, Sunderland **S** August 1978 from Newcastle Utd, £330,000 **D** 19.8.1978 v Queen's Park Rangers, lg **L** September 1985 to Sunderland, £100,000 **Apps** 359, 21 gls **Hons** EC 1981–82, 1983–83, 1984–85 finalist; Div1 CH 1978–79, 1979–80, 1981–82, 1982–83, 1983–84; LC 1980–81, 1981–82, 1982–83, 1983–84; CS; 1979, 1980, 1982 **OC** Junior Football, Newcastle Utd, Sunderland, Hartlepool Utd, Beerschot (Belgium), Wigan Athletic, Wrexham

AFTER BEING AN FA CUP loser against Liverpool in the 1974 final, the ex-Newcastle full-back went on to win a hatful of honours with the Reds. As the replacement for the hugely popular Joey Jones, he could have had a difficult time winning over the Anfield fans. But his speed, bravery and direct approach were much appreciated by Kopites, who quickly gave him the nickname 'Barney Rubble'.

Kennedy was a stalwart of the team that conceded just 16 League goals in the 1978–79 season. As well as his abilities at the back, he possessed an attacking instinct that brought a series of crucial goals. Probably the most famous was the 1981 European Cup final winner against Real Madrid – a fierce shot that surprised Kennedy as much as the thousands of Liverpudlians in the Paris crowd. Three years later it was his final spot-kick that settled the famous penalty shoot-out against Roma: for the second time in succession, the Geordie defender had won the European Cup for Liverpool. Despite his consistent form at Anfield, Kennedy won just two England caps. He left for Sunderland in 1985 and is now one of the army of former Liverpool players working as a media pundit.

Kennedy, Ray

1974/5-1981/2 (Forward) **B** 28.7.1951, Seaton Delaval, Northumberland **S** July 1974 from Arsenal, £180,000 **D** 31.8.1974 v Chelsea, lg (scored) **L** January 1982 to Swansea C, £160,000 **Apps** 393, 72 gls **Hons** EC 1976–77, 1977–78, 1980–81; UEFA 1976–76; Div1 CH 1975–76, 1976–77, 1978–79, 1979–80, 1981–82; LC 1980–81; FAC finalist 1976–77; CS 1976, 1979, 1980, 1982; 17 caps for England **OC** South Northumberland Schools, New Hartley Juniors, Arsenal, Swansea C, Hartlepool Utd, Sunderland (coach)

LIVERPOOL PAID A record £180,000 for the Arsenal striker in July 1974, but his signing hardly merited a mention in the press. Why? Because it was on the very same day Bill Shankly resigned as boss.

But it was Shankly's successor who should take most credit for Kennedy's glittering Anfield career. Bob Paisley put him through an intensive training regime that reduced his weight from 14 stone to 12 stone, 10 pounds. Most crucially, when the player struggled to make an impression in the forward line, Paisley converted him into a midfielder. As a result, he became – in the former manager's own words – "one of Liverpool's greatest" players. He won 17 England caps and was one of the rocks on which Paisley's all-conquering 1970s side was built.

"His contribution to Liverpool's achievements was enormous and his consistency remarkable," the manager wrote. "So much so, that on the rare occasions he missed a match his absence was felt deeply, simply because he was a midfield powerhouse with tremendous vision and knowledge of the game.

"He showed the ability to open up the game and give you the width of the park. When intercepting a loose ball he would invariably hit a telling pass – and running on to one himself he was as good as anyone I've seen. He was many people's choice of English football's player of the seventies. You can't quibble with his honours. Amongst them are four seasonal Doubles – he achieved the domestic Double with Arsenal, twice helped Liverpool win the League and a European trophy in the same season and then

the League Cup and European Cup in 1980–81, his last full season at Anfield. But, above all, you can't quibble with Ray's performances at Liverpool, which were a credit to him."

It was the emergence of Ronnie Whelan, and the transfer of Kennedy's close friend Jimmy Case, that finally led Kennedy to ask for a move. He signed for John Toshack's Swansea at the beginning of 1982, helping them to the Welsh Cup for two years in succession. He left the game to run a pub in his native North-East, but later had to retire due to the onset of Parkinson's Disease.

Kennedy, Mark

1994/5-1997/8 (Winger) **B** 15.5.1976, Dublin, Rep I **S** March 1995 from Millwall, £1 million **D** 9.4.1995 v Leeds Utd, lg **L** March 1998 to Wimbledon, £2 million **Apps** 21, 0 gls **Hons** 17 caps for Rep I **OC** Millwall, Quens' Park Ranger's (loan), Wimbledon, Man C, Wolves

GREAT THINGS WERE EXPECTED from the 18-year-old when he arrived from Millwall for £1million. However, despite winning Republic of Ireland caps, he failed to make any meaningful

impression in his handful of senior games. At least Liverpool made a profit out of the youngster, as Wimbledon paid £2million for his signature in 1998.

Kettle, Brian

1973/4-1979/80 (Left-back) **B** 22.4.1956, Prescot, Lancashire **S** May 1973 from Junior football **D** 4.11.1976 v Real Sociedad, UEFA **L** September 1980 to Wigan Athletic, £25,000 **Apps** 4, 0 gls **Hons** England youth caps **OC** Junior Liverpool football, Wigan Athletic; manager: South Liverpool, Southport, Stalybridge Celtic & Rhyl

FORMER ENGLAND YOUTH international and a key member of the Reds' reserves who dominated the Central League throughout the 1970s. Unfortunately the local-born left-back always faced fierce competition for a first-team place, first from Alec Lindsay, then Joey Jones and Alan Kennedy. He left the club for Wigan Athletic in 1980, after making just four senior appearances. He later managed South Liverpool, Southport, Stalybridge Celtic and the Welsh league side, Rhyl.

Kippe, Frode

1998/9-2001/2 (Defender) **B** 17.1.1978, Oslo, Norway **S** January 1999 from Lillestrom, £700,000 **D** 21.9.1999 v Hull, WC **L** July 2002 to Lillestrom – on loan prior to re-signing **Apps** 2, 0 gls **Hons** U-21 honours for Norway **OC** Lillestrom (twice)

GIANT NORWEGIAN, signed from Lillestrom in 1998 for £700,000. Kippe made his Reds debut in a Worthington Cup win against Hull City in 1999, but played just one more game before being loaned to Stoke City. He left Anfield when his contract expired in July 2002.

Paisley's Pride: the popular former boss rated Kennedy as one of Liverpool's greatest players

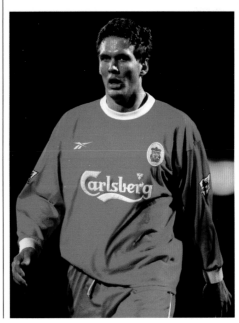

Kirkland, Chris

2001/2-present (Goalkeeper) **B** 2.5.1981, Leicester **S** 31 August 2001 from Coventry C, £6 million **D** 9.10.2001 v Grimsby T, WC **Apps** 19 **Hons** England U-21 caps **OC** Leicester C

THE OUTSTANDING YOUNG Coventry goalkeeper caught Gerard Houllier's eye when he denied Michael Owen an almost certain hattrick in a 2001 League game at Highfield Road. Five months later, he was an Anfield player, as Houllier shelled out more than £6million – a record British fee for a goalkeeper. Despite his price tag, the England Under-21 international went straight into the reserves, due to the arrival of Jerzy Dudek from Feyenoord. But when the big Pole suffered a loss of form and confidence in the 2002–03 season, Kirkland was given the chance to impress with an extended run in the first team.

Although that run coincided with the club's worst sequence of results for years, his own performances oozed class. One brilliant display against Southampton even had Saints' manager Gordon Strachan declaring him to be one of the world's best 'keepers. Unfortunately, his run was shattered by a serious knee ligament injury in an FA Cup tie at Crystal Palace in February. He was forced to sit the rest of the season out, but is sure to be challenging for a senior team place – and full England honours – when his recovery is complete.

Kop

➡ See Spion Kop

Kop Kat

MUCH-LOVED CARTOON character from the club's official magazine during the 1980s. Kop Kat supposedly lived in the Boot Room and claimed to answer fans' letters by using Bob Paisley's typewriter!

Kozma, Istvan

1991/2-1992/3 (Midfield) **B** 3.2.1964, Paszto, Hungary **S** January 1992 from Dunfermline A, £300,000 **D** 16.2.1992 v Ipswich T, FAC **L** 1993 to Ujpest Doza **Apps** 10, 0 gls **Hons** caps for Hungary **OC** Ujpest Doza (twice), Dunfermline A

HUNGARIAN MIDFIELDER, often referred to as one of Graeme Souness's biggest mistakes in the transfer market. The Liverpool boss gave Kozma his debut in the 1992–93 season. Unfortunately the midfielder's limitations were embarrassingly obvious and, by the end of the campaign, he was on his way back to Hungary.

Kvarme, Bjorn Tore

1996/7-1998/9 (Centre-back) **B** 17.6.1972, Trondheim, Norway **S** January 1997 from Rosenborg on Bosman transfer **D** 18.1.1997 v Aston Villa, lg (Man of the Match) **L** 1999 to St Etienne **Apps** 54, 0 gls **Hons** 1 cap for Norway **OC** Rosenborg, St Etienne, Real Sociedad

NORWEGIAN DEFENDER signed as a replacement for centre-back John Scales at the beginning of 1997. The speedy ex-Rosenborg man fitted well into Roy Evans' three-man back line and won rave reviews at first. After some awful mistakes in games against Everton and Manchester United which cost Liverpool points, Kvarme's confidence evaporated. He spent time in the reserves with the odd first-team comeback but it was no surprise when he was sold to St Etienne in 1999.

They shall not pass: Chris Kirkland has proved a very effective last line of defence for the Reds in his time at Anfield

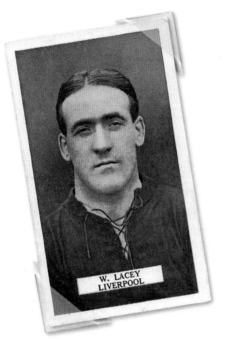

W. LACEY
LIVERPOOL

Lacey, William 'Billy'

1911/12-1923/24 (Half-back) **B** 24.9.1889, Wexford, Rep I

S February 1912 from Everton **D** 2.3.1912 v Middlesbrough, lg

L Aug 1924 to New Brighton **Apps** 258, 29 gls **Hons** Div1 CH 1921–22,
1922–23; FAC 1913–14 finalist; Lancs Snr Cup 1918–19, 1923–24
finalist, 1922–23 finalist; Liv Snr Cup 1911–12; international honours
for Rep I **OC** Shelbourne (twice), Everton, New Brighton **d** 30.5.1969

FORMER EVERTON STAR who crossed the
park in a 1912 exchange deal and quickly
became one of the great characters of the era.
Lacey was fast and versatile, capable of playing
in any midfield position, but who particularly
excelled on the flanks.

He was part of the 1914 FA Cup Final line-
up and a key figure in the two Championship-
winning sides of the early 1920s. Born in
Wexford, Lacey also gained honours with Eire
and the League of Ireland, winning his final
international cap at the age of 40.

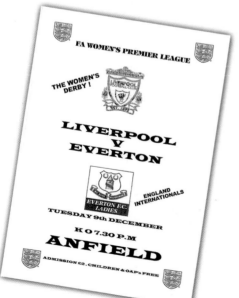

Coming of age: Ray Lambert was just 13 when he signed but didn't play a senior game until his twenties

Ladies' Team

LIVERPOOL LADIES WAS formed in 1989 as
Newton Ladies and, two years later, entered the
first National League as Knowsley WFC. The
team changed its name to Liverpool FC Ladies
at the beginning of the 1994–95 season and has
enjoyed the full financial backing of the club
ever since. They currently play in the FA
Women's Northern Division, with home fixtures
at Poulton Victoria FC's ground in Wallasey.

Lambert, Ray

1935/6-1956/7 (Right/left-back) **B** 18.7.1922, Bagillt, Flintshire

S January 1936 from Flint Schools **D** 5.1.1946 v Chester C, FAC

L Retired in 1956 **Apps** 341 (+ 113 WW2 games), 2 gls **Hons** Div1
CH 1946–47; FAC 1949–50 finalist; capped for Wales **OC** Flint
Schools, wartime guest: New Brighton, Reading

LIVERPOOL WERE SO impressed with the
Flintshire schoolboy's performances that they
persuaded him to sign at the tender age of 13.
He would certainly have been a teenage debutant but the outbreak of war meant he didn't
play a senior game until 1946 when he was in
his early twenties. That was the season the
Reds stormed to League title success, with
Lambert making 36 appearances both in
defence and midfield. He went on to play more
than 300 games for the club and won five international caps before retiring to run a
newsagent's business back in North Wales.

Lancashire Cup

LIVERPOOL COMPETED FOR this regional
trophy, as well as the FA Cup, in their very first
season of existence. They beat Southport, West
Manchester and Darwen before losing 2-1 to
Bootle in a Fourth Round tie at Anfield. They
continued to take part in this local competition
for several years and succeeded in lifting the
trophy in 1898.

Lancashire League

WHEN THE NEWLY formed Liverpool FC failed in their application to join the Football League in 1892, they had to compete in the Lancashire League instead. The club's first-ever competitive game took place on September 3rd, 1892, when they took on Higher Walton at Anfield – and won 8-0. By the end of the season, they had won 17 of their 22 fixtures and finished on top with 36 points. Just a few weeks later, the Football League accepted a second application from the club and Liverpool were able to leave rivals like South Shore, West Manchester and Fairfield behind.

The full list of their 1892-93 Lancashire League fixtures is as follows:

Date	Opposition		Score	Att
03/09/92	Higher Walton	H	8-0	200
24/09/92	Bury	H	4-0	4,000
01/10/92	West Manchester	H	3-1	3,000
22/10/92	Higher Walton	A	3-1	150
05/11/92	Blackpool	A	0-3	3,000
12/11/93	Fleetwood	A	4-1	2,000
26/11/92	Rossendale Utd	A	2-0	1,500
03/12/92	Fleetwood	H	7-0	1,000
17/12/92	Blackpool	H	0-2	4,000
24/12/92	South Shore	A	1-0	2,000
31/12/92	Heywood Central	H	6-2	1,000
02/01/93	Fairfield	A	4-1	3,000
07/01/93	Heywood Central	A	2-1	1,000
14/01/93	West Manchester	A	0-0	2,000
11/02/93	Bury	A	0-3	8,000
18/02/93	Nelson	A	3-2	1,500
25/02/93	Southport	H	2-0	1,500
04/03/93	Nelson	H	3-0	2,000
16/03/93	Fairfield	H	5-0	2,000
18/03/93	South Shore	H	4-1	2,000
25/03/93	Rossendale Utd	H	2-1	1,200
15/04/93	Southport	A	1-1	1,500

Lawler, Chris

1959/60-1974/75 (Right–back) **B** 20.10.1943, Liverpool **S** May 1959 from Liverpool schools **D** 20.3.1963 v West Bromwich Albion, lg **L** October 1975 to Portsmouth **Apps** 549, 61 **Hons** UEFA 1972–73; CWC 1965–66 finalist; Div1 CH 1965–66, 1972–73; FAC 1964–65, 1970–71 finalist; CS 1965, 1966, 1971 finalist; 4 caps for England **OC** Portsmouth, Stockport C, Bangor

A QUALITY FULL-BACK with a scoring record that would put many midfielders to shame. The so-called Silent Knight was one of the most consistent performers of the Shankly era, making 241 consecutive appearances

Chris Lawler, head and shoulders above the rest

between October 1965 and April 1971. His ability to go forward added a new dimension to Liverpool's attack and his accuracy in the opposition penalty box brought him 61 goals.

The Merseyside-born defender joined the club after winning England schoolboy honours. He was later capped at Youth and Under-23 level and went on to play four senior international games. In 1975 he left to join Portsmouth where his 1960s team-mate Ian St John had taken over as manager. A decade on, he returned to Anfield as Reserve team trainer, but quit the game for good in 1986.

Lawrence, Tommy

1957/58-1970/71 (Goalkeeper) **B** 14.5.1940, Dailly, Ayreshire **S** 30.10.1957 from Warrington **D** 27.10.1962 v West Bromwich Albion, lg **L** September 1971 to Tranmere R **Apps** 390 **Hons** Div1 CH 1963–64, 1965–66; FAC 1964–65; CWC 1965–66 finalist; CS 1964, 1965, 1966; 3 caps for Scotland **OC** Warrington, Tranmere R, Chorley (player-trainer)

BURLY, 14 STONE GOALKEEPER whose acrobatic saves earned him the nickname the 'Flying Pig'. Lawrence joined Liverpool in 1957 and became the first choice No.1 soon after promotion to the First Division five years later. He was an amazingly consistent performer who missed just four games in the eight seasons following his debut. His speed off the line meant he was often able to cover for his defenders and his brilliant performance in the 1966 Charity Shield led to the label 'sweeper keeper'. Three seasons later, Lawrence set a Division One record by conceding a meagre 24 goals in 42 games. However, with the brilliant Ray Clemence waiting in the wings, the Scottish international's time was coming to an end. He lost his place in 1970 and moved to Tranmere soon afterwards.

Sweeper-keeper: 'Flying Pig' Tommy Lawrence kept the goalkeeper's jersey for eight years

Lawrenson, Mark T

1981/2-1987/8 (Left-back/central defender) **B** 2.6.1957, Preston **S** August 1981 from Brighton, £900,000 **D** 29.8.1981 v Wolverhampton W, lg **L** March 1988 retired through injury **Apps** 356, 16 gls **Hons** EC 1983–84, 1984–85 finalist; WCCH 1981 finalist; Super Cup 1984–85 finalist; Div1 CH 1981–82, 1982–83, 1983–84, 1985–86; FAC 1985–86; LC 1981–82, 1982–83, 1983–84, 1986–87 finalist; CS 1982, 1983 finalist, 1984 finalist; Screen Sport SC 1985–86 **OC** Preston schools, Preston NE, Brighton, Oxford Utd (manager), Newcastle Utd (coach)

BOB PAISLEY SURPRISED everyone when he shelled out a record £900,000 for the Brighton defender in 1981. But within weeks the Kopites were hailing the Republic of Ireland international as one of the classiest players ever to wear a red shirt.

It's certainly hard to think of a better tackler. Blessed with lightning pace and superb timing, his interventions at the back were often as entertaining to watch as a Liverpool goal. In countless games, opposition attackers thought they had a clear run with the ball, only to see it whipped away from them by a long, gangly Lawrenson leg. Just as impressively, he would then use the ball to set up an immediate counter attack.

His centre-back pairing with Alan Hansen was probably the strongest the club has ever known. Like his partner, he was formidable in the air. And, with Steve Nicol and Phil Neal as the full-backs, Liverpool's defence looked almost invincible. Not surprising, then, that Lawrenson won so many honours in a compara-

tively short Anfield career. Troubled with achilles damage in the 1985–86 season, he was eventually forced to quit playing two years later at the age of 30. He went on to manage Oxford United and coach Newcastle, before reuniting with Hansen as a leading BBC football pundit.

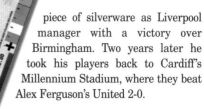

League Cup

IT MAY BE THE LEAST prestigious of the domestic trophies, but victory in the tournament has helped kick-start Liverpool's season more than once. It also remains a guaranteed route to lucrative European competition and therefore demands to be taken seriously.

Not that Liverpool did for many years. Bill Shankly's team first took part in the League Cup back in 1960, then refused to compete for seven years because of fixture congestion fears. It wasn't until 1978 that Bob Paisley first took a Reds side to the final, and it was 1981 before they finally lifted the trophy.

But they've made a habit of it since then. Under its various names – Milk Cup, Littlewoods Cup, Rumbelows Cup, Coca-Cola Cup and Worthington Cup – the Reds have now won the trophy a record seven times. They beat Tottenham in the 1982 final, Manchester United in 1983 and Everton a year later. In 1995, Roy Evans' team beat Bolton at Wembley and in 2001 Gerard Houllier landed his first

piece of silverware as Liverpool manager with a victory over Birmingham. Two years later he took his players back to Cardiff's Millennium Stadium, where they beat Alex Ferguson's United 2-0.

Lee, Sammy

1977/8-1985/6 (Midfield) 1991/2–present (Coaching staff) **B** 7.2.1959, Liverpool **S** 1977 as apprentice from Merseyside schools **D** 8.4.1978 v Leicester City, lg **L** August 1986 to QPR, £200,000 **Apps** 259, 19 gls **Hons** EC 1980–81, 1983–84, 1984–85 finalist; WCCH 1981 finalist, 1984 finalist; Super Cup 1984–85 finalist; Div1 CH 1981–82, 1982–83, 1983–84, 1985–86; LC 1980–81, 1981–82, 1982–83, 1983–84; CS 1982, 1986, 1983 finalist, 1984 finalist; Screen Sport SC 1985–86; 14 caps for England **OC** QPR, Osasuna, Southampton, Bolton W

BUSTLING MIDFIELDER with a powerful shot and biting tackle. He began his career as an Anfield apprentice and marked his 1978 debut with a goal against Leicester. It was another two years before he got an extended first-team run but, once in, he was almost impossible to shift. Bob Paisley had a special affection for the youngster, whose stocky, 5ft 7in frame and phenomenal workrate reminded him of himself when he was a player. Lee won a cascade of medals, and the first of his 14 England caps, under Paisley. But it was in 1983–84, with Joe Fagan as boss, that he had his best year. An ever-present in the League matches, he also played in all the Milk Cup and European Cup games as the Reds stormed to their unique Treble. Lee left two years later, joining QPR for £200,000. After a spell with Osasuna in Spain, he returned as reserve-team coach under Roy Evans. His responsibilities were extended to the senior team in 1999 and then to England's U-21 side. In 2001 Sammy was promoted to work for England alongside Sven-Goran Eriksson.

Mark Lawrenson operated in tandem with Alan Hansen in one of the strongest centre-back pairings ever

Leishman, Tommy

1959/60-1962/3 (Left-half) **B** 3.9.1937, Stenhousemuir **S** November 1959 from St Mirren, £9,000 **D** 28.12.1959 v Charlton Athletic, lg **L** January 1963 to Hibs, £10,000 **Apps** 118, 7 gls **Hons** Div2 CH 1961–62 **OC** Camelon Juniors, St Mirren, Hibernian, Linfield (player-manager)

FORMER ST MIRREN part-timer whose £9,000 signing came just weeks before the arrival of another Scot, Bill Shankly. Leishman was a shaven-headed, six-footer who possessed pace as well as a crunching tackle. He played in all but one game in the 1961–62 promotion-winning campaign, but lacked the ability required for Division One. With the new campaign just a couple of months old, Shankly brought Willie Stevenson to Anfield – and Leishman was sold to Hibernian for £10,000.

Leonhardsen, Oyvind

1997/8-1998/9 (Midfield) **B** 17.8.1970, Kristiansund, Norway **S** June 1997 from Wimbledon, £3.5 million **D** 15.10.1997 v West Bromwich Albion, Coca-Cola Cup **L** August 1999 to Tottenham, £3.5 million **Apps** 49, 7 gls **Hons** caps for Norway **OC** Molde, Rosenborg, Wimbledon, Spurs, Aston Villa

AFTER SIGNING FOR £3.5 million, the Norwegian international struggled to repeat the impressive goalscoring form he'd shown at Wimbledon. Roy Evans tried him in a variety of midfield positions, as well as on the flanks, but he failed to make any real impression and found the net just seven times. When new boss Gerard Houllier took sole charge, he was reluctant to give Leonhardsen any more first-team chances. In August 1999, he accepted a £3.5 million bid from Tottenham.

Lewis, Henry 'Harry'

1916/7-1922/3 (Inside-forward) **B** 19.12.1896, Birkenhead **S** September 1916 from The Comets FC **D** 30.8.1919 v Bradford C, lg (scored) **L** Oct 1923 to Hull C **Apps** 70, 12 gls **Hons** Div1 CH 1921–22; CS 1922 finalist **OC** The Comets, Hull C, Mold **d** 11.7.1976

BIRKENHEAD-BORN FORWARD who made 12 appearances in the 1921–22 title-winning team. He lost his place the following season and moved to Hull City, eventually finishing his career with the Welsh League side Mold.

Lewis, Kevin

1960/1-62/3 (Outside-right/left) **B** 19.9.1940, Ellesmere Port **S** June 1960 from Sheffield Utd, £13,000 **D** 20.8.1960 v Leeds Utd, lg (scored) **L** August 1963 to Huddersfield T, £18,000 **Apps** 82, 44 **Hons** Div2 CH 1961–62; England youth honours **OC** Sheffield Utd, Huddersfield T, Port Elizabeth, SA

THE SHEFFIELD UNITED striker cost Liverpool a record £13,000 in the summer of 1960. Two years later he repaid every penny as his two goals against Southampton sealed the team's promotion to Division One. Lewis, who was born in Ellesmere Port, was a tall and fast forward whose pre-match nerves often caused him to be violently sick. But once on the pitch he was extremely effective, as his 44 goals in 82 appearances show. Unfortunately for him, the likes of Ian St John and Peter Thompson were displaying even more impressive form, and his first-team chances became increasingly limited. He moved to Huddersfield Town for £18,000 at the start of the 1963–64 season and later finished his playing career in South Africa.

Liddell, William 'Billy' B

1937/8-1960/1 (Forward) **B** 10.1.1922, Townhill, Dunfermline **S** July 1938 from Lochgelly Violet, £200 **D** 5.1.1946 v Chester C, FAC (scored) **L** 1961 retired **Apps** 534, 229 gls + WW2 26, 18 gls **Hons** Div1 CH 1946–47; FAC 1949–50 finalist; 28 caps for Scotland + 8 WW2 caps; 2 GB caps **OC** Kingseat Jrs, Hearts of Beath, Lochgelly Violet, Blairhill Colliery **d** 3.7.2001

LEGENDARY SCOTTISH WINGER, still regarded by many older fans as Liverpool's greatest player of all time. Combining the strength of an ox and the speed of a gazelle, Liddell shattered the club's appear-ance and goalscoring records during a 14-year

Tried out in every area of midfield, Oyvind Leonhardsen never quite consolidated his first-team place

BILLY LIDDELL

average footballer. Throughout his time at Anfield, he held down a nine-to-five job as an accountant. He was a committed Christian who neither drank nor smoked. He was also a tireless charity worker, a voluntary DJ for hospital radio and a Merseyside Justice of the Peace.

In August 1960, just a few months before his 40th birthday, he made his final League appearance. A few weeks later, almost 40,000 fans turned up for his testimonial against an International Xl. "Not once throughout his long service has he given the club a moment's anxiety," said the then chairman Tom Williams.

"Whatever he has been asked to do he has done willingly and with good grace, content with the knowledge that, even if it was occasionally not just what he would have preferred, it was for the good of the Liverpool club.

"He has added much lustre to Liverpool's name by his sporting behaviour, the high standard of his play and his scoring exploits. Never have I seen him guilty of a deliberate foul, or arguing with the referee, or anything else which would tend to lower the reputation of himself, his club or football in general. He has been a credit to the game throughout his long career."

League career. But for the outbreak of World War Two, some of his records would still stand.

He was only 16 when Liverpool boss George Kay persuaded him to move south of the border. Within a year he was a professional, on the brink of first-team action. However, war was then declared and Liddell was called up to the RAF, serving in Britain and Canada. He was demobbed just a few weeks into the 1946–47 season, then made 35 League appearances for a Liverpool team that went on to lift the Championship. Team-mate Bob Paisley recalled how he routinely terrorised defences and how the Kop responded to his mix of brute force and skill. "Billy was so strong he was unbelievable. From beginning to end, he would battle, challenge and show tenacity."

Although the Reds went into swift decline after that Championship win, Liddell remained in outstanding form. He topped the Anfield scoring charts for eight years, won 28 Scotland caps and was twice chosen for Great Britain representative sides. It was largely because of his virtuoso performances that home gates stayed high during Liverpool's lengthy spell in Division Two. His conduct on the field was without parallel: not a single booking in all his senior outings. His loyalty was also superb: despite being condemned to play in the lower reaches, he rejected transfer bids from home and abroad.

Off the field too, Liddell was anything but an

The King of the Wing, that's the way many Reds fans remember Billy Liddell, the Flying Scot

Lime Street Station

LIVERPOOL'S MAINLINE RAILWAY station and the starting point for many great LFC homecomings. Probably the noisiest was in 1965 when the team arrived back from London Euston two days after winning the FA Cup for the first time. The police allowed just a couple of hundred fans onto the concourse, but there were an estimated half a million more waiting in the streets outside.

Hundreds of thousands of travelling Reds supporters have passed through Lime Street over the years. For trips to Wembley – and, more recently, Cardiff – the station has been a riot of colour as fans have unfurled banners specially made for the occasion. But, for atmosphere, no night will beat May 23rd, 1977 when some 5,000 Liverpudlians boarded special trains to the club's first-ever European Cup final 48 hours later. The stamp on their return tickets bore the simple legend: 'Rome And Back'.

Lindsay, Alec

1969/70-1976/7 (Left-back) **B** 27.2.1948, Bury **S** March 1969
from Bury, £67,000 **D** 16.9.1969 v Dundalk, E Fairs Cup (scored)
L September 1977 to Stoke C, £20,000 **Apps** 248, 18 gls
Hons UEFA Cup 1972–73; Div1 CH 1972–73; FAC 1973–74,
1970–71 finalist; CS 1974, 1971 finalist; 4 caps for England
OC Bury, Stoke C, Oakland (USA)

"THE FINEST FULL-BACK passer of a ball I ever played with," is how Kevin Keegan described Liverpool's classiest defender of the early 1970s. But accuracy was only one aspect of the former Bury man's game. There was also his precise, clean tackling ability, his calmness under pressure and a fierce shot that brought 18 goals in an illustrious Anfield career.

With Lindsay partnering Chris Lawler on the right, Liverpool had probably the most

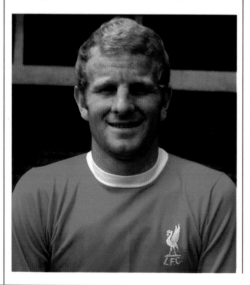

attack-minded full-backs in Britain. Both were willing to dribble their way out of trouble, link up with wingers and end the moves by getting into scoring positions themselves. Throughout his eight seasons with the club, Linday's form was so consistent that he was almost taken for granted. The only surprise was that he managed just four caps for England.

Although on the losing side in the 1971 FA Cup final against Arsenal, Lindsay made amends with a commanding Wembley display against Newcastle three years later. Liverpool won the game 3-0, and his only disappointment was when the referee wrongly disallowed his screaming left-foot shot for supposed offside. In between those two finals, he also played a major part in the club's 1973 League and UEFA Cup double. However, by the time the team repeated that feat in 1976 he had lost his regular first-team place to Joey Jones. He moved to Stoke a year later, then finished his career with the

What a Finnish! Litmanen celebrates with strike partner Michael Owen

American side Oakland. He's been involved in a number of businesses since retiring and is now a pub licensee in Lancashire.

Litmanen, Jari

2000/01-2001/2 (Forward) **B** 20.2.1971, Lahti, Finland **S** January
2001 from Barcelona, free **D** 10.1.2001 v Crystal Palace, LC
L August 2002 to Ajax **Apps** 43, 9 gls **Hons** UEFA Cup 2000–01;
FAC 2000–01; LC 2000–01; Super Cup 2002; CS 2002; 76 caps for
Finland **OC** Reipas Lahti, HJK Helsinki, MyPa, Ajax (twice), Barcelona

THE MOST FAMOUS and talented Finnish footballer of all time fulfilled a childhood dream when he joined Liverpool. As a boy he had watched English football on TV, falling in love with Anfield and the goalscoring skills of Kenny Dalglish and Ian Rush. By the time he pulled on a red shirt himself, he had become a legendary international and the star of the great Ajax side of the 1990s.

After leaving Amsterdam for Barcelona, Litmanen's glittering career hit trouble. A series of injuries kept him out of the first team for months, then, with the arrival of a new manager, he was told he didn't feature in the club's future plans.

It was in January 2001 that manager Gerard Houllier offered him the chance to rejuvenate his career in the Premiership, and Litmanen jumped at it.

An instant favourite with the Kop, he immediately showed the creativity that had opened up defences throughout Europe. His performances were peppered with delightful touches, memorable moments and some outstanding goals.

Yet, despite all his skill and popularity, he was never able to command a regular place and became increasingly frustrated by the Anfield rotation system. In August 2002 he returned to Ajax – and a hero's welcome from his adoring Dutch fans.

Little Known Facts...

...about Liverpool Football Club

• The first player to sign was the Glasgow Rangers inside-right Tom Wyllie, who had previously turned out for Everton and Bury.

• The club's first-ever game was a friendly against Rotherham Town on September 1st, 1892 – a match they won 7-1.

• The team's original nickname was 'The Anfielders'.

• In a 1902 game at Anfield, the Stoke City team was ravaged by food poisoning. At one stage they were reduced to just seven men as a number of players rushed to the gents. Liverpool won 7-0, with striker Andy McGuigan hitting five.

• During ground redevelopment in 1906, the Anfield pitch was raised five feet.

• When the Kop was opened that same year, the cost of a season ticket was just seven shillings and six-pence (the equivalent of 38 pence at today's prices).

• On February 19th, 1910, Old Trafford staged its first-ever game. The result of that Division One clash? Manchester United 3, Liverpool 4.

• In 1914, manager Tom Watson led the team on their first international pre-season tour – to Scandinavia.

• During the First World War, the club sent footballs to the Western Front to help raise morale among British troops. The players gave 12 per cent of their salaries to needy families, while soldiers on leave were allowed into the ground free.

• The tradition of Liverpool and Everton players running out side-by-side for derby matches began in 1927.

> Manchester United Football Club, Ltd.,
>
> WINNERS OF THE LEAGUE CHAMPIONSHIP, 1907-8.
> WINNERS OF THE MANCHESTER CUP, 1908.
> WINNERS OF THE FOOTBALL ASSOCIATION CHARITY SHIELD, 1908.
> WINNERS OF THE ENGLISH CUP, 1909.
>
> TELEPHONE 68, OPENSHAW.
> TELEGRAMS:
> "MANGNALL, CLAYTON, MANCHESTER."
> SECRETARY:
> J. E. MANGNALL.
>
> BANK STREET, CLAYTON,
> MANCHESTER,
>
> February 15th, 1910.
>
> OPENING OF NEW GROUND,
>
> Manchester United v. Liverpool,
>
> FEBRUARY 19th, 1910.
>
> Dear Sir,
>
> The President (Mr. J. H. Davies) and Directors of the Manchester United Club ask your acceptance of enclosed, and extend a cordial invitation to attend the opening Match on Saturday next.
>
> The ground is situate at Old Trafford near the County Cricket Ground, and can be reached by three tram routes—Deansgate, Piccadilly and St. Peter's Square.
>
> The ground when completed will hold over 100,000 people. The present Stand will accomodate 12,000 people seated.
>
> An early reply will greatly oblige.
>
> Yours truly,
>
> J. E. MANGNALL,
> Secretary.

• In a 1943 wartime Northern League game against Chester, centre-forward Cyril Done scored seven goals. Liverpool won the match 9-0.

• During a 1945 tour of Germany, the club were presented with shirts made from material set aside for Nazi flags. These came in very useful at a time of clothing rationing back in Britain.

• Bill Shankly's first signing for Liverpool was the Motherwell forward Sammy Reid. Apart from a Liverpool Senior Cup outing, he never appeared for the first team.

• In all their 14 years together at Anfield, Shankly and Bob Paisley missed only two games between them. Shankly went on a scouting mission before a 1965 FA Cup tie against Stockport, and Paisley was absent for the Cup defeat by Chelsea the following season.

• In 1971 Anfield staged a Division One game between Manchester United and Arsenal after Old Trafford had been closed due to repeated crowd trouble. United won 3-1 in front of a 27,000 crowd.

• At age 16, Alan Hansen had a trial at Melwood – and was rejected for failing to reach "the standard required".

• In 1984 an estimated quarter-of-a-million people visited Anfield for a series of prayer meetings led by the American evangelist Billy Graham – probably the first time a packed football ground was free of swearing!

• When Liverpool beat Everton 3-1 at Wembley in 1986, they were the first team to win the FA Cup without a single Englishman in the line-up.

• In the 2000–01 season the Reds became the first team to complete every possible fixture in a season.

Littlewoods Cup

 See League Cup

L

Triumvirate: Livermore, Evans and Moran

Livermore, Doug

1965/6-1970/1 (Midfielder) 1994/5-1998/99 (Assistant manager) **B** 27.12.1947, Liverpool **S** November 1965 from Bolton W (amateur) **D** 20.4.1968 v West Ham, lg **L** November 1970 to Norwich C, £22,000 **Apps** 17, 0 gls **Hons** LC 1994–95; FAC 1995–96 finalist (both as asst manager) **OC** Norwich C (twice), Bournemouth (loan), Cardiff C, Chester C, Swansea C; Wales national side (assistant manager); Tottenham Hotspur (reserve-team manager)

THE LIVERPOOL-BORN midfielder made only 17 appearances in a five-year Anfield career, but life under Shankly and Paisley clearly had an effect. After retiring from the game he became a widely respected coach with Norwich, Cardiff and Swansea. He was appointed assistant to the Welsh national team and, in 1987, became Tottenham's caretaker manager between the reigns of David Pleat and Terry Venables. In 1994, Liverpool's newly appointed boss Roy Evans invited his old colleague to become first team coach at Anfield. He stayed throughout Evans's management, helping plot the 1995 Coca-Cola Cup victory, but returned to Norwich when Gerard Houllier took sole charge.

Liverpool Echo

MERSEYSIDE'S TOP-SELLING newspaper and a vital source of daily information for Reds fans. *The Football Echo*, printed and on the streets less than half an hour after the final whistle, contains ball-by-ball match reports of Liverpool and Everton games. However, readers with a short attention span can simply refer to the cartoon Kopite on the paper's masthead, who will be – depending on the Reds' result – either dancing, sobbing or holding a spike, representing a single point. The 'Footy Echo' was first published in 1889 and has been a Saturday night institution ever since.

Liverpool Senior Cup

A KNOCKOUT COMPETITION for the professional and amateur sides affiliated to the Liverpool County FA. Liverpool first won the trophy in 1893 following a bad-tempered clash with Everton before 10,000 spectators at Bootle. The Everton officials made an official complaint about some of the refereeing decisions and were later censured by the FA for their lack of sportsmanship. Reds' Chairman John Houlding put the trophy on display at the Sandon Hotel – then had to pay for a replacement when a thief made off with the original!

As expected, Merseyside's two biggest clubs were to dominate the competition for many years to come. The most popular matches were held when the teams were in different divisions and the tournament provided the only opportunity for derby clashes. Throughout the 1950s, it was common for Senior Cup games to be played before packed houses at Anfield and Goodison.

When Liverpool were promoted back to the top flight in 1962, the club stopped entering its senior side. The Cup is still staged annually, but these days it's the Reds' reserves who compete.

'Liverpool Way, The'

ORIGINALLY A TERM for the famous pass-and-move tactics, 'The Liverpool Way' has since come to describe the guiding principles on which the entire club is run. Traditions matter at Anfield, and there are certain codes of behaviour that continue to set Liverpool – its players, officials and supporters – apart from the rest.

In an era when Premiership clubs are traded on the stock market, Liverpool's board is made up of genuine fans rather than institutional investors. Some rivals may exist simply to make money but, as Anfield chairman David Moores once put it, "Liverpool FC is all about winning things and being a source of pride to its fans. It has no other purpose." For Moores and his fellow directors, The Liverpool Way involves taking commercial decisions with ordinary fans – and their economic circumstances – in mind (it's no accident that Anfield admission prices have always been among the cheapest for a top-flight club). It also means open and honest dealings with others, and showing loyalty to their manager during difficult times. For boss Gerard Houllier, it means finding players with

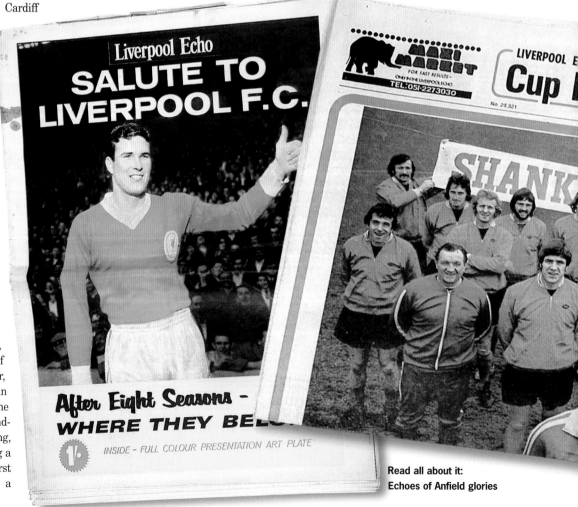

Read all about it:
Echoes of Anfield glories

The founder of the Liverpool Way, the Merseyside messiah, Bill Shankly

the right attitude as well as skills ("When a player puts on a red shirt I expect him to die for it," as the Frenchman once said). And, for those who are chosen to play, it means putting the team – rather than themselves – first at all times.

The Liverpool Way also dictates behaviour on the terraces. At Anfield, opposition goalkeepers can always expect to be applauded, and ex-players cheered rather than booed. Fierce loyalty to their own team never blinds Reds fans to the achievements of others, as the incredible ovations for Leeds and Arsenal – when they won the title at Anfield in 1969 and 1989 – showed. But it's the passionate support for their own team, through bad times and good, that makes them stand out.

In a 2001 interview, chief executive Rick Parry attributed the continuing closeness of club and supporter to Bill Shankly. It was the legendary Scot who began The Liverpool Way traditions and, more than two decades after his death, his legacy is as powerful as ever. "Shankly

forged a special bond with the fans and the people in the city because he understood them and he treated them with openness, honesty and respect. He had huge enthusiasm for the game, which rubbed off on everyone around him. Players and supporters had self-belief and pride, they had passion. There was no place for losers, no place for anyone prepared to give less than one hundred per cent.

"Off the pitch, the club also had a reputation for doing things the right way. Nothing flash, nothing pretentious. Envied by others but always respected, never despised. Always planning ahead, never resting on recent glories. Simply put, what matters for this club, moving forwards, is to win trophies and stay close to its supporters. Easy to say – a little more difficult to do. But guiding values should be simple so that they are understood and remembered by everyone."

Livingston, George T

1902/3-1902/3 (Inside-right) **B** 5.5.1876, Dumbarton **S** May 1902 from Celtic **D** 6.9.1902 v Blackburn R, lg (scored) **L** May 1903 to Manchester C **Apps** 32, 4 gls **Hons** caps for Scotland **OC** Sinclair Swifts, Artizan Thistle, Parkhead FC, Dumbarton (twice, once as manager), Hearts, Sunderland, Celtic, Manchester C, Rangers (twice, once as trainer), Manchester Utd, Bradford C (trainer) **d** 15.1.1950

L Left Liverpool | **LC** League Cup | **n/k** not known | **OC** Other Clubs | **P** Premiership | **S** Signed | **Sb** Substitute | **SSSC** Screen Sport Super Cup | **UEFA** UEFA Cup | **WCCH** World Club Championship

129

Lloyd, Larry V

1969/70-1973/4 (Centre-half) **B** 6.10.1948, Bristol **S** April 1969 from Bristol R, £50,000 **D** 27.9.1969 v WBA, lg **L** August 1974 to Coventry C, £225,000 **Apps** 218, 5 gls **Hons** UEFA Cup 1972–73; Div1 CH 1972–73; FAC 1970–71 finalist; CS 1971 finalist; 4 caps for England **OC** Bristol R, Coventry, Nottm Forest, Wigan (player-manager), Notts County (manager)

ONE OF THE FEW PLAYERS to leave Liverpool in the prime of his career… then go on to even better things. Not that it seemed that way when he went through the Anfield exit door. At that stage, the giant centre-back was the holder of a League Championship and UEFA Cup medal, having helped the team to their 1973 Double. After losing his place through injury the following year, Liverpool sold him to Coventry for £225,000 and his career seemed set for an inevitable decline.

Then, in 1976, Brian Clough took him to Nottingham Forest for the bargain-basement price of £60,000. It proved to be a steal. Lloyd rediscovered the powerful, domineering form that had made him such a hit in his early days at Anfield and became a key link in the most successful Forest team of all time. After winning two European Cups, a League Championship and League Cup medal at the City ground, Lloyd became player-manager at Wigan and boss of Notts County.

Longworth, Ephraim

1910/11-1927/8 and 1928/9-1939/40 (reserve-team trainer) (Right/left-back) **B** 2.10.1887, Halliwell, nr Bolton **S** 9.6.1910 from Leyton **D** 19.9.1910 v Sheffield Utd, lg **L** May 1928 retired **Apps** 370, 0 gls (plus 120 wartime apps, 1 gl) **Hons** Div1 CH 1921–22, 1922–23; FAC 1913–14 finalist; Lancs Snr Cup 1918–19, 1923–24, 1922–23 finalist; Liv Snr Cup 1911–12; 5 caps for England **OC** Bolton St Luke's Junior, Chorley Road Congregationals, Bolton St Lukes (Lancs Combination), Halliwell Rovers, Hyde St George, Bolton W, Leyton **d** 7.1.1968

LONG-SERVING DEFENDER, two-time Championship winner – and the first Liverpool player to captain England. Longworth arrived at Anfield after spells at his hometown team, Bolton and the Southern League club Leyton. Manager Tom Watson's last signing for the club was a refined full-back who could play on the left or right. He made the first of his five England appearances in 1920 as his country came from 4-2 down to beat Scotland 5-4. A year later, he led out the national side as they took on Belgium.

By the time he reached 40, Longworth had featured in 370 senior games and spent several of his 18 years at Anfield as captain. But for all his skill at the back he never once found the net and still holds the club record for the highest number of games without scoring. After retiring in 1928 he joined the coaching staff, and finished his working life as groundsman.

Lowe, Henry C

1911/12-1919/20 (Centre/wing-half) **B** 20.3.1886, Whitwell, Derbyshire **S** 5.5.1911 from Gainsborough Trinity **D** 4.9.1911 v Bolton W, lg **L** March 1920 to Nottm Forest **Apps** 135, 2 gls **Hons** Liv Snr Cup 1911–12 **OC** Whitwell FC, Gainsborough Trinity, Nottm Forest. **d** 25.10.1958

CONSISTENT AND RELIABLE captain whose absence from the 1914 FA Cup Final through injury may well have cost Liverpool the trophy. Lowe could play in any position along the half-back line and his coolness under pressure led one journalist to praise his "admirable powers of imparting steadiness and solidarity to his colleagues". Like many great players of the time, his career was interrupted by the First World War. When the fighting ended he left Liverpool for Nottingham Forest.

Lucas, Thomas

1916-1933 (Right/left-back) **B** 20.9.1895, St Helens **S** May 1916 from Eccles Borough **D** 13.9.1919 v Aston Villa, lg **L** July 1933 to Clapton Orient **Apps** 365, 3 gls **Hons** Div1 CH 1921–22; ; Liv Snr Cup 1919–20, 1926–27, 1928–29 **OC** Sherdley Villa, Sutton Commercial, Heywood Utd, Peasley Cross, Eccles Borough, Clapton Orient, Ashford (manager) **d** 11.12.1953

AFTER CONTESTING LIVERPOOL'S full-back berth with Eph Longworth, Lucas emulated his team-mate by captaining England. The former St Helens schoolboy joined the club in 1916 and was a key member of the team that won the 1922 Championship. He lost his place to Longworth the following year but then got back into the team, as the defence was reorganised to accommodate them both. In all, Lucas won three England caps, skippering the side in a 5-3 victory over Belgium in 1926. He later joined Clapton Orient before retiring at the age of 39 to run a Buckinghamshire pub.

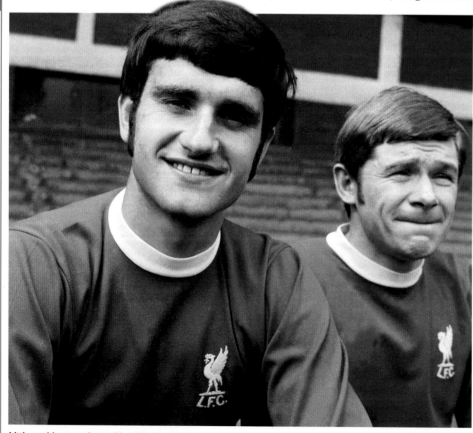

Little and Large – Larry Lloyd (left) with his team-mate Brian Hall pictured at a pre-season Anfield

KEY Apps Appearances | **B** Born | **CH** Championship | **CWC** Cup Winners' Cup | **CS** Charity Shield | **D** Debut | **d** Died | **EC** European Cup | **FAC** FA Cup | **gls** Goals | **Hons** Honours | **lg** League

Macs, Team Of The

IN THE SIX MONTHS between LFC's formation and its first-ever game, team manager John McKenna went on a frantic search to recruit players. His inquiries led him to Scotland where the game was still strictly amateur, and where part-time footballers were keen to escape their jobs in the shipyards, mines and steel mills.

His recruitment success north of the border meant that Liverpool's early sides were overwhelmingly Scottish. By the time they played their first Football League match in September 1893, the line-up – the famous 'Team Of the Macs' – was: McOwen; Hannah, McLean; McCartney, McQue, McBride; Gordon, McVean, M McQueen, Scott, H McQueen.

Ten of the players were Scots. The 11th, goalkeeper Bill McOwen, was from Darwen in Lancashire.

McAllister, Gary (MBE)

2000/1-2001/2 (Midfield) **B** 25.12.1964, Motherwell **S** July 2000 from Coventry C, free **D** 19.8.2000 v Bradford C, lg **L** Summer 2002 to Coventry C as player-manager **Apps** 87, 10 gls **Hons** UEFA 2000–01; FAC 2000–01; LC 2000–01; CS 2001; Super Cup 2001 **OC** Motherwell, Leicester C, leeds Utd, Coventry C (twice)

RECKONED BY SOME to be Gerard Houllier's most inspired signing, the 35-year-old McAllister arrived at Anfield on a 'Bosman'-style free transfer in July 2000. Already a Championship winner with Leeds, the Scottish veteran had also enjoyed distinguished spells at Leicester and Coventry, as well as captaining his country at Euro 96.

While most observers thought he was bought merely to provide midfield cover, McAllister turned out to be one of the most influential figures in Liverpool's 2000–01 Treble season, or, in Houllier's own words, "a real diamond". He scored four goals in the Premiership run-in, including an unforgettable 44-yard free kick that beat Everton at Goodison Park, plus a semi-final penalty that dumped Barcelona out of the UEFA Cup. His late appearance as a substitute in the FA Cup Final against Arsenal helped spark Liverpool's triumphant fightback. And, nine days later, he picked up the Man Of The Match accolade as the Reds beat Alaves in the UEFA Cup Final in Dortmund.

Bringing class and experience to Liverpool's young midfield, McAllister stayed with the club for one more full season, bowing out as a substitute in a 5-0 victory over Ipswich, and with the adoring Kop's ironic "What A Waste Of Money" chant ringing in his ears. McAllister returned to his old club Coventry City and is now viewed as a promising coach for the future.

Indian summer for the veteran Gary McAllister who came to the club on a free and dazzled in midfield

McAteer, Jason

1995/6-1998/9 (Utility) **B** 18.6.1971, Birkenhead **S** September 1995 from Bolton W, £4.5 million **D** 16.9.1995 v Blackburn R, lg **L** January 1999 to Blackburn R **Apps** 139, 6 gls **Hons** 50 caps for Rep I **OC** Bolton W, Blackburn R, Sunderland

BIRKENHEAD-BORN MIDFIELDER who slipped through the Liverpool and England net – surfacing at Bolton, and as part of Jack Charlton's Irish national side. McAteer shone at the 1994 USA World Cup finals, starring alongside the likes of John Aldridge and Ray Houghton – two other players who owed their international places to Irish ancestry.

The following year he was on the losing side when Liverpool beat Bolton in the Coca-Cola Cup Final, but within six months he had arrived at Anfield in a £4.5million deal. In just over three seasons with the club, McAteer made 139 appearances, either in midfield or as an attacking right full-back.

A broken leg sidelined him for most of the 1997–98 season and, although he eventually battled his way back to fitness, he didn't fit in with new manager Gerard Houllier's plans. He joined Blackburn in 1999, helping them win promotion back to the Premiership, before moving to Sunderland at the beginning of the 2001–02 season.

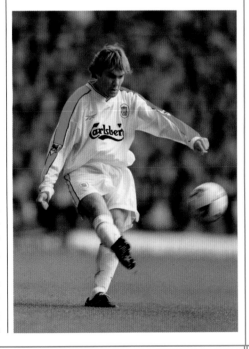

M

McBride, James

1892/3-1894/5 (Left-half) **B** 30.12.1873, Renton, Dumbartonshire
S 1892 from Renton FC **D** 3.9.1892 v Higher Walton, Lancs Lg
(scored) **L** Nov 1894 **Apps** 56, 13 gls **Hons** Div2 CH 1893–94;
Lancs Lg 1892–93 **OC** Renton Wanderers, Renton FC **d** n/k

McCartney, John

1892/3-1897/8 (Right-half) **B** Newmilns, Ayrshire **S** September 1892
from St Mirren **D** 22.10.1892 v Higher Walton, Lancs Lg **L** 1898 to
New Brighton Tower **Apps** 165, 5 gls **Hons** Div2 CH 1893–94,
1895–96; Lancs Lge 1892–93 **OC** Newmilns FC, St Mirren, New
Brighton Tower **d** n/k

McConnell, John M

1909/10-1911/2 (Left-half) **B** 9.12.1890, Cambusnethan, Lanarkshire
S April 1909 from Airdrie, £80.00 **D** 18.12.1909 v Aston Villa, lg
L 1912 to Aberdeen **Apps** 53, 1 gl **Hons** Liv Snr Cup 1911–12
OC Junior football, Motherwell, Airdrie, Aberdeen. **d** n/k

McConnell, William

FORMER LIVERPOOL DIRECTOR who
served as immediate post-war chairman. 'Billy
Mac' was a caterer who ran a string of dockside
cafes during World War Two. When the fighting
ended, he organised the club's famous 1946 tour
of America and Canada, in order for the players
to escape food rationing.

Food aid: Chairman of the board, Bill McConnell

McCowie, Andrew

1896/7-1898/9 (Inside-forward) **B** 1876, Cambuslang, Scotland **S** Oct
1896 **D** 3.4.1897 v The Wed, lg **L** 1899 to Woolwich Arsenal **Apps**
35, 11 gls **OC** Woolwich Arsenal, Middlesbrough, Chesterfield **d** n/k

Taking a breather: Terry McDermott waits for a corner to be taken in the 1979 Charity Shield v Arsenal

McDermott, Terry

1974/5-1981/2 (Midfield) **B** 8.12.1951, Kirkby, Liverpool
S November 1974 from Newcastle Utd, £170,000 **D** 16.11.1974 v
Everton, lg **L** September 1982 to Newcastle Utd, £100,000 **Apps**
329, 81 gls **Hons** EC 1976–77, 1977–78, 1980–81; Super Cup
1977, 1978 finalist; Div1 CH 1976–77, 1978–79, 1979–80,
1981–82; FAC finalist 1976–77; LC 1980–81, 1981–82, 1977–78
finalist; CS 1979, 1980; WCCH 1981 finalist; England U-23 honours
OC Liverpool Schools Football, Bury, Newcastle Utd (twice), Cork C,
Apoel FC

REPRESENTED KIRKBY schoolboys alongside
Phil Thompson and later joined his old friend in
one of the best Liverpool sides of all time.

Despite his local roots, McDermott evaded the
attention of the Anfield talent scouts and began
his professional career at Bury. He then joined
Newcastle United and was on the losing side
when they faced Liverpool in the 1974 FA Cup
Final. But just a few months on, his disappointment was wiped away when Bob Paisley's
£170,000 bid was accepted, opening the door to
a future at Anfield.

It was a glorious one. In a 329-game career,
the wiry, workaholic midfielder won four
Championship and three European Cup
medals. He also gained 25 England caps and, in
1980, became the first ever player to win both
the PFA and Football Writers' Player Of The

Year Awards in the same season. McDermott's passing and off-the-ball running were second to none, but he'll also be remembered for his habit of scoring breathtaking goals. One, a header against Tottenham in a 7-0 home win in 1978, is still regarded as one of the finest ever seen at Anfield. Another, a curled free-kick against Tottenham, became famous in the opening titles of the BBC's *Match of the Day* programme.

After nine years at Anfield, McDermott returned to Newcastle for £100,000. He later played abroad, then drifted out of the game altogether before Kevin Keegan lured him back to St James' Park as assistant manager in 1992.

McDonald, John

1909/10-1911/2 (Outside-left) **B** 1886, Kirkcaldy, Scotland **S** May 1909 from Rangers **D** 4.9.1909 v Chelsea, lg **L** May 1912 to Newcastle Utd, £650.000 **Apps** 81, 4 gls **OC** Wemyss Harp, Vale of Wemyss, Raith Rovers (twice), Rangers, Newcastle Utd **d** n/k

MacDonald, Kevin D

1984/5-1987/9 (Midfield) **B** 22.12.1960, Inverness **S** November 1984 from Leicester C, £400,000 **D** 29.12.1984 v Luton T, lg **L** July 1989 to Coventry C **Apps** 63, 5 gls **Hons** Div1 CH 1985–86; FAC 1985–86; Super Cup 1985 finalist; SSSC 1985–86 **OC** Inverness Caledonian, Leicester C, Rangers (loan), Coventry C

AN EARLY SIGNING of Joe Fagan's, arriving from Leicester City as a potential replacement for fellow Scot Graeme Souness in November 1984. MacDonald initially struggled to make a mark at Anfield, but then seized his first-team

One of Fagan's gang: Kevin MacDonald

Jack McDougall of Sunderland and Jim McDougall of Liverpool FC before a cup-tie in the 1930s

chance when Steve McMahon got injured midway through the 1985–86 campaign. Liverpool went on to win the League and FA Cup Double that season, with skipper Alan Hansen declaring MacDonald to be "far and away our most influential player".

Sadly, he broke a leg the following season and, despite regaining fitness, could never recapture his best form. After loan periods with a previous club, Leicester City, and Glasgow Rangers, he took up the offer of a permanent move to Coventry City in the Midlands. After retiring as a player, he joined Aston Villa's coaching staff.

McDougall, Jimmy

1927/8-1937/8 (Left-half/inside-left) **B** 23.1.1904, Port Glasgow **S** April 1928 from Partick Thistle **D** 25.8.1928 v Bury, lg **L** 1938 to S Liverpool as player-coach **Apps** 356, 12 gls **Hons** 2 Scotland caps **OC** Port Glasgow Athletic, Partick Thistle, S Liverpool **d** July 1984

CULTURED EX-PARTICK THISTLE winger who, along with Matt Busby and 'Tiny' Bradshaw' formed an all-Scottish international half-back line at Anfield in the mid-1930s. McDougall stayed at Liverpool for a decade and, after retiring, set up a successful chandlery business in the city.

McGuigan, Andrew

1900/1-01/2 (Inside-left) **B** 24.2.1878, Newton Stewart, Dumfriesshire **S** May 1900 from Hibs **D** 6.10.1900 v Derby C, lg **L** 1902 to Middlesbrough **Apps** 37, 14 gls **Hons** Div1 CH 1900–01 **OC** Newton Stewart FC, Hibs, Middlesbrough, Accrington Stanley, Exeter C, Burslem Port Vale, Bristol C **d** n/k

MEMBER OF LIVERPOOL'S first title-winning side, and the first Reds player to score five goals in a single match. The ex-Hibernian forward spent two seasons at Anfield before moving on to a succession of clubs including Middlesbrough, Accrington Stanley, Exeter, Port Vale and Bristol City. He later returned to the Anfield staff, helping to coach the Championship teams of 1922 and 1923. After leaving the game, he ran a newsagents' shop and became well-known for his work for pensioners' charities.

McInnes, James S

1937/8-45/6; sec:1955/6-1964/5 (Left-half) **B** 1911, Ayr **S** March 1938 from Third Lanark, £5,500 **D** 19.3.1938 v Brentford, lg (scored) **L** Retired August 1946, joined LFC admin staff **Apps** 51, 2 gls **OC** Third Lanark; wartime guest: Brighton, Newcastle Utd, York C, Leeds Utd, Luton T, Millwall, QPR, Fulham and Manchester Utd **d** 5.5.1965

ALTHOUGH AN accomplished pre-war player, McInnes is remembered for tragic reasons: in May 1965, in the week of Liverpool's first-ever FA Cup final victory, his body was found hanging in the turnstile area of the Kop. McInnes, who gained a BSc at Edinburgh University during the war, had returned to Anfield as secretary in 1955. However, as the club became ever more successful under Bill Shankly, he was ill-equipped to handle the increasing pressures of the job. He committed suicide while apparently suffering from extreme stress.

McKenna, John

LIVERPOOL'S FIRST-EVER team manager who went on to become one of the game's guiding lights, serving as president of the Football League for 26 years. McKenna was an Ulsterman whose early passions were Rugby Union and rifle shooting. He joined the Everton board in 1887 and was one of the handful of members who remained loyal to chairman John Houlding when the club left Anfield in 1892.

When Houlding decided to set up an entirely new club, he invited McKenna to share the managerial duties with William Barclay. McKenna accepted, gave up his job as a vaccinations officer with the local health authority and dedicated the remainder of his life to football.

The man who built the Kop – John McKenna

It was he who masterminded the trips to Scotland to recruit the so-called Team of the Macs. He guided the new team to the top of the Lancashire League, then drafted the successful bid to join the Football League's Division Two. In 1896, he persuaded Sunderland's Championship-winning manager Tom Watson to become his successor at Anfield. Then, as Watson built the teams that would lift the title in 1901 and 1906, McKenna replaced the increasingly fragile Houlding as LFC's driving commercial force.

As the most senior director, he took a firm hold on the finances, oversaw transfer dealings and boosted the Anfield capacity by authorising the building of the Spion Kop. He stayed on the board until 1922, enjoying two spells as chairman, and retained the Football League presidency until his death in 1936.

MacKinlay, Donald

1909/10-1928/9 (Left-half/forward) **B** 25.7.1891, Newton Mearns, nr Glasgow **S** January 1910 from Newton Villa **D** 20.4.1910 v Nottm Forest, lg **L** July 1929 to Prescot Cables **Apps** 434, 34 gls **Hons** Div1 CH 1921–22, 1922–23; FAC finalist 1913–14; CS 1922 finalist; Lancs Snr Cup 1918–19, 1923–24, 1922–23 finalist; Liv Snr Cup 1911–12; Lancs Sr Cup 1918–19, 1919–20, 1923–24, 1922–23 finalist; Scottish caps **OC** Newton Swifts, Newton Villa, Prescot Cables **d** 16.9.1959

ONE OF THE MANY great Scots in the club's history, MacKinlay made the journey to Liverpool after being spotted playing junior football in his native Glasgow. He went on to make 434 appearances and captain the side during an Anfield career lasting almost 20 years. Although usually appearing as left-back, MacKinlay was versatile enough to operate as a wing-half and striker. Fast and strong, he was adept at going forward and getting goals. Among the 34 he scored for the club was a spectacular shot at West Ham in 1926 – fired from 10 yards inside his own half.

As part of the 1914 team that reached the FA Cup Final, MacKinlay collected a loser's medal. But within a decade he had skippered the team to two consecutive League Championship triumphs. He retired from first-class football in 1928 following a series of injuries. He later went into the licensed trade, running a pub in the city until his death in 1959.

McLaughlin, John T

1967/8-75/6 (Midfield) **B** 25.2.1952, Kirkby, Liverpool **S** 1967 from Kirkby Schools **D** 18.4.1970 v Chelsea, lg **L** April 1976 to Barrow **Apps** 55, 3 gls **OC** Portsmouth (loan), Barrow, Wrexham

AFTER JOINING LIVERPOOL as an apprentice, McLaughlin signed professional terms on his 17th birthday. Manager Bill Shankly gave him his senior chance in May 1970, then made him a midfield regular during the transitional 1970–71 campaign. An injury to the slightly built teenager cleared the way for Ian Callaghan's comeback after cartilage surgery. He then faced keener competition for a first-team place due to the emergence of Brian Hall and the arrival of Peter Cormack. Frustrated by a lack of playing opportunities, McLaughlin left to join Portsmouth on loan, before playing out his career with non-League clubs.

McMahon, Steve

1985/6-1990/1 (Midfield) **B** 20.8.1961, Liverpool **S** September 1985 from Aston Villa, £350,000 **D** 14.9.1985 v Oxford Utd, lg **L** 1991 to Manchester C, £900,000 **Apps** 276, 50 gls **Hons** Div1 CH 1985–86, 1987-88, 1989-90; FAC 1988–89; CS 1988, 1989; Screen Sport SC 1985–86; 17 caps for England **OC** Everton, Aston Villa, Manchester Ci, Swindon T (player-manager), Blackpool (manager)

KENNY DALGLISH'S first signing as manager – and one of only two players to captain both Liverpool and Everton. McMahon began his career at Goodison Park before heading off to Aston Villa in 1983. Within 18 months he was back on his native Merseyside, shoring up a Liverpool midfield that was still missing Graeme Souness.

McMahon made up for the ex-skipper's absence, combining aggression and bite with subtle skills and fine passing. Although he missed the run in to Liverpool's Double-winning 1985–86 season through injury, he was a key figure throughout the triumphant 1987–88 campaign. "He is the midfield engine and when he is firing on all cylinders he's a fearsome sight," wrote team-mate Ray Houghton. "He chases, intimidates and simply refuses to give up. He has a reputation for being too hard but I can't agree with that. He is simply an out and out winner. We call him the 'main man' in midfield."

McMahon's form earned him 17 England caps. But despite his continued effectiveness on the field and his enduring popularity on the terraces, he found himself transfer-listed when Souness returned to Anfield as manager in 1991. He was sold to Manchester City for £900,000 and later went into management at Swindon and Blackpool.

The Main Man: Steve McMahon fought many a hard battle in the Liverpool midfield and came out on top in most of them

McManaman, Steve

1989/90-1998/9 (Midfield) **B** 11.2.1972, Kirkdale **S** 1989 from
Liverpool youth football **D** 15.12.1990 v Sheffield Utd, lg **L** July 1999
to Real Madrid, free **Apps** 364, 66 gls **Hons** FAC 1991–92, 1995–96
finalist; LC 1994–95; 37 caps for England **OC** Real Madrid

THERE WERE TIMES during the 1990s when
a dazzling run from 'Shaggy' was the only thing
Liverpool fans had to cheer. The boyhood
Evertonian broke into the Reds' first-team in
1991, running opposing defences ragged with
his breathtaking speed and dribbling skills, and
quickly earning the first of many England call-
ups. His body may have been slight and his legs
spindly, but he could shake off the strongest
challenges and often finish his runs with a
fierce shot.

In a first-team career spanning eight years,
three appearances still stand out: the 1992 FA
Cup final when he switched wings at half-time
to help open up the Sunderland defence; the
1995 Coca-Cola Cup final against Bolton when
his two virtuoso goals settled the match; and the
1997 UEFA Cup clash at Celtic Park, when his
60-yard run resulted in a goal, and Liverpool's
passage into the next round. Sadly, his Anfield
career was to end 18 months later as his contract finished and Real Madrid stepped in with
an eye-watering £15million offer. As one of the
world's highest-paid players, McManaman
found himself under intense scrutiny in Spain.
But he won over Madrid's notoriously fickle fans
when his stunning goal in the 2000 European
Cup final helped secure victory over Valencia.
Playing alongside the likes of Ronaldo, Zidane
and Figo, McManaman has shown himself
capable of competing alongside the world's best.
Surprisingly he found himself frozen out of the
England international picture by manager
Sven-Goran Eriksson.

McMullan, David

1925/6-1927/8 (Right-half) **B** date n/k, Belfast **S** October 1925 from
Belfast Distillery **D** 17.10.1925 v Manchester C, lg **L** July 1928 to
New York Giants, USA **Apps** 35, 0 gls **Hons** caps with NI
OC Belfast Distillery, New York Giants, Belfast Celtic, Exeter C **d** n/k

McNab, John "Jock" S

1919/20-1927/8 (Right-half) **B** 17.4.1894, Cleland, Lanarkshire
S November 1919 from Bellshill Athletic **D** 1.1.1920 v Manchester
Utd, lg **L** June 1928 to QPR **Apps** 222, 6 gls **Hons** Div1 CH
1921–22, 1922–23; CS 1922 finalist; Lancs Snr Cup 1922–23 finalist; Scottish caps **OC** Army Football, Bellshill Athletic, QPR **d** 2.1.1949

THE SCOTTISH-BORN midfielder joined the
club after playing for the British Army and his
local team Bellshill Athletic.

From Kirkdale to the Bernabeu, Macca has gained two Champions League winners' medals with Real

Jack McNab (centre) enjoys a round of golf

His tough-tackling made him a regular in the Championship sides of 1922 and 1923 and won him an international call-up. He transferred to Queens Park Rangers in 1928, but later moved back to Merseyside to run a Bootle pub.

McNULTY, Thomas

1953/4-1957/8 (Full-back) **B** 30.12.1929, Salford **S** February 1954 from Manchester Utd, £7,000 **D** 24.2.1954 v Sheffield Wed, lg **L** 1958 to Hyde Utd **Apps** 36, 0 gls **Hons** none **OC** Salford Boys Club, Manchester Utd, Hyde Utd **d** n/k

McOWEN, William A

1892/3-1893/4 (Goalkeeper) **B** 1871, Blackburn **S** 1892 from Darwen **D** 13.4.1893 v Southport Central, Lancs Lg **L** 1894 to Blackpool **Apps** 26, 0 gls **Hons** Div2 CH 1893-94 **OC** Blackburn R, Darwen, Blackpool **d** 27.12.1950

THE SOLE ENGLISHMAN among the regular Team of the Macs who lifted the Second Division Championship in 1893-94.

Liverpool remained unbeaten throughout that campaign, with the former Blackburn 'keeper conceding just 16 goals. After leaving Anfield he resumed his earlier career as a dentist.

McPHERSON, Archie

1929/30-1934/5 (Inside-left) **B** 10.2.1910, Alva, Clackmannanshire **S** November 1929 from Rangers **D** 23.11.1929 v Leeds Utd, lg **L** December 1934 to Sheffield Utd **Apps** 132, 19 gls **Hons** none **OC** Bathgate, Rangers, Sheffield Utd, Falkirk, Dundee Utd, Alloa Athletic (manager) **d** 1969

FORMER GLASGOW RANGERS forward whose impressive form led to six appearances for the Scottish League. His five years at Anfield coincided with a barren spell for the club. He later made an FA Cup final appearance with Sheffield United and became Alloa Athletic's coach.

McPHERSON, William

1906/7-1907/8 (Inside-left) **B** Date n/k Beith, Ayrshire **S** 1906 from St Mirren **D** 6.10.1906 v Arsenal, lg (scored) **L** 1908 to Rangers **Apps** 55, 16 gls **Hons** none **OC** Beith FC, St Mirren, Rangers, Hearts **d** n/k

McQUE, Joe

1892/3-1897/8 (Centre-half) **B** Scotland, date n/k **S** 1892 from Celtic **D** 3.9.1892 v Higher Walton, Lancs lg (scored twice) **L** 1898 to Third Lanark **Apps** 142, 12 gls **Hons** Div2 CH 1893-94, 1895-96; Lancs Lg 1892-93 **OC** Celtic, Third Lanark **d** n/k

SCOTTISH CENTRE-HALF who joined from Celtic and featured in Liverpool's first-ever line-up. He appeared in more than 140 games, including the original Derby clash with Everton where he was said to have played "like a man possessed". He also won two Second Division Championship medals with the club.

McQUEEN, Hugh

1892/3-1894/5 (Outside-left) **B** 1.10.1867, Harthill, Lanarkshire **S** October 1892 from Leith Athletic **D** 5.11.1892 v Blackpool, Lancs Lg **L** July 1895 to Derby C **Apps** 52, 13 gls **Hons** Div2 CH 1893-94; Lancs Lg 1892-93 **OC** Leith Athletic, Derby C, QPR, Gainsborough Trinity, Fulham (trainer), Norwich C (trainer) **d** 8.4.1944

ANOTHER MEMBER OF the Team Of The Macs, recruited from the Scottish side Leith Athletic. He was an impressive goalscoring winger, and younger brother of team-mate – and future Liverpool manager – Matt McQueen. He left Anfield for Derby County in 1895, and was voted Man of the Match in the FA Cup Final three years later, despite being on the losing side. He later played for Queen's Park Rangers and Fulham before joining the coaching staff at Norwich City.

McQueen, Matt

1892-1899 and 1922/3-1927/8 (director-manager) **B** 18.5.1863, Harthill, Lanarkshire **S** October 1892 from Leith Athletic **D** 2.9.1893 v Middlesbrough **L** 1899 left to become a referee, **Apps** 87 + 16 Lancs Lg, 2 gls **Hons** Div 2 CH 1893–94, 1895–96; Lancs Lg 1892–93; Scotland caps **OC** Leith Athletic (twice), Hearts **d** n/k

PROBABLY THE MOST versatile figure in Liverpool's history, having featured in every single playing position, before serving as a director, then as the manager.

McQueen was already a Scottish international when John McKenna recruited him and his brother, Hugh, from Leith Athletic in 1892. He operated mainly as an inside-forward, but soon showed the capacity to play anywhere, including in goal.

After twice helping Liverpool to promotion to Division One, McQueen retired from playing to become a football referee. In a further shift of role, he was later elected to the Anfield board and, in January 1923, was asked to take over as manager after the shock resignation of David Ashworth.

The team went on to lift the title that year, although much of their healthy points lead was eroded during McQueen's three months in charge. He remained at the helm for another five years but was never able to add to the trophy tally. He was forced to quit in 1928 after losing a leg in a car crash, and spent his retirement at home in Kemlyn Road.

McRorie, Daniel

1930/1-1933/4 (Outside-right) **B** 25.6.1906, Glasgow **S** November 1930 from Morton **D** 29.11.1930 v Sheffield Utd, lg **L** October 1933 to Rochdale **Apps** 36, 6 gls **Hons** 1 Scottish cap **OC** Queen's Park Strollers, Airdrieonians, Stenhousemuir, Morton, Rochdale, Runcorn **d** 26.7.1963

McVean, Malcolm

1892/3-1896/7 (Outside/inside-right) **B** 7.3.1871, Jamestown, Dunbartonshire **S** 1892 from Third Lanark **D** 3.9.1892 v Higher Walton, Lancs Lg **L** March 1897 to Burnley **Apps** 126, 51 gls **Hons** Div2 CH 1893–94, 1895–96; Lancs Lg 1892–93 **OC** junior football, Third Lanark, Burnley, Dundee, Bedminster **d** 6.6.1907

THE FORMER SHIPYARD worker scored 51 times in his Anfield career – including the club's first-ever League goal. He also hit a hat-trick in the record 10–1 League victory over Rotherham United in 1896, and was a member of the two teams who won the Second Division Championship during the 1890s.

Managers

LIVERPOOL FC HAVE HAD 14 managers in the first 110 years of their history. The longest-serving boss is Tom Watson, who died in 1915 after 19 years at the helm. Joe Fagan, who retired after just two seasons in charge, is the manager with the shortest reign. The club has twice operated under a joint manager system, and – between 1915 and 1920 – had no recognised boss at all. The full list of managers reads:

1892–1896:	John McKenna & WE Barclay
1896–1915:	Tom Watson
1915–1920:	Vacant
1920–1923:	David Ashworth
1923–1928:	Matt McQueen
1928–1936:	George Patterson
1936–1951:	George Kay
1951–1956:	Don Welsh
1956–1959:	Phil Taylor
1959–1974:	Bill Shankly
1974–1983:	Bob Paisley
1983–1985:	Joe Fagan
1985–1991:	Kenny Dalglish
1991–1994:	Graeme Souness
1994–1998:	Roy Evans
Aug-Nov '98:	Roy Evans & Gerard Houllier
Nov 1998–:	Gerard Houllier

Manager of the Year Award

THE NUMBER OF TIMES Liverpool bosses have carried off this honour reflects the club's dominance during the 1970s and 1980s. Bill Shankly received the award in 1973, while his successor Bob Paisley won it six times. Joe Fagan rounded off his Treble-winning 1984 season by being named Manager Of The Year, while Kenny Dalglish was honoured in 1986, 1988 and 1990. Despite winning a unique treble of domestic and European knock-out trophies, Gerard Houllier was overlooked in 2001.

138

KEY Apps Appearances | **B** Born | **CH** Championship | **CWC** Cup Winners' Cup | **CS** Charity Shield | **D** Debut | **d** Died | **EC** European Cup | **FAC** FA Cup | **gls** Goals | **Hons** Honours | **lg** League

Top boss: Shankly rounds off a Double-winning season by lifting the 1973 Manager of the Year award, the first of 11 that have so far come to Anfield

L Left Liverpool | **LC** League Cup | **n/k** not known | **OC** Other Clubs | **P** Premiership | **S** Signed | **Sb** Substitute | **SSSC** Screen Sport Super Cup | **UEFA** UEFA Cup | **WCCH** World Club Championship

Matteo, Dominic

1993/4-1999/00 (Defender) **B** 24.4.1974, Dumfries **S** 1985 from Birkdale Utd, 1993 **D** 23.10.1993 v Manchester C, lg **L** Summer 2000 to Leeds Utd, £4 million **Apps** 155, 2 gls **Hons** none **OC** Birkdale Utd, Leeds Utd

RECRUITED BY KENNY DALGLISH, who watched him play alongside his own son Paul for Birkdale United, Matteo joined Liverpool's School of Excellence as an 11-year-old. By the time he was 20, he had graduated to the first team, later proving his versatility by appearing as a full-back, central defender and midfielder.

During the 1995–96 season Roy Evans handed him a sweeper's role – and Matteo responded with a series of performances that led to an international call-up. However, a number of injuries – coupled with Evans' departure – meant he had trouble regaining his first-team place during the next few seasons. As Gerard Houllier strengthened his squad with a number of foreign defenders, Matteo finally decided the time had come to leave. In the summer of 2000 he joined Leeds United for £4million.

Maxwell, Layton

1999/00-2000/01 (Midfielder) **B** 3.10.1979, St Asaph **S** From LFC Youth academy, 1999 **D** 21.9.1999 v Hull C, Worthington Cup (scored) **L** July 2001 to Cardiff C on free transfer **Apps** 1, 1 gl **Hons** Wales U21 honours **OC** Cardiff C

THE WELSH UNDER-21 international could lay claim to Liverpool's best-ever goals-to-games ratio – even though he only ever made one appearance. That came in a Worthington Cup tie with Hull City in September 1999. Despite netting in front of the Kop, Maxwell was never seen in a Red shirt again. He spent the whole of the 2000–01 season on loan to Stockport County, before joining Cardiff City in July 2001.

Utility man: Marsh was a useful player at Anfield

Marsh, Mike A

1987/8-1992/3 (Forward) **B** 21.7.1969, Liverpool **S** 1987 from Kirkby Town **D** 1.3.1989 v Charlton Athletic, lg **L** 1993 to West Ham **Apps** 101, 6 gls **Hons** FAC 1991–92 **OC** Kirkby Town, West Ham, Coventry C, Galatasary, Southend Utd, Kidderminster Harriers, Southport

DISCOVERED BY PHIL THOMPSON while playing for Kirkby Town, Marsh was given his debut by Kenny Dalglish – and later inherited the Scot's famous No.7 jersey. Under Graeme Souness he initially flourished, making 18 starts in the 1991–92 season and impressing the Anfield crowd with his subtle skills and outstanding passing. He also scored six goals in his Liverpool career, with the most memorable coming in the UEFA Cup tie with Auxerre when the Reds overturned a 2-0 deficit to win 3-2 at Anfield.

Despite his obvious midfield abilities, Marsh also found himself used as a right-back – a position where he was clearly uncomfortable. His early promise faded and, to the disgust of many Kopites, Souness sold him and David Burrows in an exchange deal that brought Julian Dicks to Anfield.

Following a relatively short spell at Upton Park, Marsh moved to Coventry and the Turkish club Galatasaray, before joining Ronnie Whelan's Southend United. He was forced to retire from the professional game following a knee injury, though he later turned out for non-league teams Kidderminster, Southport and Accrington Stanley.

Local hero: Dominic Matteo finally moved on to Leeds when there was no place in the team for him

Meijer, Erik

1999/00-2000/01 (Striker) **B** 2.8.1969, Meerssen **S** 1.7.1999 from Beyer Leverkusen, free **D** 7.8.1999 v Sheffield Wed, lg **L** 11.12.2000 to Hamburg **Apps** 27, 2 gls **Hons** 1 cap for Holland **OC** SV Meersen, MVV Maastricht, MVV Fortuna Sittard, EVV Eindhoven, PSV Eindhoven, Bayer Uerdingen, Bayer Leverkusen, SV Hamburg

POWERHOUSE STRIKER from Holland, who arrived on a free transfer from Germany's Bayer Leverkusen in the summer of 1999. Meijer partnered Titi Camara in attack, making 27 appearances but never scoring a League goal. A self-confessed boyhood Liverpudlian, 'Mad Erik' enjoyed a strong rapport with the crowd and seemed to celebrate his team-mates' goals with as much enthusiasm as the most ardent Kopite. Even after he left – bound for SV Hamburg in December 2000 – he maintained a strong interest in Liverpool's fortunes, gaining folk-hero status by joining Reds fans in a sing-song before the 2001 UEFA Cup Final in Dortmund.

'Mad Erik' was well loved by the Anfield crowd if perhaps more for his personality than goals he scored

Scotland Road's very own Jimmy Melia

Melia, James 'Jimmy'

1953/4-1963/4 (Inside-left) **B** 1.11.1937, Liverpool **S** 1953 from LFC groundstaff **D** 17.12.1955 v Nottm Forest, lg (scored) **L** March 1964 to Wolverhampton W **Apps** 286, 79 gls **Hons** Div1 CH 1963–64; Div2 CH 1961–62 **OC** Wolverhampton W, Southampton, Aldershot (player-coach), Crewe Alexandra (player, then player-manager), Southport (manager), Brighton (manager), Belenenses (coach), Stockport C (manager)

AS ONE OF 11 CHILDREN from a Scotland Road family, Melia was always likely to be a local favourite. But it was his habit of getting on the scoresheet that really endeared him to the Anfield crowd.

After winning England caps at schoolboy and youth level, he broke into the Liverpool first team in December 1955, scoring on his debut against Nottingham Forest. He finished top scorer in the 1958–59 season with 21 goals in 40 games – enough to convince new boss Bill Shankly to make him part of his future plans. He was an ever-present in the 1961–62 promotion campaign, and part of the squad that helped Shankly land the title two years later. But it was the emergence of Alf Arrowsmith – an even more effective goal-grabber – that cost Melia his place that season, and in March 1964 he was transferred to Wolves for £50,000.

He went on to play for – and coach – a string of clubs, including Crewe, Aldershot, Southport, and Belenenses of Portugal. The high point of his managerial career came in 1983 when his Brighton side won a fifth round FA Cup tie at Anfield en route to a final against Manchester United. That clash ended all square, before Melia's team were beaten 4-0 in the replay.

Mellor, Neil

2002/3- present (Striker) **B** 4.11.82, Sheffield **S** From LFC Academy 2002 **D** 4.12.2002 v Ipswich T, Worthington Cup. **Apps** 6, 1 gl **Hons** FA Youth Cup semi-final

SON OF EX-MANCHESTER CITY star Ian Mellor, this powerful striker averaged more than a goal a game for the Reds' Reserves during the 2001–02 campaign. Impressive pre-season friendly displays meant he was soon knocking on the door for a first-team place – and he was given his chance in a Worthington Cup tie against Ipswich in the 2002–03 season. Mellor went on to score a crucial goal in the semi-final against Sheffield Utd. Shortly afterwards, he was rewarded with a new three-year contract.

Face for the future: Mellor celebrates his first senior goal after being the reserve league's top-scorer

L Left Liverpool | **LC** League Cup | **n/k** not known | **OC** Other Clubs | **P** Premiership | **S** Signed | **Sb** Substitute | **SSSC** Screen Sport Super Cup | **UEFA** UEFA Cup | **WCCH** World Club Championship

141

Melwood

LIVERPOOL'S FAMOUS TRAINING ground was once owned by the city's Saint Francis Xavier college, and named after two of its most prominent Jesuit priests: Fr Melling and Fr Woodlock. The club bought the land in 1952, but it wasn't until Bill Shankly's arrival seven years later that it began to play such an important role in the club's affairs.

Under his personal supervision, Melwood was extended, renovated and equipped with some of the best training and medical facilities in the country.

Each weekday morning, his players would board a bus at Anfield before being driven the three miles out to West Derby, where they'd be subjected to the 'Sweat Box' the 'Shooting Boards' and endless five-a-sides. Afterwards, the coach would take them back to Liverpool 4 where they showered and changed. "It gave them time to warm down properly after training. That way they didn't suffer from strains," said Shankly. "It also helped to build up a great team spirit."

The Melwood facilities remained largely unaltered until the 1970s when the wood pavillion-style dressing rooms were demolished to make way for a new gym and administration offices.

After Gerard Houllier's arrival it was given another radical overhaul, as the new manager began to organise training on more scientific lines. Today the gym is split into two areas: one containing cardiovascular equipment like running machines and steppers, the other kitted out with weights, bars and dumb-bells for strength training.

All the equipment is computer-controlled so the players, using their own individual key cards, can store their fitness and performance details throughout the week. There are extensive rehabilitation rooms for those on the injury list, along with a full-time team of masseurs – plus a hydrotherapy pool – to help players back to fitness.

As for the outdoor facilities, Melwood houses a number of full-size pitches as well as those used for five-a-side.

Two of them were relaid at the same time as the Anfield pitch, giving players an opportunity to become used to the match-day quality. A third was given a synthetic surface, as well as floodlights, to ensure that training can take place in all weathers.

Back in the Shankly era it was common for fans to call in to see the players being whipped into shape out on the training ground for the big games ahead. Today, public interest is too overwhelming for that to happen.

➔ See also 'Training'

Metcalf, Arthur

1912/3-1918/9 (Inside-forward) **B** 8.4.1889, Sunderland **S** May 1912 from Newcastle Utd, £150 **D** 28.9.1912 v WBA, lg **L** 1919 to Stockport C **Apps** 63, 28 gls **Hons** FAC 1913–14 finalist **OC** Herrington Swifts, North Shields Athletic, Newcastle Utd, Stockport C, Swindon T, Accrington Stanley, Aberdare Athletic, Norwich C **d** n/k

EX-NEWCASTLE striker who played in every position for the Reds, averaging nearly a goal every two games, which more than justified his £150 transfer fee.

Milk Cup

➔ See League Cup

Millennium Stadium

"WE ALWAYS WIN in Wales," sing the Kopites. And, after the stirring 2003 Worthington Cup final, who could blame them? The 2-0 victory over Manchester United made it four wins in five visits to Cardiff's showpiece arena. Wembley may have been 'Anfield South' – but no-one's in a hurry for it to be rebuilt.

Liverpool's initial Millennium Stadium triumph came in the 2001 Worthington Cup clash with Birmingham – the first time a domestic final had been staged outside England. After winning the game on penalties, they scored a 2-1 victory over Arsenal in the FA Cup final, then beat United 1-0 in the Charity Shield.

After losing to the Gunners in the same fixture in 2002, some may have thought Cardiff had lost its shine. But nine months later, under the stadium's closed, retractable roof, Messrs Gerrard and Owen put them right.

Fighting fit: Melwood is where players spend most of the week and plays a vital role in match preparation

The teams are introduced to dignitaries before the 2001 Cup Final in the Millennium Stadium, Cardiff

M

Miller, Tom

1911/12-1919/20 (Centre-forward) **B** 29.6.1890, Motherwell
S February 1912 from Hamilton Academical **D** 17.2.1912 v The
Wednesday, lg **L** September 1920 to Manchester Utd **Apps** 146, 56
gls **Hons** FAC 1913–14 finalist; Lancs Snr Cup 1918–19; Scotland
caps **OC** Larkhill Hearts, Glenliven, Lanark Utd, Third Lanark, Hamilton
Academical (twice), Manchester Utd, Hearts, Torquay Utd, Raith R
d 3.9.1958

SCOTTISH INTERNATIONAL centre-forward,
signed from Hamilton Academical in 1912.
Miller appeared in the 1914 FA Cup final defeat
by Burnley, but a year later was suspended by
the FA for his part in a match-fixing scandal
involving Liverpool and Manchester United.
His ban was lifted following the First World War
when he promptly asked for a transfer... to Old
Trafford.

Milne, Gordon

1960/1-1966/7 (Right-half) **B** 29.3.1937, Preston **S** August 1960
from Preston NE, £12,000 **D** 31.8.1960 v Southampton, lg **L** May
1967 to Blackpool, £30,000 **Apps** 280, 18 gls **Hons** Div1 CH
1963–64, 1965–66; Div2 CH 1961–62; CS 1964, 1965; 14 caps for
England **OC** Preston Amateurs, Morecambe, Preston NE, Blackpool,
Wigan Athletic (player-manager); England youth team (manager);
Coventry C (manager), Leicester C (manager), Besiktas (manager),
Nagoya Grampus 8 (manager), Newcastle Utd (director of football)

ARRIVING FROM PRESTON in August 1960,
the stylish half-back was one of the first pieces
in Bill Shankly's new Liverpool jigsaw. Milne,
whose father had played alongside Shanks,
became an immediate and automatic first-team
choice, helping drive the team to promotion in
his second full season. He was an ever-present
as the Reds stormed to the title in 1964, and one
of only 14 players used as Liverpool claimed
another Championship two years later. Sadly,
he missed out on the 1965 FA Cup Final due to
an injury picked up earlier in the season.

During the 1966–67 season, Milne began to
find it harder to command a regular first-team
place and, as the campaign ended, he switched
to Blackpool for £30,000 – more than twice what
Liverpool had paid for him seven years earlier.
When his playing days ended, he became a
respected figure in management, taking charge
of Coventry, Leicester and the England youth
team, moving on to coaching positions abroad.

Molby, Jan

1984/5-1994/5 (Midfield) **B** 4.7.1963, Kolding, Denmark **S** August
1984 from Ajax, £200,000 **D** 25.8.1984 v Norwich C, lg **L** 1996 to
Swansea C as player-manager **Apps** 291, 60 gls **Hons** Div1 CH
1985–86, 1987–88, 1989–90; FAC 1985–86, 1991–92, 1987–88
finalist; CS 1986; 33 caps for Denmark **OC** Kolding, Ajax Amsterdam,
Barnsley (loan), Norwich C (loan), Swansea C (player-manager),
Kidderminster Harriers (player-manager), Hull C (manager)

LIVERPOOL'S FIRST 'EUROPEAN' signing,
and the player who helped boost the team's legendary following in Scandinavia. Joe Fagan
spotted the so-called Great Dane after he'd broken into the Ajax first team as a 21-year-old. In
1984 he switched to Anfield for £200,000, quickly building a reputation as one of the finest
passers in the game, and the possessor of a
lethal shot.

His all-round talents quickly caught the eye
of several clubs scattered round the continent,
particularly Barcelona who had him watched a
number of times. At one stage – when Molby lost
his place in the first team – a move to the
Spanish side seemed likely. However, failure to
agree personal terms meant he was to continue
his stay at Anfield.

Molby's physique may have been bulky but
he could never be considered in any way a physical player, preferring instead to operate in
space while spraying inch-perfect balls around
the pitch. He was a key figure in the 1985–86
Double-winning team, as well as the sides that
lifted the Championship title in 1987 and 1990,
plus the 1989 FA Cup.

He spent a total of seven years on
Merseyside, scoring 60 goals in 291 games,
establishing new records for penalty-taking
accuracy... and picking up the most authentic of
scouse accents along the way.

The Great Dane delivers another perfect penalty in the 1-0 victory over Manchester United in 1988

KEY Apps Appearances | **B** Born | **CH** Championship | **CWC** Cup Winners' Cup | **CS** Charity Shield | **D** Debut | **d** Died | **EC** European Cup | **FAC** FA Cup | **gls** Goals | **Hons** Honours | **lg** League

Molyneux, John

1955/6-1961/2 (Right-back) **B** 3.2.1931, Warrington **S** June 1955
from Chester, £4,500 **D** 3.9.1955 v Blackburn R, lg **L** August 1962
to Chester, £2,000 **Apps** 249, 3 gls **Hons** England Youth caps **OC**
Orford Youth Club, Chester (twice), New Brighton

POPULAR DEFENDER
throughout the club's 1950s
wilderness years in Division
Two. The Warrington-born
Molyneux was a strong
tackler with a tremendous
physique, but not good
enough to survive Bill
Shankly's early clear-out.
After losing his place to
Gerry Byrne, the former
Chester player moved
back to his old club.

Money, Richard

1980/1-1981/2 (Defender) **B** 13.10.1955, Lowestoft **S** May 1980
from Fulham, £50,000 **D** 13.9.1980 v WBA, lg **L** April 1982 to Luton
T, £100,000 **Apps** 17, 0 gls **Hons** none **OC** Lowestoft Town,
Scunthorpe Utd (twice), Fulham, Derby C, Luton T, Portsmouth,
Aston Villa (coach), Notm Forest (coach), Manchester C (coach),
Coventry C (coach)

ALTHOUGH SIGNED AT THE same time as
Ian Rush, the former Fulham defender enjoyed
nothing like the same success at Anfield. Money
was a useful full-back, but the phenomenal consistency of Phil Neal and Alan Kennedy made it
impossible for him to get a decent run in the
first team. He made disappointingly few senior
appearances before moving to Luton in 1982.
He's since managed Scunthorpe and worked as
a coach at Aston Villa, Nottingham Forest,
Manchester City and Coventry.

Moran, Ronnie

1952-1969 (player) and 1969-1999 (coaching staff) (Left-back)
B 28.2.1934, Crosby, Liverpool **S** January 1952 from Crosby Schools
D 22.11.1952 v Derby C, lg **L** 1969 joined LFC coaching staff
Apps 379, 17 gls **Hons** (as player) Div1 CH 1963–64; Div2 CH
1961–62; CS 1964; (on coaching staff) all LFC hons from 1964–65
FAC to LC1994–95 **OC** none

WITH 49 YEARS AT ANFIELD, Moran must
rank as the club's longest-serving employee. But
it's his tremendous achievements in that career
that make him a true Liverpool legend.

After signing professional terms in 1952,
Moran took four years to establish himself as
the club's left-back. He became a model of consistency, missing just six games between 1955
and 1959, and ending the decade as captain. A

One club, one passion, one love: Moran as player (above) and coach (below), the ultimate Anfield servant

survivor of Bill Shankly's ruthless cull, he went
on to help the Reds win promotion and the First
Division title. He missed out on a place in the
1965 FA Cup final, but returned to play his last
two games in the legendary European Cup
semi-final against Inter Milan.

On retirement as a player, he joined the
coaching staff and guided the Reds' reserves to
a string of Central League Championships. But
his tactical awareness and unrivalled knowledge of every player's strengths and weaknesses made him a vital part of the first-team set-up.
By the time Kenny Dalglish took over as manager, he was the club's acknowledged second-in-
command. And, when the Scot dramatically
stepped down in 1991, the board turned to him
to see the team through its period of turbulence.
He remained as caretaker boss for 10 games,
gladly stepping aside when Graeme Souness
was given the job full-time. Just a year later,
though, he was back in the limelight, leading
Liverpool out for their triumphant 1992 FA Cup
final appearance, as the manager recovered
from heart surgery. He remained at the club
until the end of the decade, serving under his
long-time friend Roy Evans and enjoying a well-
deserved testimonial against Celtic in 2000.

Those who worked with 'Bugsy' describe a
down-to-earth character who demanded 100 per
cent effort at all times. At Melwood, he drove the
players relentlessly, while at Anfield, his voice

could be heard booming from the dug-out. He
was also a fierce proponent of The Liverpool
Way – a philosophy that kept the players
focused on what lay ahead, rather than behind
them. Usually the first to bring them down to
earth after a trophy was won, he was always the
one looking forward when a game was lost.
When the dejected team trooped into the dressing room after the shattering 1988 FA Cup final
defeat by Wimbledon, not a word was said for 10
minutes. Moran then came in and started to
pick up the discarded kits. "Pre-season training
begins on July 12th," were his only words.

L Left Liverpool | **LC** League Cup | **n/k** not known | **OC** Other Clubs | **P** Premiership | **S** Signed | **Sb** Substitute | **SSSC** Screen Sport Super Cup | **UEFA** UEFA Cup | **WCCH** World Club Championship

145

Morgan, Hugh

1897/8-1899/1900 (Inside-left) **B** 20.9.1869, Longriggend, Lanarkshire **S** March 1898 from St Mirren **D** 2.4.1898 v Notts County, lg **L** June 1900 to Blackburn R **Apps** 68, 18 gls **Hons** 2 caps for Scotland **OC** Junior football, St Mirren, Blackburn R **d** n/k

Morris, Frederick W

1958/59-1959/60 (Outside-right) **B** 15.6.1929, Pant, nr Oswestry **S** March 1958 from Mansfield T, £7,000 **D** 3.9.1958 v Brighton, lg **L** June 1960 to Crewe Alexandra, £4,000 **Apps** 48, 14 gls **Hons** none **OC** Oswestry T, Walsall, Mansfield T, Crewe Alexandra, Gillingham, Chester, Altringham

Morris, Richard

1902-1905 (Inside-left) **B** 1879, Newtown, Montgomeryshire **S** 31 March 1902 from Newtown FC **D** 19.4.1902 v Bury, lg **L** July 1905 to Leeds City **Apps** 39, 5 gls **Hons** caps for Wales **OC** Druids (Ruabon), Newtown FC, Leeds City, Grimsby T, Plymouth Argyle, Huddersfield T

Morrison, Tom

1928/9-1935/6 (Right-half) **B** 21.7.1904, Coylton, Ayrshire **S** February 1928 from St Mirren, £4,000 **D** 11.2.1928 v Portsmouth, lg **L** November 1935 to Sunderland **Apps** 254, 4 gls **Hons** 1 cap for Scotland **OC** Troon Athletic, St Mirren, Sunderland, 1936–37 assisted Cambridgeshire junior team under the pseudonym 'Anderson', Ayr United, Drumcondra (coach) **d** n/k

Tom Morrison, Depression-era player

Morrissey, John J

1957/8-61/2 (Outside-right/left) **B** 18.4.1940, Liverpool **S** April 1957 from Liverpool schools **D** 23.9.1957 v Stoke C, lg **L** August 1962 to Everton, £10,000 **Apps** 37, 6 gls **Hons** England schoolboy honours **OC** Liverpool Schools, Everton, Oldham Athletic

THE FORMER ENGLAND schoolboy made his debut at 17 to become one of the youngest-ever players to turn out for the Reds' first team. He was a hard, tenacious winger who combined skilful dribbling with a powerful shot. Despite his obvious ability he was unable to displace Alan A'Court from the senior side and, in 1962, Liverpool were happy to accept a £10,000 bid from Everton. Morrissey became a star player at Goodison for the next decade, winning two Championships and an FA Cup winners' medal.

Mosaics

THE TRADITION OF mosaics on the Kop began in 1995 – the idea of fans who wanted a new way of generating atmosphere following the demolition of the terraces. There have been seven mosaic displays, organised by the fanzine *Red All Over The Land*, and fully supported by the club. Among the most memorable images were the French national flag, displayed shortly after Gerard Houllier's illness, the 'Allez' mosaic – unveiled on his emotional return to the dugout before the European tie against Roma – and the giant 'This Is Anfield' message, displayed before the 2002 Premiership clash with Manchester United.

Murphy, Danny

1997/8-present (Midfield) **B** 18.3.1977, Chester **S** 1997 from Crewe Alexandra, £2 million **D** 9.8.1997 v Wimbledon, lg **Apps** 206, 36 gls **Hons** UEFA Cup 2000–01, FAC 2000–01, LC 2000–01, 2002–03; Super Cup 2001; CS 2001, finalist 2002; 6 caps for England **OC** Crewe Alexandra

GOALSCORING MIDFIELDER who was spotted playing for Crewe in 1997 and immediately given his chance in the Liverpool first team by Roy Evans. Although he showed much potential, Murphy's early form was erratic, prompting a spell in the Reserves, bust-ups with the club management and an eventual loan spell back at Crewe. A series of heart-to-heart chats with new boss Gerard Houllier cleared the air and led to a change of attitude, as the Chester-born player threw himself into training with renewed vigour.

Breaking back into the first team in 1999, Murphy was a regular by the time of the Treble season, contributing 10 goals throughout that campaign, including a memorable free-kick curler that beat Manchester United at Old Trafford. His ability to score – and create

The Hallowed Murph – Danny was voted Liverpool's Player of the Season in 2002–03

Celebrating all things past and present, the LFC Museum is an Aladdin's cave of priceless memorabilia – and memories; below: the 1978 European Cup

chances for others – led to an England call-up in 2001, and he was only prevented from appearing at the following year's World Cup after breaking a bone in his foot.

He was back in shape for the start of the 2002–2003 season, and part of the team that went on to lift the Worthington Cup. Murphy finished the season on a high after topping the fans' poll as Player of the Year. Contributing 12 goals from midfield, he was second only to Owen in the scoring charts. But it was his skill, consistency and work rate that marked him out as one of the most improved players at Anfield.

Museum

SITUATED AT THE BACK of the Kop, the Liverpool FC Museum & Tour Centre is home to the biggest and most impressive collection of club memorabilia on show anywhere. Fans have made the pilgrimage from all over the world since its opening in 1997, passing through an original Anfield turnstile and soaking up the authentic atmosphere of days gone by.

Among the original exhibits are medals and shirts loaned or donated by former players like Billy Liddell and Kenny Dalglish; Michael

Owen's *Ballon D'Or* sits proudly in one of the display cabinets as does Roger Hunt's 1966 World Cup winners' medal and Jerzy Dudek's Man of the Match award from the 2003 Worthington Cup final. There are also actual-size replicas of the club's domestic and European trophies, plus a huge ceramic memorial to the 96 victims of Hillsborough.

In a spine-tingling recreation of the 1960s, the museum has constructed a 'virtual' Kop – complete with crush barriers, film show and the soundtrack of a packed, swaying terrace.

Other fascinating and rare collections include matchday tickets and programmes from the Victorian age, boots and kits worn by the Championship sides of the 1920s, along with badges, banners, scarves, rattles and scrapbooks, all donated by supporters.

There's a 60-seat cinema showing four films charting the history of England's most successful club, including the 2000–01 Treble.

The stadium tour allows fans behind-the-scenes access to the ground. There's a chance to visit the dressing room, walk down the tunnel to the sound of 45,000 cheering fans, touch the famous 'This Is Anfield' sign – and even sit in the dug-out.

The museum and stadium tour has won a number of recent awards for tourism and customer care. It has also won the enthusiastic support of many ex-Reds. Among those who've enjoyed the full experience are Kevin Keegan – and the entire 1965 FA Cup Final team.

N

Neal, Phil

1974/5-1985/6 (Right-back) **B** 20.2.1951, Irchester **S** October 1974 from Northampton T, £66,000 **D** 16.11.1974 v Everton lg **L** December 1985 to Bolton W, player-manager **Apps** 650, 60 gls **Hons** Most decorated player for any one club: EC 1976–77, 1977–78, 1980–81, 1983–84, 1984–85 finalist; UEFA 1975–76; Div1 CH 1975–76, 1976–77, 1978–79, 1979–80, 1981–82, 1983–84; FAC 1976–77 finalist; LC 1981–82, 1982–83, 1983–84; Super Cup 1977, 1978, 1985 finalist; WC CH 1981 finalist, 1984 finalist; CS 1976, 1979, 1980, 1982, 1977 finalist, 1983 finalist, 1984 finalist; 50 caps for England **OC** Northampton T, Bolton W (player-manager), England (coach), Coventry C (manager), Cardiff C (manager), Manchester C (manager)

LITTLE WAS EXPECTED of the Division Four full-back when he arrived from Northampton Town – but he went on to win 50 England caps and finish his career as the most decorated player in Liverpool's history.

At £66,000, Neal was Bob Paisley's first sign-

The master of penalties: Phil Neal on the mark at Goodison and (right) he scores Liverpool's goal in the 1-1 draw with Roma, 1984. The Reds won 4-2 on penalties

KEY Apps Appearances | **B** Born | **CH** Championship | **CWC** Cup Winners' Cup | **CS** Charity Shield | **D** Debut | **d** Died | **EC** European Cup | **FAC** FA Cup | **gls** Goals | **Hons** Honours | **lg** League

ing. Just weeks after joining in October 1974, the manager gave him a surprise debut in the Goodison derby, alongside another new recruit Terry McDermott. "I couldn't get out there fast enough, and what a sight and sound it was," he wrote later. "I stood there taking it all in and happy that I had been lucky enough to move. If I could make myself a regular, I told myself, I would be playing in front of crowds like that every week."

And he did. In fact, after pulling on the No.2 shirt for the first time, Neal made a record 253 consecutive appearances between 1976 and 1982. He never missed a day's training in those years and was so determined to keep his place that he even played with a broken foot, using a specially adapted boot to ease the pain. By the time his Anfield career finished he had featured in 650 senior matches and been an ever-present in nine different seasons. Brilliantly consistent in defence, he was also a master at going for-

ward, setting off on lightning quick raids down the right flank and getting into scoring positions. One such run produced a goal in the 1984 European Cup final, ensuring that Liverpool went into a victorious penalty shoot-out against Roma. Seven years earlier, in the same Rome stadium, his cool penalty had helped the Reds to their first European Cup final win against Borussia Moenchengladbach.

Neal left Anfield in 1985 after a short spell as captain. He was appointed player-coach at Bolton, then went on to manage Coventry and assist Graham Taylor during his period as England boss.

'Nearly Men'

LIVERPOOL'S SQUADS OF the last 40 years are impressive enough. Were it not for lack of cash, health problems and personal ambition, the quality could have been even higher.

Just imagine, for example, three more of England's 1966 World Cup winning team joining Roger Hunt at Anfield. It almost happened. Early in his reign Bill Shankly made a bid for Leeds United centre-back Jack Charlton, but was prevented by the board from raising his bid from the initial £18,000. He also tried to sign Blackpool's Alan Ball – but looked on appalled as the fiery midfielder chose Everton's bigger fee. And when Gordon Banks wanted to leave Leicester, he decided to take Shankly up on a long-standing offer to move to Liverpool. Unfortunately for the England No.1, the manager had just discovered the young Ray Clemence – and opted to show faith in an England international of the future.

In subsequent years, various transfers have fallen down due to last-minute hurdles. In 1974 Leicester striker Frank Worthington agreed personal terms, only to be rejected when a medical revealed high blood pressure. Celtic's Lou Macari looked Liverpool-bound until he was tempted by a rival offer from Manchester United in 1976. Another Parkhead hero, Charlie Nicholas, chose Highbury ahead of Anfield seven years later. And in 1993, Southampton 'keeper Tim Flowers was set to exchange places with David James, before deciding on a future with Blackburn instead.

Since the arrival of Gerard Houllier, it's the club, rather than the player, that's been more likely to bring potential deals to a halt. Apart from passing up a chance to buy the Brazilian star Rivaldo, Houllier surprised many fans when he decided against making Nicolas Anelka's loan arrangement permanent. But in aban-

Big Frank Worthington was nearly a Red

doning negotiations with Leeds United's Lee Bowyer – citing the player's lack of real desire to play for LFC – the manager left many of those same supporters feeling relieved.

Neill, Robert S G

1894/5-1896/7 (Centre-half) **B** 24.9.1875, Govan, Glasgow **S** Jan 1895 from Hibernian **D** 27.4.1895 v Bury, test. match **L** April 1897 to Rangers **Apps** 27, 3 gls **Hons** 2 caps for Scotland **OC** Glasgow Ashfield, Hibernian, Rangers **d** 7.3.1913

THE VICTORIAN DEFENDER is worth a mention, if only for his height. At 5ft 4in, Neil is almost certainly the shortest centre-back in Liverpool's history. He joined the club from Hibernian, then spent a season at Anfield before becoming a Scottish League and Cup winner with Glasgow Rangers.

Newby, Jon

1997/8-2000/1 (Striker) **B** 28.11.1978, Warrington **S** 28.5.1997 from LFC Academy **D** 21.9.1999 v Hull City, LC **L** 22.3.2001 to Bury **Apps** 4, 0 gls **Hons** 1995–96 FA Youth Cup **OC** LFC Academy, Sheffield Utd (loan), Crewe Alexandra (loan), Bury

ALTHOUGH HE FEATURED alongside Michael Owen in Liverpool's 1996 FA Youth Cup-winning side, the striker's Anfield career was never destined to be as successful. After making his debut in a 1999 Worthington Cup tie against Hull City, Newby managed just a handful of first-team appearances. He was later loaned out to Crewe and Sheffield United before being sold to Bury in March 2001.

Nicholl, James

1913/4-1914/5 (Inside-left) **B** Port Glasgow **S** Jan 1913 from Middlesbrough **D** 24.1.1914 v WBA, lg **L** 1915 **Apps** 59, 14 gls **Hons** FAC 1913–14 finalist **OC** Middlesbrough **d** n/k

L Left Liverpool | **LC** League Cup | **n/k** not known | **OC** Other Clubs | **P** Premiership | **S** Signed | **Sb** Substitute | **SSSC** Screen Sport Super Cup | **UEFA** UEFA Cup | **WCCH** World Club Championship

149

Nicknames

ANFIELD MAY BE A SHRINE, but it's also a workplace. And, just like any office or factory floor, the dressing room is a breeding ground for aliases. Some, like 'Shanks' and 'Saint' are obvious. Others need some explaining: Bob Paisley's 'Gunner' derived from his rank in the Army, while David Johnson's habit of carrying a bag containing every type of pill and cream led to the nickname 'Doc'. Here's a selection of dressing-room names for some Reds legends: (N.B. John Barnes' initials are JCB.)

John Barnes	Digger
Kenny Dalglish	Super
Alan Hansen	Jockey
Robbie Fowler	God
Rob Jones	Trigger
Alan Kennedy	Barney Rubble
Ray Kennedy	Razor
Steve McManaman	Shaggy
Ronnie Moran	Bugsy
Phil Neal	Zico
Steve Nicol	Chico
Ian Rush	Omar
Graeme Souness	Charlie
Ron Yeats	Rowdy

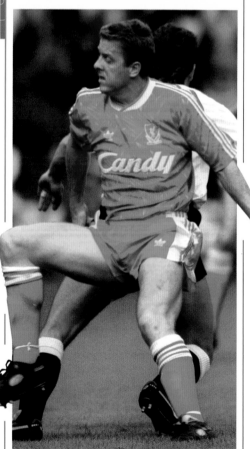

The man in Size 12s: junk-food junkie Stevie Nicol

Nicol, Steve

1981/2-1994/5 (Defender/midfielder) **B** 11.12.1961, Irvine **S** October 1981 from Ayr Utd, £300,000 **D** 31.8.1982 v Birmingham C, lg **L** January 1995 to Notts County **Apps** 466, 46 gls **Hons** EC 1983–84, 1984–85 finalist; Super Cup 1985 finalist; WC CH 1984 finalist; Div 1 CH 1983–84, 1985–86, 1987–88, 1989–90; FAC 1985–86, 1988–89, 1991–92, 1987–88 finalist; CS 1988, 1989, Screen Sport SC 1985–6; 72 caps for Scotland **OC** Ayr Utd boys, Ayr Utd, Notts County, Sheffield Wed, WBA

COSTING JUST £300,000 in October 1981, the former Ayr United full-back proved to be one of Anfield's greatest bargains. In fact, 20 years later, Ronnie Moran named him in his best Liverpool team of all time.

Two-footed, fast and versatile, Nicol could play in any defensive or midfield position. He was noted not just for his perfectly timed tackles, but also for his heading ability, willingness to take men on and knack of getting into scoring positions. He made his breakthrough in the 1983–84 season and, despite missing his spot kick in the penalty shoot-out with Roma, ended the campaign with a treble of medals. He went on to be one of the most consistent performers of the next decade, earning 27 Scotland caps, plus the 1989 Footballer Of The Year award.

With his Size 12 boots, junk food diet and mad sense of humour, Nicol was a dressing room legend. His team-mates subjected him to merciless ribbing, but had huge respect for his skills on the field. "When my knee problems had taken their toll on my running, it made me feel I could light a cigar and read a newspaper to have Steve on the outside," recalled Alan Hansen. "His fitness was astonishing. Dieticians would be horrified at the amount he ate. He could eat for Britain. He and I once went on a Norwegian cruise and he probably consumed more than the rest of us put together. It was not unusual for him to go through six or eight packets of crisps in one go. But he never carried any excess weight, hardly missed a tackle and gave the impression of being able to bomb up and down that right touchline forever. Suffice it to say that after our first match together on the right, I thought, 'Where have you been all my life?'"

After serving under Bob Paisley, Joe Fagan, Kenny Dalglish, Graeme Souness and Roy Evans, Nicol left Anfield in 1995 to become player-coach at Notts County. He later turned out for Sheffield Wednesday and Doncaster before becoming head coach with the American side Boston Bulldogs. In 2001, he joined New England Revolution and, 12 months later, was named American Major League Soccer's 'Coach of the Year' and given a new two-year contract.

Nieuwenhuys, Berry (Nivvy)

1933/4-1946/7 (Outside-right) **B** 5.11.1911, Boksburg, Transvaal, SA **S** September 1933 from Germiston Calies, SA **D** 23.9.1933 v Tottenham, lg **L** 1947 – retired **Apps** 260, 79 gls **Hons** Div1 CH 1946–47 **OC** Boksburg FC, Germiston Calies; wartime guest: Arsenal, West Ham **d** June 1984

SOUTH AFRICAN WINGER renowned for his lean frame, lightning pace and fierce shot. Nicknamed Nivvy – because no-one could work out how to pronounce his surname – he was a crowd favourite who joined in 1933 and ended his Anfield career with a Championship medal. In between he served in the wartime RAF, guested for West Ham and Arsenal and collected £658 from a benefit game between Liverpool and Everton. Shortly after helping the Reds to the 1947 title, Nivvy went back to South Africa to pursue a professional golf career.

Berry Nieuwenhuys, wing wizard from South Africa

Northern Ireland

DESPITE THE CITY'S HISTORICALLY strong links with Ulster, Liverpool have fielded just a tiny number of full Northern Ireland internationals. Winger Billy Lacey – a regular in the club's 1922 and 1923 Championship teams – played for his country 12 times during his Anfield career, while Belfast-born half-back David McMullan also won three international call-ups in the 1920s. But with 27 appearances for his country, the legendary goalkeeper Elisha Scott easily holds the club record for Northern Ireland caps.

KEY Apps Appearances | **B** Born | **CH** Championship | **CWC** Cup Winners' Cup | **CS** Charity Shield | **D** Debut | **d** Died | **EC** European Cup | **FAC** FA Cup | **gls** Goals | **Hons** Honours | **lg** League

Oggy, Oggy, Oggy: veteran Steve Ogrizovic in goal for the Sky Blues thwarts up-and-coming young whippersnapper Emile Heskey

O

Ogrizovic, Steve

1977/8-1981/2 (Goalkeeper) **B** 12.9.1957, Mansfield **S** November 1977 from Chesterfield. £70,000 **D** 8.3.1978 v Derby, lg **L** August 1982 to Shewsbury Town, in part exch for Bob Wardle **Apps** 4, 0 gls **Hons** none **OC** Chesterfield, Shrewsbury T, Coventry C

A FINE 'KEEPER WHOSE first-team chances were always severely limited due to the presence of the outstanding Ray Clemence. After five years as Anfield understudy, he moved to Shrewsbury in an exchange deal involving Bob Wardle. He later played for Coventry and won an FA Cup winners' medal as the Sky Blues beat Tottenham in the 1987 final. Ogrizovic played with Coventry until his early forties, and now runs the club's youth academy.

Orr, Ronald 'Wee'

1907/8-1911/2 (Inside-left) **B** 6.8.1880 Bartonholm, Ayreshire **S** April 1908 from Newcastle, £350 **D** 4.4.1908 v Aston Villa, lg (scored) **L** Jan 1912 to Raith Rovers **Apps** 112, 13 gls **Hons** caps for Scotland **OC** Kilwinning Eglinton 1896, Glossop North End, St Mirren, Newcastle, Raith Rovers, South Shields. **d** n/k

Otsemobor, Jon

2000/1-present (Defender) **B** 23.3.1983, Liverpool **S** Joined LFC Academy 2000, July 2002 to senior squad **D** 6.11.2002 v Soton, LC **Apps** 1, 0 gls **Hons** England youth international **OC** Hull (loan)

LIGHTNING-QUICK defender, seen as one of the club's brightest home-grown prospects. Otsemobor is a former England schoolboy international and captain of the Liverpool youth side. He made his debut in a Worthington Cup victory over Southampton in 2002, but went on loan to Hull City soon afterwards. Sometimes compared to Rio Ferdinand, 'Semi' is capable of playing anywhere along the back-line.

Owen, Michael

➡ **See page 152-153**

Oxley, Cyril

1925/6-1927/8 (Outside-right) **B** 2.5.1904 Worksop **S** Oct 1925 from Chesterfield, c£250 **D** 31.10.1925 v Sunderland, lg **L** Sept 1928 to Southend Utd **Apps** 34, 6 gls **Hons** none **OC** Whitwell Colliery, Chesterfield, Southend Utd (twice), Kettering T, Morecambe **d** 20.12.1984

L Left Liverpool | **LC** League Cup | **n/k** not known | **OC** Other Clubs | **P** Premiership | **S** Signed | **Sb** Substitute | **SSSC** Screen Sport Super Cup | **UEFA** UEFA Cup | **WCCH** World Club Championship

151

Owen, Michael

1996/7–present (Striker) **B** 14.12.1979, Chester **S** To LFC School of Excellence 1990; to first team 18.12.1996 **D** 6.5.1997 v Wimbledon, lg (scored) **Apps** 258, 139 gls, **Hons** UEFA 2000–01; FAC 2000–01; LC 2000–01, 2002–03; Super Cup 2001; CS 2001, 2002 finalist; European Footballer of the Year 2001; BBC Sports Personality of Year 1998; PFA Young Player of the Year 1997–98; 1995–96 FA Youth Cup; 47 caps for England **OC** None

Liverpool star at 17, national hero at 18, European Footballer of the Year at 22. Already it seems as if Owen has been on the scene for an age. But the frightening fact – for opponents at least – is that his best years are still in front of him.

By any standards Owen is a phenomenon. Since he passed Ian Rush's schoolboy landmark by hitting 97 goals in a single season, the records around him have steadily crumbled. He's now topped the Anfield scoring charts for six consecutive seasons, equalled Rush's feat of 20 goals in European competition, and become only the second Reds player to score a Premiership century. On the mark 20 times for his country, he's also eclipsed Roger Hunt as the Liverpool striker with most goals for England.

Owen's chief weapons are his close control, the timing of his runs, and the ability to get into scoring positions. Then there's the devastating turn of speed that can destroy the best defences in the world – plus his knack of performing at his best on the biggest of occasions.

It all came together most spectacularly at the 1998 World Cup when Owen – then the youngest England international of the 20th century – humbled the entire Argentina defence with one of the most dazzling goals in the tournament's history. Three years later he left Arsenal's Lee Dixon and Tony Adams for dead as he sprinted almost 60 yards to score Liverpool's last-gasp FA Cup winner in Cardiff. Then, within the space of four months, he demolished Germany with an unforgettable hat-trick in his country's 5-1 victory in Munich.

That performance helped convince leading continental sports journalists to give Owen the *Ballon D'Or* trophy for 2001. It made him the first British-based footballer to be voted Europe's top player since Denis Law, and put him in the company of such all-time greats as Matthews, Cruyff and Eusebio.

So how does he handle all the attention and adulation? With the same maturity and level headedness he has shown since first breaking into the first team back in 1997, then lifting the PFA Young Player Of The Year award within 12 months. He may since have developed into a global star – conservatively valued at around £45 million – but he has remained fiercely close to his North Wales roots, staying under the watchful eye of his father Terry, a former Everton pro. Any fears that he might waste his prodigious talent were banished long ago. Owen is determined to be the world's best striker, and is willing to work harder than anyone to achieve his ambition.

The single-minded professionalism, and confidence in his own ability, has seen him silence his critics repeatedly throughout his career. No left foot? Look at the shot that beat England's No. 1 David Seaman at the Millennium Stadium. Not good enough in the air? Witness the header that sunk Paraguay at Anfield, a game in which Owen became the youngest player to captain his country since the legendary Bobby Moore.

During the 2002–03 season the doomsayers were at it again, seizing on a barren goalscoring run, and a brief recurrence of his old hamstring trouble, as evidence that he had lost his spark. But the striker forced his way back, fitter and stronger than ever, finishing the campaign with 28 goals, including three hat-tricks. The season also brought his 100th goal in the League, and a trademark blistering run and shot past Manchester United's Fabien Barthez to seal Worthington Cup final victory.

As the campaign ended, Liverpool immediately signalled their intention to offer him a new long-term contract. Boss Gerard Houllier underlined his crucial importance to the club, and had a chilling prediction for the Premiership's defenders: "Our vision is to win the title, and we want to do it with Michael in our team. He is a genuinely world class player, and physically now he is much stronger. As well as his goals, he works extremely hard for the team, running across defences, dropping back when he has to, and winning the ball. He has had a great year – but I think he will be even better next season."

Above left: Owen after hitting the net against Arsenal

(Above) He shoots, he scores... Owen has developed into one of the world's deadliest strikers. Here he shows his technique against Newcastle at Anfield

L Left Liverpool | LC League Cup | n/k not known | OC Other Clubs | P Premiership | S Signed | Sb Substitute | SSSC Screen Sport Super Cup | UEFA UEFA Cup | WCCH World Club Championship

Pagnam, Frederick

1914/5-1919/20 (Inside-right) **B** 4.9.1891, Poulton-le-Fylde, Lancs
S 21.5.1914 from Blackpool **D** 10.10.1914 v Chelsea, lg (scored)
L October 1919 to Arsenal, £1,500 **Apps** 39, 30 gls (48 apps, 42
gls WWI) **Hons** Liv Snr Cup 1914–15 **OC** Lytham, Blackpool
Wednesday, Huddersfield T, Southport Central, Blackpool, Arsenal,
Cardiff C, Watford (manager), Turkey (national coach) **d** 7.3.1962

BLACKPOOL-BORN CENTRE-FORWARD
whose 30 goals in 39 games give him one of the
best scoring ratios of all Liverpool strikers down
the years. His League goals all came in the last
season before World War One and, during
wartime itself, he got on the score sheet 42
times in 48 matches. In 1919 he transferred to
Arsenal, where his prolific ways attracted a
then huge £3,000 bid from Cardiff two years
later. He went on to play for – then manage –
Watford before becoming boss of the Turkish
national side, then coaching in Holland.

Paisley, Bob (OBE)

1939/40-1953/4 (Left-half) & 1954/5-1982/3 (Coach/Manager)
B 23.1.1919, Hetton-le-Hole, Co Durham **S** May 1939 from Bishop
Auckland **D** 5.1.1946 v Chester, FAC **L** July 1954 retired, to LFC
backroom staff **Apps** 277, 12 gls **Hons** (as player) Div1 CH
1946–47; (as manager or asst manager) all LFC honours from
1961–62 to 1982–83 **OC** Bishop Auckland **d** 14.2.1996

HE WAS THE MOST successful manager in
Liverpool's history. But, if he'd had his own way,
Paisley would never have emerged from the
Anfield shadows.

His elevation to the boss's chair came on the

day Bill Shankly
stunned everyone
by quitting. "I did-
n't want his job,"
Paisley revealed.
"I even tried talk-
ing him into stay-
ing. I suggested
that if he went
away on a world
cruise to recharge
his batteries we
could see if we
could handle it
together when he came back. But Bill just said
he'd had enough, and that was that."

Paisley feared he was on a hiding to nothing.
If Liverpool were successful, people would give
the credit to Shankly; if the team failed, the
blame would be his alone. And there were critics of his style, especially when the Reds ended
his first season in charge without a trophy.
From then on, though, they began to play like
world-beaters, and no one could deny that it was

The Main Man – manager Bob Paisley with his Anfield backroom staff and fellow members of the Boot Room

Above right: Bob Paisley with television presenter Eamonn Andrews on the set of *This Is Your Life*

Paisley, rather than his predecessor, who had brought out the best in them. The new boss built a team that would win a Championship/UEFA Cup Double in 1976 and an unforgettable League/European Cup Double a year later.

When Kevin Keegan left for Hamburg after that triumphant night in Rome, Paisley came up with the masterstroke of signing Kenny Dalglish. With him leading the attack, and fellow Scots Alan Hansen and Graeme Souness joining shortly afterwards, Paisley assembled arguably Liverpool's greatest side ever. They retained the European Cup in 1978, then lost just four games out of 42 as they ran away with the League Championship the following year.

By the time Paisley stood down in 1983, his teams had landed six titles, three European Cups and as many League Cups. He was Britain's most successful football manager of all time, with six Manager Of The Year awards to his credit. He also commanded ultimate respect from those around him. "He may have been regarded as a fatherly figure by the supporters but, let me tell you, he ruled Anfield with a rod of iron," said Souness. "You could tell when he was about by the changed atmosphere in the dressing rooms and training ground. There were few who dared mess with him. If we were not performing, Bob would say, 'If you have all had enough of winning, come and see me and I will sell the lot of you and buy 11 new players.'"

Paisley had shown the same toughness in his days as an Anfield half-back. "I would not like to play against him," wrote a journalist, reviewing Liverpool's 1947 title-winning team. "This North-East young man has little height, two stout limbs, a heart of gold and a tackle that is riotous. He has tenacity written all over his face." It was that winning mentality that persuaded the club to offer him a position on the backroom staff when he hung up his boots. Paisley accepted the challenge, became reserve team coach and was appointed second-in-command to the newly arrived Bill Shankly in 1959. The legendary Scot went on to dominate Anfield for the next 15 years. Little did anyone realise his modest and unassuming assistant would one day become an even greater manager.

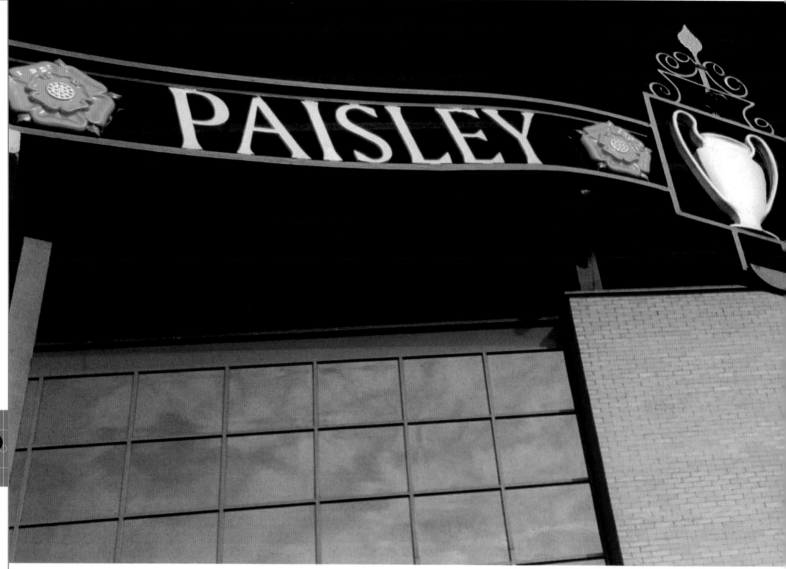

The Paisley Gateway, opened by Bob's widow Jessie – "He deserved this honour 100 per cent," she said

Paisley Gateway

A PERMANENT MEMORIAL to Liverpool's most successful boss, unveiled by his widow Jessie in 1999. The gates, at the front of the Kop entrance, show an artist's impression of three European Cups won under his management, plus the coat of arms for Hetton-le-Hole, Bob's birthplace in County Durham.

Parkinson, Jack

1901/2-1913/4 (Centre/inside-forward) **B** 9.1883, Bootle **S** 1901 from Hertford Albion & Valkyrie FC **D** 3.10,1903 v Small Heath, lg (scored) **L** 1914 to Bury **Apps** 220, 130 gls **Hons** Div2 CH 1904–05; Dewar Shield 1906; Liv Cup 1905–06; Liv Snr Cup 1911–12; 2 caps for England **OC** Hertford Albion & Valkyrie FC, Bury **d** 13.9.1942

ONE OF THE CLUB'S EARLIEST goalscoring heroes, Parkinson was striking partner for the equally prolific Sam Raybould as Liverpool clinched promotion to Division One in 1905. Injuries forced him to miss much of the following season's Championship-winning campaign, but he later bounced back to help spearhead the Reds' attack until the outbreak of the First World War. He retired in 1915 and later ran a string of newsagents in the city. He remains one of only 11 Liverpool players to score more than 100 League goals for the club.

Parry, Maurice P

1900/1-1908/9 (Right-half) **B**1878, Trefonen, nr Oswestry **S** Aug 1900 from Brighton Utd **D** 13.10.1900 v Bolton W, lg **L** May 1909 to Partick Thistle **Apps** 221, 4 gls **Hons** Div1 CH 1905–06, Div2 CH 1904–05; Dewar Shield 1906; Liv Cup 1905–06; 16 Welsh caps **OC** Newtown, Long Eaton Rangers, Leicester Fosse, Loughborough, Brighton Utd, Partick Thistle; Rotherham County (manager), Barcelona (coach), Frankfurt (coach), Cologne (coach) **d** 24.3.1935

WELSH HALF-BACK who spent nine years at Anfield before going on to coach some of Europe's greatest clubs, including Frankfurt, Cologne and Barcelona. Parry was a regular member of the 1906 Championship-winning side and his skill and consistency brought him 16 international caps.

He left the club in 1909, joining Partick Thistle before starting his coaching career. His son Frank later played outside-right for Everton.

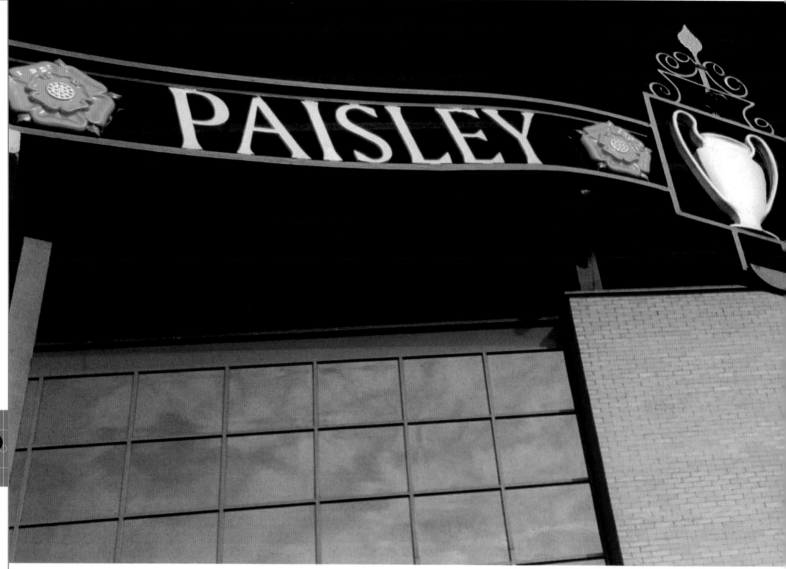
PROMINENT FOOTBALLERS.

J. PARKINSON,
LIVERPOOL.

Jimmy Payne, dubbed 'the Merseyside Matthews'

suffering from the stress of the job, decided to hand over the reins to George Kay.

Payne, Jimmy

1942/3-1955/6 (Outside-right) **B** 10.3.1926, Bootle **S** 1942 from Bootle ATC **D** 11.9.1948 v Bolton W, lg **L** April 1956 to Everton, £5,000 **Apps** 244, 43 gls **Hons** FAC 1949–50 finalist **OC** Bootle Schools, Bootle ATC, Everton FC, England B Honours **d** n/k

DUBBED 'THE MERSEYSIDE Matthews' because of his close control and ball skills, Payne was a gifted winger who never quite achieved his full potential. The former Bootle schoolboy joined in 1942 but had to wait six years for his full debut. He earned a place in the 1950 FA Cup Final side, and it was only the presence of the great Stanley Mathews and Tom Finney that prevented him winning full caps for England. In 1956 he was sold to Everton.

Peake, Ernest

1908/9-1913/4 (Centre/left-half) **B** 1888, Aberystwyth **S** May 1908 from Aberystwyth **D** 20.2.1909 v Woolwich Arsenal, lg **L** 1914 to Third Lanark **Apps** 55, 6 gls **Hons** Liv Snr Cup 1909–10; caps for Wales **OC** Aberystwyth, Third Lanark, Blyth Spartans, Aberaman (manager), Caerphilly (manager) **d** 19.11.1931

Pearson, Albert V

1919/20-1920/1 (Outside-left) **B** 6.9.1892, Tynemouth **S** 24.4.1919 from Port Vale **D** 30.8.1919 v Bradford C, lg (scored) **L** 1921 to Port Vale **Apps** 51, 4 gls **Hons** Lancs Sr Cup 1918–19, 19191–20 **OC** Hebburn Argyle, Sheffield Utd, Port Vale (twice), Llanelli, Rochdale, Stockport C, Ashton National **d** 24.1.1975

Parry, Rick

THE CLUB'S CHIEF EXECUTIVE since 1988. Before this, he spent six years as Chief Executive of the Premier League, helping broker the ground-breaking live TV deals with Sky. A lifelong Liverpudlian, he could not turn down the top job at Anfield when it became free.

Partridge, Richie

1999/00-present (Midfielder) **B** 12.9.1980, Dublin **S** September 1999 from LFC Academy **D** 29.11.2000 v Stoke City, LC **Apps** 1, 0 gls **Hons** U21 honours for Rep I **OC** Bristol R (loan), Coventry C (loan)

THE DUBLIN-BORN Academy graduate made his debut in the 8-0 destruction of Stoke during the 2001 Worthington Cup run. His skilful reserve performances have led to his inclusion in the senior squad for European games, plus useful loan spells with Bristol Rovers and Coventry.

Patterson, George

LIVERPOOL'S DEPRESSION-ERA manager never managed to land any silverware, but he did succeed in bringing some influential players to Anfield. Matt Busby, the England full-backs Tom Cooper and Ernie Blenkinsop, plus future manager Phil Taylor, were all among his signings as he fought a fraught campaign to keep Liverpool in the top-flight throughout the 1930s.

Patterson joined as an assistant to the highly successful Tom Watson in 1907. He later served as club secretary, but took over team affairs when ill health forced Matt McQueen's retirement as boss in 1928. Patterson inherited a high-scoring but under-achieving team and, despite his best efforts, was unable to bring success. At the end of the 1935–36 season, Liverpool were in 19th place and perilously close to relegation. It was then that Patterson,

Shoot-out at Anfield: El Hadji Diouf's spot-kick sinks Ipswich Town in a 2002 Worthington Cup tie

Penalty Shoot-Outs

WHEN ALAN KENNEDY converted his 1984 penalty in Rome's Olympic Stadium, he not only clinched the European Cup, he also set a trend. Liverpool have since taken part in four shoot-outs, emerging victorious in all but one.

In 1992 they booked a place at Wembley by beating Portsmouth 3-1 on penalties in an FA Cup semi-final replay. They landed the 2001 Worthington Cup with a spot-kick victory over Birmingham. And – in the same tournament two seasons later – they needed penalties to get past Ipswich Town in the fourth round.

The one time the Reds came off worst was in 1994, when Wimbledon put them out of the League Cup after a third round shoot-out at Selhurst Park.

Penalty-Takers

"Confidence is everything. There are players who can take penalties by the dozen on the practice ground, and even do better than the regular taker. But the practice ground is not the match pitch. There is no point in pressing anyone into

the job. If he doesn't want it, then he won't have the necessary nerve on the vital occasion." – Phil Neal

Luckily, Liverpool have never been short of players with the nerve – and accuracy – to take their spot kicks. From Ronnie Moran to Gordon Milne, to Tommy Smith and Kevin Keegan, the Reds usually made the most of their penalty-taking opportunities throughout the 1960s and 1970s. But it was a Keegan miss in a UEFA Cup tie against Real Sociedad that led to Neal volunteering for the responsibility in the

Cup victory over Coventry, as well as tucking away five spot-kicks in a six-game spell during the 1990–91 season. But one of his most important goals of all came in the 1986 FA Cup quarter-final at Watford, when Liverpool were within a whisker of elimination.

Molby equalised from the spot after 86 minutes, before Ian Rush grabbed an extra-time winner. Eight weeks later the Reds were at Wembley – for a famous 3-1 Cup victory over Everton.

Recent penalty-takers have included Robbie Fowler, Gary McAllister and Jari Litmanen, with Danny Murphy emerging as the latest spot-kick favourite.

Perkins, William H

1898/9-1902/3 (Goalkeeper) **B** 26.1.1875, Wellingborough **S** March 1898 from Luton T **D** 3.4.1899 v Newcastle Utd, lg **L** 1903 to Northampton T **Apps** 117 **Hons** Div1 CH 1900–01 **OC** Kettering, Luton T, Northampton T **d** n/k

AS THE EVER-PRESENT 'keeper in Liverpool's first Championship side, Perkins conceded only 35 goals in the 1900–01 season.

The former Luton Town player left Anfield two years later to finish his career with Northampton.

PFA Player Of The Year

FOUR LIVERPOOL PLAYERS have been honoured by their professional colleagues since this award began in the 1970s. When Terry McDermott received it in 1980, he became the first player to lift the Football Writers' Footballer Of The Year award in the same season. Three more Reds' players have won the award since then: Kenny Dalglish (1983), Ian Rush (1984) and John Barnes (1988).

PFA Young Player Of The Year

Liverpool have been marginally more successful when it comes to recognition for their youngsters. After Ian Rush's 1983 honour, Robbie Fowler took the award in both 1995 and 1996. Michael Owen carried it off two years later, and in 2001 it was Steven Gerrard's turn to receive the PFA accolade.

1975–76 season. After scoring twice from the spot to earn a 2-2 draw with Arsenal, the job became permanent. He went on to score 37 penalties for the Reds and became the recognised taker for England.

Yet even the cool-headed full-back doesn't rank as the club's most successful spot-kicker. That honour goes instead to Jan Molby, who took over from Neal in the mid-1980s and went on to convert 42 times. Molby's fierce and devastatingly accurate shot brought some memorable victories during his Anfield career. He once hit a hat-trick of penalties in a 3-1 League

Sven-Goran Eriksson presents Steven Gerrard with the PFA Young Player of the Year award, 2001

Piechnik on the park

Piechnik, Torben

1992/3-1993/4 (Central defender) **B** 21.5.1963, Copenhagen, Denmark **S** Summer 1992 from BK Copenhagen, £500,000 **D** 19.9.1993 v Aston Villa, lg **L** Summer 1994 to AEF Aarhus **Apps** 24, 0 gls **Hons** caps for Denmark **OC** BK Copenhagen, AEF Aarhus

AFTER HELPING DENMARK to the 1992 European Championships, the tall central defender became an early target for Graeme Souness. He worked hard to establish himself in English football, but the constantly changing line-up under Souness made it difficult for him to strike up an understanding with his team-mates and, after just two years at Anfield, he moved back to Denmark.

Platt, Peter

1902/3-1903/4 (Goalkeeper) **B** 23.1.1883, Oldham **S** May 1902 from Blackburn R **D** 11.10.1902 v West Brom Albion, lg **L** 1904 to Nuneaton **Apps** 45 **Hons** none **OC** Oswaldtwistle Rovers, Blackburn R, Nuneaton **d** 11.1.1922

Pop Songs

With over 80 different songs recorded, LFC tops the charts for music. The quality veers from the charming 'Roarin' and Scorin'' by a nameless 1966 band to the 1983-84 squad's 'We're Never Gonna Stop'. Prize for best-named band goes to the Scousemartins or Kop Unlimited Orchestra.

Fellow travellers: May 1939, and the team finds itself in Sweden. The itinerary (right) is from a 1936 European tour

Pratt, David

1922/3-1927/8 (Centre/left-half) **B** 5.3.1896, Lochore, Fife **S** Jan
1923 from Bradford C **D** 17.2.1923 v Blackburn R, lg **L** Nov 1927 to
Bury **Apps** 85, 1 gl **Hons** none **OC** Hill o' Beath, Celtic, Bradford C,
Yeovil & Petters Utd (player-manager), Notts County (manager), Hearts
(manager), Bangor C (manager), Port Vale (manager) **d** n/k

Premiership

LIVERPOOL HAVE COMPETED in the FA
Premier League since its inception in 1992. The
Reds' lowest position came at the end of the
1993–94 season when they finished eighth, and
their highest was in 2001–02 when they ended
as runners-up to Arsenal.

Pre-Season Tours

EXPOSURE TO CONTINENTAL styles may
have begun in earnest in the 1960s, but the
club's experience of foreign travel goes back
much further. As long ago as 1914, manager
Tom Watson led the Reds on a two-week tour of
Scandinavia, taking in seven games in
Stockholm, Gothenburg and Copenhagen.

In a letter to the *Liverpool Echo*, defender
Tom Fairfoul gave an early description of the
Swedes' famous enthusiasm for LFC. "We
played our third and last match in Stockholm on
Sunday 17th May against a select Swedish XI...

It was a big compliment to Liverpool FC to find
9,000 people (amongst those present were the
two children of the Crown Prince) when they
turned out in sweltering heat, more suited to
cricket than football... Our boys did as they
liked and kept the Swedes on the trot. The
crowd cheered continually and kept up a con-
stant cry for more goals! It seemed funny for
spectators to want more goals against their own
club. The game ended up eight goals to nothing.
Later on some of the players and Mr Watson
were tossed up in the air by the Swedish team."

Other early tours included Italy in 1922 and
France a year later. In 1935, the team escaped
Depression-era Britain aboard a cruise ship to
the Canaries for three matches in Las Palmas.
The following summer they toured
Czechoslovakia, Yugoslavia and Romania,
drawing major crowds in all three countries and
wearing – for the first time – black shirts. "A
football event was the visit to Bucharest of the
famous Liverpool," reported one Romanian
newspaper. "They were full of professionals and
the team had an incredible presence."

Immediately after the Second World War the
team went on a tour of Germany. A year later
they drew record crowds to American soccer stadiums during a month-long visit to the US and
Canada. That tour, during which the players
put on weight thanks to unrationed food, was
the first of three American trips in seven years.

The last, in
1953, was by
plane, as a
new era of
fast and conven-
ient international travel dawned.
Liverpool have toured far and wide since then,
entertaining crowds throughout Europe, Israel,
the Far East and South Africa. In recent years
the team's taken part in high-profile pre-season
tournaments in Spain, Holland, Scandinavia
and Ireland.

Priday, Robert H

1945/6-1948/9 (Outside-left/right) **B** 29.3.1925, Cape Town, SA
S Dec 1945 from South African football **D** 31.8.1946 v Sheffield Utd,
lg **L** March 1949 to Blackburn R **Apps** 40, 7 gls **Hons** none **OC**
South African football, Blackburn R, Clitheroe, Northwich Victoria,
Accrington Stanley, Rochdale (loan) **d** n/k

A QUICK AND SKILFUL South African who
would have played a bigger part in Liverpool's
post-war line-up had it not been for another
winger named Billy Liddell. The flame-haired
Priday joined in 1945 and was in the side at the
start of the 1946–47 Championship-winning
campaign. But when Liddell returned from RAF
service, he lost his place. He made a number of
first-team appearances the following season
before accepting a move to Blackburn.

Programmes

LIVERPOOL'S FIRST MATCH programme consisted of two sides of A4 paper and contained little more than the team sheet and an explanation of the new offside rule. It cost just one half-penny, although an original would sell for many hundreds of pounds today.

The club's long involvement in historic games makes a number of programmes keenly sought after by collectors. Rare items include the programme for the 1914 FA Cup final with Burnley – the first to be attended by a reigning monarch – and another, issued for a wartime friendly with Everton, containing Bill Shankly's name on the Liverpool team-sheet.

The two Merseyside clubs once issued a joint matchday programme – a tradition that lasted throughout the early part of the 20th Century. After the war, Reds' fans became used to the traditional pocket-sized *Anfield Review*. Then, at the start of the new millennium, they were treated to the *Official Matchday Magazine*, a high-class glossy publication, noted for its quality writing and expert use of photography. The 68-page, brochure-sized magazine won awards, glowing reviews and an avid readership. At the beginning of the 2002–03 season the publishing contract was taken over by Trinity Mirror, owners of the *Liverpool Echo*.

Hospitality on tap: there's a friendly welcome at most pubs around Anfield, but don't expect instant service on match days

Pubs

FOR A TEAM SPONSORED by Carlsberg, it's fitting that Liverpool has strong historical links with the drinks trade. Founder chairman John Houlding was a brewing magnate who once ran Everton's affairs from the Sandon Hotel, just a short walk from the Kop entrance on Oakfield Road. The pub later doubled as the Liverpool players' dressing room, and its bowling green – now the rear car park – also provided the background for the earliest team photos.

In a bid to persuade top players to move to the city, the Houlding family sometimes promised them the tenancy of one of their pubs, so boosting their incomes. When Sunderland's goalkeeper Ned Doig was in talks to join in 1905, the chairman's son invited him to be landlord of The Arkles on Anfield Road (an offer he turned down on account of having young children). A century on, The Arkles is no longer family-owned, but it remains one of the most popular drinking places on match days.

Visitors to Anfield have dozens of other pubs around the ground to choose from. Those noted for their pre-match atmosphere include The Albert, The Park and The Flat Iron (all in Walton Breck Road), Sam Dodds' Wine Bar in Oakfield Road and The Salisbury in Granton Road.

Pundits

GONE IS THE TIME when when footballers were mocked for their one-word answers and clichés. These days, the quickest route to a TV studio is through a dressing room – preferably the one at Anfield.

Ian St John blazed the media trail by becoming a World Cup commentator in 1970, then teaming up with Jimmy Greaves for one of the most entertaining television sports programmes of the 1980s. But it was Alan Hansen's clear and intelligent analysis on BBC's *Match Of the Day* that set TV executives on a mad search for other articulate ex-players. Today it seems the easiest way to find a former Reds star is to look first for a microphone. Among those working for the national media are: Mark Lawrenson (BBC) John Barnes, Barry Venison (ITV), Nigel Spackman and Ray Houghton (Sky Sports), Jim Beglin (Channel 5), Phil Neal and David Fairclough (Radio 5 Live). Several more, including John Aldridge, Alan Kennedy and Gary Gillespie, are used as match analysts on local radio and both Kenny Dalglish and Roy Evans are regulars in the television studios. Even the foreign media isn't free from the influence of ex-LFC players. Over in Spain, the most popular TV football pundit is the 1980s striker Michael Robinson.

Pursell, Robert R

1911-1920 (Left-back) **B** 18.3.1889, Campbeltown **S** 29.8.1911 from Queen's Park **D** 30.9.1911 v Sunderland, lg **L** May 1920 to Port Vale **Apps** 112, 0 gls **Hons** FAC 1913–14 finalist; Liv Snr Cup 1911-12 **OC** Aberdeen University, Queen's Park, Port Vale **d** 24.5.1974

THE SCOTTISH FULL-BACK twice got Liverpool into trouble during his nine years with the club.

In 1912 they were fined £250 for failing to talk with his club Queen's Park before persuading him to sign. And in 1915 he was one of four Reds players found guilty of fixing a Division One match against Manchester United at Old Trafford. The Football League banned him from playing until after World War One, when he joined Port Vale.

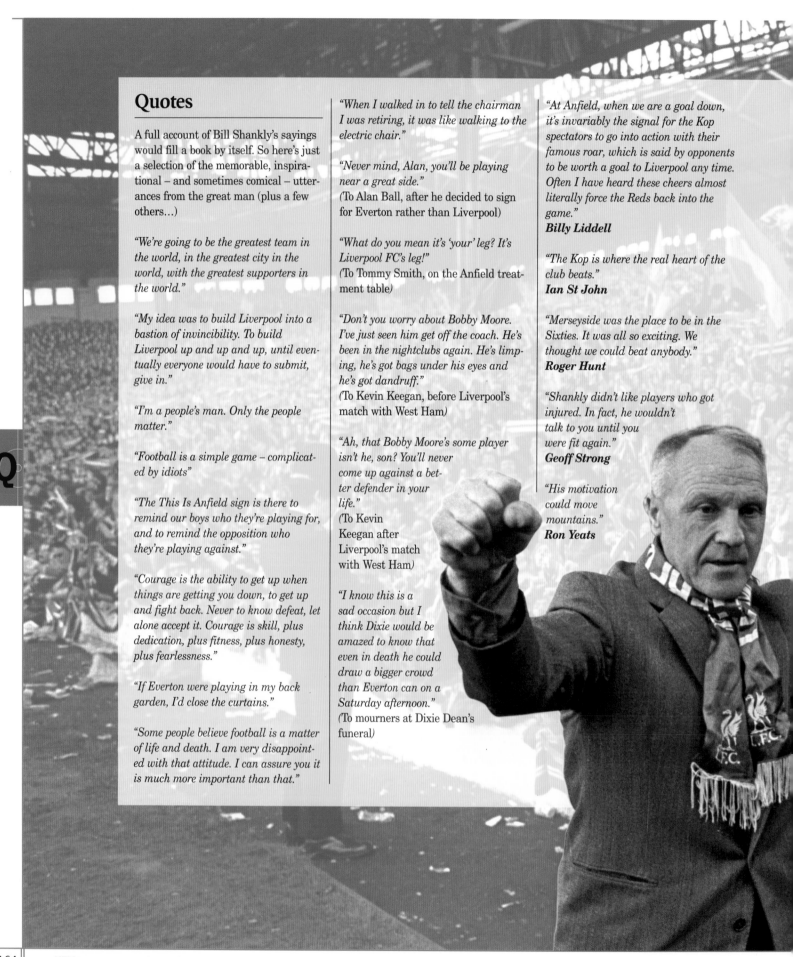

Quotes

A full account of Bill Shankly's sayings would fill a book by itself. So here's just a selection of the memorable, inspirational – and sometimes comical – utterances from the great man (plus a few others…)

"We're going to be the greatest team in the world, in the greatest city in the world, with the greatest supporters in the world."

"My idea was to build Liverpool into a bastion of invincibility. To build Liverpool up and up and up, until eventually everyone would have to submit, give in."

"I'm a people's man. Only the people matter."

"Football is a simple game – complicated by idiots"

"The This Is Anfield sign is there to remind our boys who they're playing for, and to remind the opposition who they're playing against."

"Courage is the ability to get up when things are getting you down, to get up and fight back. Never to know defeat, let alone accept it. Courage is skill, plus dedication, plus fitness, plus honesty, plus fearlessness."

"If Everton were playing in my back garden, I'd close the curtains."

"Some people believe football is a matter of life and death. I am very disappointed with that attitude. I can assure you it is much more important than that."

"When I walked in to tell the chairman I was retiring, it was like walking to the electric chair."

"Never mind, Alan, you'll be playing near a great side."
(To Alan Ball, after he decided to sign for Everton rather than Liverpool)

"What do you mean it's 'your' leg? It's Liverpool FC's leg!"
(To Tommy Smith, on the Anfield treatment table)

"Don't you worry about Bobby Moore. I've just seen him get off the coach. He's been in the nightclubs again. He's limping, he's got bags under his eyes and he's got dandruff."
(To Kevin Keegan, before Liverpool's match with West Ham)

"Ah, that Bobby Moore's some player isn't he, son? You'll never come up against a better defender in your life."
(To Kevin Keegan after Liverpool's match with West Ham)

"I know this is a sad occasion but I think Dixie would be amazed to know that even in death he could draw a bigger crowd than Everton can on a Saturday afternoon."
(To mourners at Dixie Dean's funeral)

"At Anfield, when we are a goal down, it's invariably the signal for the Kop spectators to go into action with their famous roar, which is said by opponents to be worth a goal to Liverpool any time. Often I have heard these cheers almost literally force the Reds back into the game."
Billy Liddell

"The Kop is where the real heart of the club beats."
Ian St John

"Merseyside was the place to be in the Sixties. It was all so exciting. We thought we could beat anybody."
Roger Hunt

"Shankly didn't like players who got injured. In fact, he wouldn't talk to you until you were fit again."
Geoff Strong

"His motivation could move mountains."
Ron Yeats

"Shanks had so much enthusiasm for football. When training was over at Melwood, he used to hold five-a-side matches with the local bin men. There we were – the League Champions – playing a team of bin men."
Tommy Smith

"I'm only a modest Geordie – but get me cornered and I am a mean bastard."
- Bob Paisley

"I never wanted this job in the first place, and I'm not sure that I can do it. I need all the help I can get from you players. There will be no disruptions to the team. Let's just keep playing it the Liverpool way."
Paisley, talking to the team after his appointment as manager.

"Just go out there and grab a piece of something."
Paisley to David Fairclough before sending him on as substitute against St Etienne

"Supersub – you've done it again!"
Kevin Keegan to Fairclough, 10 minutes later

"I hope I am not being boastful when I say 'I think this is only the start.' There is no team in the world we need fear. Obviously we will miss Kevin Keegan but we have plans for a replacement who could bring a new dimension to our play."
Paisley after the 1977 European Cup final

"He is the best player that Liverpool have signed this century. It was the best decision we have ever made."
Club Chairman John Smith on Kenny Dalglish

Interviewer: "Bob Paisley has described you as the complete professional. In all his years in the game he says he has never come across a finer footballer than you."
Dalglish: "Must have been before Saturday."
Granada TV interview, 1981

"As far as Dalglish and Souness are concerned, they've never lost an argument in their lives."
Alan Hansen

"You greedy sod!"
David Johnson to Alan Kennedy after the full-back's virtuoso winner in the 1981 European Cup final

"If I told other coaches we are successful because we bathe in the Mersey, I not only think they would believe me, I think the Mersey would be full of footballers from all over the country."
Ronnie Moran at the height of Liverpool's 1980s success

"Mind, I've been here during the bad times, too. One year we came second."
Paisley on his time as manager.

"The best strikers have to be selfish."
Ian Rush

"During his 33 months in charge, he sold 18 players and brought in 15. Liverpool were in a permanent state of flux."
John Barnes on the Souness era

"I couldn't settle in Italy – it was like living in a foreign country."
Ian Rush

"The intensity of management takes its toll on your health. Some people want to go on forever and I obviously don't."
Dalglish on leaving Anfield

"The pride I feel is almost indescribable. I stood on the Kop as a youngster and I understand the expectations of all our supporters."
Roy Evans on becoming boss

"I would like to pay tribute to all Roy has done for the club over 35 years. I offered him another position but he has decided to take a break. I could talk for hours about Roy and my respect for him."
Chairman David Moores on Evans' departure

"To be the best you have to forget the partying and concentrate all your energies on football."
Michael Owen

"If we aim for the moon, maybe we'll land among the stars."
Gerard Houllier on the 2001 Treble

"It was a special atmosphere only this ground can produce. St Etienne: Pt II."
Phil Thompson on 2002 Champions League victory over Roma at Anfield

"If he stays out of nightclubs for a few years, then he can buy one."
Houllier on Steven Gerrard

"What We Achieve In Life Echoes In Eternity"
LFC banner at the 2003 Worthington Cup final

Race, Henry

1927/28-1929/30 (Inside-left) **B** 7.1.1906, Evenwood, Co Durham
S 1927 from Raby Utd **D** 15.2.1928 v Derby Co, lg (scored) **L** July
1930 to Manchester C, £3,000 **Apps** 43, 18 gls **Hons** none
OC Raby Utd, Manchester C, Nottm Forest, Shrewsbury T **d** 1941

Raisbeck, Alexander G

1898/9-1908/9 (Centre-half) **B** 26.12.1878, Wallacetown, Stirlingshire
S May 1898 from Stoke C, £350 **D** 3.9.1898 v The Wednesday, lg
L 1909 to Partick Thistle, £500 **Apps** 341, 20 gls **Hons** Div1 CH
1900–01, 1905–06; Div2 CH 1904–05; Dewar Shield 1906; Liv Cup
1905–06; caps for Scotland **OC** Blantyre Boys Brigade, Larkhall
Thistle, Royal Albert, Hibernian, Stoke, Partick Thistle, Hamilton
Academical, Bristol C (secretary-manager), Halifax T (secretary-manager), Chester C (secretary-manager), Bath C (manager); LFC (scout)
d 12.3.1949

FOOTBALL'S ORIGINAL PIN-UP boy, and the
first Liverpool captain to lift the League
Championship. Routinely referred to as the best
defender in Britain during the Victorian era,
Raisbeck was a £350 capture from Stoke in
1898. He went on to play 341 first-team games,
win eight international caps and represent the
Scottish League three times.

At 5ft 9¾in, the centre-back was certainly no
giant. Yet his speed, strength and ability
brought rave notices from his earliest days at
Anfield: "Raisbeck dropped from the clouds,"
said one sports magazine. "He employs pace and
great judgement in tackling. In feeding his forwards he has few superiors." As for the fairhaired Scot's appearance, another journalist
noted: "A man of his proportions, style and carriage would rivet attention anywhere. He is a
fine and beautifully balanced figure."

After leading the Reds to that first 1901
Championship, it looked as if he might leave
due to the Football League's imposition of a £4
maximum weekly wage. But so desperate were
Liverpool for him to stay, they gave him the
additional job of 'bill inspector', supposedly
checking on the public
hoardings and notice
boards advertising the
club's matches. His
salary suitably protected, Raisbeck stayed on,
captaining the team to
the Second Division
Championship in 1905
and another League
title the following year.

He stayed with the
club until 1909 when
he was sold to Partick
Thistle for £500. He
later managed Bristol

Capt. A. G. Raisbeck (Liverpool).

OGDEN'S CIGARETTES

City, Halifax and Chester before returning to
Anfield as a talent scout.

Ramsden, Bernard

1932/3-1947/8 (Left-back) **B** 8.11.1917, Sheffield **S** March 1933
from Sheffield Victoria **D** 28.8.1937 v Chelsea, lg **L** March 1948 to
Sunderland **Apps** 66, 0 gls **Hons** none **OC** Hampton Sports, Sheffield
Victoria, wartime guest: Brighton & Hove Albion, Leeds Utd, York C,
Sunderland, Hartlepool Utd **d** March 1976

SHEFFIELD-BORN DEFENDER who formed
an effective full-back pairing with Jim Harley in
the 1930s. The partnership resumed after the
war, but the ageing Ramsden lost his place to
Ray Lambert during the 1946–47
Championship campaign.

Rawlings, Archibald

1923/4-1925/6 (Outside-right) **B** 2.10.1891, Leicester **S** March 1924
from Preston NE **D** 15.3.1924 v Blackburn Rovers, lg **L** June 1926 to
Walsall **Apps** 67, 10 gls **Hons** 1 cap for England **OC** Wombwell,
Shirebrook, Northampton T, Barnsley, Rochdale, Dundee, Preston NE
(twice), Walsall, Bradford C, Southport, Dick Kerr's FC, Burton T
d 11.6.1952

Raybould, Samuel F

1900/1-1906/7 (Centre-forward) **B** 1875, Chesterfield **S** January
1900 from New Brighton Tower **D** 13.1.1900 v W B A, lg **L** May 1907
to Sunderland **Apps** 226, 128 gls **Hons** Div1 CH 1900–01,
1905–06; Div2 CH 1904–05; Dewar Shield 1906; Liv Cup 1905–06
OC Ilkeston Town, Chesterfield Town, Derby County, New
Brighton Tower, Sunderland, Woolwich Arsenal **d** n/k

SCORING LANDMARKS
CAME easily to the
Chesterfield-born striker.
He was leading marksman
in Liverpool's original
Championship side, the
first to hit a hat-trick
past Manchester United,
and the quickest off the
mark in a Merseyside
derby – grabbing his 1900
Goodison opener after just
30 seconds. But it was his
exploits in the 1902–03 season that kept him in the
record books for almost three
decades. With 31 goals in a
League campaign, he remained at
the top of Anfield's all-time scoring charts –
until Gordon Hodgson hit 36 in 1930–31.

A turn-of-the-century signing from New
Brighton Tower, Raybould stayed at Anfield for
seven seasons, finishing four of them as top
scorer and helping the Reds to their first two

titles. He moved to Sunderland in 1907 and
ended his career with Woolwich Arsenal.

Redknapp, Jamie F

1991-2002 (Midfield) **B** 25.6.1973, Barton-on-Sea **S** 1991 from
Bournemouth, £350,000 **D** 23.10.1991 v Auxerre, UEFA
L 16.4.2002 to Tottenham, free **Apps** 308, 41 gls **Hons** LC
1994–95; 17 caps for England **OC** Bournemouth, Tottenham

ONE OF THE REDS' MOST popular servants
of recent years, but one who'll be remembered
for his injuries as much as his talent. Signed
from Bournemouth by Kenny Dalglish, the 17-
year-old Redknapp made his first-team breakthrough under Graeme Souness, establishing
himself as a powerful presence in the centre of
midfield and becoming the youngest Liverpool
player to appear in a European tie. He went on
to play a valuable role in the triumphant 1995
Coca-Cola Cup campaign and won full England
honours shortly afterwards.

Impressive performances at Euro 96 led to
another international call-up a year later.
However, a broken ankle in a 1997 match
against South Africa brought his season to an
abrupt end and signalled the start of a seemingly endless series of treatments for the next
few years. He missed out on a place in the 1998
World Cup finals, then – after being named
Liverpool captain at the start of the 1999–2000
season – was forced to sit out most of the campaign because of knee trouble.

After surgery in America he did manage a
short-term return to action.
Unfortunately, when he lifted the
2001 FA Cup at the Millennium
Stadium, he was in a shirt and
tie, sidelined once again by
injury. Nine months later,
following yet another failed
fightback to fitness,
Redknapp took advantage
of the Bosman ruling by
joining Tottenham on a
free transfer. "He's a class
player, one I had in the
England squad when I was
manager, and an excellent
professional," said Spurs boss
Glenn Hoddle. "If he can steer
clear of injuries, he could prove to
be one of the best signings we've ever
made." He made an emotional return
when his new club visited Anfield during the
2002–03 season, and was given a rapturous
reception by the Kop.

**Above: Sam Raybould, the first Reds striker to
reach 30 goals in a season; (right) Jamie Redknapp**

KEY Apps Appearances | **B** Born | **CH** Championship | **CWC** Cup Winners' Cup | **CS** Charity Shield | **D** Debut | **d** Died | **EC** European Cup | **FAC** FA Cup | **gls** Goals | **Hons** Honours | **lg** League

R

The "Reds" Start To Train For The Fight Back

When Liverpool F.C. players reported at Anfield to-day for training they were welcomed by Mr. W. J. Harrop, the club chairman. Left to right (back row): Underwood, Evans, Rudham, Molyneux, Parker, Healey, Rowley, and Perry. Front row): Mr. Harrop, Hughes, Lambert, McNulty, Payne, Liddell, Moran, Acourt, Campbell (D.), Mr. Don Welsh (manager), Scogings, Jackson, Twentyman, Anderson, South, and Saunders.

Hope in their hearts: the relegated 1954 team aimed for promotion, but it took another eight years

F.A. PREMIER RESERVE LEAGUE CHAMPIONS

Every trophy counts… success for the reserves

Homegrown stars from Jimmy Case to Robbie Fowler and Michael Owen also spent their early days plying their trade in the Central League. More recently, Gerard Houllier's rotation system, and the establishment of a much larger senior squad, has meant the regular appearance of top-rated internationals in reserve-team fixtures.

Reid, Thomas J

1925/6-1928/9 (Centre-forward) **B** 15.8.1905, Motherwell **S** April 1926 from Clydebank, £1,000 **D** 1.5.1926 v Sheffield United, lg (scored twice) **L** 1.2.1929 to Manchester Utd **Apps** 55, 30 gls **Hons** none **OC** Blantyre Victoria, Clydebank, Manchester Utd, Oldham, Barrow, Rhyl Athletic **d** 1972

Relegation

LIVERPOOL HAVE SUFFERED the humiliation of the drop only three times in their history. They fell into Division Two in 1895 and 1904, but got back to the top flight at the first attempt on both occasions. It was another half a century before Don Welsh's Reds were relegated – after losing 23 games in the 1953–54 season. The team stayed in the lower reaches until Bill Shankly led them to the Second Division Championship in 1962.

Republic Of Ireland

A DOZEN LIVERPOOL PLAYERS have won senior caps for Eire. Dublin-born Steve Heighway was the first, making his international debut against Poland in 1971, and going on to win 34 caps.

Others include Ronnie Whelan – whose 51 appearances make him Liverpool's most capped player for the Republic – and Ray Houghton, who played 34 of his 73 Ireland matches while at Anfield.

Steve Staunton, with 89 games, is the country's most capped player of all time, although only 38 of those appearances took place while he was with Liverpool. And Ken de Mange, who made his international debut in 1987, is the only player to win a full cap without appearing for the Reds' first-team.

Reserve Team

THE REDS' RESERVES WON their first Central League title in 1958 – with a certain Bob Paisley guiding them to the top as team coach. They've since won it more than any other club, and established a record by lifting the trophy an incredible 10 times between 1969 and 1980.

The success is probably down to the high-quality teams that the club have always fielded. Once, Anfield tradition dictated that top-flight players spend time in the Reserves learning The Liverpool Way, before being blooded in the senior side. Legends like Ray Clemence, Ray Kennedy and Terry McDermott all spent lengthy periods in the second string line-up before graduating as first-team regulars.

Riedle, Karl-Heinz

1997/8-1998/9 (Forward) **B** 16.9.1965, Weiler, Germany **S** July 1997 from Borussia Dortmund **D** 9.8.1997 v Wimbledon, lg **L** 28.9.1999 to Fulham, £200,000 **Apps** 76, 15 gls **Hons** caps for Germany **OC** TSV Ellhofen, SV Weiler, Augsburg, Blau-Weiss Berlin, Werder Bremen, Lazio, Borussia Dortmund, Fulham

AFTER HELPING BORUSSIA Dortmund to two successive Bundesliga titles, the German international sealed their European Cup final triumph with two goals against Juventus. Liverpool boss Roy Evans then beat off stiff competition for his signature as he sought a high-profile replacement for the departing Stan Collymore. Riedle brought experience and class to the Liverpool front line, but a combination of

Vorsprung durch Technik: former striker Karl-Heinz Riedle hits the mark with German precision

KEY Apps Appearances | **B** Born | **CH** Championship | **CWC** Cup Winners' Cup | **CS** Charity Shield | **D** Debut | **d** Died | **EC** European Cup | **FAC** FA Cup | **gls** Goals | **Hons** Honours | **lg** League

The best left foot in the business, John Arne Riise lets fly with a typical rocket shot

injuries – plus the presence of Robbie Fowler and the emerging Michael Owen – meant he was never a first-team regular. When First Division Fulham stepped in with a £200,000 offer in 1999, he decided to help their push for a Premiership place.

Riise, John Arne

2001/2-present (Defender) **B** 24.9.1980, Molde, Norway **S** July 2001 from Monaco, £4 million **D** 10.7.2001 v Bayer Leverkusen, friendly **Apps** 111, 14 gls **Hons** LC 2002–03; CS 2001; CS 2002 finalist; 25 caps for Norway **OC** Aalesund, Monaco

THE NORWEGIAN INTERNATIONAL made an explosive start with the opening goal in the 3-2 European Super Cup victory over Bayern Munich. Within a year, he had established himself as the Reds' most consistent performer and more than justified Gerard Houllier's £4million fee to Monaco.

Blessed with lightning pace, an immense throw-in and a rocket of a shot, the powerfully built Riise proved equally effective on the left side of midfield or defence. He enjoyed a tremendous 2001–02 debut season, showing the confidence and ability to run at opposing defences and get on the scoresheet. Among his eight goals were a brilliant run and shot that squared the League game at Highbury and a stunning 30-yard free-kick against Manchester United that confirmed his status as a new Anfield hero.

Riise found himself less of a regular in the early part of the 2002–03 campaign but gradually fought his way back to automatic selection. He was in the team that won the Worthington Cup against United, and delighted Reds fans by signing a contract extension that tied him to Anfield until 2007.

"I am very pleased to have the opportunity of playing for Liverpool because this is the club I always wanted to join," he said afterwards. "They have a fantastic reputation and history; they take young players and make them into great ones. Plus they have a really great following in Norway.

"There have always been great players here and we have a great squad at the moment. It was the biggest step of my life to come to Anfield, and I want to stay as long as possible."

Riley, Arthur J

1925/6-45/6 (Goalkeeper) **B** 26.12.1903, Boksburg, SA **S** August 1925 from Boksburg FC **D** 24.10.1925 v Tottenham, lg **L** c1945–46 to South Africa **Apps** 338, 0 gls **Hons** caps for South Africa **OC** Boksburg FC **d** n/k

LIVERPOOL RECRUITED THEIR first-ever foreign player after he took part in South Africa's 1924 tour of Britain. Manager Matt McQueen saw the 6ft 1in goalkeeper as a long-term replacement for Elisha Scott, and Riley had to wait four years before eventually usurping the Irishman as first-choice Number One. He stayed with the Reds throughout the 1930s,

eventually returning to South Africa with the outbreak of war, and with more than 300 senior appearances to his credit.

Roberts, Sydney

1929/30-1936/7 (Inside-left) **B** 1911, Bootle **S** 1929 from Bootle JOC **D** 23.4.1932 v Portsmouth, lg **L** August 1937 to Shrewsbury T **Apps** 62, 13 gls **Hons** none **OC** Bootle JOC, Shrewsbury T, Chester, Northfleet **d** n/k

Robertson, John 'Jack T

1900/1-1901/2 (Right-back) **B** 1877, Newton Mearns, Renfrewshire **S** 1900 from Stoke C **D** 1.9.1900 v Blackburn Rovers, lg **L** May 1902 to Southampton **Apps** 47, 0 gls **Hons** Div1 CH 1900–01 **OC** Newton Thistle, Edinburgh St Bernard's, Stoke, Southampton, Brighton & Hove Albion **d** n/k

Robertson, Thomas

1897/8-1901/2 (Outside-left) **B** n/k, Lanarkshire **S** March 1898 from Hearts, £350 plus John Walker **D** 11.4.1898 v The Wednesday, lg (scored) **L** May 1902 to Hearts, £300 plus 'Sailor' Hunter **Apps** 141, 34 gls **Hons** Div1 CH 1900–01; 1 cap for Scotland **OC** East Benhar Heatherbell, Motherwell, Fauldhouse, Hearts (twice), Dundee **d** n/k

Robinson, Michael J

1983/4-84/5 (Forward) **B** 12.7.1958, Leicester **S** August 1983 from Brighton, £200,000 **D** 20.8.1983 v Manchester Utd, CS **L** December 1984 to QPR, £100,000 **Apps** 52, 13 gls **Hons** EC 1983–84; Div1 CH 1983–84; 23 Caps for Rep I **OC** Waterloo Wanderers, Dolphinstone FC, Preston NE, Manchester C, Brighton, QPR, Osasuna FC

THE EIRE INTERNATIONAL spent just 16 months at Anfield, yet won both Championship and European Cup winners medals – and appeared in the first all-Merseyside Cup Final.

An early signing of Joe Fagan's, Robinson was an aggressive forward who provided powerful back-up for Ian Rush and Kenny Dalglish. He was never likely to displace those two Anfield legends, but was frequently used as a third striker, contributing valuable goals, including a memorable League hat-trick at West Ham. His appearance against Everton came when he replaced Craig Johnston in the 0-0 draw at Wembley. He won his European medal after making six appearances in the tournament, and coming on as a late substitute for Kenny Dalglish in Rome.

Unable to command regular first-team foot-

In good company: Michael Robinson played alongside Anfield legends such as Graeme Souness and Alan Hansen

ball, Robinson moved to Queens Park Rangers in December 1984. He later joined ex-Anfield teammate Sammy Lee at Osasuna in Spain, then launched a new career as a soccer pundit on Spanish television.

Robinson, Peter

LIVERPOOL FC'S YEARS OF domestic and European dominance were a triumph for their managers and players. But success wouldn't have been possible without the massive contribution of club secretary Peter Robinson, the man widely acknowledged as British football's finest administrator during the 1970s and 1980s.

He took the job following the suicide of Jimmy McInnes, shortly after the 1965 FA Cup final, and quickly developed a close friendship and understanding with Bill Shankly. "He was very astute," recalled Tommy Smith. "With him there, Shankly was able to segregate everything. The football side was for the manager, the trainers and the players themselves. The administration side should be left to somebody who knew what he was doing. That was the Peter Robinson side."

It was Robinson who brought a new controlled approach to Liverpool's travels around Europe. Rather than rely on scheduled flights which played havoc with players' body clocks, he began chartering planes to carry the team on dates and times to suit them. He booked the best hotels, far away from the noise and distractions of the big cities. And he bypassed the sub-standard food on offer in Eastern Bloc countries by taking along trained chefs. At home, Robinson helped supervise the gradual and increasingly ambitious redevelopment of Anfield. He also helped negotiate transfers, TV contracts and shirt sponsorship deals.

His reaction to the disasters at Heysel and Hillsborough also brought respect and admiration. It was Robinson who drew up a whole new business plan based on the potentially ruinous loss of revenue resulting from the post-Brussels European ban. And he was one of the key figures who insisted on sensitivity and togetherness after the events of Saturday April 15th, 1989. "On the Sunday morning I went down to the Shankly Gates end of the ground and people were just wandering around there in a daze," he told a Radio City interviewer some years later. "I spoke to a few people and they really didn't know what to do. I just said to one or two of them, 'Would you feel better if you went in to the ground?' and they said, 'Yes, I think we would.' So I said to our people, 'Throw open the gates and let them in.' A couple of people said, 'What about the pitch?' and I said, 'I don't think in cir-

Decision-maker: long-serving secretary, Peter Robinson

cumstances like this the pitch matters. Who knows what the future holds for Liverpool? The important thing is the people at the moment, and if they think they're going to get some comfort from going into the ground we must let them in.' Anfield became a shrine for people to come along and express their sorrow, and I think that brought it home to everyone, seeing those thousands and thousands of people, day in, day out, all wanting to pay their respects to the people who had died."

Robinson stayed with the club for another decade, becoming a director in 1993. He witnessed the return to European football, the resignation of Kenny Dalglish and the unhappy periods under Graeme Souness and Roy Evans. It was also his congratulatory call following France's 1998 World Cup triumph that helped persuade his old friend Gerard Houllier to come to Anfield as joint manager. However, shortly after the Frenchman took sole command, Robinson himself decided to leave, handing over his duties to the current chief executive Rick Parry, and beginning a new career as an agent.

Robinson, Robert S

1903/4-11/2 (Right-half) **B** 1.10.1879, Sunderland **S** February 1904 from Sunderland **D** 13.2.1904 v Stoke C, lg **L** 1912 to Tranmere Rovers **Apps** 271, 64 **Hons** Div1 CH 1905–06; Div2 CH 1904–05 **OC** Sunderland Royal Rovers, Sunderland, Tranmere Rovers **d** n/k

PROMINENT FOOTBALLERS

R. ROBINSON,
LIVERPOOL.

AS LEADING GOAL-SCORER in the 1904–05 season, Robinson did more than most to haul the Reds out of Division Two. The ex-Sunderland striker was given a deeper role in the following year's Championship-winning campaign, then switched to half-back later in his Anfield career. He kept up a decent strike rate despite changing positions, and had found the net 66 times by the time of his 1912 transfer to Tranmere Rovers.

Rogers, Fred 'The Bullet'

1933-40 (Right/centre-half) **B** 17.4.1910, Frodsham, Cheshire **S** March 1933 from Helsby Athletic **D** 27.10.1934 v Preston NE, lg **L** Retired 1940 **Apps** 75, 0 gls **Hons** none **OC** Helsby Athletic, Tranmere R **d** 1.4.1967

Rosenthal, Ronny 'Rocket'

1989/90-1993/4 (Striker) **B** 11.10.1963, Haifa, Israel **S** March 1990 from Standard Liege, £1 million **D** 31.3.1990 v Southampton, lg **L** January 1994 to Tottenham, £250,000 **Apps** 97, 22 gls **Hons** caps for Israel **OC** Maccabi Haifa, FC Brugge, Standard Liege, Luton Town (loan), Tottenham, Watford

FEW PLAYERS HAVE MADE such an explosive impact on the title race as the former Israeli international back in 1990. There were just eight League games to go when the striker arrived from Belgium's Standard Liege – but that was enough for him to turn the season Liverpool's way. "Ronny gave us the momentum," gushed boss Kenny Dalglish afterwards. "He had five starts, three appearances as sub and seven goals. It was that which helped us to win the Championship."

The first three of those goals came at Charlton, his hat-trick capping a brilliant full debut and helping Liverpool to a 4-0 win. He was on the scoresheet as the team beat Chelsea, he grabbed a vital equaliser in a home draw with Nottingham Forest, then scored twice as the Reds hit six past Coventry on the last day of the campaign.

'Rocket' Ronny, the Israeli international who helped tilt the 1990 title race Liverpool's way

Within weeks, Dalglish paid £1 million to make Rosenthal's move permanent. However, despite his obvious ability to barge past defences and find the net, the player was largely restricted to a substitute's role.

He continued to score spectacular goals – including a memorable last-minute Anfield derby winner in 1993 – but, just six months later, moved to Tottenham for £250,000. He later played for Graham Taylor's Watford before retiring to become a football agent.

Ross, Ian

1963/4-1971/2 (Utility player) **B** 26.11.1947, Glasgow **S** 1963 from junior football; 8.8.1965 turned professional **D** 14.1.1967 v Sheffield W, lg **L** February 1972 to Aston Villa, £60,000 **Apps** 69, 4 gls **Hons** none **OC** Aston Villa, Notts County (loan), Northampton T (loan), Peterborough Utd, Wolverhampton W, Hereford Utd, Berwick Rangers, Keflavik

THE FORMER CAPTAIN of Liverpool's all-conquering Central League side always found his first-team chances limited. However, he was an effective midfielder whose ability to man-mark led to his starring appearance in the 1971 European Fairs Cup tie at Bayern Munich. Manager Bill Shankly gave him the task of shackling the great Franz Beckenbauer – a job he performed to per-

fection, as Liverpool drew 1-1 in Germany to preserve their home advantage and go through to the next round. The Glaswegian left Anfield for Villa Park the following year, captaining the resurgent Midlands team to immediate promotion from Division Three and a League Cup triumph in 1975. He later played for Peterborough, then managed Huddersfield, Berwick Rangers and the Icelandic club Keflavik.

Ross, James D

1894/5-1896/7 (Inside-right) **B** 28.3.1866, Edinburgh **S** 1894 from Preston NE, £75 **D** 13.9.1894 v Bolton W, lg (scored) **L** March 1897 to Burnley **Apps** 85, 40 gls **Hons** Div2 CH 1895–96 **OC** Edinburgh St Bernard's, Preston NE, Burnley, Manchester C **d** 12.6.1902

LIVERPOOL BROKE THE BANK to land the outstanding Scot back in 1894… paying Preston a record £75 to bring him to Anfield.

Already a two-time Championship winner when he arrived, Ross went on to captain the side and help them to the Second Division title in 1896. Ross and his brother Nick, who played for Preston and Everton, were both celebrated stars of the Victorian age. But their decision to

go south of the border caused huge criticism back in Scotland and, as a result, they were never capped for their country.

Rotation System

FORMER CHELSEA BOSS Ruud Gullit first introduced the Premiership to rotation, recruiting an enlarged squad of first-team players to Stamford Bridge in the mid-1990s. Manchester United and Newcastle quickly followed suit, with Gerard Houllier embracing the system even more enthusiastically when he took sole charge at Anfield.

It proved to be a radical departure from Liverpool's past. Under previous managers, stability was considered precious, with the club using as few senior players as injuries would allow. Under Houllier, the team sheet began to change by the week, with up to four players challenging for each individual position. Although it caused an outcry among some fans – and several players – Houllier was adamant that football had developed into a 14-man game. "Those who say football hasn't changed and that players should be able to play every three days are wrong," he informed one interviewer. "These days there are more sprints for strikers, more challenges, less space because teams are cleverer and the pace of the game has changed. There are more injuries and we need to have a bigger squad to cope with this."

It was the rigours of the 63-game Treble season that began to sway the critics. Houllier used 28 players during that marathon campaign, often using two, even three substitutes, to devastating effect for short spells of individual games. "Subs won the Champions League for Manchester United and substitutes won the Euro 2000 final for France," he explained. "You send on someone fresh and quick in the last half hour and it can make a very big difference, but the key to the whole thing is the attitude of the sub himself. He has got to share your vision, to understand how he is being used. If he is fed-up because he is on the bench, if he is not in the correct frame of mind when he gets to play, it won't work."

By the 2002–03 season Houllier had more than 30 players – most of them internationals – challenging for a first-team place. Although such fierce competition would once have caused an exodus, it's now a fact of life at all leading Premiership clubs. "One of my principles is 'Think Team First,'" says the manager. "I do not want players who only think of themselves."

Franz who? Ian Ross was on of the few players ever to eclipse Beckenbauer out on the pitch

Antonio Rowley – dream debutant

The captain and the King – Phil Taylor meets George VI at Wembley

Rowley, Antonio Camilio

1953/4-1957/8 (Inside-right) **B** 19.9.1929, Porthcawl **S** October 1953 from Stourbridge **D** 19.4.1954 v Middlesbrough, lg (scored) **L** March 1958 to Tranmere R £3,500 **Apps** 63, 39 gls **Hons** caps for Wales **OC** Wellington Town, Birmingham C, Stourbridge, Tranmere R, Bangor C, Northwich Victoria, Mossley

ONE OF A HANDFUL OF LIVERPOOL players to score a hat-trick on his debut, Rowley went on to average more than a goal every other game for the Reds. The Welshman was with the club during its Division Two doldrum years but, despite his scoring ability, was never given a prolonged first-team run. He left for Tranmere in 1958 and went on to find the net more than 50 times in 108 games for the Birkenhead club.

Royalty

THE CLUB'S LINKS WITH royalty go back to 1914, when George V became the first reigning monarch to attend an FA Cup final. Several other members of the Royal Family have been present at Liverpool's finals since that first clash with Burnley, including the Queen in 1965 and Princess Anne in 1974.

Liverpool FC has also received several Royal visits down the years. The first came in 1921 when King George and Queen Mary coupled a trip to the Aintree Grand National with an FA Cup semi-final between Cardiff and Wolves at Anfield. The Duke of Kent opened the Main Stand in 1973 and both the Queen and Prince Charles toured the ground following the 1989 Hillsborough disaster.

Ruddock, Neil 'Razor'

1993/4-1996/7 (Defender) **B** 9.5.1968, Wandsworth **S** July 1993 from Tottenham, £2.5million **D** 14.8.1993 v Sheffield Wed, lg **L** July 1998 to West Ham **Apps** 152, 12 gls **Hons** LC 1994–95; 1 cap for England **OC** Tottenham (twice), Southampton, Millwall, QPR (loan), West Ham, Crystal Palace, Swindon T (asst-manager)

THE FORMER TOTTENHAM centre-back lived up to his 'hard man' reputation the very first time he pulled on a red shirt. In a 1993 testimonial for Ronnie Whelan, he managed to fracture Peter Beardsley's cheekbone!

For a while the £2.5million signing found it difficult to settle in Graeme Souness's side, with many fans complaining about his lack of finesse on the ball. But his enthusiasm and fighting spirit gradually won over the doubters, and his late equaliser in a dramatic 3-3 fightback against Manchester United gained him a new band of admirers on the Kop.

Ruddock's best season came in 1994–95 when he was one of three central defenders used in a new formation by Roy Evans. He was a commanding presence in a back line that conceded just 36 goals throughout the Premiership campaign. And, by the time it was over, he'd also won a Coca-Cola Cup winners' medal and an England call-up.

The following season, though, the player suffered a devastating blow when he lost his place in the FA Cup Final line-up to Phil Babb –

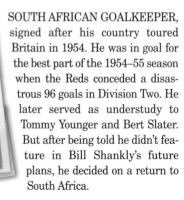

a decision which Evans later admitted was a mistake. He then injured his groin before the new campaign started and from then on spent much of his Anfield career on the treatment table.

As the the 1997–98 season drew to a close, the club sold Ruddock to West Ham. He later moved to Crystal Palace, before again teaming up with Evans as his managerial assistant at Swindon. One story about him has become legend. Although still on the playing staff, Ruddock's frame had grown ever more burly. After trying on a reputed 86 pairs of shorts, the club had to ask their Far Eastern kit manufacturers to make a specially large pair to fit him.

Rudham, Kenneth R 'Doug'

1954/5-1959/60 (Goalkeeper) **B** 3.5.1926, Johannesburg, SA **S** October 1954 from Jo'burg Rangers **D** 20.11.1954 v Nottm Forest, lg (clean sheet) **L** May 1960 to Johannesburg Ramblers **Apps** 66, 0 gls **Hons** caps for SA **OC** Johannesburg Rangers, Jo'burg Ramblers **d** August 1991, Hong Kong

SOUTH AFRICAN GOALKEEPER, signed after his country toured Britain in 1954. He was in goal for the best part of the 1954–55 season when the Reds conceded a disastrous 96 goals in Division Two. He later served as understudy to Tommy Younger and Bert Slater. But after being told he didn't feature in Bill Shankly's future plans, he decided on a return to South Africa.

Hell Razor: Neil Ruddock took no prisoners at the heart of Liverpool's defence in the 1990s

L Left Liverpool | **LC** League Cup | **n/k** not known | **OC** Other Clubs | **P** Premiership | **S** Signed | **Sb** Substitute | **SSSC** Screen Sport Super Cup | **UEFA** UEFA Cup | **WCCH** World Club Championship

175

Rush, Ian (MBE)

1980/1-1986/7 & 1988/9-1995/6 (Striker) & 2002/3-present (striker's coach) **B** 20.10.1961, St Asaph **S** April 1980 from Chester, £300,000 **D** 13.12.1980 v Ipswich T, lg **L** June 1987 to Juventus, £3.2 million; he returned in 1988 and then left for Leeds Utd in 1996, free **Apps** 659, 346 gls **Hons** EC 1983–84, 1984–85 finalist; Super Cup 1985 finalist; WCCH 1984 finalist; Div1 CH 1981–82, 1982–83, 1983–84, 1985–86, 1989–90; FAC 1985–86, 1988–89 and 1991–92, 1995–96 finalist; LC 1980–81, 1981–82, 1982–83, 1983–84, 1994–95, 1982–83 finalist; CS 1982, 1986, 1989, 1990; SSSC 1987; Footballer of the Year (twice), 73 caps for Wales **OC** Chester C, Juventus, Leeds Utd, Wrexham (player-coach), Sydney Olympic (Australia); LFC (coach)

THE WELSHMAN BEGAN his Anfield career with a rollicking – but ended it as Liverpool's all-time goalscoring king. Rush arrived from Chester for £300,000, a then record fee for a British teenager. He made just a handful of appearances in his first season, then demanded an explanation for his lack of first-team chances. "You don't score enough goals," was Bob Paisley's simple and brutal reply, "so you're not worth your place."

Rush briefly considered quitting, but decided to answer his manager by becoming more selfish in the box – the response Paisley had wanted all along. By the end of the 1981–82 campaign he had notched 30 goals in all competitions and discovered a vein of form that would cause scoring records to tumble in the seasons ahead. He was, quite simply, a goal machine, combining pace, aerial power, the ability to shoot accurately with both feet and the unerring instinct of when to be in the right place at the right time. For five years his partnership with Kenny Dalglish was the most feared in Britain, and one of the main reasons Liverpool were able to sustain their place as Europe's premier club. In a second period at Anfield – preceded by a year-long spell with Juventus – he reclaimed his position as the Reds' leading marksman and shattered what few scoring records were still left.

Rush's medal toll alone gives a pointer to his brilliant career, but doesn't begin to describe all of his achievements. With 346 goals in all competitions, he's the most prolific striker in Liverpool's history. His total of 44 FA Cup goals is a 20th century record while his five-goal total in FA Cup finals is an all-time best by an individual. He shares with Geoff Hurst the League Cup scoring record of 49 and was the first player to win that trophy five times. With 20 goals for Liverpool in Europe, only Michael Owen has scored as many. And, with 28 goals for Wales, he's his country's all-time top scorer.

But it's his exploits against Liverpool's oldest rivals that are most fondly remembered by Reds' fans. In 1982 he spearheaded Everton's destruction, finding the net four times in a 5-0 League win at Goodison. He struck twice to help win the first all-Merseyside FA Cup final in 1986 and hit another double as Liverpool again beat the Blues at Wembley three years later. By the time he left Anfield he had found the net 25 times against Everton – more than anyone else in the history of Merseyside derbies.

He had also won Europe's Golden Boot Award, a double Footballer of the Year accolade and an MBE. He may have been past his peak but, when granted a free transfer in the summer of 1996, there was a string of Premiership clubs eager for his signature. He played for Leeds, then moved to Newcastle where Dalglish had taken over as manager. In 1998, shortly after being inducted into the Premier League's Hall of Fame, he began a brief period as player-coach with Wrexham.

But after a Liverpool career that brought him every trophy worth winning – both at home and abroad – Rush's first loyalties will always lie at Anfield. In January 2003 he accepted an offer to join Gerard Houllier's backroom team as a part-time striking coach, working with the likes of Emile Heskey, Milan Baros and Michael Owen. "I'm just delighted to be back," he told reporters at Melwood. "It's a privilege to have anything to do with Liverpool Football Club."

Goal Rush: the Welsh wizard finds the target yet again

The Sandon, John Houlding's watering hole

Sandon Hotel

HUGE VICTORIAN PUB once owned by Liverpool FC founder John Houlding. Following Everton's move to Anfield in 1884, Houlding _ then their chairman – ran all their affairs from his upstairs office at the Sandon. He also made the players use the pub as their dressing room, attracting press criticism for "forcing them to make their way through hordes of fans on match days". When Houlding's new Liverpool club took over the ground eight years later, their players also used the Sandon's changing facilities. And its bowling green – now the rear car park – provided the backdrop for the first-ever photograph of the team. More than a century on, the Sandon still stands on Oakfield Road, just 50 yards from the Kop's flagpole corner. The pub's five bars and lively pre-match atmosphere make it a favourite meeting place for Reds fans.

Satterthwaite, Charles O

1899/00-1901/2 (Inside-left) **B** 1877, Cockermouth, Cumberland **S** 8.12.1899 from Burton Swifts **D** 16.12.1899 v Nottm Forest, lg **L** 1902 to New Brompton **Apps** 45, 12 gls **Hons** Div1 CH 1900–01 **OC** Workington, Bury, Burton Swifts, New Brompton, West Ham, Woolwich Arsenal **d** 25.5.1948

Saul, Percy

1906/7-08/9 (Right/left-back) **B** 1881, Rotherham **S** 30.4.1906 from Plymouth Argyle **D** 22.9.1906 v Birmingham, lg **L** 1909 to Coventry C **Apps** 83, 2gls **Hons** none **OC** Thornhill FC, Gainsborough Trinity, Plymouth Argyle, Coventry C, Rotherham County, Rotherham T **d** n/k

Record-breaker: Dean Saunders was the first Liverpool player to hit four in a European tie

Saunders, Dean N 'Deano'

1991/2-92/3 (Striker) **B** 21.6.1964, Swansea **S** July 1991 from Derby C, £2.9 million **D** 17.8.1991 v Oldham A, lg **L** October 1992 to Aston Villa, £2.3 million **Apps** 61, 26 gls **Hons** FAC 1991–92; 61 caps for Wales **OC** Swansea C, Cardiff C (loan), Brighton, Oxford Utd, Derby C, Aston Villa, Galatasary, Nottm Forest, Sheffield Utd, Bradford C, Blackburn R

GRAEME SOUNESS HAD BEEN in the manager's chair for just a matter of months when he smashed the British transfer record to land Derby's free-scoring striker. Sadly, after just one season, he was keen to send his £2.9 million signing back on his travels. Saunders certainly hadn't lost his natural scoring ability when he joined Liverpool – as his four goals in an early European tie against Kuusysi Lahti showed. But, in a team that was being constantly chopped and changed, he simply failed to settle and find consistency.

With Ian Rush and John Barnes injured for the best part of the campaign, the scoring onus fell firmly on his shoulders: he responded with just nine League goals, as Liverpool hit a miserable 47 all season.

By September 1992, Souness was convinced he'd made a mistake, and was happy to accept a £2.3million bid from Aston Villa. In one of those mystifying – and infuriating – twists, the player rediscovered his best form the very moment he arrived at the Midlands club.

Saunders, Roy

1948/9-58/9 (right-half) **B** Salford, 4.9.1930 **S** May 1948 from Hull City (amateur) **D** 7.2.1953 v Middlesbrough, lg **L** March 1959 to Swansea Town **Apps** 146, 1 gl **Hons** Youth honours for England **OC** Hull City, Swansea Town (twice, once as trainer), Ammanford FC (manager)

THE FATHER OF WELSH international striker Dean Saunders spent six seasons vying for a regular place in the Liverpool first team. Unfortunately his Anfield career coincided with the club's worst period in history, as they tried – and repeatedly failed – to climb out of Division Two. Saunders managed more than 140 appearances for the Reds, earning a reputation for speed and bravery in midfield. He moved to Swansea in 1959 and later became team trainer at The Vetch.

Saunders, Tom

AS A HEADMASTER in Liverpool's West Derby district, Saunders saw thousands of youngsters hoping to make a career in professional football.

His skill as a talent-spotter was then honed during a decade managing the Liverpool Boys side. After a spell coaching England Schoolboys, Saunders was invited to join Bill Shankly's backroom staff in 1970. He became Liverpool's Youth Development Officer, laying on trials for hundreds of youngsters – including Kenny Dalglish and Alan Hansen – and supervising the progress of apprentices as they passed through the Youth and Reserve systems on their way to the senior squad.

A key member of the Boot Room, Saunders was also charged with 'spying missions', travelling the continent to compile dossiers on Liverpool's upcoming opponents. In the early days of European competition, Shankly cared little for such analysis. But, following the 1966 mauling by Ajax, he and Bob Paisley learned how crucial it was to do their homework on likely rivals. Saunders, with his teacher's brain and ability to spot strengths and weaknesses, was the ideal man for the role. Although he retired shortly after the Heysel disaster, he retained close contacts with the club. He was made a director in 1993 and remained on the board until shortly before his death in 2001.

Savage, Robert Edward 'Ted'

1931-1937 (Right-half) **B** Jan 1912, Louth, Lincs **S** May 1931 from Lincoln C, £2500 **D** 26.9.1931 v Grimsby T, lg (scored twice) **L** Dec 1937 to Manchester Utd **Apps** 105, 2 gls **Hons** none **OC** Lincoln C, Manchester Utd, wartime guest; Carlisle Utd, West Ham Utd, Chelsea, Fulham, Millwall, Southport, York C, South Liverpool (manager) **d** 30.1.1964

Scales, John 'Bond'

1994/5-1996/7 (Centre-half) **B** 4.7.1966, Harrogate **S** September 1994 from Wimbledon, £3.5 million **D** 10.9.1994 v West Ham Utd, lg **L** December 1996 to Tottenham Hotspur, £2.5 millon **Apps** 94, 4 gls **Hons** LC 1994-95; 3 caps for England **OC** Bristol Rovers, Wimbledon, Tottenham Hotspur, Ipswich Town

AS A MEMBER OF WIMBLEDON'S 1988 FA Cup winning side, Scales brought back some uncomfortable memories for Liverpool fans. But once at Anfield his stylish play and composure quickly soon won over the doubters. In fact, he was always an unlikely member of the Dons' so-called Crazy Gang. An intelligent, pacy centre-back, he also showed great anticipation in defence and was equally adept at setting up attacks.

Roy Evans used him as one of three central defenders in the 1994–95 season – a campaign in which he collected a Coca-Cola Cup winners' medal. He went on to partner a rejuvenated

178

KEY Apps Appearances | **B** Born | **CH** Championship | **CWC** Cup Winners' Cup | **CS** Charity Shield | **D** Debut | **d** Died | **EC** European Cup | **FAC** FA Cup | **gls** Goals | **Hons** Honours | **lg** League

Mark Wright at centre-back, but then fell victim to a series of niggling injuries which prevented him from commanding a regular starting place. Evans sold him to Tottenham at the end of 1996, in a deal worth £2.6million. He stayed at White Hart Lane for nearly four years before moving to Ipswich.

Scotland

WITH 102 INTERNATIONAL appearances, Kenny Dalglish is the most capped Scottish player ever. And, with 30 goals, he also shares Denis Law's all-time scoring record. Dalglish won 55 of his caps while with Liverpool. One of his most memorable goalscoring performances came in the 2-0 World Cup qualifying victory over Wales in 1977 – a game actually played at Anfield.

Liverpool's other notable Scottish internationals down the years include Alex Raisbeck, Billy Liddell, Ian St John, Graeme Souness, Alan Hansen and Steve Nicol. Former Scotland captain Gary McAllister had already announced his retirement from international football by the time he arrived at Anfield.

Shaken not stirred, the stylish John Scales was nicknamed "Bond" because he always kept his cool

Great Scot: Kenny Dalglish won a record 102 international caps for Scotland

Scott, Elisha

1912/3-1933/4 (Goalkeeper) **B** 24.8.1894, Belfast, NI **S** 3.9.1912
from Broadway Utd, Belfast **D** 1.1.1913 v Newcastle Utd, lg (clean
sheet) **L** 25.6.1934 to Belfast Celtic as player/manager **Apps** 468 +
15 WW1, 0 gls **Hons** Div1 CH 1921–22, 1922–23; Lancs Cup
1918–19, 1919–20, 1930–31; Liv Snr Cup 1914–15; CS 1922 finalist; 31 caps for NI **OC** Belfast Boys Brigade, Linfield, Broadway Utd,
Belfast Celtic **d** 16.5.1959

THE LEGENDARY ULSTERMAN spent more
than 20 years at Anfield, earning a reputation
as the country's – and possibly the world's – best
'keeper.

His elder brother Billy – who kept goal for
Everton in the 1906 FA Cup final – tipped
Liverpool off about the 17-year-old's extraordinary talent. Manager Tom Watson tempted him
across the Irish Sea as an understudy for his
Scottish international Kenny Campbell. But, by
the outbreak of World War One, Scott was
already staking his claim to be first-choice No.1.

When the hostilities ended he was duly
installed between the posts, attracting rave
reviews from football writers around the country. "He has the eye of an eagle, the swift movement of a panther when flinging himself at a
shot and the clutch of a vice when gripping the
ball," wrote one. Playing behind an equally formidable defence – comprising the likes of Don
McKinlay and Eph Longworth – he was quick
and agile enough to deny even the most-feared
strikers. During Liverpool's successive
Championship years in 1922 and 1923, he conceded just 61 goals in 81 games.

Scott was also the Kop's favourite, and one of
the first players to inspire his own chant
("Lisha, Lisha") from the terraces. He was
famous for his Merseyside derby duels with
Everton's Dixie Dean – and for the bad language
which so disgusted his churchgoing teammate
Jimmy 'Parson' Jackson.

He was also noted for being 'careful' with his
cash – even walking the three miles from
Anfield to catch the Mersey ferry home, rather
than paying for a tram.

Although his form began to fade by the early
1930s his popularity never waned. Reds supporters were outraged when Everton made a
£250 bid for his signature, and forced the
Anfield board to reject the offer by bombarding
the *Liverpool Echo* with protest letters.

But even fan-power wasn't enough to stop
him leaving when his old club Belfast Celtic
asked him to be player-manager. Scott left in
1934 after making 468 appearances and winning 27 Northern Ireland caps. He played his
final international game two years later, at the
age of 42, and subsequently retired from management in 1949.

All-time legend Elisha Scott had the "clutch of a vice when handling the ball"

'Scouser Tommy'

EPIC TERRACE ANTHEM in honour of Liverpool soldiers who died at the battle of Spion Kop and in the Second World War desert campaign against the Nazis. Self-penned by the Kop's wordsmiths, Scouser Tommy's first four stanzas are sung to the tune of the American ballad *Red River Valley*. The remaining verses borrow the tune of the Ulster Orangemen's 'The Sash My Father Wore'.

Although still sung regularly – particularly by Liverpool's travelling supporters – 'Scouser Tommy"s heyday was in the early 1980s, when Sammy Lee was often filmed teaching his team-mates the words after numerous Wembley victories. It was also in that period that the Kop added an entirely new verse – to celebrate a legendary Ian Rush performance at Goodison Park.

Lyrics

Let me tell you the story of a poor boy
Who was sent far away from his home
To fight for his king and his country
And also the old folks back home

So they put him in a Highland Division
Sent him off to a far foreign land
Where the flies swarm around in their thousands
And there's nothing to see but the sand

As the battle was starting next morning
Under a Libyan Sun
I remember that poor Scouser Tommy
He was shot by an old Nazi gun

As he lay on the battlefield dying (dying, dying)
With the blood gushing out of his head (of his head)
As he lay on the battlefield dying (dying, dying)
These were the last words he said...

Oh! I am a Liverpudlian
I come from Spion Kop
I like to sing, I like to shout
I go there quite a lot (every week)

We support a team that's dressed in red
A team that you all know
A team that we call LIVERPOOL
And to glory we will go

We've won the League
We've won the Cup
And we've been to Europe, too
We played the Toffees for a laugh
And we left them feeling blue (five-nil)

1, 2, 1-2-3, 1-2-3-4, five-nil
Rush scored one, Rush scored two, Rush scored three
And Rush scored four, La, la la, la...La, la, la, La, la.

The Voice of Anfield – George Sephton is the man for a tongue-twister

Screen Sport Super Cup

A SHORT-LIVED TOURNAMENT for the English clubs who would have qualified for Europe had it not been for UEFA's post-Heysel ban. Liverpool beat Southampton, Tottenham and Norwich in the knock-out stages, before meeting Everton in the 1986 final. They recorded a 7-2 aggregate victory over the Blues, winning 3-1 at Anfield and 4-1 at Goodison.

Sephton, George

THE SO-CALLED 'VOICE OF ANFIELD' began his PA announcing duties in the 1971–72 season, just as Kevin Keegan was making his Liverpool debut. His unmistakably rich tones have guided fans through thousands of half-time scores, dedications and 'Golden Goal' competition winners since then. And, as the man charged with reading out the team line-ups, he's also had to deal with some memorable European tongue-twisters.

"Luckily I took Russian and Spanish at school, which means I can cope with most East European and Latin names," says the man behind the Tannoy. "But I've always had trouble with the Greek ones. When we played AEK Athens back in the 1970s, they made five late changes and used a set of subs who weren't listed in the programme. It was a nightmare."

The influx of overseas players into the Premiership means domestic games aren't as simple any more either: "The corkers are the likes of Kishishev at Charlton, or – my favourite – Svetaslav Todorov, once of West Ham and now at Portsmouth. And the big worry now is the number of Chinese players who are on their way up." As the man who wrestled successfully with the likes of Mylnarczyk from Poland's Widzew Lodz, and Puotiniemi from the Finnish side Oulu Palloseura, George will surely handle it.

Shankly, Bill

ANYONE DOUBTING THE lasting influence of Liverpool's legendary manager need only look to the 2003 Worthington Cup final for proof. There were hundreds of banners on display as the Reds took on Manchester United at the Millenium Stadium. But the flag that caught the eye showed Shankly in his most famous pose: arms held aloft, acknowledging the cheers of his adoring fans.

It's now nearly 30 years since he relinquished control at Anfield, and more than two decades since his death, yet he remains the most revered figure ever to be associated with Liverpool FC. His sayings have entered into common language. And team and fans alike still look to his period in charge for inspiration.

Just how did a miner's son from Ayrshire come to command such enduring respect, affection and loyalty on Merseyside? He brought success, without a doubt, but his successor Bob Paisley enjoyed even more. He landed Liverpool's first FA Cup, but later managers won European Cups and Trebles. What none of them could ever match, though, was Shankly's unique affinity with the fans. "I understand the Liverpool people," he told one interviewer. "They're spirited, they have life in them, they're arrogant, they're cocky and proud – and I'm just the same as them."

Those characteristics were evident in his days as a player but it was at Liverpool that they found an echo on the terraces. From the day he arrived in December 1959 he spoke of the fans' importance in making Liverpool great again. His ambition was to build Anfield into a "bastion of invincibility", and he wanted those who stood on the terraces to help strike fear into all Liverpool's opponents. As they came up with the vocal backing, the new manager began delivering his own side of the bargain. "I learned more in his first three months than I'd done in the previous seven years that I'd been a pro," said ex-captain Ronnie Moran. "He was the real start of this football club. It needed a bloke like him to explode it on its way."

Explode it certainly did. By 1962, Liverpool were back in the top flight. By 1964 they were Champions. Shankly had put together a side brimming with home-grown talent and big-name buys from outside. He had trained them to be the fittest players in Britain, instilled in

"Spirited, arrogant, cocky and proud" – Ayrshire-born Shankly believed he had a Liverpudlian's personality

them a massive self-belief – and constantly reminded them of the debt they owed their supporters: "You are going to win today because you must not disappoint the finest spectators any club has in the world," he told them before that famous 1965 FA Cup clash with Leeds. "If necessary, you should be prepared to die for them."

Victory at Wembley, plus another Championship success a year later, guaranteed Shankly his place in Anfield folklore. But it was his ability to build a second great team that marked him out as one of the all-time greats of British football management. By the turn of the decade, Liverpool had experienced four trophy-less years. Showing a new ruthlessness, Shankly axed many of his old favourites and invested in a fresh crop of exciting youngsters. Around such figures as Ray Clemence, Kevin Keegan and John Toshack, he constructed a side that went on to dominate the domestic game throughout the early 1970s. They also landed a European trophy for the first time ever.

But in July 1974, with another FA Cup safely in the bag, Shankly shocked everyone at the club. Citing tiredness, and a wish to look after his wife Nessie, he announced his departure just weeks before the start of the new season. The news every fan had secretly dreaded for years was suddenly, and horribly, real.

Sadly, while Liverpool coped unexpectedly well with the loss, he quickly came to regret his decision. Almost from the day he announced his decision until his sudden death seven years later, he missed involvement with the club. Unable to find a new role at Liverpool, he took up a string of consultancy jobs with other clubs. But, as Paisley later wrote, it didn't satisfy him: "There was no way he could really be a part-time adviser. He had to be completely involved or he was like a caged lion. This, I'm sure, caused him a great deal of frustration." Shankly's health suddenly deteriorated at the age of 68. His death from a heart attack in 1981 robbed the game of its greatest character. But, to this day, he is the guiding spirit behind Liverpool FC.

S

L Left Liverpool | **LC** League Cup | **n/k** not known | **OC** Other Clubs | **P** Premiership | **S** Signed | **Sb** Substitute | **SSSC** Screen Sport Super Cup | **UEFA** UEFA Cup | **WCCH** World Club Championship

183

end. Tom Murphy's bronze statue, sponsored by Carlsberg in 1998, has become the favourite backdrop for fans wanting their photographs taken outside the ground. It shows the great man with arms outstretched and Liverpool scarf around his neck. And it bears the simple phrase: 'He Made The People Happy'.

Sheedy, Kevin M

1980/1-1981/2 (Midfield) **B** 21.10.1959, Builth Wells **S** July 1978 from Hereford Utd, £80,000 **D** 14.2.1981 v Birmingham C, lg **L** May 1982 to Everton, £100,000 **Apps** 5, 2 gls **Hons** 45 caps for Rep I **OC** Hereford Utd, Everton, Newcastle Utd, Blackpool

LIKE JOHNNY MORRISSEY a generation earlier, Sheedy was a talented player who went on to greater things across Stanley Park. The former Hereford apprentice made just one full appearance for the Reds when Blues boss Howard Kendall offered £100,000 for his signature. He then waved goodbye to reserve team football to become one of the driving forces behind Kendall's resurgent Everton during the mid-1980s.

An intelligent left-sided midfielder with a superb shot, Sheedy went on to win Championship medals in 1985 and 1987. He also helped lift the 1985 European Cup Winners Cup and won a clutch of Republic of Ireland caps.

Looking at Liverpool's midfield during his Anfield career, it's easy to see why he was 'the one that got away'. Competing with the likes of Kennedy, McDermott and Case, then Souness, Lee and Whelan could never have been easy, even for a player of international potential. However, in the modern era of rotation, it's unlikely that Liverpool would let a player of such quality slip through their fingers.

Sheldon, John 'Jackie'

1913/14-1921/2 (Outside-right) **B** 1887, Clay Cross **S** Nov 1913 from Manchester Utd **D** 29.11.1913 v Tottenham, lg **L** Retired 1922 through injury **Apps** 147, 20 gls **Hons** FAC 1913–14 finalist **OC** Nuneaton, Manchester Utd, WWI guest: Fulham, Forest **d** 19.3.1941

Shelley, Albert

POST-WAR TEAM TRAINER who helped manager George Kay whip the 1946–47 Championship side into shape. Shelley remained on the backroom staff for many years and had the distinction of leading the 1950 FA Cup Final team out at Wembley, due to Kay's illness. It was his retirement in 1959 that paved the way for Bob Paisley to become trainer.

Shankly Gates

A PERMANENT MEMORIAL to the former manager, put in place the year after his death. The wrought iron structure, standing at the corner of the Main Stand and Anfield Road End, was unveiled by Bill's widow Nessie, who herself died in 2002. The image of the gates – topped out with the words You'll Never Walk Alone – is replicated on the official Liverpool FC crest.

Shankly Statue

ANFIELD'S SECOND SHANKLY memorial stands at the entrance to the Museum and Tour Centre at the Kop

Top: the Shankly gates mark the entrance to Anfield; right: the Great Man immortalised in bronze

The goalkeeper who packed a punch – Cyril Sidlow in action during the 1940s

Shepherd, J.William 'Bill'

1945/6-1951/2 (Right-back) **B** 25.9.1920, Liverpool **S** December 1945 from Elm Park FC **D** 21.8.1948 v Aston Villa, lg **L** 1952 to Wigan Athletic **Apps** 58, 0gls **OC** Elm Park FC, Wigan A **d** 1983

Shone, Daniel

1915/6-1927/8 (Centre-forward) **B** 27.4.1892, Wirral **S** 1915 from Earl FC (amateur); prof May 1921 **D** 27.8.1921 v Sunderland, lg **L** June 1928 to West Ham **Apps** 81, 26 gls **Hons** Div1 CH 1921–22 **OC** Earle FC, Grayson's Garston, West Ham, Coventry C **d** 1974

Shortest Players

UNRELIABLE STATISTICS FOR Liverpool's earliest teams make it impossible to name the smallest player ever to turn out for the Reds. Raby Howell, a Sheffield-born gypsy who played in the 1890s, is described in some early reports as "diminutive", while Ronald Orr, a tiny Scottish international who played before the First World War, was often referred to in print as "The wee Orr".

Two other Scots from the Victorian era, James McBride and Robert Neil, were said to have had their height recorded at 5ft 4in. In Neil's case that would have been remarkable, given that he played at centre-half throughout his career with Liverpool, Hibernian and Rangers. Since World War Two, Liverpool have fielded very few players under 5 ft 8in. They include Bob Paisley, Brian Hall and Sammy Lee (all 5ft 7in), Roy Saunders and Nick Barmby (5ft 6½in) and the 1950s winger Mervyn Jones, who measured just 5ft 4in.

Sidlow, Cyril

1945/6-1951/2 (Goalkeeper) **B** 26.11.1915, Colwyn Bay, Wales **S** February 1946 from Wolves, £4,000 **D** 31.8.1946 v Sheffield Utd, lg (clean sheet) **L** August 1952 to New Brighton **Apps** 165, 0 gls **Hons** Div1 CH 1946–47; FAC 1949–50 finalist; 7 caps for Wales **OC** Llandudno, Colwyn Bay, Wolves, wartime guest for: Notts C, Wrexham, Darlington, Burnley, Hartlepool Utd, New Brighton

GOALKEEPER IN LIVERPOOL'S 1946–47 Championship-winning side. The Welsh international came from Wolves in a £4,000 deal – then a record fee for a 'keeper – and remained an Anfield regular for nearly five years. He was a great crowd favourite, with a reputation for throwing the ball as powerfully as other goalkeepers could kick it.

L Left Liverpool | **LC** League Cup | **n/k** not known | **OC** Other Clubs | **P** Premiership | **S** Signed | **Sb** Substitute | **SSSC** Screen Sport Super Cup | **UEFA** UEFA Cup | **WCCH** World Club Championship

185

Singing

TERRACE SINGING WAS FIRST heard at Anfield almost a century ago, as fans celebrated their team's 1906 Championship victory. A year later, reporters described "weird, unearthly cries" on the newly built Kop – although the noise came from Blackburn Rovers supporters rather than Liverpool's. It was the covering of the Kop in 1928 that gave Anfield a distinctive sound, as the roars of almost 30,000 fans were amplified by a cantilever metal roof. But it wasn't until the early 1960s that those roars were turned into rhythmic chants and songs.

The televised 1962 World Cup finals in Chile provided the supporters with their inspiration. The sight of thousands of South Americans performing their 'Bra-zil – cha cha cha' routine was quickly taken up and customised by the Kopites. Film of the Reds winning promotion in 1962 shows the players going up to the Main Stand to collect the Second Division Championship, then joining the fans in a rous-ing rendition of 'Liv-er-pool – clap, clap, clap'.

The repertoire grew rapidly the following season. An FA Cup fourth round replay against Burnley in February 1963 brought the crowd's first rendition of early Beatles songs. A few weeks on, they turned The Routers' surfing hit 'Let's Go' into a celebration of their idol Ian St John. By the end of the year they were welcoming the entire team out to a spine-tingling version of 'You'll Never Walk Alone'.

Nobody was more delighted with this development than Bill Shankly. Seeing how the noise intimidated opposing teams, he positively encouraged the supporters to get involved. It was during a guest appearance on Radio Four's *Desert Island Discs* that he revealed how Gerry Marsden's song inspired him and his players as the noise filtered through to the Anfield dressing room. According to Bob Paisley's account, Shankly took the pre-match anthem particularly seriously – and once complained bitterly that the crowd "should have given us another verse".

The Anfield fans were gaining national celebrity status. On the last day of the 1963–64 season, the BBC's *Panorama* programme visited the "birthplace of a new cultural phenomenon". "The 28,000 people standing here on the Kop begin singing together – they seem to know intuitively when to start," the reporter told his millions of viewers. "Throughout the match they invent new words, usually within the framework of old Liverpool songs. But, even when they begin singing these new words, they do so with one immediate, huge voice. They seem, instinctively, to be in touch with one another."

Not surprisingly, the trend was quickly followed at every major football ground throughout Britain. But, as one football historian later noted, "The Liverpool crowds have been imitated but never adequately, no other fans being able to match their invention, to say nothing of the sustained indecency." More than any other terrace, the Kop had wordsmiths who seemed able to take any tune and give it a football twist. Great European occasions often brought out the best in them, starting with the night when Inter

The real Mersey Sound: Reds fans in full cry before the UEFA Cup tie against Celtic, 2002–03

Milan were told to 'Go Back To Italy', to the tune of 'Santa Lucia'. A decade on, when facing French Champions St Etienne, the Kop gave a first airing to 'Allez Les Rouges'. For the 1977 European Cup final, 'Arrividerci Roma', became 'We're on Our Way To Roma'.

The Kop's wall of sound finally began to subside in the 1980s, when safety regulations cut its capacity by more than 10,000. The later introduction of seats reduced the noise further, as small groups of singers found themselves isolated from each other in different parts of the stand. But, in recent seasons, singing has made a major comeback, thanks to renewed success on the field and the introduction of regular mosaics and flag nights. Away from Anfield, Liverpool's travelling support is the most vocal in Britain – as a packed Parkhead found when it was outsung by just 2,500 Reds fans in 2003. And on the Kop, the wit and invention remains unmatched anywhere. Just who else could have transformed the naff 1980s party hit 'Agadoo' into a hymn of praise to El Hadji Diouf?

Vladimir Smicer, aka 'Vlad the Impala' for his pacy style, is one of three Czechs to have played for LFC

Slater, Robert 'Bert'

1959-1962 (Goalkeeper) **B** 5.5.1936, Musselburgh, Midlothian **S** June 1959 from Falkirk, exchange for Tommy Younger **D** 22.8.1959 v Cardiff C, lg **L** July 1962 to Dundee **Apps** 111, 0 gls **Hons** Div2 CH 1961–62; Scotland U-23 honours **OC** Airth Castle Rovers, Tranent Juniors, Falkirk, Dundee, Watford (player and coach)

Smicer, Vladimir

1999/00-present (Midfield/forward) **B** 24.5.1973, Degin, Czech Rep **S** 1.7.1999 from Lens, £3.75million **D** 7.8.1999 v Sheff Wed, lg **Apps** 143, 14 gls **Hons** UEFA 2000–01; FAC 2000–01; LC 2000–01, 2002–03; Super Cup 2001; CS 2001, 2002 finalist; 61 caps for Czech Rep **OC** Slavia Prague, Lens

THE CZECH REPUBLIC international first made his mark at Euro 96, with a series of skilful displays helping his country reach the final. A year later he moved from Slavia Prague to RC Lens and was a driving force behind the French club's first domestic title triumph.

He teamed up with his close friend Patrik Berger at the start of the 1999–2000 season, helping Liverpool plug the midfield gap left by Steve McManaman. He initially found it difficult to adjust to the pace of the Premiership, but by his second season in England was regularly showing the form that had made him such a class performer for his country.

Fast, agile and tricky, Smicer performed consistently well throughout the Treble campaign, giving the Reds width and fresh attacking options. Gerard Houllier saw him playing a key part in the Reds' future, and duly offered him a new contract tying him to Anfield until 2005.

Smith, James 'Jim'

1929/30-1932/33 (Centre-forward) **B** 12.3.1902, Old Kilpatrick, Dunbartonshire **S** Sept 1929 from Ayr Utd, £5,500 **D** 21.9.1929 v Man Utd, lg (scored twice) **L** July 1932 to Tunbridge Wells Rangers **Apps** 62, 38 gls **Hons** none **OC** Dumbarton Harp, Clydebank, Rangers, Ayr Utd, Tunbridge Wells Rangers, Bristol R, Newport C, Notts C, Dumbarton (player/manager) **d** 1975

AS A STRIKER WITH AYR United, found the net an incredible 66 times in the 1927–28 season. Liverpool paid a reputed £5,500 for his services two years later and he went on to average more than a goal every two games for the Reds. After just two seasons at Anfield he moved to Tunbridge Wells Rangers, then a succession of clubs including Bristol Rovers, Newport County and Dumbarton. Smith emigrated to the USA following the outbreak of World War Two – and to this day holds the British seasonal goalscoring record.

Smith, John T 'Jack'

1951/2-53/4 (Centre-forward) **B** 21.12.1927, Birkenhead **S** March 1951 from Brombrough Pool **D** 29.9.1951 v Derby Cy, lg (scored) **L** May 1954 to Torquay Utd, £1,500 **Apps** 59, 14 gls **Hons** none **OC** Brombrough Pool (twice), Torquay Utd

Smith, Sir John W (CBE)

AS LIVERPOOL FC'S CHAIRMAN from 1973 to 1990, Sir John was in charge of the club as it enjoyed its greatest triumphs, and suffered its worst tragedies. He served for many years as a director before his appointment to the top job, and within just 12 months had to tell a disbelieving world that Bill Shankly was quitting. In persuading Bob Paisley to take on the role, he

Smith oversees Kevin Keegan's move

Man of Iron Tommy Smith, but his tough reputation belied his subtle footballing skills

KEY **Apps** Appearances | **B** Born | **CH** Championship | **CWC** Cup Winners' Cup | **CS** Charity Shield | **D** Debut | **d** Died | **EC** European Cup | **FAC** FA Cup | **gls** Goals | **Hons** Honours | **lg** League

performed a masterstroke. And, in lobbying for the untried Kenny Dalglish to replace Joe Fagan, he again showed his ability to spot managerial potential.

Sir John was a respected administrator whose talent was recognised with an invitation to chair the Sports Council in 1985. That same year he helped steer Liverpool through the tragedy of Heysel, co-operating with the Belgian authorities to help find the fans responsible. Four years on, he was also one of the key figures who dictated Liverpool's widely admired response to Hillsborough. In 1990, he handed over the chairmanship of the club to fellow director Noel White. He remained an active member of the board for the remaining five years of his life.

Smith, Tommy

1960/1-1977/8 (Midfield/defender) **B** 5.4.1945, Liverpool **S** May 1960 from Liverpool Schools **D** 8.5.1963 v Birmingham C, lg **L** August 1978 to Swansea C **Apps** 638, 48 gls **Hons** EC 1976–77; UEFA 1972–73, 1975–76; Super Cup 1977; CWC finalist 1965–66, Div1 CH 1965–66, 1972–73, 1965–76, 1976–77; FAC 1964–65, 1973–74, 1970–71 finalist, 1976–77 finalist; LC finalist 1977–78; CS 1965, 1966, 1974, 1971 finalist; 1 cap for England **OC** Liverpool Schools, Swansea C

BORN JUST A FEW STREETS away from Anfield, the boyhood Liverpudlian broke into his beloved team as a teenager and soon earned a reputation as the hardest man in football. But, for all his tough-guy image, Smith was a player of rare talent, whose subtle touches played a huge part in the development of the Reds' famous passing game.

Bill Shankly gave him his Euro debut in the 1964 European Cup tie against Anderlecht, judging correctly that his "additional defender" role would confuse the Belgian champions. What he didn't guess was that the 19-year-old would then demand a regular first-team place on the strength of this outing. It was the start of an intense, if often prickly, relationship between the two men, and an event that later led the manager to declare, "Tommy Smith could start a riot in a graveyard."

Dressing room bust-ups aside, the so-called Anfield Iron gave his boss a decade of unfailing service. He was one of the few players to survive Shankly's ruthless 1970 first-team cull and, whether playing in midfield, central defence or

We've only got one Song: Cameroon defender Rigobert Song enjoyed a cult following

at full-back, never showed anything less than 100 per cent commitment. As captain of the 1973 UEFA Cup-winning side, he became the first Liverpool player ever to get his hands on a European trophy. But his greatest moment came four years later, as he emerged as an unlikely hero in the European Cup final against Borussia Moenchengladbach.

He was making his 600th Liverpool appearance on that night in Rome. With an hour gone and the game all-square at 1-1, the Reds won a corner. "Steve Heighway drove this ball over – it's got to be the greatest ball I've ever seen, and at a perfect height," he later recalled. "I'm not the fastest person in the world but I can steal a yard on anyone, and the defence just seemed to stand there like they were frozen, including the goalkeeper. So I went in and met the ball with my head – and as soon as I hit it I knew I was on target."

The goal set Liverpool on their way to their most famous victory ever. Two nights later, Smith led the team out for his dream testimonial in front of a packed and delirious Anfield. The TV and press journalists were out in force, but the man of the moment had just one quote: "I'm changing my name to Roy of the Rovers!"

After one more year with the club, Smith moved to Swansea, then finished his career

with the American club Tampa Bay Rowdies. He later enjoyed a spell on the Anfield backroom staff before becoming involved in several business ventures. Today, sadly crippled with injury from his playing days, he works as a newspaper columnist and after-dinner speaker.

Smyth, Samuel

1952/3-1954/5 (Centre-forward) **B** 25.2.1925, Belfast **S** Dec 1952 from Stoke C, £12,000 **D** 3.1.1953 v Stoke C, lg **L** January 1955 to Bangor, £2,000 **Apps** 44, 20 gls **Hons** Caps for NI **OC** Linfield, Dundela FC, Wolves, Stoke C, Bangor

Song, Rigobert

1999-2000/1 (Defender) **B** 1.7.1976, Nkenlicock, Cameroon **S** January 1999 from Salernitana **D** 30.1.1999 v Coventry C, lg **L** 8.11.2000 to West Ham, £2.5 million and Daniel Sjolund swap **Apps** 38, 0 gls **Hons** 67 caps for Cameroon **OC** Tonnerre Yaounde, Metz, Salernitana, West Ham, Koln (loan), Lens

THE CAMEROON INTERNATIONAL spent less than two years at Anfield but established a cult following with his buccaneering style. He arrived fresh from a second World Cup finals appearance for his country. The recruitment of Sami Hyypia meant he was unable to play in his preferred position of centre-half, but he put in impressive performances at right-back and was regularly seen charging up the flanks. Sadly, as the 1999–2000 season progressed, his form faded and he became increasingly error-prone. Gerard Houllier sold him to West Ham for £2.5million shortly after the campaign ended.

Souness, Graeme J

1977/8-1983/4 (Midfield) 199/2-1993/4 (Manager) **B** 6.5.1953, Edinburgh **S** January 1978 from Middlesbrough, £352,000 **D** 14.1.1978 v WBA, lg **L** June 1984 to Sampdoria, £650,000 **Apps** 359, 56 gls **Hons** EC 1977–78, 1980–81, 1983–84; Super Cup 1978 finalist; Div1 CH 1978–79, 1979–80, 1981–82, 1982–83, 1983–84; LC 1980–81, 1981–82, 1982–83, 1983–84; CS 1979, 1980; FAC 1991–92 (as manager); 54 Scotland caps **OC** Tottenham, Boro, Sampdoria, Rangers (player/manager), Blackburn R (manager)

COMBINING STRENGTH and subtlety, commitment and cunning, Souness was possibly the most complete midfielder British football ever produced. If Reds' fans were given the chance to pick an all-time Liverpool XI, his name would be among the first on the team sheet. If former players were given the opportunity, many would make him captain.

Signing for a bargain £352,000 fee in 1978, the Scottish international made an immediate impact, dominating the midfield, protecting his defence and getting forward to score with some spectacular strikes. He supplied the pass for Kenny Dalglish's winner at the 1978 European Cup final, missed just one game in the majestic 1978–79 Championship season and played a pivotal role as the Reds stormed to a domestic and European Double in 1981.

Awarded the captaincy shortly afterwards, Souness made sure that his win-at-all-costs attitude was adopted by all his team-mates. With him as the driving force, Liverpool stormed to three more Championships and cemented a four-year domination of the League Cup. In 1984 he secured the last of those knock-out trophies, hitting the winner in the final replay against Everton. Two months later he scored from the spot as the team won their European Cup final penalty shoot-out against Roma.

That night marked the end of his Liverpool playing career. The following season he moved to the Italian Serie A side Sampdoria for £650,000, broadening his own horizons but leaving a gap at Anfield that was virtually impossible to plug. Two years later he took the manager's chair at Rangers, using his ambition and determination to haul the Glasgow club back to the summit of Scottish football – and to keep it there for the next four seasons.

His huge success at Ibrox made him the obvious candidate to succeed Kenny Dalglish as Liverpool boss in 1991. But, for all his previous success as a player, his managerial reign became associated with underperformance, poor transfer dealings and dressing room disquiet. In a turbulent 33 months, he sold 18 squad members and brought 15 in. He shipped out good players, some still at their peak, and replaced them with big-money signings who often failed to live up to expectations. It was the club's busiest ever period in the transfer market. In an interview several years later, Souness himself admitted that he'd tried to do too much too soon.

On the plus side, he did land the 1992 FA Cup, despite sudden health problems that resulted in heart surgery just days before the trip to Wembley. He also demonstrated his ability to spot and nurture young talent, giving debuts to the likes of Steve McManaman, Jamie Redknapp and Robbie Fowler. But his efforts were never enough to prevent Liverpool's seemingly endless slide into mid-table mediocrity. In January 1994, three days after the team's humiliating Third Round FA Cup defeat by lowly Bristol City, manager and club parted by mutual consent.

His unhappy experiences behind him, he went on to manage Benfica and the Turkish club Galatasaray. He then made a return to the domestic game with Southampton, before leading his new team Blackburn to League Cup victory and European competition. Souness has undoubtedly developed into a successful and respected Premiership manager. But it's for his awesome playing abilities that he'll always be admired at Anfield.

Souness, the no-nonsense boss

Spackman, Nigel J

1986/7-1988/9 (Midfield) **B** 2.12.1960, Romsey **S** February 1987 from Chelsea, £400,000 **D** 25.2.1987 v Southampton, LC **L** Feb 1989 to QPR, £500,000 **Apps** 63, 0 gls **Hons** Div1 CH 1987–88; FAC 1987–88 finalist; LC 1986–87 finalist **OC** Andover Town, AFC Bournemouth, Chelsea (twice), QPR

VERSATILE MIDFIELDER WHOSE valuable contribution to the 1987–88 Championship campaign is often overlooked. The ex-Chelsea star made 27 League appearances during that exhilarating season, filling in for the injured Ronnie Whelan and playing one of the games of his life in the famous 5-0 destruction of Nottingham Forest.

Whelan's return made it difficult for him to

Determination, skill and commitment were the hallmarks of Graeme Souness's game

retain his place the following year and, when QPR offered him the chance of regular first-team football, he decided to leave. He went on to enjoy a second spell at Chelsea, before managing Sheffield United and Barnsley. He's now a regular football pundit with Sky Sports.

Speedie, David

1990-91 (Forward/midfield) **B** 20.2.1960, Glenrothes, Fife **S** 30.1.1991 from Coventry, £700,000 **D** 3.2.1991 v Manchester Utd, lg (scored) **L** August 1991 to Blackburn R, £500,000 **Apps** 14, 6 gls **Hons** 10 caps for Scotland **OC** Barnsley, Darlington, Chelsea, Coventry C, Blackburn R, Southampton, Birmingham C, WBA (loan), West Ham (loan), Leicester C

WITH EARLY GOALS AGAINST Manchester United and Everton, the well-travelled Scot made the brightest possible opening for Liverpool. But, as an early casualty of the Souness reign, Speedie lasted at Anfield for less than a year.

He was always considered one of Kenny Dalglish's odder signings. The wrong side of 30 when he arrived from Coventry City, Speedie had a reputation as a combative player who wound up referees and opposing fans. Aggression and commitment aside, he had little to offer the Reds' attack – and Souness wasted no time in offloading him to Blackburn.

Spicer, Edward W

1937/8-1952/3 (Left-back/wing-half) **B** 20.9.1922, Liverpool **S** 1937 from school football **D** 30.1.1946 v Bolton W, FAC **L** Retired through injury 1954 **Apps** 168, 2 gls **Hons** FAC 1949–50 finalist; England schoolboy honours **OC** Liverpool schools

TOUGH FORMER ROYAL MARINE who just missed out on a 1946–47 Championship medal to go with his WW2 decorations because of too few appearances. The Liverpool-born half-back was a first-teamer for several years and made the line-up for the 1950 FA Cup Final against Arsenal.

L Left Liverpool | **LC** League Cup | **n/k** not known | **OC** Other Clubs | **P** Premiership | **S** Signed | **Sb** Substitute | **SSSC** Screen Sport Super Cup | **UEFA** UEFA Cup | **WCCH** World Club Championship

191

Spion Kop

FOOTBALL'S MOST FAMOUS enclosure began life as a ramshackle wooden stand on what was once known as the Oakfield, or Walton Breck Road end of Anfield. With attendances booming during the 1905–06 Championship season, the Liverpool board decided to demolish it and replace it with a huge bank of rubble and cinders, capable of housing 28,000 spectators.

It derived its name from Spioenkop, a hill in South Africa's Natal province and scene of one of the bloodiest battles of the Boer War six years earlier. During that battle, 320 troops from the Lancashire Fusiliers were killed and more than 500 wounded. As many of the victims had been recruited from Merseyside, it seemed a fitting tribute to their memory. Several other grounds also had their own 'Kops', notably Arsenal, but Liverpool's rapidly became the most famous.

Later, it was extended further and topped out with a 45,000 square-foot cantilever roof. With a height of 125 feet and a slope measuring 425 x 131 feet, it was the largest covered terrace in Europe. The Football League's President declared the new Kop open on August 25, 1928, as Liverpool celebrated with a 3-0 victory over Bury. Further limited modernisation took place afterwards – notably the fitting of concrete steps and iron crush-barriers after World War Two – but its image as a vast, grey, swaying terrace remained unchanged for generations.

By 1980, having gained worldwide fame for its passion, wit and sportsmanship, the Kop succumbed to new safety regulations that reduced its capacity to 21,500. Almost a decade on, it was cut to just 16,480, with its fans penned in behind brutal steel fencing. Happily, those fences were torn down in the wake of the 1989 Hillsborough disaster, but it was that same tragedy that led to the once unthinkable.

On April 30, 1994, the Kop played host to its last standing spectators, as Liverpool took on Norwich in the last home game of the season. Legendary figures from the club's past – including Albert Stubbins, Ian Callaghan and Joe Fagan – came on the pitch to say their farewells. Within weeks, it was levelled to make way for a single-tiered grandstand with 12,000 seats.

➲ Also see: Anfield, Singing

Sponsors

LIVERPOOL'S ORIGINAL SPONSORS were the Japanese hi-fi firm Hitachi, whose 1979 deal was the first-ever involving an English League club. Four years later the club negotiated a new deal that put the Crown Paints name on the team shirts, and in 1988 the electrical goods company Candy took over. They were then succeeded by Carlsberg, who've been team sponsors since 1992.

The new Kop has become famous for its mosaics; inset: how it used to look before seats were installed

Stanley House

IMPOSING RED-AND-WHITE brick structure, situated at 73 Anfield Road, opposite the entrance to the Centenary Stand. This was the Victorian home of Liverpool's founder chairman John Houlding. It was also the venue for the historic meeting on March 15th, 1892, that brought the club into existence.

Stanley Park

THE MUNICIPAL SPACE separating the grounds of Liverpool and Everton FC. Created in 1870 by the Victorian designer Edward Kemp, the park was actually home to Everton for the team's first five years.

They left in 1883 and, a year later, moved to Anfield, courtesy of a loan from future Reds' founder John Houlding. Today the park is back in the spotlight as the proposed venue for a new Anfield.

Liverpool FC are seeking permission for a new 60,000 all-seater stadium. If the plan is approved, the park's boundaries will be re-drawn so there's no net loss of public space.

Birthplace of the Reds – John Houlding's home at 73 Anfield Road

Staunton, Steve 'Stan'

1986/7-1990/1 & 1998/9-2000/1 (Defender) **B** 19.1.1969, Drogheda, Rep I **S** 2.9.1986 from Dundalk **D** 17.9.1988 v Tottenham, lg **L** August 1991 to Aston Villa, £1.1 million (and again in December 2000 to Aston Villa, free) **Apps** 147, 6 gls **Hons** Div1CH 1989–90; FAC 1989–90; 89 caps for Rep I **OC** Dundalk, Bradford C (loan), Aston Villa (twice), Crystal Palace (loan)

THE ONE-TIME GAELIC footballer made his first-team breakthrough during an injury-ravaged 1988–89 campaign. He made the left-back position his own with a series of controlled and confident performances but, despite winning Championship and FA Cup medals, found himself surplus to requirements when Graeme Souness took over as boss.

Aston Villa paid £1.1 million for his signature, but there's no doubt that Liverpool were the losers. He played some of the best football of his career at Villa Park, making more than 200 appearances, earning the bulk of his record 89 Republic of Ireland caps and appearing in World Cup final tournaments. Roy Evans acknowledged the club's mistake by mounting a successful bid to bring him back to Anfield in the summer of 1998. He stayed for another two years before returning to Villa on a free transfer.

Steel, William G

1931/2-1934/5 (Right-back) **B** 6.2.1908, Blantyre, Lanarks **S** Sept 1931 from St Johnstone, £1,000 **D** 19.12.1931 v Derby County, lg **L** March 1935 to Birmingham C, £5,000 **Apps** 128, 0 gls **Hons** none **OC** Bridgton Waverley, St Johnstone, Birmingham, Derby C, Airdrieonians (trainer/manager), Third Lanark (manager)

Stevenson, Willie

1962/3-1967/8 (Left-half) **B** 26.10.1939, Leith **S** October 1962 from Rangers, £27,000 **D** 3.11.1962 v Burnley, lg **L** Dec 1967 to Stoke C, £48,000 **Apps** 241, 17 gls **Hons** CWC 1965–66 finalist; Div1 CH 1963–64, 1965–66; FAC 1964–65; CS 1964, 1965, 1966 **OC** Edina Hearts, Dalkeith, Rangers, Stoke C, Tranmere R

AFTER WINNING SCOTTISH League and Cup medals, the former Rangers half-back was planning a new life in Australia. But, just as his emigration was about to be made permanent, Bill Shankly persuaded him to return to Britain for a new life with Liverpool.

The decision proved crucial as the newly promoted Reds sought to establish themselves in Division One. His fierce tackles added bite to the half-back line, and his passing ability helped set up countless scoring opportunities for the likes of Roger Hunt and Ian St John.

As consistent as he was classy, Stevenson missed just nine League games in his first four seasons. He picked up Championship medals in 1964 and 1966 and, in between, put in a man-of-the-match performance in Liverpool's first FA Cup Final victory.

BILLY STEVENSON

But along with midfield colleague Gordon Milne, he paid the price for Liverpool's defeat by Everton in the same tournament in 1967. With his team failing to challenge for honours for the first time in years, Bill Shankly decided to axe them both. The arrival of Emlyn Hughes from Blackpool further undermined Stevenson's position and he accepted a £48,000 move to Stoke.

Stewart, James M

1908/9-1913/4 (Inside-right) **B** Dumbarton **S** April 1909 from Motherwell **D** 4.9.1909 v Chelsea, lg **L** Jan 1914 to Hamilton Academical **Apps** 63, 26 gls **Hons** none **OC** Motherwell, Hamilton Academical, Portsmouth (training staff) **d** n/k

The Saint strikes again – this 1967 goal against Fulham was among the 118 he scored for the club

Stewart, Paul

1992/3-1995/6 (Forward/midfielder) **B** 7.10.1964, Manchester **S** July 1992 from Tottenham, £2.3 million **D** 8.8.1992 v Leeds Utd, CS **L** March 1996 to Sunderland after lengthy loans out **Apps** 42, 3 gls **Hons** none **OC** Blackpool, Manchester C, Tottenham, Liverpool, Crystal Palace (loan), Wolves (loan), Burnley (loan), Sunderland, Stoke C, Workington

HE MAY HAVE HAD A fine record with Manchester City and Tottenham, but Stewart turned into one of the most disappointing buys of the Graeme Souness era. With the impressive Steve McMahon banished from the first team, Stewart was supposed to bring steel to the midfield. In his White Hart Lane days, he converted from striker to goal-scoring central midfielder, winning three England caps under Graham Taylor. But a series of lacklustre performances soon led to him being loaned out to other clubs. New boss Roy Evans showed little faith in the £2.3 million man's potential and granted him a free transfer to Sunderland in 1996.

St John, Ian

1961/2-1970/1 (Centre-forward) **B** 7.6.1938, Motherwell **S** 2 May 1961 from Motherwell, £37,500 **D** 9.5.1961 v Everton, Liv Snr Cup (scored hat-trick) **L** August 1971 to Coventry C **Apps** 425, 118 gls **Hons** Div1 CH 1963–64, 1965–66; Div2 CH 1961–62; FAC 1964–65; CWC 1965–66 finalist; CS 1965, 1966; 21 caps for Scotland **OC** Motherwell Bridge Works FC, Douglas Water Thistle, Motherwell (twice, player-manager), Coventry C (player-assist manager), Portsmouth (manager), Sheffield Wed (coaching staff)

A TRUE ANFIELD IMMORTAL whose signing sparked Bill Shankly's 1960s revival, and whose performances inspired one of the earliest terrace chants. Shankly spotted the 5ft 7in striker playing against the giant Ron Yeats in a Scottish League friendly fixture. It was, according to the manager, the most important game he ever witnessed. "If I hadn't seen this match the history of this present Liverpool Football Club might have been written in a different way," he said in 1966. "It filled me with ambition and elation. For here were a couple of players I was

194

KEY Apps Appearances | **B** Born | **CH** Championship | **CWC** Cup Winners' Cup | **CS** Charity Shield | **D** Debut | **d** Died | **EC** European Cup | **FAC** FA Cup | **gls** Goals | **Hons** Honours | **lg** League

Storer, Harry

1895/6-1901 (Goalkeeper) **B** 24.7.1870, Ripley **S** Dec 1895 from Woolwich Arsenal **D** 1.1.1896 v Manchester City, lg **L** c1901 **Apps** 121 **Hons** Div2 CH 1895–96 **OC** Ripley Town, Derby Midland, Gainsborough Trinity, Woolwich Arsenal **d** 25.4.1908

Strong, Geoffrey H

1964/5-1969/70 (Utility player) **B** 19.9.1937, Kirkheaton, Northumberland **S** November 1964 from Arsenal, £40,000 **D** 7.11.1964 v Fulham, lg **L** August 1970 to Coventry C, £40,000 **Apps** 201, 33 gls **Hons** Div1 CH 1965–66; FAC 1964–65; CS 1964, 1965, 1966 **OC** Stanley Utd, Arsenal, Coventry C

BOUGHT AS BILL SHANKLY'S "twelfth man" in 1964, the lanky Geordie proved to be one of Liverpool's most versatile players ever. In six years at Anfield, the former Arsenal inside-forward played in every outfield position, proving himself as an effective goalscorer, tough tackling full-back and fine midfield distributor.

Strong was chosen as a replacement for the injured Gordon Milne in the 1965 FA Cup final, winning plaudits for his midfield dual with Footballer of the Year Bobby Collins. The following year he showed his bravery, battling through the European Cup Winners' Cup semi-final against Celtic despite a severe knee injury. Midway through the second half of that Anfield clash, he defied excruciating pain to meet an Ian Callaghan cross – and head Liverpool into a place in the final.

By the end of the decade, Strong had inherited Gerry Byrne's old left-back position. But, following the watershed 1970 FA Cup defeat by Watford, he found himself dropped in favour of the emerging Alec Lindsay. That summer he moved to Coventry City and stayed with the Sky Blues until his retirement in 1973.

going to do my utmost to sign. I felt that if I could secure their signatures I would be laying the foundation stone of a terrific new team at Anfield."

It was St John who arrived first, signing from Motherwell in May 1961 for a record £37,500, and immediately bagging a hat-trick in a Liverpool Senior Cup debut against Everton. The next season his prolific partnership with Roger Hunt produced 59 goals as Liverpool stormed to the Second Division title. He hit 21 in the Reds' 1963–64 Championship campaign. And the following year he headed the winner that brought the FA Cup to Anfield for the first time.

As well as goals, he brought creativity and anticipation to Liverpool's attack. Shankly called him a "soccer artist" who could mould a forward line, sense situations before they happened and outjump the tallest of defenders despite his own size. But what really endeared him to his manager was his passion and willingness to give everything for the full 90 minutes. "St John is a footballer with a tiger in his tank," he wrote. "He's a player who has got the one thing so necessary for success: a heart the size of himself. He has helped us soar to the top in a tremendous manner. Nothing I can say can add to my admiration of this bubbling, skilful, courageous, non-stop player."

Committed, and sometimes hot-headed, he could whip opposing fans into a frenzy of temper – particularly those at Goodison Park. But the Anfield crowd idolised him, adopting When The Saints Go Marching In and the famous "1-2, 1-2-3, 1-2-3-4, St John!" chant at every home game. In later years, only the most revered players would be deemed worthy of that last honour, Dalglish and Fowler among them.

But, like team-mates Yeats and Tommy Lawrence, St John stayed in the team until he was past his best. Finding himself sidelined in Shankly's great 1970 clear-out, he moved to Coventry before taking up managerial positions at Motherwell and Portsmouth. He also had a spell coaching Sheffield Wednesday but then began a highly successful career as a TV and radio sports presenter.

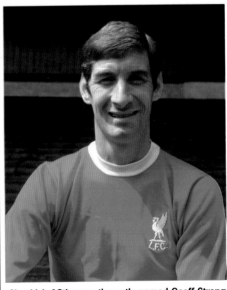

Shankly's 12th man: the aptly named Geoff Strong

Geordie goal-king Albert Stubbins was famous for his amazing flying headers

Stubbins, Albert

1946/7-1952/3 1954-1960 (scout) (Centre-forward) **B** 13.7.1919, Wallsend **S** 12.9.1946 from Newcastle Utd, £12,500 **D** 14.9.1946 v Bolton W, lg (scored) **L** September 1953, Ashington **Apps** 178, 83 gls **Hons** Div1 CH 1946–47; FAC 1949–50 finalist; Liv Snr Cup 1946–47, 1947–48, 1951–52; Football League rep hons **OC** Whitley & Monkseaton FC, Newcastle Utd, Wartime guest: Sunderland, Ashington, USA national team (coach), New York (coach) **d** 28.12.2002

TO SIXTIES FANS HE WAS the player whose photo made it onto the cover of the Beatles' Sgt Pepper album. To an earlier generation of supporters, he was the scoring hero who helped deliver Liverpool's first post-war Championship.

The prolific Geordie signed in 1946 for a then mammoth £12,500 fee. He went on to score 28 goals in his opening season, teaming up with the equally deadly Jack Balmer to drive the Reds towards their first title for a quarter of a century.

"He was a brilliant centre-forward, with most delicate and accomplished ball control and a terrific shot," said team-mate Billy Liddell. "I would say he was one of the most popular players with the crowd during my 21 years at Liverpool."

One sign of that popularity came in 1948 when Stubbins got involved in a contract wrangle that kept him out of action for three months. When it was resolved, he was given a run-out in a reserve team match at Anfield – and 20,000 fans turned up to watch. He retired as a player in 1953, his once-golden scoring touch dented by a series of injuries. He spent time as an Anfield scout before travelling to America to coach the US national team, and later worked as a sports journalist in his native North-East.

Substitutes

ON SEPTEMBER 15TH, 1965, Geoff Strong replaced Chris Lawler in a home league fixture against West Ham. He became the first Liverpool substitute ever to come off the bench – and marked his historic appearance with a goal in the 1-1 draw.

There've been many famous substitute appearances since then. They include David Fairclough's dramatic match-winning effort against St Etienne in 1977, Howard Gayle's tormenting of Bayern Munich in the 1981 European Cup quarter-final and Ian Rush's two-goal, extra-time performance against Everton at Wembley in 1989.

Gayle's appearance in Germany became famous for another reason: he was the first sub in Liverpool's history to be withdrawn before the final whistle. Seven other players have since suffered the same experience, the last being Milan Baros at the 2003 Worthington Cup final.

With 18 goals as Number 12, Fairclough is easily Liverpool's highest-scoring substitute. On four occasions he came off the bench to score twice. And, with goals in the League, FA Cup, European Cup and League Cup, he was the first Liverpool substitute to score in four different competitions. But even 'Supersub' himself never bagged a hat-trick after replacing a team-mate. The only Liverpool player to achieve that was Steve Staunton, in a League Cup tie against Wigan in 1989.

Super Cup

➔ See European Super Cup

Supporters' Clubs

LIVERPOOL FC BOASTS a massive worldwide following, and a simple click on its website will reveal messages from as far afield as Australia, North America, the Far East and South Africa. The Association Of International Branches – formerly the LFC International Supporters' Club – now has almost 140 affiliated groups around the globe. The largest organisation is the LFC Official Supporters' Club, which offers discounted club merchandise, free admission to reserve games plus entry to pre-season 'fans' days' at Anfield and Melwood. Meetings are held regularly, with the club supplying one player for a Q&A session each month. For those wanting a more 'detached' organisation, there's also the Independent Liverpool Supporters Association. Set up in 2001, ILSA provides "an organised and independent voice for Liverpool fans and seeks to maintain the pride, traditions and dignity for which Liverpool and its fans have become famous over the years."

Come in Number 12: David Fairclough scored 18 goals as substitute

Tallest Players

EVEN ALLOWING FOR statistical errors, it's unlikely Liverpool have had a taller outfield player than former centre-back Frode Kippe. Measuring 6 ft 5in, the giant Norwegian would appear to have a full inch on his nearest rival, 1950s inside-forward, Hugh Gerhardi. Between the posts, the Reds have had two 'keepers who also stretched to 6ft 5in: Steve Ogrizovic and David James – but at 6ft 6in, current stopper Chris Kirkland tops the lot.

Tanner, Nicky

1989/90-1992/3 (Full-back) **B** 24.5.1965, Bristol **S** July 1988 from Bristol R, £30,000 **D** 2.12.1989 v Manchester C, lg **L** 1993 retired through injury **Apps** 59, 1 gl **Hons** none **OC** Mangotsfield Utd, Bristol R, Norwich C (loan), Swindon T (loan), Bath City

AFTER A CAREER with Bristol Rovers and non-league Mangotsfield United, a move to Anfield was something of a leap. Still, Tanner proved to be an effective utility player, taking Gary Ablett's place in the 1991–92 season and later deputising in central defence for captain Mark Wright.

Always prone to injuries, he was more often out of the side than in during the Souness era. After a long lay-off in the 1993–94 season, he went to Norwich, then Swindon on loan. He was forced to retire due to serious back problems shortly afterwards and Liverpool rewarded him with a testimonial match at Yeovil, in 1995.

Taylor, Harold

1932/33-1936/7 (Left-half/forward) **B** 1912, Hanley **S** July 1932 from Stoke C **D** 5.11.1932 v Leeds Utd, lg **L** Summer 1937 **Apps** 72, 6 gls **Hons** none **OC** Stoke St Peter's, Stoke C **d** n/k

Taylor, Phil

1936/7-1953/4 (player) 1956/7-1958/9 (manager) (Right-half/inside-right) **B** 18.9.1917, Bristol **S** March 1936 from Bristol R, £5,000 **D** 28.3.1936 v Derby C, lg (scored) **L** Retired July 1954, later joined LFC coaching staff **Apps** 345, 34 **Hons** Div1 CH 1946–47; FAC 1949–50 finalist; 3 caps for England; Football League **OC** Bristol R, wartime guest: Brighton, Newcastle Utd, Leeds Utd

SUPERB ANFIELD SERVANT whose distinguished playing career was later overshadowed by his period as boss. The former England Schoolboys captain started as an apprentice with his local club Bristol Rovers. But when Liverpool came in with a £5,000 offer in 1936, they decided to cash in on their 18-year-old prodigy.

Taylor took his place alongside Matt Busby in Liverpool's half-back line and helped the club

Up for it: 1940s skipper Phil Taylor wins an aerial duel, while Bob Paisley looks on

stave off the real threat of relegation in manager George Kay's first full season. He made his name as a classy right-sided player and soon won the first of his three England caps. He also kept up his keen interest in cricket, even making a first-class appearance for Gloucestershire in 1938.

When war broke out the following year, Taylor served in the 9th King's Regiment, guarding the viaducts on the Liverpool to London train line. He made wartime guest appearances for Brighton, Newcastle and Leeds, then – when hostilities ended – formed part of the Liverpool team that lifted the 1946–47 Championship. He took over the captaincy from Jack Balmer soon afterwards and, in 1950, led the Reds out for their FA Cup final clash with Arsenal.

He played on until he was 35, making his last appearance as Liverpool dropped to Division Two in 1954. He then spent two years on the coaching staff before the board appointed him managerial successor to the sacked Don Welsh. Although

he took the Reds to within a whisker of promotion – twice finishing third – he could never quite manage to get them out of the lower reaches. Gradually the stress of that challenge took its toll and it was an exhausted Taylor who decided to step down from his duties in November 1959.

"No matter how great has been the disappointment of the directors at our failure to win our way back to the First Division, it has not been greater than mine," he told the press. "I made it my goal. I set my heart on it and strove for it with all the energy I could muster. Such striving has not been enough and now the time has come to hand over to someone else to see if they can do better."

Although he dropped out of the game to become a sales representative, Taylor remained an honoured guest in the Anfield directors' box. His successor Bill Shankly took his beloved club to new heights – and no Reds fan could have been more delighted.

You're on Sky Sports! Liverpool take on Forest in the channel's first-ever live game

Televised Matches

ON AUGUST 22ND, 1964, Kenneth ("they think it's all over") Wolstenholme appeared on the Anfield pitch to welcome BBC2 viewers to "Beatleville" – and a brand new sports programme called *Match Of The Day*. Liverpool's 3-2 victory over Arsenal may have been watched by less than 100,000 viewers, but it marked the birth of a TV institution. It also helped spread Anfield's reputation as the noisiest, most atmospheric ground in Britain.

The club has been involved in three more historic TV 'firsts' since then. In 1967, the FA Cup fifth round clash with Everton was beamed 'live' to giant closed-circuit screens at Anfield – in front of 40,000 fans who'd been unable to get tickets for Goodison Park. Two years later, *Match Of The Day* marked the introduction of colour broadcasting by showing Liverpool's 2-0 home League victory over West Ham. And on

August 16th, 1992, Sky TV visited Nottingham's City Ground to screen its first-ever live Premiership game. The result: Nottingham Forest 1 Liverpool 0.

Television Programmes

ONE OF LIVERPOOL'S first appearances on a non-sports programme came in 1964 when the BBC's Panorama made an 'anthropological' film about crowd behaviour. A few weeks later – with Beatlemania and America's fascination with Liverpool at its height – the team were invited on to the US's top-rated *Ed Sullivan Show* in front of an audience of 60 million.

Documentaries featuring the team include *The Kop Flies East*, Granada TV's film about the 1966 trip to Honved, famous for the shots of Ron Yeats doing the Twist in a Hungarian nightclub. In 1983, ITV also screened *Home And Away*, a fly-on-the-wall programme following Liverpool

and Everton fans to Wembley for the first all-Merseyside cup final.

Liverpool playwright (and Reds' fan) Alan Bleasdale has used Anfield as a backdrop for television drama, most memorably for the dream sequences in his 1970s BBC series *Scully*. And, in 1982, he persuaded the then captain Graeme Souness to play the part of himself in the award-winning *Boys From The Blackstuff*… opposite the terrifying fictional character 'Yosser' Hughes. Several people associated with the club have also been featured on TV's *This Is Your Life*, including Bill Shankly, Bob Paisley and John Barnes.

Tennant, John W 'Jack'

1933/4-1935/6 (Left-back) **B** 3.8.1907, Newcastle **S** 16 May 1933 from Torquay Utd **D** 9.9.1933 v Aston Villa, lg **L** January 1936 to Bolton W **Apps** 42, 0 gls **Hons** none **OC** Washington Colliery, Stoke C (twice), Torquay Utd, Bolton W, wartime guest: Wrexham, Southport **d** 1978

KEY Apps Appearances | **B** Born | **CH** Championship | **CWC** Cup Winners' Cup | **CS** Charity Shield | **D** Debut | **d** Died | **EC** European Cup | **FAC** FA Cup | **gls** Goals | **Hons** Honours | **lg** League

Testimonial Matches

THE PROMISE OF a money-spinning testimonial game was often a powerful incentive when trying to recruit players during the club's formative years. It was almost certainly a factor in luring original captain Andrew Hannah, who was awarded an 1894 benefit match against Accrington Stanley – at the age of only 29. A year after that first recorded testimonial, Liverpool laid on a fund-raising game for new captain – and future manager – Matt McQueen, against an England International XI at Anfield. And in 1896 around 5,000 fans turned up for striker Joe McQue's benefit match against Burnley, a ticket for which is on display at the Liverpool FC Museum.

Increased wages have reduced the need for such events today, but former players and managers have managed to attract huge crowds to their testimonials down the years. In 1960 almost 38,000 fans came to honour Billy Liddell's years of remarkable service. Bill Shankly's 1975 testimonial – featuring Liverpool against a Don Revie Select XI – brought 39,000 fans to Anfield. And three years earlier, 'Sir' Roger Hunt signed off his career with an emotional benefit match – in front of more than 50,000 spectators.

Thomas, Michael

1991/2-1997/8 (Midfield) **B** 24.8.1967, Lambeth
S Dec 1991 from Arsenal, £1.5 million **D** 18.12.1991 v Tottenham, lg **L** 1998 to Benfica **Apps** 163, 12 gls
Hons FAC 1991–92; LC 1994–95; 2 caps for England **OC** Arsenal, Portsmouth (loan), Middlesbrough (loan), Benfica, Wimbledon

FAST AND POWERFUL midfielder, forever associated with one of the most miserable nights in Anfield history. Liverpool were just a minute away from clinching the 1989 Championship on goal difference when Thomas broke through the Reds' defence to score – sending the title to Arsenal instead.

Graeme Souness paid £1.5 million to prise him away from Highbury in 1991. And by the end of the season, he'd helped banish his previous scoring exploits by volleying the Reds into the lead in their FA Cup final victory over Sunderland.

Although beginning to show the form that had made him such a highly rated property at Arsenal, Thomas soon succumbed to a series of injuries that kept him sidelined for the best part of two seasons. He never returned to his best and, after a period on loan to Middlesbrough, was transferred to Benfica.

Heartbreaker... Michael Thomas scores the last-minute goal that silenced the Anfield terraces and took the 1989 Championship trophy to Arsenal

L Left Liverpool | **LC** League Cup | **n/k** not known | **OC** Other Clubs | **P** Premiership | **S** Signed | **Sb** Substitute | **SSSC** Screen Sport Super Cup | **UEFA** UEFA Cup | **WCCH** World Club Championship

199

Thompson, David

1994/95-1999/2000 (Midfielder) **B** 12.9.1977, Birkenhead
S 8.11.1994 from School of Excellence **D** 19.8.1996 v Arsenal, lg
L July 2000 to Coventry C, £2.5m **Apps** 56, 5 gls **Hons** FA Youth
Cup 1995–96; England U-21 hons **OC** Swindon T (loan), Coventry C,
Blackburn R

AFTER GRADUATING FROM Liverpool's
School of Excellence, the Birkenhead-born
teenager went on to play a key role in the FA
Youth Cup triumph in 1996. He made his senior
team debut later that year, then spent a successful loan period with Steve McMahon's
Swindon Town.

Thompson was given new opportunities to
prove himself in the 1998–99 season, and
responded with a number of fine wide-midfield
performances. In one substitute appearance
against Southampton, he got on the scoresheet
only 15 seconds after coming off the bench. It
seemed like he was on the brink of a regular
first-team place but, in the summer of 2000,
Gerard Houllier accepted a £2.5million bid from
Coventry City. After a troubled two years at
Highfield Road – during which he collected two
red cards and nine bookings – Thompson was
transferred to Blackburn Rovers.

Thompson, Peter

1963/4-1973/4 (Outside-left) **B** 27.11.1942, Carlisle **S** August 1963
from Preston NE, £40,000 **D** 24.8.1963 v Blackburn R, Lg **L** January
1974 to Bolton W, £18,000 **Apps** 415, 54 gls **Hons** Div1 CH
1963–64, 1965–66; FAC 1964–65, 1970–71 finalist; CWC 1965–66
finalist; CS 1964, 1966; 16 caps for England **OC** Preston NE,
Bolton W

A RECORD £40,000 signing from Preston who
soon became one of the
greatest Liverpool wingers
of all time. Thompson's dazzling show for England
against Brazil in 1964 led to
the press nickname of 'The
White Pele'. But at Anfield
his performances were even
more impressive.

For that was the year that
he became the last piece in
Bill Shankly's Championship-
winning jigsaw, tormenting
defences with his speed and
trickery down the left flank.
Often his jinking runs would
finish with perfectly weighted
crosses for Ian St John and
Roger Hunt. But, just as often,
he'd cut inside to unleash thunderous shots past
a helpless 'keeper. On the day Liverpool

clinched their title against Arsenal, Thompson
capped a devastating display by getting on the
scoresheet twice. A year later he hit a piledriver
past Chelsea to seal the Reds' passage to their
historic FA Cup final against Leeds.

Without doubt the most 'individual' of
Liverpool's 1960s stars, Thompson began an
exhilarating, crowd-pleasing tradition that
would later be followed by Steve Heighway and
John Barnes. His ball control was unmatched
and, at his peak, few defenders ever managed to
dispossess him. As Shankly once remarked in
the dressing room, "Boys, if you're feeling tired,
pass the ball to Peter and let him go for a run
with it."

By the early 1970s Thompson had become
prone to knee injuries and, with the young
Heighway in superb form, he found it difficult to
re-establish himself in the first team. He moved
to Bolton in 1974 and retired four years later to
concentrate on a range of business interests.

Thompson, Phil

1970/1-1985 (player) 1986/7-1991/2 (Coaching staff) 1999/00-
present (assistant manager) (Central defender) **B** 21.1.1954, Liverpool
S 22 Jan 1971 from Kirkby Schools **D** 3.4.1972 v Manchester Utd, lg
L March 1985 to Sheffield Utd, after loan **Apps** 477, 16 gls
Hons EC 1977–78, 1980–81; UEFA 1975–76; Super Cup 1977,
1978 finalist; Div1 CH 1972–73, 1975–76, 1976–77, 1978–79,
1979–80, 1981–82, 1982–83; FAC 1973–74, 1976–77 finalist; LC
1980–81, 1981–82; CS 1974, 1976, 1977, 1979, 1980, 1982,
1983 finalist; 43 caps for England **OC** Kirkby Schools, Sheffield Utd

AS A FAN HE STOOD on the Kop; as a man he
won every major honour in the game. In a
decade when Liverpool rose to dominate
English and European football, Thompson was
at the heart of the Reds'
defence. He captained his club
and his country and developed
a deep tactical knowledge that
would serve the Reds so well
in later years.

Bill Shankly gave the ex-
Kirkby schoolboy his senior
debut in the 1971–72 season.
Tall, skinny and awkward,
he looked ill-equipped to
deal with the demands of
the game. But, within a
year, he'd proved himself
capable of handling the
First Division's biggest
and roughest strikers. He
won League titles,
European trophies and
England caps. Then, when Emlyn
Hughes left Anfield, he helped form a legendary
defensive pairing with Alan Hansen. "Our part-

nership was phenomenal," the Scot later
recalled. "Our rapport, stemming from our ability to read the game, seemed almost telepathic."

It was as skipper that Thompson enjoyed his
greatest professional moment, lifting the
European Cup after the team's 1981 victory
over Real Madrid in Paris.

So determined was he to keep hold of the trophy that he took it to bed. The next day he took
the Cup back to his local pub in Kirkby so his
old friends and fellow fans could have their photographs taken with it.

But by the time of the Reds' 1984 European
Cup triumph, Thompson had lost the captaincy
to Graeme Souness, and his regular place to
Mark Lawrenson. He left the following year for
Sheffield United but, as the most diehard of
Reds' supporters, couldn't wait to get back to
Anfield.

His first stint on the coaching staff may have
ended in an acrimonious bust-up with Souness,
but when he was asked back to assist the newly
appointed Gerard Houllier, he didn't hesitate for
a second. As first team coach, and Houllier's
motivator-in-chief, he's played a huge role in the
Reds' resurgence over the last four years. And,
with him in the dressing room, Reds fans can be
sure that pride and passion are alive and well.

P. Thompson (Liverpool)

Double act: Phil Thompson and Gerard Houllier

KEY Apps Appearances | **B** Born | **CH** Championship | **CWC** Cup Winners' Cup | **CS** Charity Shield | **D** Debut | **d** Died | **EC** European Cup | **FAC** FA Cup | **gls** Goals | **Hons** Honours | **lg** League

The pride of Kirkby: Thompson shows off the 1981 European Cup to his friends and family in the crowd

L Left Liverpool | **LC** League Cup | **n/k** not known | **OC** Other Clubs | **P** Premiership | **S** Signed | **Sb** Substitute | **SSSC** Screen Sport Super Cup | **UEFA** UEFA Cup | **WCCH** World Club Championship

Toshack, John B (OBE)

1970/1-1977/8 (Centre-forward) **B** 22.3.1949, Cardiff **S** November 1970 from Cardiff C, £110,000 **D** 14.11.1970 v Coventry C, lg **L** 1 March 1978 to Swansea C, (player-manager) **Apps** 246, 96 gls **Hons** UEFA 1972–73, 1975–76; Div1 CH 1972–73, 1975–76, 1976–77; FAC 1973–74, 1970–71 finalist; CS 1976; 40 caps for Wales **OC** Cardiff C, Swansea C (player/manager then manager), Sporting Lisbon (manager), Real Sociedad (manager three times and coach), Real Madrid (manager twice), Wales (manager), Deportivo La Coruna (manager), Besiktas JK Istanbul (manager), St Etienne (manager)

A KEY PLANK IN Bill Shankly's rebuilt 1970s side and one half of a legendary goalscoring partnership. The manager broke his own spending records to prise the 20-year-old centre-forward from Cardiff City. But his £110,000 fee was justified almost immediately, as Toshack helped the Reds to an epic fight-back, resulting in a 3-2 win in the 1970 Anfield derby.

The following year saw him team up with Kevin Keegan and form British football's most lethal strike partnership. The understanding between the two was unique, with Toshack dominant in the air and his smaller colleague feeding off his delightful flicks and touches. Together, they contributed 31 goals as Liverpool landed a League and UEFA Cup double in 1973. A year later they added nine more during the team's triumphant FA Cup run.

His most effective season came in 1975–76 when he hit 23 goals in 53 appearances. One of those came in the Nou Camp stadium when his smart 'one-two' move with Keegan led to a decisive strike past the Barcelona 'keeper. Liverpool won the game 1-0, in what Bob Paisley described as one of their best-ever performances on the Continent.

But by the following season Toshack was struggling to keep his place, due to a combination of injuries and competition from the newly arrived David Johnson. He left in 1978 to become player-manager of Swansea City, a club he duly took from Fourth Division to First in successive seasons. His obvious talent as a manager was recognised by some of Europe's top clubs, and he later was appointed to the boss's chair at Portugal's Sporting Lisbon and Spain's Real Sociedad. In recent years he's had a brief period in charge of the Welsh national team, as well as two spells at Real Madrid.

Training

"My players could never play at the pace we train. If they drop to half training pace in a match it's quick enough."
– **Bill Shankly**

DURING THE 1960s Liverpool were undoubtedly the fittest side in Britain. Shankly's team became used to playing up to 60 games a season. Injuries were a rarity. Matches were often won in the dying stages as opposing teams wilted.

Asked for the reasons, the boss pointed to the work they put in at Melwood and the methods he introduced, based on his own regime while playing at Preston. He had little time for tactics or strategy. Training was simply there to achieve the five things he considered essential for a top professional footballer: skill, speed, strength, stamina and flexibility.

Many players have written about how straightforward, but hard, the training could be. The 90-minute sessions would involve running, turning, shooting and ball practice. Then there was the so-called Sweat Box – a fenced-in area known by some as 'Torture Square' – in which players hit the ball against numbered boards, collected the return, hit again... until Shankly or Bob Paisley finally blew the whistle. Lastly, there were the five-a-sides, played between members of the first team, the reserves and coaching staff.

Although Bob Paisley, Joe Fagan and Kenny Dalglish all modified the training programme over the next three decades, the five-a-side tradition survived throughout. John Barnes, who arrived in 1987, has described how seriously they were taken. "Liverpool believed everything we faced in five-a-sides would be encountered again on match day. That was why they were so competitive. No one ever cheated. No one ever attempted a one-two without being prepared to make the run.

"No one ever thought this was only training and they were not going to track back. At some clubs, players often do not try in training. If someone went past them, it was not the end of the world.

"That never happened at Melwood. Every player treated five-a-sides as if they were cup finals on a small pitch. Liverpool's training

Target man: Toshack spearheaded the Reds' attack in the early seventies

'Legs out, stomach in': Anfield training, 1940s-style

characterised Liverpool's play – uncomplicated but devastatingly effective."

Both Graeme Souness and Roy Evans brought in their own training methods in the 1990s, but, by the time of Gerard Houllier's arrival, there was room for improvement. Noting how the game had become faster and more physical, the new manager called for changes in both technique and attitude. "I don't think some players felt the relationship between the training and the game was important," he told one interviewer. "They didn't understand the connection. Players thought training was something to pass the time between matches."

Like Shankly 40 years earlier, Houllier took charge of a major redevelopment of Melwood. Training is now designed to take account of the modern demands of the Premiership. And, if the team's recent success is anything to go by, the new methods are working.

Transfer Deals

ALTHOUGH BETTER NOTED for finding bargains in the transfer market, Liverpool haven't been afraid to shell out big money down the years. Kenny Dalglish's £440,000 signing from Celtic in 1977 was a record between British clubs, and the £1.9million paid to Newcastle for Peter Beardsley a decade later represented a record between English clubs. In 1995, Roy

Evans broke all British records by paying Nottingham Forest £8.5million for Stan Collymore. The estimated £11million purchase of Emile Heskey from Leicester in 2000 remains a club record.

On the sales front, Liverpool took in a record £3.2million from Ian Rush's move to Juventus in 1986. They collected £7million from Collymore's 1997 sale to Aston Villa and another £11million from Robbie Fowler's switch to Leeds in 2001.

→ Also see Bargain Buys

Traore, Djimi

(Defender) **B** 1.3.1980, Laval **S** February 1999 from Laval, £550,000 **D** 14.9.1999 v Hull City, LC **Apps** 63, 0 gls **Hons** FA Premier Reserve Championship North 1998–99; France U-13 hons **OC** Laval, Lens (loan)

TALENTED, BALL-PLAYING DEFENDER whose performances with the French club Laval made him one of the most sought-after teenagers in Europe. AC Milan, Lazio and PSG were all chasing his signature, but Liverpool won the race with a £550,000 bid in February 1999. The lean, 6ft 3in Taore made several appearances but spent the 2001–02 season on loan to Lens. He returned to provide vital cover for a number of injured team mates during the new campaign, playing at full-back and centre half. "It's not important where I play," he told the club's website. "I just hope I can be a regular in the side."

Trebles

LIVERPOOL'S CLEAN SWEEP of knock-out cups in 2001 brought the club its second Treble of trophies. The first time they lifted three pieces of silverware was in 1984, when Joe Fagan landed the League Championship, European Cup and Milk Cup – in his first season as manager.

Three times a winner: the 1984 team

Twentyman, Geoffrey

1953-1959 & 1967/8-1985/6 (Left-half) (Chief scout) **B** 19.1.1930, Carlisle **S** December 1953 from Carlisle Utd, £10,000 **D** 19.12.1953 v Manchester Utd, lg **L** match 1959 to Ballymena Utd (player-manager) **Apps** 184, 19 gls **Hons** honours with Irish league **OC** Swifts Rovers, Carlisle Utd (twice), Ballymena Utd (player-manager), Morecombe (player-manager), Penrith FC (manager-coach), Rangers (scout)

ALTHOUGH HE PLAYED throughout much of Liverpool's Second Division period, Twentyman is best remembered as the man who helped bring the likes of Alan Hansen, Phil Neal and Ian Rush to Anfield.

He joined the club from Carlisle, converting from centre-back to right-half in the 1953–54 relegation season. He stayed for five years before joining Ballymena United. It was Bill Shankly – Twentyman's old boss at Brunton Park – who brought him back to Anfield as chief scout in 1967. He became a respected member of the Boot Room, toured every ground in the country and tipped the club off about emerging talent like Ray Clemence and Steve Heighway. But, after 20 years in the job, Twentyman and the club parted ways. After being replaced at Anfield by Ron Yeats, he became chief scout for Glasgow Rangers.

UEFA Cup

LIVERPOOL FIRST COMPETED in this tournament under its original name, the Inter Cities Fairs Cup, qualifying in successive years between 1968 and 1971. Bill Shankly landed the newly named trophy for the first time in 1973, after a two-legged final victory over Borussia Moenchengladbach. Three years later Bob Paisley repeated the feat, guiding his team to a 4-3 aggregate win over the Belgian side FC Bruges.

In 1991, Liverpool emerged from their post-Heysel European ban to take their place in the tournament. Sadly, their six-year absence from European competition showed and they were comprehensively beaten by the Italians of Genoa in the fourth round. A decade later, though, Gerard Houllier's new-look team re-established the winning tradition, beating Alaves 5-4 in the most exciting UEFA Cup final of all time.

Unbeaten Runs

LIVERPOOL HAVE ONLY once gone through an entire season unbeaten – back in 1893–94, when they won the Second Division championship at the first time of asking. The team played 28 games during that promotion campaign, winning 22 and drawing the rest.

In 1987–88 the Reds equalled Leeds United's feat of going 29 games unbeaten from the start of the season. Their record came to an end at Goodison Park, where a single Wayne Clark goal gave Everton victory.

There have been nine separate seasons in which the team haven't lost a game at Anfield. Their longest unbeaten home run stretched for 85 domestic and European matches between January 1978 and January 1981.

Underwood: relegation-season 'keeper

Underwood, E. David

1953/4-1955/6 (Goalkeeper) **B** 15.3.1928, St Pancras, London **S** December 1953 from Watford, £7,000 **D** 19.12.1953 v Manchester Utd, lg **L** July 1956 to Watford, £1,250 **Apps** 50

Hons none **OC** Edgeware T, QPR, Watford (three times), Dartford, Fulkham, Dunstable Town, Hastings Utd, Barnet **d** 25 Jan 1984

That completes the set: the Reds lift the 2001 UEFA Cup, to go with the FA and Worthington trophies

Upset? Grimsby's Phil Jevons certainly isn't as he dumps LFC out of the Worthington Cup, Oct 2001

Upsets

FREAK RESULTS ARE PART and parcel of knock-out competitions – and Liverpool have suffered their share over the years. In 2002 they went out of the Worthington Cup after losing to Grimsby – the fifth time they'd been eliminated by lower league clubs in that competition.

In the FA Cup, 22 teams from the lower divisions have had the better of the Reds. And, in 1959, even the amateurs of Worcester City managed to score a 2-1 victory in the Third Round. Despite that embarassment, some fans still cite the 1988 FA Cup final as the biggest upset of all. It was virtually impossible to get odds on Kenny Dalglish's Double-chasers losing to Wimbledon at Wembley – yet it was the Division One minnows who eventually lifted the trophy following a single Lawrie Sanchez goal.

While upsets often knock a season off course, they can have long-term positive effects. It was the 1970 FA Cup defeat by Second Division Watford that convinced Bill Shankly to break up his great 1960s side and put together a new team that would go on to dominate English football. And in 1994 it was the Third Round home loss to Bristol City that finally brought down the curtain on Souness's reign as manager.

Uren, Harold J

1907/08-1911/12 (Outside-left) **B** 23.8.1885, Barton Regis, Bristol **S** 4.10.1907 from Hoylake FC **D** 16.11.1907 v Man City, lg **L** February 1912 to Everton, in exchange for Billy Lacey and Tom Gracie **Apps** 46, 2gls **Hons** none **OC** Northern Nomads, Hoylake FC, Everton, Wrexham **d** 7.4.1955

Venison, Barry

1986/7-1991/2 (Right-back) **B** 16.8.1964, Consett **S** July 1986 from Sunderland, £250,000 **D** 16.8.1986 v Everton, CS **L** July 1992 to Newcastle Utd, £250,000 **Apps** 157, 2 gls **Hons** Div1 CH 1987–88, 1989–90; FAC 1988–89; CS 1986, 1988, 1989, 1990; SSSC 1986; 2 caps for England **OC** Sunderland, Newcastle Utd, Galatasaray, Southampton

AFTER CAPTAINING SUNDERLAND at the age of 20, the Geordie full-back was determined to make his mark on a bigger stage. So determined that he wrote to every First Division manager asking if they wanted to sign him when his contract was up. Amazingly, Kenny Dalglish was the only one who expressed an interest, paying £250,000 to bring him to Anfield in the summer of 1986.

Venison went on to make more than 150 appearances for the club, picking up Championship and FA Cup medals along the way. He was a consistent performer, noted for his clean tackling and willingness to go forward. He also packed a vicious shot, although he rarely managed to get on to the scoresheet.

Graeme Souness sold him to Newcastle in 1992 after a period of injuries. But, back in his native North-East, Venison played some of the best football of his career, converting to midfield and winning two full England caps to go with the Under-21 honours he had collected while with Sunderland. He finished his playing career following spells with Turkey's Galatasaray and Southampton, and is now one of ITV's leading football pundits.

Vignal, Gregory

2000/1-present (Defender) **B** 19.7.1981, Montpellier **S** Sept 2000 from Montpellier, £500,000 **D** 6.1.2001 v Rotherham Utd, FAC **Apps** 20, 0 gls **Hons** U-18 caps for France **OC** Montpellier, Bastia (loan)

ONE OF A CROP OF promising French youngsters signed by Gerard Houllier. Vignal joined from Montpellier shortly after helping his country's Under-18 side win the 2000 European Youth Championships. He made his debut as a substitute full-back in an FA Cup Third Round tie against Rotherham in January 2001, and went on to make six appearances throughout the Treble season, impressing fans with his strength and willingness to burst down the left flank. "I find it incredible that I am only 19 and yet playing for one of the biggest clubs in Europe," he said shortly after joining. Unfortunately, a broken foot kept him sidelined for most of the following campaign and he was loaned out to the French club Bastia during the 2002–03 season.

"Gizza job!"... Venison was signed after offering his services to the club in writing

KEY Apps Appearances | **B** Born | **CH** Championship | **CWC** Cup Winners' Cup | **CS** Charity Shield | **D** Debut | **d** Died | **EC** European Cup | **FAC** FA Cup | **gls** Goals | **Hons** Honours | **lg** League

Striking achievement: Ian Rush won more international caps with Liverpool than anyone else

Waddle, Alan R

1973/4-1976/7 (Centre-forward) **B** 9.6.1954, Wallsend **S** June 1973 from Halifax T, £40,000 **D** 1.12.1973 v West Ham, lg **L** Sept 1977 to Leicester C, £450,000 **Apps** 22, 1 gl **Hons** none **OC** Wallsend Boys Club, Halifax T, Leicester C, Swansea C, Newport C, Mansfield T, Hartlepool, Peterborough Utd, Swansea C, Barry T

GIANT GEORDIE STRIKER whose opportunities were always restricted by the presence of John Toshack. The ex-Halifax centre-forward – cousin of Tottenham and England winger, Chris – spent four years at Anfield, managing just 22 first-team appearances. He won a medal as an unused substitute in the 1977 European Cup final, but probably enjoyed his best Liverpool moment when he scored the winner against Everton in the Goodison derby in 1973. After moving to Leicester City for £450,000, he went on to play for Toshack's Swansea team.

Wadsworth, Harold

1918/19-1923/4 (Outside-right) **B** 1.10.1898, Bootle **S** 13.5.1919 from Tranmere R **D** 4.10.1919 v Newcastle Utd, lg **L** June 1924 to Leicester C **Apps** 55, 3 gls **Hons** none **OC** Bootle St Matthew's, Tranmere Rovers, Leicester C, Nottm Forest, Millwall **d** 2.11.1975

Wadsworth, Walter

1912/13-1925/6 (Centre-half) **B** October 1890, Bootle **S** 8.2.1912 from Ormskirk **D** 20.3.1915 v Middlesbrough, lg **L** May 1926 to Bristol C £400 **Apps** 240, 8 gls **Hons** Div1 CH 1921–22, 1922–23; rep hons for Football League **OC** Lingdale, Ormskirk, Bristol C, Flint Town (player-manager), New Brighton, Oswestry Town **d** 6 October 1951

KEY MEMBER OF LIVERPOOL'S defence as the team stormed to successive titles in 1922 and 1923. The slim Bootle-born centre-back was known as 'Big Waddy' – to differentiate him from team-mate, and younger brother, Harold (see above entry).

Wales

WITH 67 GAMES FOR HIS country while at Anfield, Welshman Ian Rush is the most-capped Liverpool player in history. He made a career total of 73 international appearances, and – with 28 goals – still holds his country's all-time scoring record.

Out of the total of 14 Reds players who've represented Wales, two others have won more than 70 caps during their careers. They are striker Dean Saunders, with 74 appearances, and defender Joey Jones, with 72.

Walker, John

1898-1902 (Inside-right) **B** 31.5.1874, Coatbridge **S** April 1898 from Hearts, £350, inc Tom Robertson **D** 11.4.1898 v The Wednesday, lg **L** May 1902 to Rangers **Apps** 120, 31 gls **Hons** Div1 CH 1900–01; caps for Scotland **OC** Armandale, Hearts, Rangers, Morton **d** n/k

Wall, T Peter

1966/7-69/70 (Left-back) **B** 13.9.1944 Westbury **S** October 1966 from Wrexham, £26,000, inc Stuart Mason **D** 16.3.1968 v Burnley, lg **L** May 1970 to Crystal Palace, £35,000 **Apps** 42, 0 gls **Hons** none **OC** Shrewsbury T, Wrexham, Crystal Palace, Orient (loan) St Louis Stars (loan), California Surf (player-trainer)

SERVED AS A PROMISING understudy to Gerry Byrne, but struggled to make the first-team position his own once his predecessor retired. The former Wrexham player did enjoy an extended run in the 1969–70 season, but became a casualty of Bill Shankly's clear-out following an infamous FA Cup defeat at Watford. He was sold to Crystal Palace at the end of the campaign and went on to make 180 appearances for the south London club.

Wallace, Gordon H

1960/1-1967/8 (Inside-left) **B** 13.6.1944, Lanark **S** Jan 1960 from Lanarkshire Schools football **D** 27.10.1962 v WBA, lg **L** October 1967 to Crewe A, £5,000 **Apps** 22, 6 gls **Hons** none **OC** Lanarkshire Schools, Crewe A

ALTHOUGH HE ARRIVED just a couple of months after his old school friend Ian St John, the little inside-left never made the same

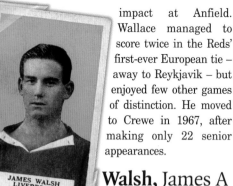

impact at Anfield. Wallace managed to score twice in the Reds' first-ever European tie – away to Reykjavik – but enjoyed few other games of distinction. He moved to Crewe in 1967, after making only 22 senior appearances.

Walsh, James A

1922/23-1927/28 (Centre-/inside-forward) **B** 15.5.1901, Stockport **S** 20.5.1922 from Stockport C **D** 29.8.1923 v Birmingham, lg (scored twice) **L** June 1928 to Hull C **Apps** 77, 27 gls **Hons** none **OC** Stockport C, Hull C, Crewe A, Colwyn Bay **d** 1971

Taking on Europe's best: Paul Walsh was one of Fagan's most gifted players

KEY Apps Appearances | **B** Born | **CH** Championship | **CWC** Cup Winners' Cup | **CS** Charity Shield | **D** Debut | **d** Died | **EC** European Cup | **FAC** FA Cup | **gls** Goals | **Hons** Honours | **lg** League

Walsh, Paul A

1984/85-1987/88 (Forward) **B** 1.10.1962, Plumstead **S** May 1984
from Luton T, £700,000 **D** 18.8.1984 v Everton, CS (scored)
L February 1988 to Tottenham, £500,000 **Apps** 112, 37 gls
Hons EC 1984–85 finalist; Div1 CH 1985–86; LC 1986–87 finalist;
CS 1984 finalist; SSpSC 1986; 5 caps for England **OC** Charlton,
Luton T, Tottenham, QPR (loan), Portsmouth (twice), Manchester C

IMMENSELY TALENTED England international who would have won far more honours had it not been for a number of serious injuries. Joe Fagan paid a club record £700,000 for the Londoner, shortly after he had carried off the Young Player of The Year award while with Luton. Walsh was exceptionally quick, with brilliant ball control and the ability to get into scoring positions. He scored within 14 seconds of his

His finest hour: Walters slides the late winner past Auxerre in the UEFA Cup

league debut against West Ham and contributed 11 goals in the 1985–86 Championship season. But, in less than four years with the club, Walsh was sidelined with cartilage damage, a broken wrist and a hernia. In 1988, following another long spell on the treatment table, he was transferred to Tottenham, where he later collected an FA Cup winners' medal.

Walters, Mark

1991/2-1995/6 (Winger) **B** 2.6.1964, Birmingham **S** July 1991 from
Rangers, £1.3 million **D** 17.8.1991 v Oldham A, lg **L** January 1996 to
Southampton, free transfer **Apps** 124, 19 gls **Hons** FAC 1991–92;
LC 1994–95; 1 cap for England **OC** Aston Villa, Rangers, Stoke C
(loan), Wolves (loan), Southampton, Swindon T, Bristol R

THE EX-RANGERS WINGER followed manager Graeme Souness to Anfield in the summer of 1991, hoping to continue the form that had set the Scottish League alight in over 150 appearances for the Glasgow side. But, despite some shows of individual brilliance, Walters soon found himself overshadowed by the emergence of another young winger, Steve McManaman.

In more than 120 senior games with the club, two displays stand out. The first was in November 1991, when he scored the late winner in the epic 3-2 UEFA Cup comeback against Auxerre at Anfield. The second was in April 1993 when he put three past Coventry – making him the first-ever Liverpool player to bag a Premier League hat-trick.

But the departure of Souness signalled the beginning of the end for the player. After placing him out on a lengthy loan spell at Wolves, Roy Evans accepted a bid from Stoke City at the beginning of 1996. Walters later continued his career with Southampton, Swindon Town and Bristol Rovers.

Wark, John

1983/4-1987/8 (Defender) **B** 4.8.1957, Glsgow **S** March 1984 from
Ipswich Town, £450,000 **D** 31.3.1984 v Watford, lg (scored) **L** Jan
1988 to Ipswich Town **Apps** 108, 42 gls **Hons** Div1 CH 1983–84,
1985–86; 29 caps for Scotland **OC** Ipswich T (twice), Middlesbrough

HE MAY HAVE BEEN bought as a midfield
replacement for Graeme Souness in 1984, but it
was as a goalscorer that Wark really made his
mark at Anfield. In his first full season, the
Scottish international eclipsed Ian Rush, finding the net 27 times thanks to his surging runs
from deep positions. He also contributed 15
goals in all competitions as Liverpool stormed to
a League and FA Cup double in 1986. Sadly, he
broke a leg before the season reached its climax
and was never able to recapture his best form.
In 1988 he rejoined his old club Ipswich, where
he'd earlier won FA Cup and UEFA Cup medals,
plus the PFA's Player of The Year accolade.

Bill Shankly (far left, middle row) with an RAF team in wartime

Wartime Football

THE TWO WORLD WARS had a huge impact
on the city of Liverpool, costing thousands of
lives and millions of pounds worth of damage.
Among the estimated 20,000 young men from
Merseyside who died in the 1914-18 war were
three Liverpool FC players: Joe Dines and Wilf
Bartrop, both killed on the Western Front, and
Tom Gracie, who lost his life while serving with

the Royal Scots Guards in Glasgow. During
World War Two, Liverpool's players were the
first to respond to the FA's appeal for Territorial
Army volunteers. Many of those who put their
names forward were drafted into the King's
Liverpool Regiment, serving their country with
distinction during the six years of fighting.
Tragically, team skipper Tom Cooper – a
Sergeant in the Military Police – was killed in a
motorcycle crash while on despatch duty.

Both wars caused havoc with the Football
League programme, leading to the suspension
of normal competitive games. During the First
World War, the authorities abandoned all fixtures in the summer of 1915, leaving clubs to
organise themselves into makeshift county
leagues for the remainder of the fighting.
Liverpool – operating without a manager following Tom Watson's death – performed surprisingly well in their Lancashire League, fin-

(Left) The team that played just three games before
war stopped the 1939 league programme; (below)
Shankly's signature on a wartime autograph book

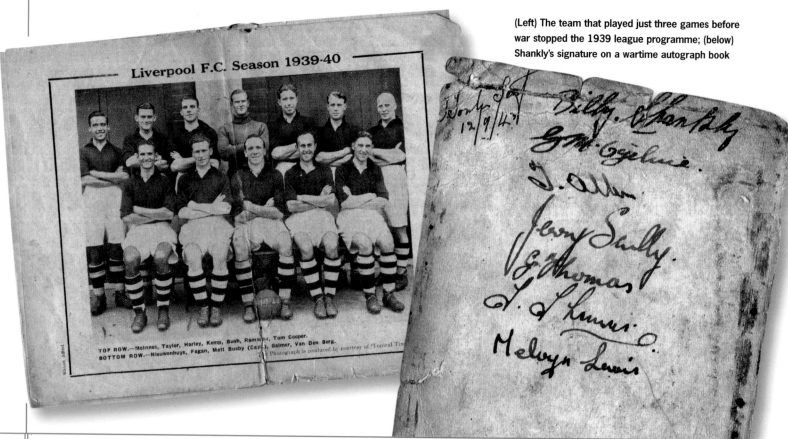

Liverpool F.C. Season 1939-40

TOP ROW.—McInnes, Taylor, Harley, Kemp, Bush, Ramsden, Tom Cooper.
BOTTOM ROW.—Nieuwenhuys, Fagan, Matt Busby (Capt.), Balmer, Van Den Berg.

ishing once as runners-up, and even carrying off the trophy at the end of the 1916–17 season.

When Britain again declared war on Germany in 1939, the national league programme was once more put on hold and replaced by a zonal competition that reduced the need for travelling. Crowds were initially restricted to a maximum of 8,000, and teams were allowed to field 'guest players' from other clubs whose barracks were situated nearby. Among those who guested for Liverpool were Manchester City and England 'keeper Frank Swift, Wolves' international captain Stan Cullis, and – on one occasion – Bill Shankly of Preston.

The club played a grand total of 287 competitive games during the long years of World War Two, winning the Football League North title in 1943 and the Lancashire Cup in 1944. Centre-forward Cyril Done was the club's most prolific striker, hitting 43 goals in the 1943–44 season, and grabbing a total of 151 throughout the entire wartime period.

Watson, Tom

ONE OF THE MOST successful managers in English football history – and the first Liverpool boss to bring the title to Anfield. The ex-teacher joined the club in 1896, after guiding his Sunderland side to three Championship successes. He introduced rigorous new training methods, changed the team colours to red and recruited a brilliant new set of players who would take the newly promoted team to the summit of Division One. By the end of the 1900–01 season he had landed the club's first League title; five years later he brought home a second. In 1914 he also took the Reds to their first FA Cup Final, but saw his team lose 1-0 to Burnley.

Throughout his career, the thick-set Geordie was known as a football visionary, a pioneer of European tours and one of the first coaches to lay down rules regarding players' diets. He was also a superb talent-spotter, bringing the legendary Scottish captain Alex Raisbeck to Anfield and recruiting a string of world-class goalkeepers like Ned Doig, Sam Hardy and Elisha Scott. During his reign, Liverpool emerged from Everton's shadow to become the pre-eminent football force on Merseyside. With success, the board were able to redevelop the ground, building the Spion Kop to house the ever-growing band of spectators.

Watson stayed with the club until the last day of the 1914–15 season when he fell ill while watching his team win at Oldham. He died at his Anfield home a fortnight later, aged 62.

Website

LIVERPOOL'S PIONEERING ONLINE operation has rapidly become one of the world's most successful sports websites, attracting up to a million hits every day. It includes extensive features about the club's history, former players, information about upcoming matches, plus a vibrant message board attracting posters from all over the globe. For a modest monthly charge, subscribers can also become holders of an 'E-Season Ticket', giving them access to exclusive interviews and video footage. During the 2002–03 season the site scored a cyberspace first by 'webcasting' Liverpool's Premiership game against Manchester United at Old Trafford. Internet surfers can find the site at **www.liverpoolfc.tv**

Welsh, Don

1951/2-1955/6 (Manager) **B** 25.2.1911, Manchester **S** Turned out for Liverpool FC as a 'guest player' during wartime **D** n/k **L** 1956, sacked **Hons** 3 caps for England and 9 WW2 caps **OC** Torquay United, Charlton Athletic (both as player)

THE EX-CHARLTON STRIKER had happy playing memories at Anfield, appearing as a frequent wartime guest and scoring six times in one amazing 12-1 win over Southport. Sadly, he was unable to repeat that sort of success as boss. And today he's remembered as the man who took the Reds into the Second Division – and the first Liverpool manager to be sacked.

Welsh took the job in 1951 after the increas-

Don Welsh – Division Two boss

ingly frail George Kay was forced into retirement. The fanatically fit former Army PT instructor did his best with an ageing crop of players but, with little money to spend, was unable to stop them spiralling downwards. In 1953 he watched his side go out of the FA Cup to non-league Gateshead, a year later they were relegated and then, in their first season in Division Two, they suffered their record 9-1 defeat at the hands of Birmingham.

Welsh's days were clearly numbered. He did manage to improve results by axing old favourites and bringing in talented youngsters like Ronnie Moran, Alan A'Court and Jimmy Melia. But midway through the 1955–56 season, with promotion miles away, the Anfield board ordered him to make way for Phil Taylor.

You'll Never Surf Alone… the LFC website attracts fans from around the world

Wembley

LIVERPOOL'S INCREASINGLY frequent trips to the national stadium during the 1980s led former chairman Sir John Smith to dub it 'Anfield South'. The club played 30 major games there before the famous Twin Towers were eventually demolished, winning 17, losing eight and drawing five.

Among the most memorable matches were the 1965 FA Cup final when Liverpool beat Leeds 2-1 to lift the trophy for the first time; the 1978 European Cup victory over FC Bruges; and the first all-Merseyside FA Cup Final in 1986, when the Reds ran out 3-1 winners against Everton.

West, Alfred

1903/4-1908/9 and 1910/11-c1911/12 (Right-back) **B** 15.12.1881, Nottingham **S** November 1903 from Barnsley, £500 **D** 7.11.1903 v Notts C, lg **L** June 1909 to Reading (but he came back in 1910!) **Apps** 141, 6 gls **Hons** Div1 CH 1905–06 **OC** Ilkeston FC, Barnsley, Reading, Notts C **d** n/k

Westerveld, Sander

1999/0-2000/1 (Goalkeeper) **B** 10.23.1974 Enschede, Holland **S** 15.6.999 from V Arnhem, £4 million **D** 7.8.1999 v Sheffield Wed, lg **L** Dec 2001 to Real Sociedad **Apps** 103 **Hons** LC 2001; FAC 2001; UEFA 2001; CS 2001; Super Cup 2001; 6 Holland caps **OC** FC Twente, Vitesse Arnhem, Real Sociedad

HIS £4 MILLION MOVE from Vitesse Arnhem to Liverpool made Westerveld the most expensive goalkeeper in British football. But his record of conceding the fewest Premiership goals in the 1999–2000 season soon made the Dutch international look cheap at the price.

After performing impressively for Holland at Euro 2000, Westerveld went on to play a crucial role in Liverpool's Treble-winning campaign, featuring in every Premiership fixture and

Home from home: Shankly leads out his men at Wembley for the 1971 FA Cup final against Arsenal

KEY Apps Appearances | **B** Born | **CH** Championship | **CWC** Cup Winners' Cup | **CS** Charity Shield | **D** Debut | **d** Died | **EC** European Cup | **FAC** FA Cup | **gls** Goals | **Hons** Honours | **lg** League

Dutch Master: Sander Westerveld

making the all-important save in the Worthington Cup final penalty shoot-out against Birmingham. His heroics in the 2001 Charity Shield against Manchester United won him the man of the match award, but a series of high-profile blunders at the start of the new League season led to him being dropped. The double signing of Dudek and Kirkland made his chances of regaining the Number One jersey look remote and, in December 2001, he opted for a move to Spain's Real Sociedad.

Wheeler, John E

1956/57-1962/63 (Right-half) **B** 26.7.1928, Crosby **S** September 1956 from Bolton W, £9,000 **D** 15.9.1956 v Stoke C, lg **L** May 1963 to New Brighton as player-manager, but instead became Bury's trainer! **Apps** 177, 23 gls **Hons** England B hons **OC** Carlton FC, Tranmre R, Bolton W, Bury

CROSBY-BORN MIDFIELDER who made many of his Anfield performances as an inside-right, combining aggressive tackling with the knack of getting into scoring positions. His committed style made him one of the more popular members of Liverpool's Second Division side of the 1950s, and in 1956 he gained a place in the club's history books by scoring a hat-trick in the space of just four minutes against Port Vale. Wheeler captained the side for a spell, but lost his regular place when new boss Bill Shankly signed Gordon Milne from Preston. He made just one appearance in the 1961–62 promotion-winning season before joining the coaching staff at Bury.

JOHN WHEELER

L Left Liverpool | **LC** League Cup | **n/k** not known | **OC** Other Clubs | **P** Premiership | **S** Signed | **Sb** Substitute | **SSSC** Screen Sport Super Cup | **UEFA** UEFA Cup | **WCCH** World Club Championship

213

Wembley hero of 1982, Whelan beats Spurs' Ossie Ardiles to the ball during his match-winning League Cup Final performance

Whelan, Ronnie

1979/1980-1993/94 (Midfield) **B** 25.9.1961,Dublin **S** 21 Sept 1979 from Home Farm, £3,500 **D** 3.4.1981 v Stoke C, lg **L** 1994 to Southend (manger) **Apps** 473, 73 gls **Hons** EC 1983–84, EC 1984–85 finalist; Div1 CH 1981–82, 1982–83, 1983–84, 1985–86, 1987–88 1989–90; FAC 1985–86, 1988–89, 1987–88 finalist; LC 1981–82, 1982–83, 1983–84; CS 1982, 1986, 1988, 1989, 1990; ScSSc 1986; 51 caps for Rep I **OC** Home Farm, Southend Utd (player and manager), Panionios (manager), Olympiakos Nicosia (manager)

BOB PAISLEY LANDED ONE of Liverpool's best-ever bargains when he signed the lean 18-year-old from the Irish club Home Farm. Within two years he was in the first team and on his way to amassing a glittering haul of domestic and European medals.

Replacing Ray Kennedy in midfield, Whelan made an immediate impression with his speed, tackling ability and perfect distribution. He also had a predator's eye for goal, often getting on the scoresheet in spectacular style. His two vital Wembley strikes against Tottenham helped Liverpool to Milk Cup success in 1982 and, just a year later, he hit a brilliant curled winner against Manchester United as the Reds won a third successive final in the competition.

Whelan was one of the Reds' most consistent performers during their 1980s decade of dominance, making more than 400 appearances and winning a record number of Republic of Ireland caps while with the club. As his career developed he switched to a deeper role, using his bulkier frame to break up opposition attacks, and sometimes switching to defence. And, as team-mate Alan Hansen gradually succumbed to injuries, Kenny Dalglish recognised his huge influence on the team by making him captain.

But by the time Graeme Souness arrived, Whelan was himself dogged by fitness problems. He stayed at Anfield until 1994 before accepting the manager's position at Southend United, then going on to work as a coach in Greece and Cyprus.

White, Dick

1955/6-1961/2 (Centre-half) **B** 18.8.1931, Scunthorpe **S** November 1955 from Scunthorpe Utd, **D** 10.3.1956 v Barnsley, lg **L** May 1962 to Doncaster R, £4,000 **Apps** 217, 1 gl **Hons** Div2 CH 1961–62 **OC** Scunthorpe Sea Cadets, Brumby Amateurs, Scunthorpe Utd, Doncaster R, Kettering T (player-manager) **d** 15.6.2002

COOL AND DEPENDABLE centre-half who lost his place – and the club captaincy – to Ron Yeats in 1961. White demonstrated his versatility by switching to a full-back role, and made 24

came in the 1971–72 season when he hit a hat-trick against the eventual champions, Derby County. But he broke a leg soon afterwards and was never able to reclaim John Toshack's first-team position. He left for Cardiff City in 1974.

Wilkie, Thomas

1895/6-1898/99 (Left-back) **B** 1876, Edinburgh **S** 18.1.1895 from Hearts **D** 7.9.1895 v Notts C, lg **L** 1899 to Portsmouth **Apps** 64, 2 gls **Hons** Div2 CH 1895–96 **OC** Hearts, Portsmouth **d** 8.1.1932

Wilkinson, G Barry

1953/4-1959/60 (Wing-half) **B** 16.6.1935, Bishop Aukland **S** Sept 1953 from Bishop Aukland **D** 5.12.1953 v Blackpool, lg **L** August 1960 to Bangor C, £500 **Apps** 79, 0 gls **Hons** England Youth hons **OC** West Auckland, Bishop Auckland, Bangor City, Tranmere R, Holyhead Town

Williams, R. Bryan

1945/6-1952/3 (Utility player) **B** 4.10.1927, Liverpool **S** August 1945 from South Liverpool **D** 12.3.1949 v Birmingham C, Lg **L** July 1953 to South Liverpool as player-coach **Apps** 34, 5 **Hons** none **OC** South Liverpool (twice), Crewe A, Rhyl

THE LIVERPOOL-BORN utility player was one of the first footballers to gain a reputation for long throw-ins – a technique later perfected by post-war team-mate Bob Paisley. He made most of his Liverpool appearances at inside-left, but also provided useful cover in midfield and defensive positions. As well as his versatility on the pitch, Williams was also a superb all-round athlete, excelling as a sprinter and swimmer. He became South Liverpool player-coach in 1953, and later played for Crewe.

Williams, Thomas Valentine (TV)

LONG-SERVING ANFIELD director, chairman and the club's first Life President. Williams was a life-long Reds fan who even remembered the birth of singing at Anfield during the team's 1906 title celebrations. He bought shares in the club at the end of World War One but didn't join the board until he retired from his job as a cotton broker in 1948. During his time on the board, Williams was responsible for many major decisions, including the deal to buy Melwood and the redevelopment of Anfield during the 1960s. But it was his offer to take Bob Paisley on to the coaching staff in 1954, and his recruitment of Bill Shankly as manager five years later, that were to have such a huge and lasting impact on Liverpool's fortunes.

Wilson, Charlie

1897/8-1905 and 1905-1939 (Backroom staff) (Wing-half) **B** Stockport **S** 15.12.1897 from Stockport C **D** 19.3.1898 v Bolton Wanderers, lg **L** c1905 joined LFC backroom staff as coach/scout **Apps** 90, 3 gls **Hons** Div1 CH 1900–01 **OC** Stockport C **d** 1947, Stockport

ONE OF ANFIELD'S most outstanding servants, helping to bring success as a player, scout and trainer. Stockport-born Wilson was a regular member of Liverpool's first-ever Championship side, but tragically a broken leg brought his playing career to an abrupt end soon afterwards.

He stayed on the Anfield staff until his retirement nearly 40 years later, and was coach of the 1922 and 1923 Title-winning sides.

W

appearances as the team clinched promotion in the 1961–62 season. But, within weeks of collecting a Second Division Championship medal, he was sold to Doncaster Rovers.

Whitham, Jack

1970/71-1973/74 (Forward) **B** 8.12.1946, Burnley **S** April 1970 from Sheffield Wed, £57,000 **D** 12.9.1970 v Newcastle Utd, lg **L** March 1974 to Cardiff C **Apps** 18, 7 gls **Hons** England U-23 hons **OC** Holy Trinity FC, Sheffield Wed, Cardiff C, Reading, Worksop T

ONE OF BILL SHANKLY'S first signings of the 1970s and a striker whose goalscoring abilities had brought England under-23 honours. Sadly, the injuries that had dogged his Sheffield Wednesday career also blighted his time at Anfield and, in four years with the club, he managed just 18 senior games. His best performance

Cap in hand: TV Williams congratulates Cyril Sidlow and Ray Lambert on receiving their Welsh caps

L Left Liverpool | **LC** League Cup | **n/k** not known | **OC** Other Clubs | **P** Premiership | **S** Signed | **Sb** Substitute | **SSSC** Screen Sport Super Cup | **UEFA** UEFA Cup | **WCCH** World Club Championship

215

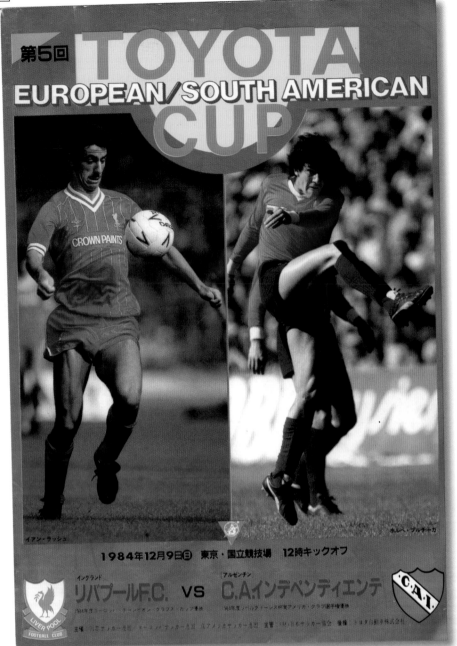

Wright, Mark

1991/2-1998/9 (Centre-half) **B** 1.8.1963, Dorchester **S** July 1991 from Derby C, £2.2 million **D** 17.8.1991 v Oldham A, lg **L** Dec 1999 retired **Apps** 210, 9 gls **Hons** FAC 1991–92, 1995–96 finalist; 45 caps for England **OC** Oxford Utd, Southampton, Derby C, Southport (manager), Oxford Utd (manager), Chester C (manager

A STRONG, COMMANDING centre-half was Graeme Souness's first priority when he became Liverpool boss – and Derby's England international seemed to fit the bill perfectly. The former manager spent £2.2million to prise him from the Midlands club and for a while it seemed an inspired move. Wright was an intelligent and courageous figure at the heart of the Reds' defence, emerging as a natural captain when

Wilson, David C

1967-68 (Outside-right) **B** 24.12.1942, Nelson **S** February 1967 from Preston NE, £20,000 **D** 13.5.1967 v Blackpool, lg **L** May 1968 to Preston NE, £4,000 **Apps** 1 (as sub), 0 gls **Hons** England U-23 Hons **OC** Burnley Schools, Preston NE (twice), Bradford City (loan), Southport (loan), Telford Utd

World Club Championship

BOB PAISLEY TWICE resisted entering his European Cup winning sides into this traditional clash with the Champions of South America. However, a rearranged League fixture programme – and a lucrative sponsorship deal – led him to accept the challenge of a match against the Brazilian side Flamengo in 1981. Unfortunately his team lost the game in Tokyo, falling victim to three first-half goals and a mesmerising performance by the Brazilian international Zico. In 1984, it was the turn of Joe Fagan's European champions to make the one-off trip to Japan. This time they faced Independiente of Argentina. It turned out to be a much tighter affair, but the Reds still lost 1-0.

Worthington Cup

→ See League Cup

Wright, David

1929/30-33/4 (Centre/inside-forward) **B** 5.10.1905, Kirkcaldy **S** March 1930 from Sunderland **D** 12.4.1930 v Burnley, lg **L** July 1934 to Hull C, £1,000 **Apps** 100, 35 gls **Hons** none **OC** East Fife, Cowdenbeath, Sunderland, Hull C, Bradford **d** August 1953

KEY Apps Appearances | **B** Born | **CH** Championship | **CWC** Cup Winners' Cup | **CS** Charity Shield | **D** Debut | **d** Died | **EC** European Cup | **FAC** FA Cup | **gls** Goals | **Hons** Honours | **lg** League

Ronnie Whelan was hit by injury. He skippered the side to the 1992 FA Cup final and enjoyed his proudest moment in a red shirt when he lifted the trophy following the 2-0 defeat of Sunderland.

For the next three years, though, his Anfield career was dogged by injuries, loss of confidence and the odd fall-out with the club management. After losing the club captaincy, he did manage to claw his way back to form, regaining his place and featuring in all but one League fixture in the 1995–96 campaign. But then he was hit by a back injury which led to his eventual retirement as a player in 1998. Since leaving Anfield, Wright has carved out a new career in management, taking charge at Southport, Oxford United and, most recently, Chester City.

Wright, Stephen

1996/7-2001/2 (Defender) **B** 8.2.1980, Ormskirk **S** 8 July 1996 to LFC Academy **D** 29.11.2000 v Stoke City, LC **L** August 2002 to Sunderland, £2m **Apps** 21, 1 goal **Hons** 9 U-21 caps for Engand **OC** Crewe A (loan), Sunderland

THE LIVERPOOL-BORN Academy graduate made his debut in the record 8-0 Worthington Cup victory over Stoke City in 2000, coming on as a half-time replacement for Babbel. Although only a fringe player during the Treble-winning campaign, he staked a strong claim for a regular place the following season, as Babbel succumbed to a debilitating virus. Fast and determined, with a biting tackle, Wright's performances brought him England Under-21 caps and a seemingly bright future at Anfield. But, given the guarantee of first-team action with Sunderland, he accepted a move to the Stadium Of Light at the start of 2002—03.

Wright, E Victor

1933/4-1936/7 (Centre/inside-forward) **B** 24.1.1909, Walsall **S** March 1934 from Rotherham Utd **D** 17.3.1934 v Birmingham, lg **L** June 1937 to Plymouth A **Apps** 85, 33 **Hons** none **OC** Bloxwich Strollers, Bristol C, Rotherham Utd, Plymouth A, Chelmsford C, wartime guest for Millwall, Crystal Palace, Walsall **d** 1964

Wright on the Mark: the former Reds skipper was a courageous and commanding centre-half

Xavier, Abel

2001/2-present (Defender) **B** 30.11.1972, Nampula, Mozambique
S 31.1.2002 from Everton FC **D** 9.2.2002 v Ipswich T, lg (scored)
Apps 21, 2 gls **Hons** 21 caps for Portugal **OC** Estrela Amadora,
Benfica, Bari, Real Oviedo, PSV Eindhoven, Everton, Galatasaray (loan)

THE PORTUGUESE INTERNATIONAL'S
move from Everton marked another stage in a
career that has taken him to six of Europe's
toughest leagues.

He first grabbed attention during Euro 2000
when his hotly disputed handball offence in the
semi-final gave France a 'golden goal' penalty
winner – and led to a lengthy European ban
because of the vehemence of his protests.

By then he was a Goodison player, following
stints in Portugal, Spain, Italy and Holland. But
after an injury-plagued stint with the Blues, he
made a dream start to his Anfield career, scoring on his debut. However, after just a year he
went on loan to Galatasaray, with Liverpool
hoping to make the deal permanent.

Yeats, Ron 'Rowdy'

1961/2-1970/1 & 1986/7-2000/1 (Chief scout) (Centre-half)
B 15.11.1937, Aberdeen **S** July 1961 from Dundee Utd, £30,000
D 19.8.1961 v Bristol R, lg **L** July 1971 to Tranmere R **Apps** 454, 16
gls **Hons** Div1 CH 1963–64, 1965–66; Div2 CH 1961–62; FAC
1964–65; CS 1964, 1965, 1966; CWC finalist 1965–66; 2 caps for
Scotland **OC** Dundee Utd, Tranmere R (player-manager, manager),
Stalybridge Celtic, Barrow (player-manager); LFC (chief scout)

ONE OF TWO INSPIRATIONAL Scottish signings by Bill Shankly, and the defensive rock on
which Liverpool's future success was built. The
ex-slaughterman arrived from Dundee United
in 1961, just two months after Ian St John made
his Liverpool debut. Together they led the Anfield
revival that took the Reds from the Second
Division to the summit of English football.

Standing at 6ft 2in and possessing a boxer's
physique, Yeats cut an impressive figure on his
Anfield debut. "I've bought a Colossus," Shankly
told reporters afterwards. "Come in the dressing
room and have a walk around him." Handed the
captaincy by his boss, he brought formidable
strength and awesome aerial power to
Liverpool's back line. With him at its heart the
formerly leaky defence became one of the mean-
est in the League. At the end of his first season,
Liverpool had made it back to the top flight.

Yeats was an integral part of all the team's
1960s adventures – the Championships and
memorable European conquests included. But
perhaps his finest moment came in May 1965
when, following Wembley victory against Leeds,
he became the first captain in Liverpool's history to lift the FA Cup. He stayed with the club for
another six years, eventually losing his place to
Larry Lloyd in 1970. He later spent time at
Tranmere Rovers, as player and manager, but
returned to Anfield in 1987 to be chief scout.

You'll Never Walk Alone

FOOTBALL'S MOST FAMOUS anthem
was written by Rodgers and
Hammerstein, and given its first-ever
public airing in their 1945 Broadway musi-
cal *Carousel*. It moved all those who heard it
from the very beginning. With America at war,
many people in the audience had relatives fighting overseas, and they found solace and inspiration in the song's message of solidarity.

It was was Hollywood's 1956 movie version
of *Carousel* that first brought it to international
attention. Hundreds of thousands of cinema-
goers were touched as Barbara Cook and
Samuel Ramey laid into the film's climactic cho-
ruses, among them a young Liverpool musician
named Gerry Marsden.

Seven years on, and with two consecutive
Number One hits to his name, Gerry and his

The Colossus: Ron Yeats with the 1964 League Championship trophy

Marsden's song – and Shankly's memory

band, the Pacemakers, asked their record company if they could release it as an unlikely single. They agreed, brought in Beatles producer George Martin, and recorded it at EMI's world-famous Abbey Road studios. "We came into the studio after recording the basic track, and as soon as I heard George's string score I just knew it was going to be massive," said the singer.

By October 1963, the song was top of the charts and being played over the Anfield PA system. Its stirring themes of pride, struggle and community had a powerful resonance with the Kop, and fans found themselves singing along to it almost instinctively. By the end of Bill Shankly's first title-winning season, the supporters had adopted it as their anthem. The manager chose it as his favourite record on BBC Radio's *Desert Island Discs*. As he later told Gerry: "I've given Liverpool a team – you've given us a song."

Dozens of other artists have since put their own versions on vinyl, including Elvis Presley, Placido Domingo, Dionne Warwick and Pink Floyd. In the USA, the song is now associated with charity telethons, and, in Britain, it's been re-released to raise funds after major disasters, notably after the Bradford City stadium fire in 1985 when it spent two weeks at Number One.

Following the Kopites' example, many other soccer fans have also taken to singing 'You'll Never Walk Alone' before matches, and the lyrics can now be heard ringing round stadiums as far afield as Germany, Holland, Belgium and Greece. The close relationship between Liverpool and Celtic has also led to its adoption at Parkhead, and some memorable moments of communal singing between the two sets of fans. They include the 2003 UEFA Cup tie in Glasgow – when Gerry led the singing – and the emotional 1989 benefit game for the Hillsborough victims, attended by 60,000 fans.

But however well it's sung elsewhere, YNWA's spiritual home will always be at Anfield... at 2.55pm on a Saturday afternoon.

Chorus:
Walk on, walk on, with hope in your heart
And you'll never walk alone
You'll never walk alone

Starting young: a 17-year-old Michael Owen gets his name on the scoresheet – there would be plenty more where that came from

Younger, Thomas

1956-1959 (Goalkeeper) **B** 10.4.1930, Edinburgh
S June 1956 from Hibs, £9,000 **D** 18.8.1956 v
Huddersfield T, lg **L** June 1959 to Falkirk (player-
manager) **Apps** 127, 0 gls **Hons** caps for Scotland
OC Hutchison Vale, Hibs (twice: as player and director), Falkirk (player-manager), Stoke City, Leeds Utd
(player and scout), Toronto City (coach)
d 13.1.1984

TOMMY YOUNGER

AFTER WINNING TWO Scottish
Championship medals with
Hibernian, Younger's signature commanded a fee of £9,000 – quite a figure
for a goalkeeper back in 1956.

Liverpool were happy to pay it,
though, and he rewarded them with
three years of solid and dependable
service.

Probably the most memorable
of his 127 games came against
Derby County in October 1957,
when he left the field injured...
and later returned as a centre-
forward.

The burly, 15-stone Younger
went on to represent Scotland in
the World Cup finals the following year. But in 1960, after losing his Liverpool first-team
place to Bert Slater, he accept-

ed an offer to be player-manager at Falkirk. He
later served Leeds and Stoke as assistant manager, before taking up a directorship of
Hibernian and the Presidency of the Scottish
Football League.

Youngest Players

A NUMBER OF LIVERPOOL players have
made their debuts before their 18th birthday,
but the youngest is believed to be Maxwell
Thompson, who made his one and only appearance against Spurs in 1974 – aged just 17 years
and 129 days.

Phil Charnock, who played in a 1992 match
against Appollon Limassol, is the youngest

Ziege, Christian

2000-2001 (Defender) **B** 1.2.1972, Berlin **S** 29.8 2000 from Middlesbrough, £5.5 million **D** 9.9.2000 v Manchester C, lg **L** July 2001 to Tottenham, £4.5 million **Apps** 32, 3 gls **Hons** 59 caps for Germany **OC** Sudstern 08, TSV Rudow, Hertha Zehlendorf, Bayern Munich, AC Milan, Middlesbrough, Tottenham

THE BERLIN-BORN international arrived at Anfield after a controversial deal involving his former club Middlesbrough. They rated him at £8million, but he had a get-out clause in his contract allowing him to leave for £3.5million less. He chose to exercise it, despite Boro's vehement objections, in order to win medals at Anfield. Sadly, his time on Merseyside was nowhere near the success he, or his new employers, had hoped.

Ziege started his career as a goalkeeper, but converted to a left-sided midfielder when he was a teenager. He was an outstanding prospect, snapped up by Bayern Munich as an 18-year-old and captaining his country at Youth and Under-21 level. By the time Liverpool made their move he was a highly experienced full international with almost 50 caps to his name.

He had played in every game in every round of Germany's triumphant Euro 96 run, collected domestic and European honours with Bayern and experienced a brief spell in the Italian league with AC Milan.

Gerard Houllier viewed him as the ideal man to fill Liverpool's troublesome left-back berth. But, while he proved highly effective going forward, Ziege's defensive qualities were less evident and a spell on the treatment table saw him lose the spot to Jamie Carragher.

He came back into the first team as a left-sided midfielder, but struggled to make the position his own. He came on as a substitute in the 2001 Worthington Cup final and scored from the spot in the penalty shoot-out victory over Birmingham. But, after failing even to make the bench for the FA and UEFA Cup finals, he demanded a move. Not long afterwards, Liverpool accepted a £4.5million bid from Tottenham manager Glenn Hoddle before the new season got under way.

European debutant, at 17 years and 215 days. And Michael Owen, who found the net against Wimbledon when 17 years and 144 days old, is the youngest player to score for the Reds.

In September 2000 he set another record, as the youngest post-war Liverpool player to make 100 league appearances. Only Owen (aged 20 years and 269 days) and Robbie Fowler (20 years and 343 days) have reached the league century before their 21st birthday. Alan A'Court, Jimmy Melia, Ian Callaghan, Phil Thompson and Jamie Redknapp all did it before they were 22. So far, only three have notched up 400 league games while in their twenties. They are Emlyn Hughes at 29 years, 127 days, Callaghan (29 years, 288 days) and Tommy Smith (29 years, 359 days).

Hard to get: Ziege's move from Middlesbrough was long and protracted

L Left Liverpool | **LC** League Cup | **n/k** not known | **OC** Other Clubs | **P** Premiership | **S** Signed | **Sb** Substitute | **SSSC** Screen Sport Super Cup | **UEFA** UEFA Cup | **WCCH** World Club Championship

221

BIBLIOGRAPHY

Ashton, K (1967)
The Liverpool FC Book
Stanley Paul

Ball, D & Rea, G (2001)
**Liverpool FC – The Ultimate
Book Of Stats And Facts**
The Bluecoat Press

Barnes, J. (1999)
John Barnes: The Autobiography
Routledge

Cooke, T (1999)
The Pubs Of Scottie Road
The Bluecoat Press

Davies, D & Cottrell, D (2002)
The Rough Guide To Liverpool
Rough Guides Ltd

Edge, A (1999)
**Faith Of Our Fathers:
Football As A Religion**
Mainstream Sport

Eaton, P (1999)
Inside Anfield
Granada Media

Heatley, M & Welch, I (1996)
**The Great Derby Matches:
Liverpool v. Everton**
Dial House

Hale, S, Ponting, I & Small, S (2001)
Liverpool In Europe
Carlton Books

Hansen, A (1999)
Alan Hansen, A Matter Of Opinion
Partridge

Hodgson, D (1978)
The Liverpool Story
Arthur Barker

Houghton, R (1989)
**Ray Houghton's Liverpool Notebook:
Inside Anfield 1988-89**
Macdonald Queen Anne Press

Hughes, E (1980)
Crazy Horse
Arthur Barker

Hunt, R (1969)
Roger Hunt: Hunt For Goals
Pelham Books

Inglis, S (1996)
The Football Grounds Of Britain
Collins Willow

Keegan, K (1994)
Kevin Keegan, The Seventies Revisited
Queen Anne Press

Keith, J (1999)
Bob Paisley, Manager of the Millennium
Robson Books

Keith, J (2001)
The Essential Shankly
Robson Books

Keith, J (1998)
Shanks For The Memory
Robson Books

Kelly, S. (2001)
The Anfield Encyclopaedia
Mainstream Publishing

Kelly, S (1991)
You'll Never Walk Alone
Queen Anne Press

Lamming, D (1989)
Who's Who of Liverpool 1892–1989
Breedon Books

Liddell, W (1960)
Billy Liddell: My Soccer Story
Stanley Paul

Liversedge, S. (1995)
Liverpool: From The Inside
Mainstream Publishing

Mason, T (1985)
**The Blues And The Reds: A History Of
Liverpool & Everton Football Clubs**
History Society of Lancashire and Cheshire

Neal, Phil (1981)
Attack From The Back
Arthur Barker

Paisley, R (1983)
Bob Paisley, An Autobiography
Arthur Barker

Pead, B (1993)
Ee-Ay-Addio, We've Won The Cup
Champion Press

Platt, M (2001)
Cup Kings 1965
Bluecoat Press

Rowlands, J (2001)
Everton FC, 1880–1945
Tempus Publishing

Rush, I (1985)
Rush: Ian Rush's Autobiography
Arthur Barker

Russell, D (1997)
Football And The English
Carnegie Publishing

Smith, T (1980)
Tommy Smith: I Did It The Hard Way
Arthur Barker

St. John, I (1966)
Boom At The Kop
Pelham Books Ltd.

St. John, I (1990)
Liverpool, The Glory Decade
Sidgwick & Jackson

Souness, G (1985)
Graeme Souness, No Half Measures
Collins Willow

Taylor, R, Ward, A & Williams, J (1993)
**Three Sides Of The Mersey: An Oral
History Of Everton, Liverpool And
Tranmere Rovers**
Robson Books

Thompson, A & Hale, S (2002)
This Is Anfield
Genesis Publications

Williams, J. (2001)
**Into The Red: Liverpool FC And The
Changing Face Of English Football**
Mainstream Publishing

Williams, J., Hopkins, S., & Long, C.(2001)
**Passing Rhythms: Liverpool FC And
The Transformation Of Football**
Berg

USEFUL CONTACTS

CLUB TELEPHONE NUMBERS

Main Switchboard **0151 263 2361**

Direct Line Enquiries **0870 220 2345**
Credit Card Booking Line **0870 220 2151**
UEFA Champions League Bookings **0870 220 0034**
FA Cup Booking Line **0870 220 0056**
Priority Booking Line (Priority Ticket Scheme – members only) **0870 220 0408**
24 hour information line **0870 444 4949**

Clubcall **09068 121 584***
(for Liverpool FC news and information by telephone) *calls cost 60p per minute

Mail Order Hotline (UK) **0870 6000532**
International Mail Order **00 44 1386 852035**

Conference and Banqueting (for your events at Anfield) **0151 263 7744**
Corporate Sales **0151 263 9199**
Public Relations **0151 260 1433**
Development Association **0151 263 6391**
Caring in the Community **0151 260 1433**
Museum & Tour Centre **0151 260 6677**
Membership Department **0151 261 1444**
Club Store (Anfield) **0151 263 1760**
Club Store (City Centre) **0151 330 3077**
Liverpool Football Club Credit Card
(available to over-18s) **0800 028 2440**

BECOME A MEMBER OF LIVERPOOL FC
& JOIN THE OFFICIAL LIVERPOOL SUPPORTERS CLUB
To join, please call: **08707 02 02 07**
International: **+44 151 702 8859**

SUBSCRIBE TO THE OFFICIAL LFC PROGRAMME AND WEEKLY MAGAZINE
To take out a subscription please call: **0845 1430001**

LFC TEXT MESSAGE SERVICE
Sign up for the official LFC Text Message Service including, Match 2 U, LFC News and LFC 4U services, allowing you to keep in touch when you're on the move.
To sign up go to **www.liverpoolfc.tv**

E SEASON TICKET
Sign up for an e Season Ticket to see Premier League goals & highlights,
7 TV channels and follow the team live through Turnstile.
To sign up go to **www.liverpoolfc.tv**

LFC SAVE & SUPPORT ACCOUNT WITH BRITANNIA
For more information visit **www.britannia.co.uk/lfc** call **0800 915 0503**
or visit any Britannia branch.

INTERNATIONAL BRANCHES OF LIVERPOOL SUPPORTERS CLUBS:

AUSTRALIA
Bob Wardle
PO Box 551
Gosford
NSW 2250

John O'Connell
257 Crimea Street
Noranda
Perth
6062 WA

Marcus Moore
GPO Box 2648
Brisbane
Queensland 4001

BELGIUM
Mikael Roufosse
Rue Colonel
Piron 159
4624 Rousse

BULGARIA
Aleksandar Darakchiev
Velingrad
5 Mayakovsky Str
Pazardjik District
4600

CANADA
Dara Mottahead
1874 Hennessy Crescent
Orleans (Ottawa)
Ontario
KA4 3XB

CYPRUS
Simos Sakka
Tritonos 2
Larnaca 6047

DENMARK
Per Knudsen
Melholtvej 10
Allborg East 9220

Carsten Lymann
Grofthojparken 152 St2
Viby
DK-8260

FRANCE
George Quintard
59 Rue de Marsinval
78540 Vernouillet

GERMANY
David Coultous
Westend Strasse 51
Kempten
D-87439

GHANA
Aristo Dotse
PO Box NT 267
Accra New Town
Accra 00233

GIBRALTAR
Julian Sene
32 Durban Road
Harbour Views
Gibraltar

GREECE
John Skotidas
PO Box 16767
Athens
11502

Nassos Siotropos
LFC – OSC Hellenic Branch
PO Box 34 111
10029
Athens

Panagioties Damianidis
Kalavriton 11
GR-564 30
Thessaloniki

HOLLAND
Herman Post
Brouwersdijk 95
Dordrecht
3314 GJ

Mick Kennedy
Dudokkeartier 6
Av Bilthoven
3723

HONG KONG
Philip Chu
RM-501-2, 5/F
Tung Wai Comm Bldg
109-111 Cloucester Road
Wanchai

ICELAND
Kristmann Palmasson
PO Box 8220
128 Reykjavik

ITALY
Filippo Rossi
CP 146
Sandicci
Firenza
50018

JAPAN
Keiko Hirano
Shinmachi 1-23-9-501
Setagaya-Ku
Tokyo
154-0014

LUXEMBOURG
Mark Clintworth
Black Stuff
Val Du Hamm
L-2950

MALAYSIA
Anand Nadason
21C Jalan Tengku
Ampuan Zabedah
F9/F Shah Alam
Selangor
Darul Ehsan 40100

MALTA
Brian Tanti
St Josephs House
Tal-Palma Road
Mtfara
RBT 15

MAURTITIUS
Jean Carl Palmyre
Morrison Street
Pamplemousses

NEW ZEALAND
John Corson
62 Nelson Street
Forbury
Dunedin
9001

NORWAY
Tore Hansen
Scandinavian Branch
PO Box 2142
Molde
N-6402

SINGAPORE
James Lim
30 Maxwell Road
#01-100 Singapore 069114

SOUTH AFRICA
Lester Smith
103 Tallent Street
Parow West
Cape Town
7500

Dan Tanne
PO Box 16778
Dowerglen
1612

SWEDEN
Rolf Rundstrom
Laxgatan 11
Skellcftea
S-931 64

SWITZERLAND
Florian Thurler
Official Swiss Branch
PO Box 945
Biel Bienne
CH-2501

George Rossier
PO Box 152
Trieng
CH-6234

THAILAND
Buke Bhornlerts
79-16 Sukhumit 15
Sukhumit Road
Klongtoey 1011
Bangkok

USA
Roy Yeats
Openwide Intl Inc
4024 Eastridge Drive
Pompano Beach
Florida
3306

Bernie Grimes
135 Eight Lots Road
Sutton
MA 01590

Daragh Kennedy
PO Box 7071
Fdr Station
New York
NY 10150

ZAMBIA
Karl O'Donohoe
17119 Katima Mulilo Rd
Olympia Park
Lusaka

For information about branches
in Republic of Ireland and the
UK please visit our website
www.liverpoolfc.tv

ACKNOWLEDGEMENTS

PICTURE CREDITS
The publishers would like to thank the following sources for their kind permission to reproduce the pictures in this book:

Colorsport: 110; 180.

County Press (Wigan): 39.

Empics: 4-5; 11b; 12b; 13bl; 19t; 19b; 20t; 22b; 26t; 27tr; 28t; 28br; 29t; 32bl; 33; 34t; 36tl; 37tc; 37br; 42br; 43t; 44t; 46tl; 46bl; 46-47b; 49b; 50tl; 50-51 (main); 52; 53b; 54tc; 54tr; 56t; 56b; 57; 61bc; 62-63 (main); 63 (inset); 65; 66-67t; 70-71 (main); 72; 73t; 76-77; 78t; 78b; 80-81t; 81b; 84; 85tr; 85br; 86-87 (main); 87br; 88-89 (main); 89br; 92bl; 92 (main); 93tr; 94b; 95 (main); 95br; 96tl; 98-99 (main); 100tl; 100bl; 102tl; 102br; 104-105 (main); 105br; 106tl; 108tl; 109; 111b; 113b; 115; 116-117 (main); 118t; 119br; 120tr; 120b; 121tr; 122br; 123bl; 123r; 124bl; 126bl; 126-127 (main); 128tl; 129t; 130bl; 131t; 131br; 132t; 133bl; 135; 136-137 (main); 138-139 (main); 140tl; 140br; 141t; 141l; 141b; 144br; 145tr; 148-149bc; 149tr; 150bl; 156-157 (main); 157tr; 158-159 (main); 159br; 160tl; 164-165; 167; 168br; 170tl; 170b; 171; 172r; 173bl; 173tc; 174tr; 175; 176-177 (main); 178t; 179t; 179b; 182-183 (main); 183tr; 184b; 185bl (x2); 186-187b; 188bl; 190bl; 190-191 (main); 191bl; 193br; 194-195 (main); 195br; 196br; 197t; 198; 200br; 204bl; 207t; 208-209b; 209tr; 212-213 (main); 213tr; 216-217 (main); 218bl; 219tr; 220-221 (main); 221br.

FA Fyffe: 133t.

Getty Images: 6-7; 20br; 23; 26b; 36br; 37tr; 37bc; 40-41bc; 45bl; 58-59 (main); 60-61 (main); 66b; 82-83; 125br; 143; 151; 176t; 188r; 189tr; 199b; 205tr; 206.

Roy Helsdown: 155tr.

Adrian Killen archive: 8-9; 10tl; 24cl; 62t.

Liverpool Echo: 16br; 30-31 (main); 51tr; 55b. (Doris Done): 29bl.

Liverpool FC: 12-13t; 24-25b; 38cl; 40t; 70bl; 142bl (x2); 168tr. (John Cocks): 10br; 13br; 24tc; 54bl; 79; 90; 96br; 97; 108bl; 108br; 146br; 152t; 152-153 (main); 169; 186tl; 204-205 (main).

Liverpool FC Museum Archives: 14-15 (main); 22tl; 25 (inset); 27bc; 30bl; 42tl; 48tl; 48tr; 48b; 68tl; 69tl; 74b; 82tl; 90tl; 90b (x3); 94tl; 101; 103; 107; 114bc; 114br; 116tl; 117 (inset); 119bl; 122tc; 132bl; 134tc; 138tl; 144l; 145br; 146l; 147t; 147br; 148l; 150r; 154bl; 154-155 (main); 161t; 166br; 174tl; 177tr; 184tl; 185t; 192-193 (main); 192 (inset); 193tr; 196t; 201; 202; 203tl; 203tr; 211bl; 211tr; 214-215t; 215br; 218-219 (main). (Tom Preston): 14tl.

Jim Lockwood: 162t (x3).

Manchester United Museum: 127r.

Harry Ormesher: 35; 36-37tr.

Reebok: 38br.

Skyscan/APS (UK): 49t.

Bob Thomas Sports Photography: 69b.

All paper memorabilia supplied by Liverpool FC Museum/Adrian Killen.
All 3-dimensional memorabilia supplied by Liverpool FC Museum and photographed by John Cocks.

Every effort has been made to acknowledge correctly and contact the source and/or copyright holder of each picture, and Carlton Books Limited apologises for any unintentional errors or omissions which will be corrected in future editions of this book.

PUBLISHERS' ACKNOWLEDGEMENTS
Thanks to Annie Tufte at Liverpool Football Club, Susanna Wadeson at Granada. Also to Matt Butler for editorial assistance.